Sam Shepard

Library of Congress Cataloging-in-Publication Data Is Available.

Jacket design by Kelly Winton
Book design by Neuwirth & Associates

ISBN 978-1-61902-708-4

COUNTERPOINT
2560 Ninth Street, Suite 318
Berkeley, CA 94710
www.counterpointpress.com

Printed in the United States of America
Distributed by Publishers Group West

10 9 8 7 6 5 4 3 2 1

Sam Shepard

A LIFE

John J. Winters

COUNTERPOINT

BERKELEY

A lot of time, you just have to go down many roads to get where you are going . . . The important thing is to keep moving.

—Bob Dylan

I shall walk the earth and search for something that I shall not find.

—Edward Albee

Contents

For Karen

Preface

On a fall day in 2004, Sam Shepard was back on the streets of New York. Over the years, he'd avoided the place. But this is where it had all begun, four decades earlier, when he'd gotten off an eastbound bus in Times Square so broke and hungry he had to sell a pint of blood to get a cheeseburger. He was known then as Steve Rogers, a lanky kid with a face as handsome as it was inscrutable, a young man full of ambition but unsure what he wanted from life. He could act, but hated auditioning. He'd been a musician, but couldn't afford a decent drum kit. Then there was writing; this he knew he could do. Specifically, he could write dialogue, drawn from the voices he was hearing both in his head and on the street. So that's what he went with. He was good and he was lucky. In short order, the new arrival was writing one-act plays that spoke to a new generation of theatergoers, making a name for himself around the small theaters of Greenwich Village and, at the age of twenty-two, being dubbed by the *New York Times* the "generally acknowledged genius" of Off-Off-Broadway. Eventually, he'd also take up both music and acting, and the ensuing years would bring a Pulitzer Prize, an Oscar nomination, awards at Cannes, a working relationship with Bob Dylan, well-regarded short story collections, and a movie star lover. Not bad for a Southern California kid whose greatest dream had once been to be "a veterinarian with a flashy station wagon, and a flashy blond wife, raising German shepherds in some fancy suburb."

Much had changed in four decades. Shepard stood on Bank Street on that fall afternoon in 2004, surrounded by memories of his earliest days in the city. He lit a cigar in the shade of a small tree, looked down, and saw a bronze plaque that read "Joseph Chaikin 1935–2003." Shepard still couldn't believe his old friend and mentor, a giant in the world of avant-garde theater, was gone. There's nothing like the memory of a lost friend to remind a man of his own mortality. Perhaps it was with a slight shudder that Shepard mused: "One day, no doubt, there'll be a little plaque like that for me somewhere. Wonder what the end date will be?"

That destiny was on Shepard's mind should not come as any surprise. Since the beginning of his career, it has been a central theme in much of his work. Even before he'd studied the ancient Greeks, for whom destiny was everything, Shepard was dealing with the immortal questions. "I find destiny and fate far more plausible than all this psychological stuff," he once told an interviewer. Shepard's greatest plays turn on the inevitability of destiny and the persistence of heredity, which he envisions coursing like poison in the blood, a trap one can't avoid.

Chronicling the life story of Sam Shepard means tracking a moving target, as he's ranged artistically and geographically all over the map in what his friend the film director Michael Almereyda refers to as Shepard's "sweeping road movie" of a life. And quite a life it has been. With more than fifty-five plays to his credit, including the 1979 Pulitzer Prize–winning *Buried Child*, Shepard has impacted American theater as much as any playwright of the past half century. Critics have enthused over how he has "forged a whole new kind of American play." Venerating him as well is a later generation of playwrights who came of age in his large shadow;

Suzan-Lori Parks, herself a Pulitzer winner, once sent Shepard a fan letter calling him her "gorgeous north star."

Shepard's achievements as a playwright would alone make him a natural subject for a comprehensive biography. However, he has triumphed in several other fields as well, most notably as an actor. Shepard's appearance onscreen powerfully evokes much about the Old West and a world gone by. *Authentic* is the word often used to describe the rare quality he possesses. Essayist John Hughes once said, "As an actor, Shepard has been America's primary heartthrob alterna-cowboy for many years. He's Gary Cooper in denim." For his portrayal of Chuck Yeager in the 1983 film *The Right Stuff*, Shepard earned an Oscar nomination. In addition to his nearly fifty roles in major films (and roughly a dozen more for television), he has also written and directed for the cinema. His screenplay for *Paris, Texas* helped that now-classic film sweep the top prizes at the 1984 Cannes Film Festival.

Shepard is also the author of five collections of prose, and his short fiction has appeared in the *New Yorker* and other prestigious publications. He's written songs with Dylan and John Cale, played drums and recorded with the seminal sixties psychedelic folk band the Holy Modal Rounders (once opening for Pink Floyd); he's hung with the Rolling Stones, and co-written films with Robert Frank and Michelangelo Antonioni. As for his personal life, Shepard has had relationships with singer Patti Smith and actress Jessica Lange. The latter affair, zealously kept from the public eye all these years, is revealed in detail for the first time in these pages.

Recent years have seen productions of two new plays, performed to middling reviews, and a series of films and television appearances that have fared far better, reaffirming Shepard's stature as an actor who brings something unique to the screen. The plays Shepard wrote in his heyday, particularly the so-called family plays, are revived constantly on stages around the world, including on Broadway. In 2015 *Fool for Love* was a hit uptown, and in early 2016, a star-studded and much-anticipated revival of *Buried Child* was presented Off-Broadway and on London's West End. Add up everything on this impressive résumé and it's clear that Sam Shepard's place in our cultural firmament is well secured for generations to come.

This book tells the story of this accomplished and much-admired artist. It examines the connections between the life and the work, detailing key people, places, and events that have influenced his writing for the stage and screen and made him the man and artist he is. Thanks to newly available letters and archival material, and the candor and eloquence Shepard demonstrates within their pages, the man himself comes into sharper focus. Readers may be surprised to learn that in reality Shepard is not the intrepid artist-cowboy of popular imagination, but a man who, despite all his accomplishments, finds himself caught in the same existential bind as most of us. Reflecting in early 2000, Shepard wrote of how he was still haunted by "essential feelings of inferiority and weakness."

Inferiority and *weakness* are not terms one regularly associates with Shepard. Nevertheless, over the years, he's also admitted to feeling like an imposter, and he speaks often of being plagued by feelings of anxiety and alienation. "Still I feel emotionally like a little boy inside—sad to confess but true," he wrote to a friend in early 2000. "I don't believe my inner self has grown an inch in all this time. Still the same un-nameable fears and anxieties, lostness, and all that harbored in the body of a 56-year-old man." His notebooks are full of similar sentiments, as well as self-lacerating comments, often about his drinking but about other perceived shortcomings as well.

All this runs counter to Shepard's reputation. Typically, he is viewed as the "desert-haunted cowboy-stranger," or the personification of the strong, silent type. The Sam Shepard familiar to most—crafted in interviews, by his writing, and by the countless tough-guy movie roles he's played—is primarily an illusion. From the outset, readers should be aware of the chasm that exists between the Shepard the public sees and thinks it knows, and the man himself. As he once wrote, "I believe in my mask/The man I made up is me." As much as this book will make the case for Shepard's importance as a writer and actor, it will also show him to be a man often uncomfortable in his own skin, who admits to needing alcohol to socialize and fit in with others, and who writes, he says, because he finds it easier than talking. His image, in other words, has all these years been a mask.

Sam Shepard is a complex man. Many of those interviewed for this book echoed this sentiment. Having spent a few years buried in his writing, letters, and archives, I heartily concur. He can be shy, difficult, reserved, obstreperous, openhearted, taciturn, sentimental, social, isolated, funny, angry, inspired, dull, brilliant, and ordinary. For as he has been asking himself for more than seven decades now, "Who am I?" These pages will provide as full an account as possible of Shepard, the man and artist.

Finally, readers should know that this book is not an examination or analysis of Shepard's work. It is for those interested in the man, his key works, his major films, his ideas, and his life. Deep analysis of his dramatic work is available in many scholarly books. My goal is to serve both the reader who comes to Shepard as a fan of his film work and those who enjoy his plays and other writing. It is my hope that by studying the key works and the life, as well as the connections in between, we can find the creative soul behind all of it, and learn as much as we can about the enigma that is Sam Shepard.

Sam Shepard

Discovery

*I'll never forget the elation of finishing my first one-act play. I felt
I'd really made something for the first time. Like the way you make
a chair or a table. Something was in the world now that hadn't
been there before.*

—Sam Shepard

Never knowing what to expect was the best part of the job. Especially these days, when new and daring ideas were seemingly in the air and young people were intent on slipping out from the tall shadows cast by their parents. Those parents had seen the world through a devastating war only to find themselves caught up in a decade, the fifties, marked by conformity and repression. Things were changing now. And fast. It was fall 1964. Kennedy was dead, but the Beatles had arrived just in time to pull the country out of its its collective grief, spurring in the youth of America a burst of optimism and a renewed sense of what was possible. Something was going on. As a theater critic, Michael Smith could see it on the streets, feel it in the places where he spent his nights. A new aesthetic, or something, an infusion of the innovative and radical, was changing the way artists were expressing themselves on stage and screen, in concert, in print, and on record. It was a middle finger to the establishment and its attack dogs in Birmingham and its ever-escalating war. It was pro-black, pro-women, pro-sex, pro-drugs, pro-do-it-if-it-feels-good.

Down here in Greenwich Village, still a bastion of individuality, the feeling of a coming insurgency was particularly palpable. Smith was lucky to have a prime seat for much of it. Especially down here, amid a scene that may have been just a few miles from the bright lights and marquee names of Broadway but that aesthetically couldn't have been further away. A playwright himself, Smith felt an affinity for the hopeful writers and actors who plied their trade on these makeshift stages. Yet, despite the challenges and lack of monetary reward, a legitimate scene was coalescing around a handful of small stages here in the Village, mostly on the East Side, where rents were still cheap. To call these places theaters would be laughable to uptown denizens, for this was a place of upstarts, and the stages they inhabited were in coffeehouses, churches, and apartments. Free or dirt-cheap tickets. Folding chairs. The smell of marijuana in the air. Homemade, stolen, or borrowed props and costumes. These were the elements of what one writer had a few years earlier dubbed Off-Off-Broadway. It was on these small stages that things were happening. "We all felt that Broadway, for all its frequent brilliance, had become too stuffy and consumeristic, and that the new stirrings below the radar had the potential to bring theater into the present and make it more relatable for our generation," Smith said.

This is what made his job so exciting, and as he made his way through the Bowery on this overcast Friday night to the rear of St. Mark's Church, he was, as ever, eager to discover something new. For mid-October, it was on the warm side, and most of the city was focused on the Yankees–Cardinals World Series, which was not going well for the locals. There were student protests in Berkeley, and kids in the know had been raving about a new British band called the Kinks, with some suggesting they might even give those other recent arrivals, the Rolling Stones, a run for their money. Smith, at twenty-nine, was one of the tuned-in writers at the *Village Voice*, the lefty newspaper founded nine years earlier by Norman Mailer, Ed Fancher, and Dan Wolf. As the main reviewer, he had his pick of new plays, and some weeks he attended as many as five or six. Smith's sensibilities, fueled by his interest in things outside the mainstream, such as the Living Theatre and the Beats, led him into places like the one he was entering on this night, down into the depths of Manhattan's Skid Row, to a second-floor meeting room in the parish hall behind St. Mark's on the Bowery called Theatre Genesis. Like other so-called little theaters around the Village—Caffe Cino, La Mama, and Judson Poets' Theatre—it promised the kind of immediacy impossible in a big theater, as well as genuinely innovative performances and alternatives to the "institutionalized professionalism" found uptown.

Smith saw in this movement a calling, of sorts, to check out these hole-in-the-wall theaters and tell his readers about what he'd discovered. "I always tried to be open to whatever it was," he said. "You never knew. I always had this sense that when the lights go down anything can happen."

He also couldn't shake the feeling that there was something in the air—beyond the weed—and felt that he was among the handful of critics ready for it, especially if it should blossom here on a tiny stage in the Village.

Smith had another reason for taking in that night's show. His companion for the evening, Bill Hart, a writer and director himself who was meeting him outside St. Mark's, knew one of the actors, Lee Kissman. It was always fun to see someone you knew onstage: it could make a bad play endurable, or, if things panned out, you could share in the triumph and afterglow of a great performance. Also, Kissman had been going on and on about the writer of the two plays on tap this evening, a brooding, good-looking redhead kid from the West Coast. True, this novice playwright was a busboy at the Village Gate, a nearby jazz club, but then again, Kissman was a waiter and the director of the play, Ralph Cook, was the maître d'. In this world, none of that mattered. Still, how special could this untried California import be? Smith tried to keep an open mind, but he'd read what his mentor, Jerry Tallmer, had written in the *Post*, trashing this double bill—at least the first half of it, since he left at intermission—as "derivative."

Inside, the men climbed the narrow stairs and cut across a cramped lobby to enter the performance space, which not long before had been converted from a Sunday school classroom. It was dubbed Theatre Genesis. The black box–style theater was literally that, a thirty-five-by-thirty-five-foot space with black walls and ceiling. The lighting system was meager. The set, such as it was, couldn't have been simpler: a wooden sawhorse with a blinking yellow light at each end. Smith and Hart found seats, easy to do after the Tallmer review. The first half of the bill was a play called *Cowboys*. *The Rock Garden* the closer. Two one-acts.

The lights went down, and two actors appeared on each side of the sawhorse. At first, they talked like young construction workers about the weather and then rose in turn to remark about the way the sky looked. At various points, they took on the voices of old men. Later they played cowboys and Indians, fighting invisible foes. The second play, *The Rock Garden*, was a familial tableau in two parts that culminated in a young man—Kissman himself—spouting forth to his old man about sex and orgasm, saying things like, "When I come it's like a river." After the boy reels off roughly another 150 words about his preferences in vagina size and sexual positions, the father falls off his chair and the lights go down. End of show.

The images, the jazzy lyricism of the language, the way the characters flipped identities on a dime, the lack of anything resembling a conventional plot—even by downtown standards this was something new. Smith and Hart met Kissman after the show, and the three men felt as if they'd been a part of something transcendent. The plays "had the sound of the day," Hart would later recall. Smith took them back to his place, where they stayed up all night parsing the meaning of the plays the busboy had written. It was a wild mix of Beckett and Brecht, but as American as if it had poured out of Bird's trumpet or been chanted by his Highness, Allen Ginsberg himself. Smith had been covering the little theater scene long enough to know that this was what he'd been waiting for: an experience akin to getting high, that altered one's mind but that sprang from the imagination of another. That other was named Sam Shepard, the California kid, the busboy, the lanky man-child nervously brooding in the shadows that night at Theatre Genesis. He'd reached into his inner life and somehow pulled out these experiences, transmogrified them, and set them aflame before the audience's very eyes, using nothing more than strings of words, a tape recording of traffic noise, a pilfered sawhorse, some battered furniture, and a small cast, mostly drawn from the server ranks of the Village Gate.

Smith knew a game changer when he saw it. When it came time to pen his review, he let the world in on it.

Theatre Genesis . . . [has] actually found a new playwright [and] he has written a pair of provocative and genuinely original plays. . . . [Sam] Shepard is feeling his way, working with an intuitive approach to language and dramatic structure and moving into an area between ritual and naturalism, where character transcends psychology, fantasy breaks down literalism, and the patterns of ordinariness have their own lives. His is a gestalt theater which evokes the existence behind behavior.

Smith couldn't have known it then, but his words may have kept the young playwright from giving up and heading back home to California, where he'd likely have become a veterinarian or found a sheep ranch to run. Tallmer's review in the *Post* had nearly sent him packing. But now, buoyed by Smith's rave and the resultant crowds that began turning up at St. Mark's for his plays, Sam Shepard was on his way. He began writing more one-acts at a furious pace, and over the years his work would grow more complex and polished without ever forsaking its spirit of independence, singular use of imagery, myth-shaking potency, and lyrical essence.

Not long after, the newly minted playwright was back busing tables at the Village Gate when he spilled candle wax on a customer. He was fired. It would be the last regular job Sam Shepard would ever have.

Beginnings

*Our dwelling is but a wandering, and our abiding is but a fleeting,
and in a word our home is nowhere.*

—Separatist leader at Plymouth, 1620

When the phone rang on the evening of November 4, 1943, Jane Rogers knew who was calling. She was alone at Fort Sheridan, just outside Chicago, and nine months pregnant. Her husband was two thousand miles away, serving with the U.S. Army Air Corps at Muroc Air Force Base. Sam Rogers was worried that his wife had yet to deliver. This time, he wasn't calling just to check on her status but to report that on this night, while preparing his plane for a flight to North Africa, he'd seen two shooting stars over the California desert. He took this as a sign. His reverie was soon over, however, and the lecture began: Rogers told his wife that if the baby didn't arrive in the next twenty-four hours, she was to get another doctor.

Fort Sheridan was established in the late 1880s, and it was thriving that November of 1943, serving as a recruitment reception center, one of four in the country, with recent draftees crammed into temporary quarters at the south end of the fort. By the following year, the fort's mission would change and it would become the control headquarters for prisoner of war camps across the state and in Michigan and Wisconsin. The best thing about the fort, as far as Jane Rogers was concerned, was that it sat on Lake Michigan. She loved walking along the shore, and that autumn northeastern Illinois had been especially lovely. In fact, Jane had spent a lot of time during the last two weeks of her pregnancy walking along the water's edge.

Samuel and Jane Rogers were living at Fort Sheridan in Unit 22 of what was deemed the lieutenants' quarters, in what to her was "a huge house." Late in life, Shepard would guess he was conceived in Texas, where his father had previously been stationed. "My mother tracked him down and jumped the fence," he joked.

The morning of her husband's phone call, the petite mother-to-be—who'd ballooned to 150 pounds—had spent the day scrubbing floors. The next morning she was up by seven, ready to go to Highland Park Hospital; however, no one was ready to take her at that hour. Eventually her mother went with her, but characteristically, on this rainy day when she would become a mother for the first time, Jane Rogers took the wheel for the short drive into town.

After checking in at the hospital's front desk, the expectant mom grabbed her bag and ran upstairs; she didn't want to wait for the elevator. She was undressed, in her hospital gown, and in bed before the nursing staff even knew she was there.

Samuel Shepard Rogers was delivered on November 5 at 3:20 p.m. His mother was, understandably, a bit groggy, but she knew it was afternoon because shortly after the delivery she could hear children kicking up a ruckus in the fall leaves and playing outside on their way home from school. That night, the first real snow of the season fell.

Thus it was that the "poet laureate of the American West" was, in point of fact, born more than 2,100 miles from the shores of the Pacific.

The *Highland Park News* carried Shepard's birth announcement six days later. Entries in that day's paper give a sense of what life was like for those living in a military stronghold during wartime. The paper reported promotions of soldiers stationed at the fort, war fund campaign news, notices asking housewives to save grease for the war effort, lists of soldiers home on furlough, and schedules of upcoming dances and USO shows. The war was everywhere, but by the time Shepard was born, the tide had begun to turn in the Allies' favor; seven months after his arrival, D-Day took place; and about the time the toddler was walking on his own, Germany surrendered.

Jane Rogers and her newborn soon decamped to the home of her in-laws in Crystal Lake, forty-five miles northwest of Chicago. The infant was given the nickname Steve to avoid confusion with his father and other relatives named Samuel. No one called him Sam. He was Steve as a baby, Steve when called for dinner, Steve in school and to everyone who knew him during the first two decades of life. He hated it when people called him Stevie, for it made him feel "impotent and inconsequential." Years later, on the brink of a remarkable career as a writer and actor, Steve Rogers would change his name to Sam Shepard.

For whatever reason, basic elements of Shepard's official biography are flat-out wrong. For instance, one can find his birth name in books and magazines given alternately as Samuel Shepard Rogers *Jr., III, IV, the seventh,* and *VII.* Nowhere in centuries of family records and documents do any of Shepard's forebears who share his birth name employ such traditional designations to distinguish one from the other. There are no juniors, seniors, firsts, or seconds. In other words, his name is simply Samuel Shepard Rogers. "That had gone on for generations, that name, seven generations of it," Shepard said. Chances are, he simply lost track. A thorough genealogy of his father's side of the family reveals that, in fact, he is only the fifth Samuel Shepard Rogers in the line.

In 2006, the reading of a new book titled *Mayflower,* by Nathaniel Philbrick, led Shepard to muse on his family's connection to the Pilgrims. "A woman named Susanna Fuller White on my Dad's father's side of the family—came over on the *Mayflower* and while it was parked in Cape Cod and they were sending out little expeditions of Pilgrims in rowboats, trying to locate the best location to start the new colony—Susanna gives birth to a boy named 'Peregrin'—the first white child born in the new colony," he wrote to a friend in 2006.

However, the in-depth genealogical study does not directly support a connection, though it's possible that an as-of-yet-unaccounted-for Rogers family line *is* connected to Peregrine White, who was indeed born to Susanna Fuller White aboard the *Mayflower* while it was in Provincetown Harbor. Nevertheless, it's interesting to note that several White descendants resided in Sheffield, Massachusetts, next to New Marlborough, where Shepard's ancestors lived around the same time. This may lend some credence to Shepard's claim.

Another question concerning the Rogers line is where the middle name Shepard comes from. There are two possibilities. A family bearing this name lived near Robert and Sally Rogers, our playwright's great-great-great-grandparents, in the area of New Marlborough in the late 1700s and early 1800s. This Shepard family may have been related to the Rogers. Another possibility is that Sally and Robert Rogers chose their son's middle name in honor of a long-serving, Calvinist-leaning pastor from Berkshire County, the Reverend Samuel Shepard. He lived in nearby Lenox, Massachusetts, until his death in 1846. One of these likely explains the recurrence of the middle name Shepard through the five generations that culminated with the playwright.

One ancestor Shepard has told of on a few occasions was a great-great-grandfather on his paternal side. The documentary evidence about the life of Lemuel P. Dodge, born September 9, 1832, is sketchy at best. Shepard gladly fills in the blanks, most likely drawing upon family lore or perhaps his own vivid imagination. In a 1997 documentary, he tells of how his great-great-grandfather Dodge not only served in the Civil War but lost an ear fighting for the South and an arm fighting for the North. Shepard adds to this legend, claiming that after the war, Lemuel Dodge was hanged for womanizing in Ojinaga, Mexico, whereupon his body was dragged through the streets until his head separated from his torso. It could be that Shepard's picaresque tale concerning the life and death of his great-great-granddad simply masks the fact of missing and contradictory information. A death certificate for him could not be found, but when his wife, Mary, remarried in 1877, she listed him as deceased. Records indicate that Dodge fought for the Arkansas infantry as part of the Confederate army and that after his marriage in 1866, he "again went south, engaging in various enterprises, but since 1900 all trace of him is lost." The source of this last bit of information is unclear, hence it opens up the possibility that Dodge was alive after 1877 and that he was living in another part of the country in the late 1800s. As for his ultimate end and the fate of his appendages, there are no records to indicate for certain if he died with or without them.

The tales concerning Shepard's "redneck grandfather" (the third Samuel Shepard Rogers in the line) also provided fodder for his imagination. If his grandson's description is to be believed, his later life revolved around baseball on television, an abiding love for President Truman, and writing letters to local newspapers signed "Plain Dirt Farmer." Shepard remembered his grandfather as an old man: "He smokes and drinks constantly and spits blood into a stand-up brass ashtray like you see in the lobbies of old hotels. Sometimes he coughs so violently that his whole body doubles over, and he can't catch his breath for a long time. His world is circumscribed around the sofa. Everything he needs is within a three-foot range."

This is the grandfather known as "the drinker" of the bunch, which among the Rogers clan would take some doing. As Shepard would say, "That side's got a real tough strain of alcoholism. It goes back generations." This grandfather had a notable fondness for muscatel and is famous for once setting his mattress on fire while lying upon it in a drunken stupor. One of his sons, Shepard's "Uncle Buzz," recalled how he was driving down Columbine Street in Crystal Lake when he spotted smoke pouring out of a second-story window of the family's house. He rushed inside, grabbed the flaming mattress, and tossed it out the window. He had to put the fire out with a hose in the front yard. The grandfather at some point must have also fancied himself an artist. Shepard remembers as a boy seeing a painting of a train conductor attributed to him hanging in his own family's house in South Pasadena.

Shepard's father was born on February 20, 1917, on the same wheat farm in McHenry, Illinois, as his father. The farm was lost, like so many others across the United States, as the Great Depression neared, forcing the family to move forty-odd miles south to Lombard just as Shepard's father was entering his teens. If one believes Shepard's take on things as represented in his 1970 play *The Holy Ghostly*, his grandfather's drinking, not the nose-diving economy, is the reason the farm was lost. As the character of the father in the play recalls, "My old man was a dairy farmer. Started hittin' the bottle and lost the whole farm. Things started goin' downhill from that point on."

There are things that don't show up in the pages of a genealogical study where Shepard gladly fills in the details. "I was born into this family of cranky men," he said. "Totally insane." Exhibits A through C in this case would be his father's brothers: the one who lost a leg when he was ten, the brother who married into the Chicago mob, and the one who raised dogs. Some of these characters, or parts of their life stories, would turn up in Shepard's writing. Later in life, Shepard would write of how his father kept old photos and tintypes of his brothers—these "irascible" men—on the mantel. The old man would sometimes sequester himself in the darkened living room to commune with their spirits, as if they held answers or proffered solace. His son viewed things differently: Shepard looked back over his lineage as depicted in these old images and saw a heritage in decline, evidenced, as he put it, by "the mysterious glint of doubt . . . creep[ing] into their eyes."

Shepard suspects that his father's side of the family had Native American or South American blood running through it. Well past middle age, he was still pondering the matter, confiding to one of his notebooks that his dark-skinned grandmother was South American or American Indian. If her skin tone wasn't a giveaway, Shepard wonders about her dark eyes and whether she kept the secret of her heritage from her husband. In an unpublished poem written in spring 2005, he claims his paternal grandmother was "the daughter of an Iroquois servant," with "deep black eyes" and a "sorrowful smile." Shepard also spelled out his suspicions in a 1986 interview in *Rolling Stone*: "And my grandmother, my father's mother, was part something . . . maybe American Indian, I'm not sure what. She was real dark, with black eyes, and I don't know what that was all about—there was a cover-up somewhere back there."

The Dark Muse/Father

L

There is no other origin of beauty than the wound, singular, different for each person, hidden or visible, which every man keeps inside him, which he preserves and where he withdraws when he wants to leave the world for a passing but profound solitude.
　　　　　—Jean Genet, *L'Atelier d'Alberto Giacometti*

I am my own father and my son.
　　　　　　　　　　　　　　　　—Flann O'Brien

S hepard has often looked into mirrors and seen the face of his father. The physical resemblance is easy to spot. But in the mirror, it was something equally spectral as genetic: "I mean every once in a while I'm just amazed when I catch a glimpse of who I really am. Just a little flash like the gesture of my hand in a conversation and WHAM there's my old man. Right there, living inside me like a worm in the wood."

It's not a stretch to believe that the genesis of the anxiety and insecurity Shepard often speaks of can be traced to his childhood, and in particular to his father's alcoholism and abuse. As he told an interviewer in 2010, "The male influences around me were primarily alcoholics and extremely violent." This taught him to play things close to his chest, to watch and speak little: "I listened like an animal. My listening was afraid," as the son Wesley says in Shepard's 1977 play *Curse of the Starving Class*. The effects were long-lasting. Shepard wrote in an unpublished poem in January 2006 about the times his father attacked him and that even at age sixty-two, "I find myself flinching."

Another biographer once said, "Perhaps every life requires a powerful but ambiguous (even empty) symbol around which it can revolve." Sam Rogers fulfilled that role for his only son. A veteran of World War II, who dropped bombs on Hitler's war machine, Shepard's father came home and found life wanting. He became a respected educator but slowly succumbed to an illness that was hard to pinpoint and for which, as his son put it, "the medicine was booze." Shepard has said he himself "was raised on a steady diet of fear and guilt," and there's little doubt as to the sources of these things. The old man's anger and violence—which his son bore the brunt of—caused Shepard to flee his family home in his late teens. The adult Shepard's primary goal in life has been to avoid becoming his father.

Samuel Rogers was a dreamy youth. As a boy, he was known to wander off on his own, invariably getting lost in a cornfield, where the stalks grew high over his head. "He'd wind up on some neighboring farm with his dog, Gyp, and have to spend the night there until my grandfather could come get him," one of his brothers recalled. The precocious youth would sometimes wander toward the family barn, where he'd climb into the hayloft for the sole purpose of watching his father oversee the breeding of one of his draft mares. This was strictly prohibited, but it gave young Samuel and his brothers, who sometimes followed, their first inkling of what they called "the deed." Afterward, while their father passed the bottle with the man who owned the stud, the brothers would have to wait to descend, hoping the hay didn't make them sneeze and give away their hideout.

Sam Rogers's dreamier side, however, was reined in quickly enough by reality. With the family's move to Lombard, his new life began. Money was tight, and as a teen he was forced to work outside the home to help the family make ends meet. Being the eldest of six, a disproportionate amount of this responsibility fell to him. He took odd jobs, selling Hershey bars door to door, and eventually working for a spell at the *Chicago Daily Tribune*. At some point, he squeezed in a year of college. With the war in Europe spreading, Samuel Rogers made a decision. Months before the attack on Pearl Harbor drew thousands of young men like him to enlist, he took the

of the family's Quonset hut. Another memory revolves around the fact that the military wives were issued pistols to keep the former Japanese soldiers from coming down from the nearby caves and stealing off the clotheslines. Shepard's mother fired off her share of rounds to keep her children—and the laundry—safe. He also recalled having his tonsils out while on the island. The operation took place in a Quonset hut-cum-hospital before he'd even turned five. Shepard could remember, more than six decades later, the journey to and from the operating room, the green canvas of the gurney, and "the sheet metal rooms where soldiers lay bandaged and silent."

Shepard has written of traveling from base to base around the United States with his mother during these years for surreptitious meetings with his father. Due to the nature of his assignments, Sam Rogers was forbidden to reveal his itinerary even to family. He developed a secret code using postcards that indicated to his wife a town, hotel, room number, and time to meet. The playwright would allude to the system of motel meetings—using the phone rather than postcards—in his 1985 play *A Lie of the Mind*, when Lorraine, the family matriarch, says:

> You-Name-It-U.S.A. Those were the days we chased your daddy from one air base to the next. Always trying to catch up with the next "Secret Mission." Some secret. He was always cookin' up some code on the phone. Trying to make a big drama out of things. Thought it was romantic I guess. Worst of it was I fell for it.

Sam Rogers was discharged on August 31, 1948, in Weaver, South Dakota, with a chest full of medals. His gravestone at Santa Fe National Cemetery indicates that he was a first lieutenant. However, documents from the National Archives and Records Administration indicate that his final rank was captain. He would continue to serve his country as a member of the U.S. Air Force Reserve through March 1955.

The war left deep scars on many of those who returned home from the skies and battlefields, and it's no secret that fighter pilots paid a heavy toll for the missions they flew. Shepard's father told of watching as his tail gunner was blasted out from underneath his plane. "My dad came from an extremely rural farm community . . . and the next thing he knows he's flying B-24s over the South Pacific, over Romania, dropping bombs and killing people he couldn't even see," Shepard said. "These men returned from this heroic victory . . . and were devastated in some basic way that's mysterious still." This is an explanation Shepard has often given when discussing the toll the war took on his father. It demonstrates the empathy he could summon toward his old man and signals his attempts later in life to forgive him for the abuse he inflicted. To Shepard, his father was a desperate alcoholic with a violent temper, but he would never forget that there were reasons for this, the war being a large part of it.

When he came home from the war, Sam Rogers first found work as a gardener. However, at the urging of his wife and her Aunt Grace, he took advantage of the GI Bill and attended Occidental College, located outside Los Angeles, in Eagle Rock, California. There, majoring in Latin, geography, and Spanish, he met a professor who saw in the young veteran an unusual proficiency with language and who steered him toward a career teaching Spanish. After taking his degree, Shepard's father found a position in September 1952 at San Marino High School, primarily teaching Spanish, as well as the occasional Latin and geography course. It's a job he kept through the end of the school year in 1969, which is when, his son explains, drinking ended his career.

By the end of the 1960s, Sam Rogers already had many years of hard drinking behind him. Still, he seems to have been a popular teacher. He was known for gently admonishing his students "en Español, por favor," so often that it became sort of a catch phrase. The students thought highly enough of him to dedicate the 1960 yearbook to him. In the same yearbook, beneath his photo in the faculty section, it says: "Free time: gardening, Dixieland music, completing master's degree in geography." Sam Rogers also sponsored the language and camera clubs and in the early 1960s was chair of the languages department. The Spanish club went by the name Los Titanos Espanoles (the school's sports teams were known as the Titans), which sponsored a canned food and clothing drive each Christmas to aid an orphanage in Ensenada, Mexico.

Mary Theriot, a member of San Marino's Class of 1957 who now lives in Liberty, Kentucky, remembers Sam Rogers as "a great guy." "Thanks to

Mr. Rogers, I can still recall enough Spanish to talk 'slang' with the local Mexican tobacco workers," she said.

Theriot recalls that Shepard's father emphasized practical, conversational Spanish versus drilling students on verb tenses. As a teacher he was "good-natured and patient," she added, even finding time to teach his students about football, including the quarterback sneak. Once Theriot ran into a teenage Shepard and his father at a local dog obedience trial. She recalled that the son was "rather cute."

Lawrence Cole, a 1967 graduate of San Marino High, now a retired professor from the University of Kentucky, has similar recollections. He never had Shepard's father as a teacher but frequently spoke with him in the school's hallways. "I found him to be very personable and affable, as did many others," he said. "He was very well thought of by almost everyone at the school." Cole added that Rogers "seemed to enjoy helping and counseling students with their problems. A real credit to the teaching profession."

The Spanish that Sam Rogers had mastered was not the type spoken in nearby Mexico but rather Castilian, the official language of Spain. Seeking authenticity, he'd even mastered the lisp that is peculiar to this dialect. In what would prove to be an important development in his life—perhaps even a turning point—Rogers was granted a three-month Fulbright Linguistic Scholarship to study in Bogota, Colombia, during the summer of 1961. There are some who say that Rogers left his heart in Colombia and was never the same after returning home. The belief was that he may have had an affair with, or at least fallen for, the daughter of his host family in Bogota. When Sam Rogers returned to his family at summer's end, he expressed a desire to move to Colombia. If tales of the affair, or near affair, are true, it raises the question as to whether unrequited love was another factor that undermined Samuel Rogers's happiness in life.

Shepard's father influenced his son in important ways. Sam Rogers read in the original Spanish the works of the great Latin American poets, particularly Federico Garcia Lorca and Pablo Neruda. Often he shared these poems with his young son. Shepard believed his father harbored ambitions of his own, that he was, "a poet himself . . . in a certain weird way. Because of circumstances he never really had the chance to prove himself. Who knows if my work is better than his?"

The son also absorbed from his father a love of music, as Sam Rogers was an aficionado of Dixieland jazz. He had a cardboard box of classic records that he often spun, and for years he played drums in a semiprofessional Dixieland band. As a boy, Shepard would jump behind his father's kit and bang away, planting the seeds for a love of rhythm and music that would never leave him.

Then there was, of course, the other side of Sam Rogers, the one those familiar with Shepard's writing will recognize—the father who drank too much and took out his life's disappointments on the people and things around him. When visiting the former Rogers family home in Southern California during the summer of 2015, the current homeowners showed me a good-sized nook that when Shepard was growing up had been a tiny kitchen. My hosts pointed to the empty door frame, retelling the famous story of how Sam Rogers ripped the doors off the kitchen in a drunken rage. Shepard often notes that his father was famous for destroying rooms in the house during his alcohol-fueled tirades. It didn't stop there. Even more troubling to the son was the father's brutality toward dogs. He recalls how the old man would beat the family pets, including one episode where he used a hose as a whip, opening up cuts on the dog's rib cage. The wounded pup hid for days in the yard among the avocado trees. Despite this, Shepard claims his father would have been shocked to hear someone describe him as violent. Yet to his son, Sam Rogers *embodied* violence: his butch haircut was an "emblem of his military life" and all that that suggested.

Sam Rogers's life must have seemed to him like one disappointment after another: in his youth sent to war, where he dropped bombs on faceless, nameless thousands; the loss of a beloved brother in the prime of life; a forbidden love that flared briefly only to be extinguished by the reality of a growing family back home; and his dreams of becoming a writer or a scholar of Latin American poetry subordinated to the daily grind of teaching high school to keep a roof over the heads of his wife and children. It's no wonder the family curse of alcoholism proved too much for him to overcome. The fathers in Shepard's family dramas are, in the end, as much victims as victimizers. For instance, in 1977's *Curse of the Starving Class*, the father, Weston, tries to explain his dissolution into drink and debt:

I just went off for a little while. Now and then. I couldn't stand it here. I couldn't stand the idea that everything would stay the same. That every morning it would be the same. I kept looking for it out there somewhere. I kept trying to piece it together. The jumps. I couldn't figure out the jumps. From being born, to growing up, to droppin' bombs, to having kids, to hittin' bars, to this. It all turned on me somehow. It all turned around on me.

However, in real life, the war and its attendant tragedy would seem to be mere fuel for a fire that was raging generations before Samuel Rogers ever took to the skies over Europe. The curse of alcoholism was fated to strike again. Ultimately, it seems the only thing Shepard the playwright has figured out about his father is that he was an enduring enigma. Many of his plays try to address the mystery but can penetrate only so far, ultimately confirming merely the absence of comprehension. "I suppose it has affected me, but I'm not sure how," Shepard said.

The Rock/Mother

My mother had a heart of gold
If you came within her reach you knew that

— Sam Shepard

A s biographer Scott Donaldson has written, "It's a curious thing, but almost all major American writers have had dominant mothers and ineffectual fathers. It's true of Fitzgerald and Hemingway, Faulkner and Frost, Melville and Hawthorne, Emerson and Thoreau." That's esteemed company in which to include Shepard, but it is true in his case as well. While his father became an alcoholic, slowly fading from his role as patriarch, his mother thrived. She was, her son claims, "a strong, solid woman, like a rock."

Shepard makes no unusual claims of his mother's side of the family; nor do the ancestors on that side figure much in his writing. Hence a rudimentary genealogical overview is all that's necessary. His mother, Jane Schook, was born on July 16, 1917, in Lombard, Illinois, the daughter of Frederick "Pop" DeForest Schook and Amy Victoria Bynon. On his mother's maternal side, Shepard's roots have been traced to London, Plymouth, and Newcastle, England; Wales; and Scotland. His mother's paternal side, including a grandfather of Pennsylvania Dutch extraction, was centered in Grand Rapids, Michigan.

Shepard's grandmother Amy Bynon was a petite woman who when young worked as an artist's model. This may have been the connection through which she met her husband, Frederick DeForest Schook. He taught at the Chicago Art Institute and ran a summer camp for shell-shocked veterans returning from World War I. The camp was held at a cabin he built himself in Baileys Harbor, Wisconsin, which is located on a finger of land that juts into Lake Michigan.

Jane Schook grew up on the opposite side of Lombard than her future husband, but they were brought together in high school. Both graduated from what was then known as Glenbard High School, which as the name indicates drew students from both Lombard and Glen Ellyn, its neighbor to the west. The Rogers boys were handsome and known for their outgoing, roughish personalities. Jane Schook and Sam Rogers got to know each other in high school, but that's as far as it went. After graduation, when she traveled to California to live with her Aunt Grace Upton and attend college, they each dated other people.

She first attended Pasadena City College, where she was a good student and a cheerleader. Jane Schook transferred to Occidental College in nearby Eagle Rock, where she majored in English and was the manager of the society page for the school newspaper and a member of the social club. When she returned to Illinois after her commencement in the spring of 1940, she and Sam Rogers "went steady," in the parlance of the day, marrying after he joined the service.

In the years after the war, Jane Rogers took a job teaching first grade at the elite K–12 Polytechnic School in Pasadena, located across the street from the California Institute of Technology. Many students at the Polytechnic School, then as now, were the children of professors and administrators at the top-flight research institute. The much-loved educator would work at the same school until retiring in her seventies.

Mention Jane Rogers to those who knew her and they can't say enough good things. "She was just kind, sweet, and attentive, and she adored her children," said Joyce Aaron, Shepard's first serious girlfriend after he arrived in New York in 1963. "His mother, Jane, was the steady, loving influence that gave him the emotional balance that he needed in his young life."

One of Jane Rogers's pupils, Mike White, would go on to become a well-known screenwriter, director, and actor, responsible for such films as *School of Rock* and *The Good Girl*, as well as the TV series *Enlightened*. Having Jane Rogers for a teacher in second grade back in 1977 helped set him on his career path. "I remember just loving her class and loving her," White said. "I was always excited to go to school. She was a small woman, but she was very cheerful and just a fun teacher. In fact, I remember my parents invited her to parties at our house. She seemed like a more sophisticated woman than some of the others."

When Shepard's 1978 play *Buried Child* came out, White carried a copy around school. He had no idea what the play was about, of course, but he wanted to impress the playwright's mother. "I just remember part of the reason I wanted to write scripts was because of some association with her being proud of her son and wanting her to like me," he said.

Shepard's mother encouraged White to write his first play, which was an adaptation of *The Emperor's New Clothes*. "She was my development executive," he said, adding that Mrs. Rogers helped him make cuts on his first draft. "'Get rid of this, she ordered," White recalled, slashing the air with an imaginary red pen.

Linda Stowitts met Jane Rogers in 1972, when she joined the faculty of the Polytechnic School. The veteran teacher welcomed the newcomer and became an instant mentor. "She was a wonderful woman and her students loved her, her colleagues loved her, the parents of the students loved her," Stowitts said. "She was full of energy, life, creativity, and when I started teaching I was pretty young and she took me under her wing. She was a very important presence in my life."

As an educator, Jane Rogers stressed creativity. At one point, the school awarded her a grant that funded a six-month tour of Europe. Her fellow teachers loved her, for her house parties and the sewing bees she held to make quilts for those in need. "She also had a bit of a rebellious side to her," Stowitts said. "Not always wanting to toe the line."

Jane Rogers was proud of her playwright son and was an important influence on him. "She was a pretty stable force in his life," Stowitts said. She remembers that when Shepard won the Pulitzer in 1979, his mother invited a bunch of her Polytechnic colleagues over to the house. She arranged chairs in a circle and then called her son and passed the phone around so each could each congratulate him. "He was a good sport about it," Stowitts recalled.

Go West

I had the feeling that not only had I already been over every inch of this fucking land, but that I'd been born here.

—Roberto Bolaño

S am Shepard's family didn't move west looking for gold or a better harvest like those of earlier generations had. But they did come to California seeking the same kind of security. They found it in a well-to-do relation who lived in South Pasadena.

Grace (Bynon) Upton, the aunt of Shepard's mother, would play an important role in the lives of the Rogers family. She'd already taken in his mother during her college years, and when Sam and Jane Rogers were looking to relocate and begin a new life out west, Aunt Grace, a widow by then, offered safe harbor. Her own story is one for the books, at least as Shepard tells it, beginning with her dating the bandleader John Philip Sousa. Whether that's true or not, it's clear that Aunt Grace ultimately did pretty well in the marriage department. She wed a man named Charlie Upton in their home state of Michigan in August 1921. He was fifty-eight, eighteen years her senior. After they moved to 344 Pasadena Avenue in South Pasadena a few years later, he became part owner of a lumberyard and a city councilman, while his wife volunteered with several local organizations.

Shepard's mother told him tales about his Uncle Charlie: how during a fight in the lumberyard his opponent had bitten off his thumb, and how he'd send his wife photos of the dead mule deer he hunted. As much as Shepard's outsized paternal uncles show up in his writing, it's surprising that Charlie Upton doesn't. He seems ready-made for one of Shepard's family dramas or outlandish prose pieces.

Charlie Upton died in November 1942, and Shepard indicates that he left his widow a sizable inheritance and a house large enough to accommodate the newly arrived Rogers clan when they came knocking in 1948. Aunt Grace was not only the family's benefactor; she also provided a built-in babysitter. She "half raised me," Shepard said.

Things were rarely boring around his aunt's house. Young Shepard was kept company by a drooling, farting bulldog mix, a Mexican parrot, and a backyard aviary full of canaries. Grace had a big Chrysler sedan with plaid upholstery that her husband had left her, and in it she'd take her young nephew on jaunts he'd remember all his life. One such excursion took them to the Mojave Desert for the annual Date Festival, where the locals "dressed up like Arabs" and actually rode down Main Street on the backs of camels. She also took him to Los Angeles to a farmer's market, where he saw myna birds for the first time. Shepard claims that if not for these boyhood trips with his great-aunt, he would have never known that L.A., so close by, even existed. In the summer of 2010, Shepard would pay homage to his great-aunt by naming his new Airedale after her.

The Rogers family lived with Aunt Grace for a few years before she helped the family settle into a tiny two-story house of its own on Adelaine Avenue in South Pasadena. The family shows up in the city directory at that address for the first time in 1952–1953. Shepard slept in one of the small bedrooms, in the bottom bunk below his sister Sandy, and now with a place of their own he felt like he and his family were smack dab amid "small-town-America-type stuff."

Shepard entered first grade at South Pasadena's Lincoln Elementary School, and it is here that he did his first writing. In the small amount of juvenilia that survives from these years, his wide-ranging imagination is already evident, as is his playfulness and an attention to detail beyond his years. The stories feel less like school assignments and more like bits of escapism captured on the page. The first story Shepard ever wrote remains in his memory, even if its written form is long gone. It was about a Coca-Cola bottle that travels the country getting filled up in one town, drank dry, and then sent on to the next.

"The Finding of Fang," the earliest surviving story, tells of two orphans, Steve and Spencer, from the town of White Horse in the Yukon. The boys are partly Indian, but "very civilized [*sic*]" and they love animals and candy but hate school. On a cold day in late December, the two friends walk six miles through the snow to get to class. On the way home, they notice the beauty of the snow-covered trees and how "the branches hung low from the weight." The boys then plan to go to the trading post to see if they have any puppies available, though they worry that their grandmother doesn't like dogs.

Another story, titled "Vacation Time Has Come," written at age seven, begins with a cock's crow, as the children awaken to the "the crackle of bacon on the grill." They get dressed and head downstairs. There are apparently pages missing from the story, but at some point the children go to the barn to help Grandpa with his chores, such as cleaning stalls and fetching water from the well. At the end, the main character, John, turns to his sister Nancy and says, "I learned a lot today, did you?" before falling fast asleep.

Another untitled, incomplete story from these early years involves two boys finding newborn puppies, or "little balls of fur," as the young author puts it. Kid stuff, no doubt, but the stories give us a glimpse into Shepard's early years, how he valued friendships and already possessed an affinity for animals. There is also an eye for detail and a better than passing proficiency with language, as well as signs that already the young Shepard was learning to weave the stuff of life into fiction.

It all sounds like so much fun, yet Shepard reports hating school. Indeed, it was as a reluctant student that he first felt the wrath of his father. "He was very strict, my father, very aware of the need for discipline, so called, very into studying and all that kind of stuff. I couldn't stand it—the whole thing of writing in notebooks, it was really like being in jail," he said.

At the Lincoln School, Shepard gravitated toward the unruly crowd. He spent his recess with these boys, sitting on the green picnic bench in the schoolyard making up semi-naughty rhymes about the recently defeated Hitler and Mussolini. To give a sense of how mature these jousts of word-play were: the Italian dictator's name was rhymed with *weenie*.

Outside school there was the usual fun. Shepard recalls that each year when the world-famous Rose Bowl Parade rolled through downtown Pasadena, he and a friend would set up stepladders along Colorado Avenue and run twelve-by-two-foot boards between them so they could sit above the crowds for a prime view. Wrapped in a blanket and sipping split pea soup from a thermos, they'd watch Leo Carrillo, Hopalong Cassidy, Roy Rogers, and Gene Autry ride by on horseback.

Even more important, there was the escapism of the movies. Shepard's favorite films were, not surprisingly, adventure movies and westerns, like *The Treasure of the Sierra Madre* (1948) and *King Solomon's Mines* (1950). His young mind was "haunted" by the latter film, since he "entered the world of the movie so completely." "There was this powerful impression when I was a kid going to those films and absolutely believing that this was a way to *be*. It wasn't just an actor acting; this was a *life form*," Shepard said. After seeing the film *Vera Cruz* (1954), the preteen Shepard walked around for months bearing the same wide grin he'd seen Burt Lancaster flash onscreen.

In his prose collection *Motel Chronicles*, Shepard writes about a youthful attempt at running away from home. Perhaps swept up by the same romantic impulse that fed his love of movies, Shepard and two older friends—brothers he claims were regular visitors to juvenile hall—stole bicycles and lit out for the great beyond. The incident ended with the South Pasadena cops stopping them. They took the bikes and called the boys' parents. Shepard's father was too angry to come, so his mother picked him up at the station. When he got home, Shepard recalled, he "got whipped three times with the buckle-end of my Dad's belt. Three times. That was it. Then he left the house. He never said a word." It was not the first time Shepard felt the wrath of the old man; nor would it be the last.

The denouement of the running away episode was a powerful moment for Shepard; he realized his vulnerability on a larger, more meaningful, scale. This feeling stayed with him. In his 1975 play *Action*, a character named Jeep has a similar epiphany after a run-in with the law. "It wasn't until I got in trouble that I found my true position. . . . I was in the world. I was up for grabs. I was being taken away by something bigger. . . . My frame of reference changed."

In real life, that something bigger was, to Shepard, scary and thrilling at the same time. As a youth, he would lie awake listening to the sounds of the night—his sisters' breathing, the dog at the back door—and worry about "how or when I'm going to die." This thought haunted him. The something bigger also hinted at something beyond, larger than the small house and the city where his family had landed. Waiting out there was possibility. He remembers even at this early age, he was "starving for a voice." Already he knew he had something to say and was worried about whether he'd ever get the chance to share it.

The Rogers family had grown by the mid-1950s. Joining Shepard and his sister Sandra was a second daughter, Roxanne, who was born during the family's short time in South Pasadena. The growing family must have made for a cramped household, and when benefactor Aunt Grace died, there was little reason to stay in South Pasadena. Jane Rogers began looking for her dream house about a dozen miles to the east, a place still within the comforting shadows of the San Gabriel Mountains.

As we drove through Duarte, California, past the rows of strip malls replete with their faux adobe exteriors, I couldn't help but think of something Shepard said to an interviewer in 1997: "Old rancho California is gone." Indeed, disappeared are any signs of the Old West, long ago swallowed by modernity's outward signs of progress—fast food joints, nail salons, and just about every other commercial venture known to just about every other American city or town of appreciable size. Get beyond the commercial areas, and Duarte seems like a fine place to live. There are the mountains to the north and the famed Route 66, known locally as the Mother Road, running through the city. Outsiders like me are likely to pronounce the city's name with a little south-of-the-border inflection: *Do-whar-tay*. But do so and the locals may have no idea what you're talking about. They say *Dwartee*, giving it just one syllable and letting it shoot quickly past their lips. Today this city of roughly 21,000, about twenty-two miles northwest of downtown Los Angeles, is known as the place Sam Shepard hails from.

His family's home was actually on Lemon Avenue in the neighboring city of Bradbury. It's true that Shepard attended Duarte High School, as all students of Bradbury did then and still do, and that he spent his spare time in Duarte, banging around the usual teen hangouts, like the Bob's Big Boy, or cruising through downtown on Route 66 in a jacked-up muscle car. But the house in which he spent his formative years—later featured, slightly disguised, in some of his greatest plays—was located half a mile away from downtown Duarte, just over the line in Bradbury.

Today Bradbury is among the most affluent zip codes in the United States. When Shepard's family lived there, beginning around the mid-1950s, this was not the case, but it was still, at the time, a step above the neighboring communities.

Bradbury and Duarte, and a handful of surrounding cities and towns, trace their roots to Andres Duarte, a retired Mexican soldier who had been posted to Mission San Gabriel and fell in love with the area. Upon leaving the army in May 1841, he was granted by Governor Juan Alvarado nearly 6,600 acres, which he named Rancho Azusa de Duarte. All this was before California was part of the United States. The climate and fertile soil on Señor Duarte's new parcel were perfect for crowing citrus, and consequently the rancho was subdivided into citrus ranches. Today, in addition to the city that bears Duarte's name, upon that original tract of land sit the communities of Bradbury, Monrovia, Irwindale, Baldwin Park, Arcadia, and Azusa, the latter known to Shepard fans as the setting of his play *The Unseen Hand*.

Duarte and Bradbury both remained unincorporated until push came to shove. In 1956, the City of Azusa filed to annex a portion of Duarte to use as a dump. According to the book *On the Duarte*, this was a wake-up call to Duarte, finally leading the city to file for incorporation. Duarte included Bradbury in its plans; however, Bradbury officials had ideas of their own. They filed a notice with the Board of Supervisors to incorporate as a separate city "for the purpose of protecting and preserving this foothill area as an exclusively residential community."

Ultimately, both Duarte and Bradbury incorporated separately in 1957, around the time Shepard's family moved to town.

Bradbury was home to only about six hundred residents when the Rogers family arrived. Much of the city featured horse-friendly zoning. Duarte, then with a population of about 13,000, was primarily an agricultural community, despite its dusty climate, and that continued to be the case through the end of World War II. The city was at that time still a leader in the citrus industry, and many area workers were employed in orchards and packinghouses. The outer limits featured more forbidding terrain. Shepard recalled: The outskirts of Duarte were "dry, flat, cracked and stripped down," nothing but "rock quarries and gravel pits." Trucks carrying the stones and gravel rolled through Duarte all day long. After the war, the city became mostly residential. Train tracks cut through the middle of the city, teaching Shepard a thing or two about issues of race and class. "It was the first place where I understood what it meant to be born on the wrong side of the tracks." In *The Tooth of Crime*, Shepard's 1972 play, the main character, Hoss, mentions a Creole boy he once knew, referring to the dark-skinned friend as "a Rock Town boy."

Duarte's population is nowadays almost 22,000, and it's known as the City of Health, thanks to the presence of a major clinical research center, City of Hope National Medical Center, founded in 1914.

Shepard didn't like leaving his friends in South Pasadena when the family moved, and his life in Bradbury was very different. The new address came with a host of chores. Next to the new house was an avocado orchard with, at first, sixty-five trees that had to be pruned, watered, and harvested on a regular basis. Shepard would spend part of his time plowing the orchard, wearing a bandanna around his mouth to keep the dust out of his throat. He also helped his father hose down the roof shingles during brush fire season. And then there were the animals to care for. But at least with the new house, he had a bedroom of his own, and as was typical for boys his age, he had model airplanes hanging from the ceiling, including copies of Japanese Zeroes and American P-38s. Years later, in his play *A Lie of the Mind*, the bedroom of the eldest son, Jake, has cobwebbed model airplanes hanging over the bed. They hover

over the scene, symbolically invoking the story's missing father, a former World War II bomber pilot who long ago abandoned the family and took to drink down in Mexico.

Shepard was all boy, playing "Apache Indians" in the backyard among the cacti, and when no one was looking, sneaking out of the yard to peek into the bedroom window of the Indian sisters who lived across the street. At night he listened to the desert wind blow, the screaming peacocks, and the coyotes, the latter often on the prowl near the family's sheep pen.

Shepard remembers the move to Bradbury as a turning point in his father's life and the beginning of his long, slow decline. "He couldn't hold things together, and then it kind of dissipated from there," he said. Samuel Rogers, however, was at this time just beginning his teaching career at San Marino High School, located ten miles from the family's new home.

Shepard remembered the family home being "like a little greenhouse that had been converted into a house" and that in its original incarnation it was used to store bird of paradise flowers before they were taken by train to Los Angeles. The original portion of the home was, in fact, built in Pasadena and brought via truck to its current address. The city directories from 1958 and 1959 show the house being at its current location since at least 1945 and being remodeled a decade later. The directories also note the avocado grove, sheep pens, and barn.

The current owners, Mary Lou and Tony, welcomed me and gave me a tour of the house and property. He's a stonemason, and the couple has substantially renovated the house since purchasing it from Shepard's mother in May 1972 for $35,000. The first thing I noticed is that the rectangular avocado orchard on the east side of the one-acre property, which had grown to have eighty trees at its peak, was long gone, replaced by a barn and horse pasture.

Initially, the home was a two-bedroom, one-and-a-half-bath affair, with a tiny kitchen. A quirk in the design meant Shepard and his sisters had to go outside to reach their bedrooms. With no master bedroom, Shepard's parents slept on a convertible couch in the living room, with bamboo shades pulled around for privacy. The garage on the east end of the house has since been converted by the current owners to a master bedroom. The concrete floors, despite the Mexican rugs Shepard's parents put down, were always cold on his feet.

Shepard stopped by one day about twenty-five years ago to visit the old homestead, hoping to show it to a friend. A son of the current owners was home alone, so Shepard had to settle for touring his friend around the property.

It's hard to say what Shepard's father had in mind with the small farm—whether it was intended as a hobby or a side business. The family kept chickens, a few horses, twenty-five sheep, and the avocado grove, irrigated by a system of hoses and pipes that Shepard spent many after-school hours and summer days working on. The overall enterprise shaped him, imbuing him with a lifelong love of animals and the outdoors.

While in his teens, sheep seem to have been Shepard's livestock of choice. A member of both Future Farmers of America and the local 4-H Club, he raised sheep that he entered into local competitions. He gave them names—Maine, Tamie, Vinewood, C.R., and Travis—and kept records in a green, hardbound book regarding their health, the vet work he had done on each, and other matters. His little operation was known as the Bradbury Southdown Flock. His diligence paid off, for he had a champion yearling ram one year at the Los Angeles County Fair. At one point, he also took up raising German shepherds.

Given all this, it's easy to believe that becoming an artist was the furthest thing from Shepard's mind throughout his school years. As a senior, Shepard reported to his 4-H Club that he planned to attend a local college for two years before advancing to the University of California at Davis, where he planned to study veterinary medicine. He gained further exposure to this life during summers off from school, which he spent walking horses at Santa Anita Park, as well as doing the most menial of work. "I was mucking out stalls and working in the alfalfa fields," he said. "You know in high school you didn't get very glamorous jobs back then." Other summers, he sheared and herded other people's sheep, picked their oranges, and, at one point, had a chance to manage a sheep ranch, but he passed.

During one summer break, Shepard's 4-H leader got him a job at Conley Arabian Horse Ranch in Chino, California, where a horse named Swaps was kept. Swaps had won the 1955 Kentucky Derby, and his name turns up at several points in Shepard's work—most notably, the thoroughbred is referenced in his 1994 play *Simpatico.* In his prose works, Swaps gets a mention or two, and in the TV movie *Ruffian*, featuring Shepard, a character mentions the great thoroughbred champion.

Upon arriving in Bradbury, Shepard began attending Royal Oaks Grammar School, which served kindergarten through grade eight. Duarte High School opened in 1957, just in time for Shepard to enroll as a member of the Class of 1961. Actually, the school wasn't ready that September, meaning Shepard and his classmates had to temporarily travel to Monrovia High School until the new building was completed, three months into the 1957 school year.

Shepard has given the impression of being a troubled youth during his high school years, but that's hard to fathom. For instance, here's the impression a writer from *Playboy* magazine got after interviewing him for a 1984 feature. "He was one of many rebels without causes who hated school and spent their time cruising, drinking cheap liquor and taking speed. Then there were the fights. 'In that area, fighting was a kind of badge. I never enjoyed it, but I never backed down,'" Shepard told the author. Likewise, in a short biographical piece Shepard wrote in 1971 for the American Place Theatre newsletter, he painted a portrait of himself as a hardened delinquent—stealing cars, driving recklessly, and going to jail for giving the finger to the wife of a police chief in Big Bear, California. In his prose collection *Motel Chronicles*, Shepard writes of taking Benzedrine during the school day and to crank him up before track meets. Shepard told another interviewer who asked about his alcohol problems: "My history with booze goes back to high school. Back then there was a lot of Benzedrine around, and since we lived near the Mexican border I'd just run over, get a bag of Bennies and drink Ripple wine. Speed and booze together make you quite omnipotent. You don't feel any pain. I was actually in several car wrecks that I don't understand how I survived."

Reading these I'm reminded of what one longtime Shepard observer told me: "Sam is a mystery and you may not find much but the stories he and others have woven around him." Indeed, for these tales of hell-raising are not what one hears from a classmate or intuits from Duarte

High School yearbooks. "He was nice, polite, quiet," said Geri Houlihan, a fellow member of Duarte High's Class of 1961. Shepard signed the former homecoming queen's yearbook: "Hope to see you during summer." Houlihan said that in senior year, Shepard got just one vote for the "Cutest Boy" award—hers. "He would have gotten more, but there was a ringer, a class Adonis, who stole the vote," she said.

Shepard's tales of booze and pills, if true, would put him out of step with many of his classmates. At the start of the 1960s at Duarte High, identification with school groups, such as the drill team, drama club, and athletics, was important, and Shepard had many such affiliations. Everyone went to the school dances, and cruising the local Bob's Big Boy was all the rage. As for drugs, they were rare, Houlihan remembers. "Beer and cheap wine was what the 'wrong crowd' indulged in."

If Shepard was a ruffian during his high school years, it's hard to imagine where he found the time—between school, working the family farm, playing music, sports, and his involvement with the local 4-H Club. Later in life, Shepard recalled how he'd even worked for the Tops Chemical Company, "loading buckets of chlorine in green flatbed trucks." His extra-curricular activities alone would leave little time for much hell-raising.

Shepard appears regularly in the 1960 and 1961 editions of the *Halconado*, the Duarte High School yearbook. He was, of all things, a yell leader his junior year in high school, meaning he led cheers at sporting events. He's pictured in the 1960 yearbook in his plaid pants and oversized sweater bearing a large "D." He harkens back to this experience in 1969, when he introduces a male cheerleader at about the halfway point of his play *The Unseen Hand*. The character enters wearing the same type of uniform and holding a giant megaphone. After students from a nearby town beat him with a belt and abuse him with a Tampax, the kid wonders if it's "just because I couldn't make second string." He adds, "I could have played Junior Varsity but I decided to be a cheerleader instead." Also, in his 1971 play *Shaved Splits*, an armed felon does a cheer in front of an apartment window as the police fire at him from the street below. Shepard has talked a lot about his time in high school; never does he mention his days leading cheers.

As an athlete, Shepard lettered in basketball, playing for three years; and as a sophomore and junior, he was a member of the track team. He's written that he broke the school record for the 220-yard dash while high on Benzedrine. Verifying this is impossible, as Duarte High School does not have its track records from the years 1957 to 1961.

One thing there's no argument about is that Shepard gained his first exposure to theater while at Duarte High. He was cast in two school plays, *Finian's Rainbow* and *Eighteenth Summer*. He was also spending time at both the Pasadena Playhouse and San Gabriel Playhouse, either taking acting lessons or actually performing onstage. (As testament to how badly Shepard wanted to be involved with theater, he had to hitchhike home at night from these venues, as his father wouldn't let him take the car. Each was ten miles from the family home.)

The truth of Shepard's high school years may exist in a two-page type-written biography that most likely served as copy for a theater program—which he was allowed to proof and make changes to. Shepard made a few handwritten edits. However, left untouched are the sentences about his high school years, which mention the 4-H Club, his love of animal husbandry, his prize-winning ram, and the band he played with. There are no pills, stolen cars, fistfights, drinking in Mexico, or anything of the kind added in.

Finally, reflecting nearly fifty years later on his high school years, Shepard wrote to a friend, "I actually aspired to a respectable position in society." These do not sound like the memories of a rabble-rouser.

Nonetheless, Shepard enjoyed most of the things his classmates did. The first car he owned was a 1932 Ford Deuce Coupe painted metallic blue and updated with a 198 Mercury flathead engine. He and his buddies also cruised around town in a low-riding 1958 Impala that was chopped and channeled, "a perfect cruising machine," he called it.

Hand in hand with the growing California car culture was the ascension of rock 'n' roll. Shepard didn't catch on immediately to this new music—though he would come to love it like most members of his generation. Feeling his father's influence, he first embraced Dixieland jazz. Modern jazz, in the guise of bebop and as embodied by artists such as Thelonious Monk, Eric Dolphy, Art Pepper, and Dizzy Gillespie, would overtake his world in a few years after he arrived in New York City.

When his son was twelve, Samuel Rogers bought him an old set of drums from a pawnshop, stripped off the paint, and revarnished the pieces, setting them out among the avocado trees to dry. It was far from a traditional setup, with a marching band–style bass drum, a couple of large Ludwig tom-toms, and a snare, but it was good enough that by the time Shepard reached high school he was ready to gig. His first real band is memorable more for its rehearsals than its music. A member of the group that hosted the band's practices collected wild animals by mail order (which was legal back then), and Nat's Cats, as the band was called, rehearsed in a backyard full of alligators, armadillos, spider monkeys, and other creatures. Somehow the trio—clarinet and trumpet set to Shepard's backbeat—managed to put together a repertoire that ranged from swing music to Dixieland. Eventually, the trio would succumb to the pull of the times and begin playing rock.

A student at Duarte High named Michael Romero was an accomplished drummer—good enough that Shepard was a tad jealous. From him he learned some of the finer points of playing jazz. "A rock 'n' roll drummer would turn the hand over and smash the snare drum, while the jazz drummer would hold the stick in his open palm so he could get this snap out of it," Shepard said. ". . . all of a sudden the drums opened up for me." Romero also introduced Shepard to the greats of modern jazz via his record collection. Perhaps just as important, he had a spare room at his house that Shepard sometimes made use of when he was "on the skids with the family."

One of Shepard's former classmates from Duarte High would prove even more instrumental to his future, and that was Charles Mingus III. Born September 12, 1944, Mingus was the son of the legendary jazzman and his first wife, Jeanne Gross. The boy was not the product of a happy marriage: "I remember being three years old, and my mom and dad having one of their huge fights, rolling on the floor, him holding her by the shoulder and smacking her, like in a movie."

The couple reconciled after that particular bout, but in late 1947, Gross packed up Charles III and his brother, Eugene, and left New York City for her parents' California farm. Mingus attended Duarte High School the same time as Shepard. However, the two met only once during their school years, according to Shepard. After graduation, Mingus would move to New York City, where he would provide friendship, a job, and a place for Shepard to stay when he subsequently landed in Greenwich Village.

Shepard's teen years weren't limited to cars, music, and animals. He did get a taste of higher culture around 1959, when an art house cinema opened on the edge of a vineyard near Cucamonga, about a half hour drive away. His friend Ed Wainwright introduced him to the little movie house, telling him about the films they showed there—ones that didn't turn up at the local theater and even included nudity. They took in a film called *Rocco and His Brothers* (1960), an Italian black-and-white film directed by Luchino Visconti. But the art house film that stayed with Shepard was Truffaut's 1959 classic *The 400 Blows*, about a troubled fourteen-year-old boy from an unhappy home who eventually winds up in juvenile hall. "That really stunned me," Shepard recalled. "It was like, 'Wow.' I saw a lot of similarities between my situation and that."

He also saw his own life reflected in Eugene O'Neill's *Long Day's Journey into Night*. As a young man, Shepard had read the play, but the 1962 Sidney Lumet film really captured his imagination. It provided Shepard with the first inkling that maybe he might have a story of his own to tell. "There was something wrong with the family. There was a demonic thing going on that nobody could put their finger on, but everybody knew the ship was sinking," Shepard said. "Everybody was going down, and nobody knew why or how, and they were all taking desperate measures to stay afloat. So I thought there was something about that that felt similar to my own background, and I felt I could maybe write some version of that." Shepard had also read a couple of O'Neill's one-act plays in his youth. The influence of the Nobel laureate on Shepard is unmistakable, especially in the progression from one-act plays to more complex family dramas, much of them laced with autobiography.

Overall, Shepard found life in small-town California not very amenable. "The fifties sucked dogs man," he'd later write. He saw how so many of his elders found themselves stuck in dead-end lives. To him, it seemed as if people came to L.A. County to work the groves or in government industries, then settled in trailers or houses like his own family's and simply stayed there long enough until any semblance of individual hopes was dashed. For the older set, it was a long, slow death. But for the young, there was still hope. It was all about the California sun, cars, drive-ins, and an emerging youth culture jumping to the incessant beat of rock 'n' roll.

At some point during his high school years, Shepard began writing in earnest. It was poetry that first drew him, for like so many of his contemporaries, he'd been swept up in the excitement of the Beat Generation. Allen Ginsberg's genre-shattering poem *Howl* was published in 1955, and Jack Kerouac's lyrical novel *On the Road* arrived in 1957, both well timed for Shepard to be caught up in the sense of freedom and possibility they represented. The bold language, the exuberance, and the situations depicted in these new works no doubt made a lifetime spent working at the local Alpha Beta supermarket a nonstarter.

On a sunny afternoon in May 1961, looking tall, thin, and handsome in his white graduation gown, arms akimbo, crew cut, Shepard posed in his family's backyard. The expression on the new graduate's face is hard to read. We know from a letter he wrote at the time that he was torn over which path he should follow, animal husbandry or something more creative. At some point, an idea began to take shape: perhaps being a writer or artist of some kind would be his ticket out of town. Yet he spent the summer after graduation in nearby West Covina working once again with animals. It could have easily become a career. If not for one of his father's alcohol-fueled rages, which eventually drove him cross-country, the life of a local veterinarian may have won out.

On the Road

There was no way I was going to stay in Duarte. What would have happened to me if I'd stayed? God knows.

—Sam Shepard

There must always be a struggle between a father and son, while one aims at power and the other at independence.

—Samuel Johnson

S am Shepard likes to tell a story about his beginnings as a writer: "I didn't have any idea about how to shape an action into what is seen—the so-called originality of the early work just comes from ignorance. I just didn't know." This is reminiscent of something Orson Welles said of his own early success: "I had the confidence of ignorance."

Such statements leave the impression of an artist emerging from nothing—of being a savant of sorts, arriving fully formed, immune to influence and belonging to no school or tradition. It can be viewed as the artistic equivalent of the self-made man, and it's a romantic notion that surrounds the arts in mystery and seeks to assign a special place to creators. As critic Harold Bloom reminds us, Whitman had made similar claims, seemingly forgetting the impact Emerson had on him. Shepard never even mentions as influences his mother's side of the family, including grandparents who worked in the arts.

While it's true that Shepard came of age as a writer at a time and place—Greenwich Village in the early 1960s—that granted the freedom to experiment untethered by the commercial pressures of Broadway and even Off-Broadway, he did not arrive as a tabula rasa. He had a very definite gift, but its seeds did not sprout in a vacuum. The fact is that when he arrived in New York City in the fall of 1963, Shepard had plenty of theater experience under his belt.

This personal creation myth—something from nothing—would fade with time. Later in life, Shepard regularly cited all of Beckett's work as a powerful and enduring influence, as well as Joseph Chaikin, jazz, and rock 'n' roll. But in the first blush of fame, he claimed no influences other than a fortuitous encounter with a dog-eared copy of *Waiting for Godot*. This would occur at a house party during his brief tenure at a local community college. It was the same school where he would also meet a locally renowned and innovative theater professor and write his first play.

In school, Shepard claimed he wanted to be a veterinarian, but it's clear that at every opportunity he drifted toward the theater. At Duarte High School, it may simply have been that the drama club was where the prettiest girls hung out. Whatever the draw, he got his first stage experience in two high school plays. He must have enjoyed the experience of being onstage, for he continued to gravitate toward the footlights.

Upon graduation from Duarte High, Shepard was unsure what to do. Even as late as the August after graduation, his head was swimming with ideas about his future. He'd registered for classes at nearby Mt. San Antonio College, and showing the influence of his parents' chosen careers, he planned to major in education. But even this was up in the air. His life with animals was still busy, with nine sheep, two dogs, and a new puppy in the offing.

A letter to his grandmother from the summer after graduation gives a sense of Shepard's demeanor and his adolescent confusion as to what to do next. Writing and acting are not mentioned. Instead, the seventeen-year-old Shepard writes of his busy summer as a veterinarian's assistant, his thriving "menagerie," and the possibility of ditching college for a trip to the Yukon to work in a lumberyard. Shepard's letter sounds relaxed and chatty, and that may be due to the fact that this was the summer his father spent in Colombia thanks to the Fulbright. After detailing in the letter his possible plans, Shepard adds that his father is due home the following Saturday and the old man will "probably shatter my dreams immediately."

In the end, Shepard would opt to continue living at home, taking care of his animals, and commuting the short distance to college, a place that would change his life's direction and open up for him a new world.

On the appointed day in late summer 1961, Shepard drove his old Chevy past a handful of farms and up a winding dirt road leading to Mt. San Antonio College, or Mt. SAC as it is usually called. As if to make him feel at home in his new environs, on one of the surrounding hills was a flock of sheep. A series of "row buildings" marked the heart of the campus, descending down a slight incline, and it was in these long narrow buildings that classes were held. A plethora of trees dotted the campus, and off in the distance stood Mount Baldy. When Shepard attended, the school served about three thousand students and was known for its agricultural program.

The campus had previously been an army hospital and later a navy hospital. Upon its founding, circa December 1945, the college was meant to provide returning soldiers with an affordable place to study. Located in Walnut, California, Mt. SAC is today among the largest of the state's community colleges, and the third largest in Southern California. Walking across campus in the summer of 2015, one wonders if Shepard would recognize the place. There are many new buildings (there was a late-1960s building boom), and more were going up across what is today a sprawling 420-acre campus.

Once Shepard settled in, it didn't take long for him to find his way to the theater department, and there he would have met a much-revered faculty member named Beulah Yeager. She founded the school's drama and speech department, but more important, she headed The Players, the college's student drama club, which produced a slate of four or five productions each academic year. Shepard joined the club and appeared in no less than four plays during his two semesters at the college. He played the character DeWitt in *High Tor*, Elwood in *Harvey*, and an attorney in *Ponder Heart*. He also filled multiple roles in *Missouri Legend*. Photos of these productions show a baby-faced Shepard, tall and handsome, dutifully playing his part in each.

Yeager is still spoken of in revered terms at the community college more than four decades after her death. "She was a real go-getter," remembered Ron Ownbey, a 1961 graduate of the school who later returned as a faculty member. "She was always very busy and students flocked to her." People today still marvel at Yeager's accomplishments, creating a theater program at Mt. SAC with essentially no money and no facilities.

A formidable presence, Yeager staged ambitious productions and occasionally added a novel twist. She also knew what it meant to deal with meager means: Immediately after the war, she used army surplus materials for her sets and costumes. Before 1957, plays were staged in the chapel, and the curtain was hung from a beam. Crossing the stage out of the audience's line of sight back then meant climbing out of one window, running around the back of the chapel, and climbing in another. The dressing rooms were located in another building, a good distance away. "[This] proved quite a problem in the rain," Yeager once told a local reporter. "It was then we employed an 'umbrella man.'" A 226-seat theater was built on the Mt. SAC campus in 1957, and this is where Shepard would have performed.

It's hard to know if this much-loved educator who directed him in a handful of plays during his short time at Mt. SAC impacted Shepard. He's never mentioned Yeager. However, a case can be made that she did influence at least his early work. At the very least, Yeager's use of makeshift props would have prepared him for the meanness of his Off-Off-Broadway days, where pawnshop goods and borrowed or "appropriated" items were employed in many a production.

Meanwhile, Yeager was not afraid to try new things. "She had wonderfully clever production ideas," remembered one veteran Mt. SAC faculty member. One year, she had the students put on three one-act plays staged around the same theater space requiring audience members to turn their seats 90 degrees for each one. She staged plays written by students, once turned the theater into a courtroom (replete with roving reporters interviewing and photographing audience members), was one of the first directors at any level to stage a play in the round, and once put a Model T onstage. Shepard's early plays *The Unseen Hand* and *Operation Sidewinder* each featured a vehicle; perhaps he got the idea from his old teacher.

It was during his time at Mt. SAC that Shepard had an experience that helped seal his future. We know little of the event, other than that it was a party near the college hosted by someone Shepard regarded as a "beatnik." Some time during the evening, as the jazz was playing and the party rolling along, the host approached and tossed him a copy of Samuel Beckett's 1953 play *Waiting for Godot*. Shepard read it, and it's not so much what the words on the page said to him but the expressive freedom he discovered within. As Ruby Cohn, a scholar of both Shepard and Beckett has claimed, "After *Godot*, plots could be minimal; exposition, expendable; characters, contradictory; settings, unlocalised, and dialogue, unpredictable. Blatant farce could jostle tragedy." Shepard's late-teen self likely had a less sophisticated take on *Godot* that night, but he knew what he was reading represented something modern and liberating. One thing's for sure, it was a long way from the plays he'd known in high school, like *Harvey* and *Finian's Rainbow*. "It just struck me that suddenly that with words you could do *anything*," he said. It was new and revelatory, and Shepard found in Beckett a role model of sorts. "Once I started writing plays I felt a connection" to the great Irish playwright, he said. Whether considering his first one-acts or his late near-masterpiece *Ages of the Moon*, Beckett is the through line connecting nearly all of Shepard's plays. The exceptions are the family plays, which hew closer to O'Neill's territory, yet each of these also contains touches of Beckett's bleak worldview and mordant humor.

Shepard's first play was written while he was a student at Mt. SAC. *The Mildew*, "a one-act comedy," takes up ten pages in the 1961 edition of the school's journal of student writing, *MoSAiC*. No one had laid eyes on it for a half century until an inquiry led to the discovery of a copy of the journal stowed away in the college's archives, uncovered with the help of Professor John Brantingham. Shepard has always contended that his first attempt at dramatic writing was a Tennessee Williams rip-off about a girl who is raped and later taunted by her stepfather. This is highly inaccurate, and it shortchanges his inaugural effort. *The Mildew* is by no means the rival of *Buried Child* or *The Tooth of Crime*, but for a community college freshman it shows a remarkable eagerness to experiment and a transgressive sense of humor. The play also features a few of what would soon become Shepard hallmarks.

Signed on the first page "Steve Rogers," his childhood name that he would still use for the better part of the next two years, *The Mildew* begins with a "respectable citizen" bearing the regal-sounding name Percival Chambers Jr., also known as Percy. He stands on a foggy downtown corner beneath the streetlights and a blinking red light. Percival immediately breaks the fourth wall and talks directly to the audience. (Perhaps this is what Shepard meant with his allusion to Williams, for Tom does this at the start of *The Glass Menagerie*. However, any resemblance ends there.) Percival tells the audience to hang out and try to keep warm, that some of his friends, the finest citizens in town, will soon be arriving. Instead, he is accosted by various lowlifes, beginning with a drunk seeking a light and asking the time. Next a long-haired boy arrives, "a hoodlum" we are told, who pokes fun at Percival before tearing off Percival's tie and ripping it in half in a fit of violence. Finally, two ruffians chase a girl, and when Percival tells the men to leave her alone, one of them asks if he's a knight. To teach him a lesson, they tear Percival's suit, force him to his knees, and have him repeat ad nauseam, "I am a bad, bad knight. I want to repent." After the trio leaves, a passerby sees Percival and joins him in his repentance. Eventually Percy gives up and leaves the man to pray on his own. When Percy's friends finally arrive, they see just the man kneeling on the street corner and ask after Percy. "He left," the man tells them. They leave, and the final image is of the kneeling man repeating, "I am a bad, bad knight. I want to repent."

The play was never performed, but in it are the seeds of Shepard's future work. The blinking light at the beginning of *The Mildew*, with its intrusive and ominous pulse, would resurface in his first performed play, *Cowboys*. Meanwhile, the fog that engulfs the set at the start is reminiscent of a handful of later Shepard plays where the stage is covered in smoke, as if a miniature apocalypse had arrived with the finale. (Fog, of course, also plays a large role in one of his favorite plays at the time, O'Neill's *Long Day's Journey into Night*.) Shepard's first play lacks a traditional ending, one that ties up and makes sense of all that goes before. This is also something Shepard would become known for, as well as the eruption of unexpected violence. Lastly, Shepard in his first effort already engages in such postmodernist flourishes as breaking the fourth wall and pulling the audience into the action. In the play's final minute, when Percy's friends are looking for him, one of them points at the audience and says, "Maybe they saw him."

All this being said, *The Mildew* ultimately lacks the things that set Shepard's later work apart. While it's strange and at times humorous, it lacks the sustained tension and the knowing irony of his produced work, as well as the dark humor and linguistic flights.

By the early 1960s, Shepard's father had become an alcoholic. He'd keep his teaching job at San Marino for the rest of the decade, but at home his demons wreaked havoc. The old "medicine"—booze—was working overtime. His teenage son got the worst of what resulted, remembered Shepard's sister Roxanne. "There was always a kind of facing off between them, and it was Sam who got the bad end of that," she said. "Dad was a tricky character. Because he was a charismatic guy when he wanted to be—warm, loving, kind of a hoot to be around. And the other side was like a snapping turtle. With him and Sam it was that male thing. You put two virile men in a room and they're going to test each other. It's like two pit bulls."

The father acted out in different ways, as Shepard has recounted in interviews and in his notebooks. In one instance, his father drove the family's Packard into a tree; other times he'd disappear for days. While AWOL, Samuel Rogers would stay at a local motel, coming home just long enough to dump his dirty laundry on the table with a note saying, "Don't starch the shirts." The Packard incident and the laundry drop-offs would both find their way into *Curse of the Starving Class*.

The final confrontation between father and son took place at the family home. No one recalls exactly what set the old man off, but on several occasions Shepard would refer to it as a "holocaust." It was a finale that had been building for years. "I had a falling-out with him at a relatively young age by the standards of that era," Shepard said. "We were always butting up against each other, never seeing eye-to-eye on anything, and as I got older it escalated into a really bad, violent situation. Eventually I just decided to get out." Shepard recalled years later in one of his notebooks, adopting the third-person perspective as if he still needed to distance himself from the memory, how on this occasion his father smashed the windows and tore the front door off its hinges and even set the backyard ablaze. This final battle would have been in early 1963. Shepard packed into his '51 Chevy everything he needed to hit the road.

Though Shepard would see his father only a handful of times in the ensuing decades, Samuel Rogers would prove to be an enduring presence in his son's life: an example to react against and, in later life, unwittingly follow. The latter impulse would be something Shepard would fight for decades.

"I've done my level best, everything I possibly could, not to become my father," he later wrote. "Gone out of my way in every department, changed my name, falsified my birth certificate . . . picked out clothing the opposite of what he would have worn, right down to the underwear. Spoke without any trace of a Midwestern twang, never kicked a dog, never lost my temper over inanimate objects and never ever hit a woman in the face. . . . I had no idea who I was but I was sure I wasn't him."

Shepard's departure seems, in hindsight, inevitable given the never-ending friction with his father and the ambition that was already stirring inside him. Nevertheless, his leaving was fraught with mixed emotions. As he remembered many years later, "I walked out of that house into the unknown and it scared the shit out of me but the adventure of hitting life straight on was a thrill I'll never forget."

After the terrible fallout with his father, Shepard ran, but at first he didn't go far. He initially took jobs in Chino, about twenty-five miles east of his parents' house, at both a ranch and thoroughbred farm. After a short while, he found his way to Pasadena and a job delivering newspapers. This second move proved lucky. One day, while tossing the day's news out the window of his old Chevy, Shepard happened to flip through the pages of the paper and came across an ad that read, "actors wanted." "I found out about an opening with a traveling ensemble called the Bishop's Company. I decided to give it a shot, thinking that this might be a way to really get out," he said.

Shepard walked into the audition and was handed a book of Shakespeare's plays. He was so nervous that he read not only the appointed dialogue but the stage directions as well. His nervousness was understandable.

Even though Shepard had roughly a half dozen plays under his belt, they were school plays, and the Bishop's Company was a step up. The troupe would never be confused with a Broadway company, but still, for an ambitious teen suddenly adrift and delivering newspapers for a living, it looked like a pretty good gig.

And he landed it. Not because he read stage directions like Olivier, more likely because of his height and angular good looks. "I think they hired everyone," Shepard later joked. When Shepard years later would say that he turned to acting as a means of escape, he meant it. The Bishop's Company was not only an acting job; it was a ride out of town: the troupe lived on the road.

A number of the company's alumni have gone on to careers in theater, television, and film. James Haire became the producing director of San Francisco's American Conservatory Theater, and he remembers touring the country in two Ford station wagons, each pulling a small trailer, and staying in the homes of local residents. His summation of the experience speaks to the Bishop Company's bare-bones approach: "Lots of one-night stands and a few occasional motels when there was no performance. There were no sets, a few props, and costumes of course," he said.

The company was founded in 1952 by Phyllis Beardsley Bokar and named after Bishop Gerald H. Kennedy, an early supporter. It was headquartered in Burbank, California, but its real home was the highways and byways of America. (In 1967 its reach would become international.) It began with just seven actors, but by the time Shepard joined, that number had swelled to more than two dozen. The company aimed to produce Broadway-caliber productions featuring professional actors, performing material of spiritual or social significance. However, to be most widely effective, the plays were nonsectarian and free of any formal theology.

Around the time Shepard joined, the Bishop's Company had two or three troupes crisscrossing the country, playing not only churches but a handful of colleges. Joyce Ellen Davis spent the summer of 1960 on the road with the Bishop's Company and provides this snapshot:

> We performed nearly every night in a different place. We each had a copy [of the itinerary], so when we woke up each

morning we'd know where we were. I remember hanging out of the Knickerbocker Hotel in NYC, four floors up, trying to see around the corner where Macy's Thanksgiving Day Parade was passing by . . . [and] rowing out on Lake Seneca in the middle of a rainstorm with lots of lightning, painting art at a summer camp for teenagers. . . . I ate my first knish in NYC and ate my first elk in Montana. We stayed mostly in Best Western motels. We were paid ten dollars a week. Sometimes we rode all night to get to the next place. One person was assigned to book hotel (or motel) rooms, or to arrange for our stay in private homes with people in the area who invited us. Most of the guys took turns driving. Our audiences varied in size, from less than a hundred to a thousand or more. We played at one huge place in Canada. Most of us took on more than one role. (After a while you knew your own and everyone else's lines.)

The language of some of the plays performed by the Bishop's Company was more poetic, bordering on stilted, than most of the drama being performed on professional stages in the United States in the early 1960s—that is, if one is to judge from these lines from a repertory mainstay, Christopher Fry's *The Boy with a Cart*:

> *This is the morning to take the air, flute-clear*
> *And, like a lutanist, with a hand of wind*
> *Playing the responsive hills, till a long vibration*
> *Spills across the fields, and the chancelled larches*
> *Sing like Lenten choirboys, a green treble;*
> *Playing at last the skylark into rising,*
> *The wintered cuckoo to a bashful stutter.*

"Lenten choirboys" and the like would never appear in any of Shepard's plays, but the lessons concerning the power of heightened language and the idea that there was a place onstage for poetry were not lost on him.

Shepard's first known review came during his time with the Bishop's Company. The article ran in the afternoon edition of the October 18, 1963,

Daily Intelligencer of Doylestown, Pennsylvania. The role called for Shepard to stand before the altar of a small-town church dressed as, of all things, the devil, bathed in a crimson spotlight, wearing a red coat with matching vest, a string bowtie, and a pocket handkerchief while in his hands was a ledger festooned with long, red ribbons containing the names of the damned.

Shepard evidently delivered his best Lucifer on this night. "The most subtle and suave performance of the evening, given before an audience that should have been twice as large as it was, came from Steve Rogers, tall, long-haired and bland-looking," the review read. Bland looking? It's no wonder the adult Shepard never cottoned to critics.

Two undated postcard-style photos from around this time feature Shepard and a few of his fellow Bishop's Company actors. They look like young people on an adventure, only a tad more serious. Later Shepard would fondly recall his experience with the company. "It was actually a great little fold-up theater. We were totally self-sufficient, we put up the lights, made the costumes, performed the play, and shut down." He learned much from being an itinerant artist, and it stoked his interest in writing for the stage. "It showed me the vitality of theater—you could cook it up. Then I saw how writing was connected to it." Already he was trying out new things and stretching his abilities, pushing himself to become a performer on the page. His experiments with writing during this time "led to rhythm, discoverings in space and time through packing up words and stretching them out along with their size and shape and sound. Once this got started lo and behold there came phantoms and ghosts speaking these words. At this point my acting stopped . . . and these things began to crackle."

The Bishop's Company gave Shepard a chance to experience theater from the inside, though it's impossible to tell exactly how many performances he participated in. In the fall of 1963, after eight months on the road, his stint with the troupe ended as abruptly as it had started. "One day we got to New York to do a production at a church in Brooklyn and I said, 'I'm getting off the bus,'" he recalled.

The experience he'd garnered onstage at Duarte High, at Mt. SAC, and with the Bishop's Company proved pivotal. Once Shepard got to New York and decided he didn't want to be an actor, his imagination didn't need to travel far to find an alternative. "One of the reasons I started writing plays was because I had some minimal experience on stage and sort of understood the spatial, the time thing of it, what the experience of being an actor onstage was," he said in 2013.

Once he'd arrived in New York, the fact that Sam Shepard quickly found his way to Greenwich Village should come as no surprise. It was the place in the city for "people who knew in their souls that they didn't belong where they came from," as Village denizen and former Dylan muse Suze Rotolo wrote in her 2008 memoir *A Freewheeling Time*.

Shepard and his ambitions would soon find a home in New York City.

Arriving

.L

The artists and the poets were the ones doing theology. They were the ones telling the truth.

—The Reverend Michael Allen

S am Shepard came of age at the perfect time. The fifties, also known as "the dullest and dreariest in all our history," according to historian Eric F. Goldman, were over. The sixties would be a decade of change, both in society and the arts. Rock music was ascendant, along with a youthful generation that didn't subscribe to the traditions of its elders and was ready, as a matter of course, to experience the new and unfamiliar.

All this was old news in New York's Greenwich Village. Being radical here on the West Side of lower Manhattan was the norm. The Village, since its earliest days, had been home to "rogues and outcasts." By the time the 1950s rolled around, this neighborhood was secure in its identity as the bohemian capital of America. As the writer John Strausbaugh notes, "The Village in the mid-1950s saw an intense explosion of creative activity. It was a culture engine—a zone that attracts and nurtures creative people, radicals, visionaries, misfits, life adventurers." The proximity of these doers and dreamers to each other resulted in a unique kind of synergy, spawning several important cultural movements. Abstract expressionism, bebop, the folk scene and its reigning avatar Bob Dylan, the Beat Generation, and avant-garde filmmaking—these were all birthed in the cradle that was the Greenwich Village of mid-century. Experimental theater had long found the Village to be friendly turf. When the groundbreaking Provincetown Players came inland in 1916, the troupe set up shop where else but on MacDougal Street, in the heart of the Village.

Things were already changing in American drama before the advent of the new decade. The 1959–1960 theater season delivered such watershed productions as *The Zoo Story*, *The Connection*, *The Prodigal*, and similarly new and bracing fare that marked the "crest of the Off-Broadway movement," according to critic Mel Gussow.

Mounting plays on Broadway had become expensive and risky for investors beginning in the 1940s, especially with television and the movies increasingly tempting away the audience. Grand productions, mostly musicals, were the safest bets for investors, and they became the order of the day, leaving actors who couldn't sing or dance scrambling for an ever-shrinking pool of roles. The news for up-and-coming playwrights was direr; no producer wanted to risk staging something unfamiliar or that lacked a writer who was a known quantity, like an O'Neill or Williams. Seeing the havoc this was wreaking, the Actors' Equity Association, the union that represents actors and stage managers, in 1949 ruled that its members could work in smaller theaters for rates below the minimums mandated on Broadway. This brought an influx of professional talent into the then-burgeoning Off-Broadway scene, along with the stamp of legitimacy, according to scholar Stephen J. Bottoms. The upshot was that new theaters began to emerge in renovated cinemas and elsewhere. "In effect, the serious drama being squeezed off Broadway by economic forces found an alternative home in these smaller theaters," Bottoms writes.

Among the new stages in New York were the Circle in the Square Theatre and the Cherry Lane Theatre, which were the first to feature a new wave of playwrights from overseas, including Samuel Beckett, Eugène Ionesco, and Jean Genet. Stateside, among the trailblazers of this time was Joseph Chaikin, who would become Shepard's close friend and mentor, and leader of the Open Theater, an experimental group established in 1963.

The Off-Broadway scene expanded throughout the 1950s and was solidified in January 1960 when *The Zoo Story*, paired with Beckett's *Krapp's Last Tape*, a double bill that had been a hit in Germany, had its American premiere at the Cherry Lane Theatre. It became, Bottoms claims, the "defining Off-Broadway play of the era." The fact that the play required little in the way of sets and actors (much like its artistic forebear *Waiting for Godot*) showed others that plays could be produced, and produced quite well, on a shoestring. In short, *The Zoo Story* was a game changer in many ways. "That was quite shocking and really kind of baffling to us," said Peter Feldman, cofounder with Chaikin of the Open Theater. "We knew we had to somehow find a way to respond to that." The great success of *The Zoo Story* had an immediate impact, and suddenly Off-Broadway was thriving, with new plays and larger audiences to see them. However, this boon lasted just a few years more. Before long, Off-Broadway followed the economic paradigm set by the Great White Way years earlier. Albee noted that by 1964, Off-Broadway was being ruined by "greedy landlords, union demands, costs." Indeed, the cadre of Off-Broadway theaters began feeling the pressure from escalating rents and a unionized workforce, resulting in higher production costs, a jump in ticket prices, and increased risks for producers. "Thus, for the most part, the supposed alternative had become simply a smaller-scale version of Broadway itself" by the early 1960s, according to Bottoms. The result was that those interested in creating original theater felt the need to develop a new tier of performance spaces where costs were next to nothing, ideas were the coin of the realm, and the playwright sovereign.

Former *Village Voice* editor and critic Michael Smith dates the beginning of Off-Off-Broadway to a September 1960 revival of Alfred Jarry's *Ubu Roi* at the Take 3 Coffeehouse on Bleecker Street. A program note for that production served as a de facto manifesto for the nascent scene: "A return to the original idea of Off-Broadway theatre, in which imagination is substituted for money, and plays can be presented in ways that would be impossible in the commercial theatre." The changes were in step with those taking place in society at large. "We were all very young, so we were kind of inventing ourselves at that point," said Smith. "Everybody that I knew had come to New York from someplace, and we felt like we were just making up ourselves from scratch, that it was completely open regarding what we should become and how we should lead our lives."

Around the Village sprung up a handful of nontraditional theater spaces, beginning in the summer of 1960 with Caffe Cino, followed by Judson Poets' Theatre in November 1961; La MaMa, which opened in 1961 and staged its first play in July of the following year; and Theatre Genesis in 1964. One could say the Off-Off-Broadway movement opened the door for a group of eager theater practitioners. However, that's putting it mildly. These young actors, writers, and directors *kicked* the door down. They staged their work in coffeehouses, underused spaces in churches, and even apartments. The results, Smith said, could be just as powerful as anything on Broadway. "The experience of Off-Off Broadway has demonstrated clearly if redundantly that the accepted methods and aims of theatrical production are no longer adequate but have become irrelevant to the concerns and appetites of the present," he said.

Europe was ahead of the United States in embracing new, and sometimes radical, voices in drama. Beckett, Ionesco, and Genet, along with Bertolt Brecht and Antonin Artaud and others, were breaking barriers and redefining what was possible to do and say onstage. Albee summed up their collective impact when he wrote that "American theater has always been more naturalistic in nature than not, and it was this infusion of the absurd, the experimental and the outrageous which broadened and redefined the boundaries of theatrical possibilities of American theater, for the playwrights and audiences alike." Beckett ranked above all others in Shepard's eyes. The great Irish playwright "made American theater look like it was on crutches," he said. His devotion to Beckett would last the rest of his life. Meanwhile, from Brecht and Artaud came the idea that audiences should not be allowed to passively take in theater as a means of enjoyment but should be roused to action or even shocked into a deeper form of engagement.

Shepard likely knew little of the theoretical aspects of drama in 1963 upon arriving in the Village. If he hadn't read the great European theorists by this time, it didn't matter; the ideas of Beckett, Brecht, and Artaud were in the air, incorporated into the productions of troupes like the Living Theatre, with its anarchistic-leaning politics, and the Open Theater. Joseph Chaikin, its leader, would distill into his work the high-flown ideas from Europe and through observation, osmosis, and discussion pass them on to Shepard. "I had a long history with Joe Chaikin from the very beginnings of the Open Theater," he said. "He included it all. He said, 'Let's include the circus, let's include Japanese theater, let's include Strasberg, let's include Artaud, and find all of the possibilities.'"

The lesson Shepard took to heart was that the old ways of making theater could be pushed aside and that there was so much more that could be done. From the first, he was ready to forsake tradition.

A thriving Off-Off-Broadway scene met Shepard when he landed in New York, with experimental theater seemingly busting out on every street. Caffe Cino featured a new play each week, with two performances a night, three on weekends. Judson Poets' Theatre was just as busy, and for two bucks a week you could see everything Café La MaMa staged. Those creating theater had the excitement of the dedicated amateur about them. Or, as Ellen Stewart, founder of La MaMa, put it: "I didn't know anything about theater to begin with. . . . It was like playing house." It was a circuit that survived on jury-rigging and the old standbys of begging, borrowing and stealing. It was all done with the determination of committed rebels intent on smashing the status quo. "We were all in the theater and we were all freaks," recalled Michael Smith. "We were all looking for a better new world." Those early days had about them an innocence—a sense that it existed outside the world of commerce. "None of us, as far as I knew, had any real ambition," Smith said. "There was no sense that we were trying to succeed or trying to have careers. We felt that the whole world was about to blow up and the economy and politics were about to collapse and we were just having a good time in the meantime. We were trying to keep ourselves entertained and enjoy life and comment on it as it went by."

L

Nineteen-year-old Steve Rogers, as Shepard was still known, got off the bus in Times Square and watched it pull away down Forty-Second Street. The sights and sounds of the city were unlike anything the new arrival had known in Southern California, and he thought to himself, "Now I'm really in for it." There was an amateur actor on the bus with him, a tall, skinny kid who'd been around a bit, and they'd chatted away the last few miles of the trip. He told Shepard about the Burns Detective Agency and how easily he could get a job there. "My immediate mission, though, was a cheeseburger, but I had zip in my pocket," Shepard recalled.

The Big Apple was not, at first, very accommodating. Shepard did indeed have to sell a pint of blood before heading over to the Times Square White Castle, where he'd seen the cook "scoop mounds of fried onions onto a row of sizzling greasy burgers and then flop slices of white cheese on top that bubbled and popped like Elmer's Glue." Shepard encountered a chorus line of hookers on that first day in the city, leading to him reflect that he'd never seen sex so out in the open—except maybe in Tijuana. Within twenty-four hours he was wearing the brown uniform and badge of the Burns Detective Agency and working the overnight shift on the East River watching coal barges. The job meant making the rounds from one end of the long dock to the other every fifteen minutes. In between, he took shelter in a four-by-fourteen-foot wooden hut. Shepard spent his downtime well. "It turned out to be a great environment for writing. I was completely alone in a little outhouse with an electric heater and a little desk."

In his 1996 prose collection *Cruising Paradise*, in a story titled "Fear of the Fiddle," Shepard writes that he was not always so alone on these long nights in his little shack. The lack of sleep that was an occupational hazard led him to experiment with crystal methedrine, which he acquired from Ansel Cartwright, an Appalachian fiddle player he'd met on the Lower East Side. The drug was a powder mixed with Coke, and it allowed Shepard to stay awake for up to five consecutive days. Eventually Cartwright began joining Shepard on the night shift. "We'd squeeze into the tiny guardhouse on chilly nights, with our king-size bottle of laced Coca-Cola tucked into a corner next to the heater," Shepard wrote. The fiddler would play while Shepard rapped out a rhythm on a pair of spoons he'd picked up at a pawnshop. When it came time to make the rounds, the pair would dance up and down the dock to the wild fiddle music. After a week of this came a night when Shepard forgot to make his rounds; he was fired the next day. When he got back to the place he was staying, he found his draft notice waiting for him. Decades later, he would recall these days in a notebook entry as the time when he was out of his mind and "every random hallucination" all too real.

Shepard's goals upon arriving in New York were not well formed. Music, acting, writing—any of these were a possibility—and of course within the decade he would be doing each. The quiet newcomer who not long before was on the verge of devoting his life to sick animals back in California admitted, albeit decades later, that as a teen he possessed a mean desire to become famous, to leave his mark. He reveled in the idea of being someone, conducting TV interviews in his head, as if he were a champion golfer or big-time horse trainer. He wanted to instill awe in others and have power over them, wanted to be the center of attention. "Famous for something," he wrote.

Having just come across the country with a theater troupe, it seemed only natural that acting was the first thing Shepard tried. The logistics of that gig, however, didn't sit well. "Actually, I was interested in music and acting, but I didn't want to do the audition thing," he said. "I hated the audition thing. I wanted to be autonomous, and writing offered me a part of myself, to take a notebook and go to a coffee shop and write. . . . I love the immediacy, and also that thing about dialogue. It's a kind of way of doing music."

He quickly found a makeshift space in the Village that he could, at least temporarily, call home. "It looked like a drug addict's apartment." That was the assessment of actor Lee Kissman, a Village regular and actor who would soon play an important role in Shepard's life. In fact, the flat near the corner of Avenue C and East Tenth Street, where Shepard first lived upon landing in New York, may have even been located in a condemned building. Accounts vary. But it was clearly a roach-infested dump. Shepard slept on a mattress on the floor with the bumper of a '57 Chevy for a head-board. His roommate painted on the walls. It was "the weirdest apartment I ever saw," said Ralph Cook, maître d' at the Village Gate, who would soon become the first director to be associated with Shepard's plays. The setting Shepard conjured for a play he'd soon write, *4-H Club*, was likely inspired by that first apartment:

> On the floor downstage left of the kitchen is a hot plate with a coffee pot on it. The floor of the kitchen is littered with paper, cans, and various trash. There is a garbage can in the upstage right corner. The walls are very dirty.

Shepard's roommate was none other than fellow Duarte High School alumnus Charles Mingus III. Mingus had moved to New York City after graduation to be near his famous father. There are different versions of the story concerning how Shepard tracked down his former classmate, but most likely he simply read in the *Village Voice* that Mingus's father was playing at the Village Gate. As it turned out, the son was working at the club busing tables. Mingus hooked Shepard up with the same gig.

Shepard remembered the fall of 1963, when he arrived in New York City, as being cold and blustery. "Just about froze my ass off," he recalled decades later. He remembers his outfit at that time consisting of a trench coat and motorcycle boots. During these years, his hair was "quite shaggy," according to Michael Smith. He was tall, thin, and handsome, and with Mingus in tow, he was a hot commodity with the ladies, even with a dumpy apartment to take them home to. The young women gladly queued up. "I rode anything with hair," Shepard boasted. When they weren't busy playing cowboys and Indians in the streets of the Village, Shepard and Mingus were on the make. Mingus, already on his way to becoming an artist, was always speckled and splattered with paint. Yet he had a knack for picking up stewardesses and secretaries and bringing them back to Avenue C and East Tenth. The women may have liked the idea of slumming on the wild side with a couple of artist types. Neither Shepard nor Mingus paid much attention to hygiene back then, "but these women would show up in their secretarial gear. It was wild. I couldn't believe it," Shepard said.

If Mingus the younger took Shepard in when he came to New York, his father, the jazz legend, took him to school. Shepard was transfixed watching the big man fill the stage of the Village Gate jazz club, wrapping himself around his double bass, his fingers plucking out a rhythm—smooth one minute, jumping the next—for the rest of the band to fall in with. At the legendary nightspot, Shepard heard not only Mingus but all the top players of the day, and they had a powerful effect on him. If the night was busy, he'd let the music wash over him as he bused his tables, but when there was a break, he'd stand and watch in awe. Listening to live jazz played by the preeminent players of the day would prove to be a transformative experience for Shepard.

The Village Gate opened in 1958, at 160 Bleecker Street. The entrance to the club was on Thompson Street, where there was an actual gate, hence the name of the club. "I also may have been thinking of the Gate of Horn, a famous folk club at the Rice Hotel in Chicago. Either way, the building had a gate, so it seemed like an appropriate name," recalled Art D'Lugoff, the club's owner.

Initially, the Gate hosted both jazz and folk, eventually adding comedians, blues, Latin, and pop music. During its thirty-six-year run, the club featured jazz musicians of such fame that only their first names need be mentioned: Dizzy, Miles, Nina, Thelonious, and Billie, along with John Coltrane, Stan Getz, Bill Evans, and of course Charles Mingus. In his collection of prose, poetry, and bits of memoir *Motel Chronicles*, Shepard recalls bringing ice backstage to the mercurial Nina Simone. "She was always nice to me. She used to call me 'Daahling.' I used to bring her a whole big gray plastic bus tray full of ice to cool her scotch. . . . Her performance was aimed directly at the throat of a white audience. Then she'd aim for the heart. Then she'd aim for the head. She was a deadly shot in those days."

Chip Monck, later to become famous as the emcee at Woodstock with his warnings to "stay off the towers" and avoid the "brown acid," installed the lights at the Village Gate when it opened in 1958 and worked there for the first year of the club's existence. There was, he said, an informality about the Gate's operations, not uncommon for the time. Contracts, agents, management teams, and big paydays were, if not unheard of, far from the norm. The same held on the floor of the landmark club, Monck said. "If there was a problem with a light or the sound system, we stopped the show, moved the front tables out of the way, put up the ladder, fixed the problem, then moved the tables back, replaced the patrons' drinks with new ones, and the show continued."

Shepard knew from jazz, but it was the old-timey stuff, the kind of music his father loved and played. What he encountered at the Gate was the newest of the new, and he took it all in. Internalizing everything, he listened not only as a drummer but as the writer he was working to become. He also learned that the very essence of jazz was improvisation and the ability to change on a whim, shooting off in multiple directions. Why couldn't other forms of art be like that? "Jazz could move in surprising territories, without qualifying itself," Shepard said. "You could follow a traditional melody and then break away, and then come back or drop into polyrhythms. You could have three, four things going on simultaneously. But, more important, it was an emotional thing. You could move in all these *emotional* territories, and you could do it with *passion*."

Speaking with the *Los Angeles Times* in 1979, Shepard was more specific: "I used to go and listen to Charlie Mingus and was stunned by his sense of polyrhythm—rhythm on top of rhythm on top of rhythm. I was fascinated by the idea of merging that with writing, seeing if there was a way of evoking the same kind of collage in the writing of plays. Sometimes there was and sometimes there wasn't, but that was definitely a strong influence, more so than literature."

Quickly, Shepard's exposure to jazz would lead to key insights about writing. Jazz would come to rival Beckett in influencing his work. The fluidity of the music and the way it changed keys, beat, tempo, and feel at the drop of a hat made the young playwright-to-be hot to transfer these same impulses to the page. In Shepard's hands, this would result in characters changing personalities, the eschewing of traditional motivation, ambiguous plots, and jam-like soliloquies, all of which became hallmarks of his early plays. Some of these things were already becoming key aspects of the avant-garde theater of the day, but to Shepard they were central to his approach to writing, often providing a sense of the surreal or the mysterious. And much of it he learned at the Village Gate. The club would also prove important to Shepard in another way.

L

As was typical for any New York club or restaurant of the time, the staff of the Gate was comprised of wannabe actors, writers, and a painter or two. When Shepard joined their ranks, he unwittingly fell in with what would turn out to be his first group of collaborators. Lee Kissman was a host at the Gate, having come to New York in May of 1963 after serving in Europe as a low-level intelligence analyst for the air force. He'd been part of a theater group during his time in Germany and upon his discharge looked up the New York–based girlfriend of someone affiliated with his old company. The woman gave him a place to stay and put him in touch with a school friend of hers named Kevin O'Connor, who was working at the Gate. Once introduced, O'Connor helped Kissman get a job at the club as host.

The youthful staff of the Gate had no intention of remaining members of the server class forever, and by early fall 1963, shortly after Shepard had been hired, they asked for and received permission to use the stage during off-hours to rehearse their work and to stage scenes for agents and casting directors. As the daylight began to fill the club, the staff members stood in the places occupied just hours earlier by the previous night's headliners and worked on their craft. It seemed like a promising idea, a way to work on new material and practice their acting chops. However, after just a few such rehearsals, President Kennedy was assassinated. The Village Gate staff, like the rest of the nation, went into a collective funk. "Our group never did get around to doing our scenes, except in front of each other, but it was a distant rumbling of things to come," Kissman recalled.

The man who would bring about those things was, like Shepard, a California transplant, maître d' Ralph Cook. A handsome man in his mid-thirties, with dark eyes, a mop of black hair, and a mustache, Cook had already had a career in the navy during World War II, had a few bit parts in Hollywood, and worked as an English teacher in Connecticut. He'd also survived a recent nervous breakdown and been through a divorce.

Cook had custody of his three children on weekends, and despite being a nonbeliever himself, he enrolled them in Sunday school at a church a mile to the east of the Village Gate, St. Mark's Church in-the-Bowery.

St. Mark's, at 103 Tenth Street, was no ordinary church. "I don't know if the East Village is 'way out' because of St. Mark's or if St. Mark's is 'way out' because of the East Village," Bishop Paul Moore Jr. said in 1986. "But certainly the church and the neighborhood share a free spirit." Opened in 1799, St. Mark's is the second-oldest church building in Manhattan. Throughout its history it has drawn as visitors and parishioners its share of artists and counterculture figures, including Edna St. Vincent Millay, W. H. Auden, Robert Lowell, Allen Ginsberg, Kahlil Gibran, and Martha Graham.

St. Mark's has a tradition of social activism and of supporting the arts that survives to this day.

Befitting this heritage, in 1959 J. C. Michael Allen, a former editor at *Look* magazine, became rector of St. Mark's. Born in Paris in 1927, Allen was a journalist who didn't consider himself religious until he interviewed a controversial Episcopal priest named James Pike, who was dean of the Cathedral of St. John the Divine in New York City. Impressed with Pike's activism, Allen told him, "If I could believe in God, I'd become a priest." And so he did. St. Mark's was his first parish after graduating from what is today Episcopal Theological Seminary in Cambridge, Massachusetts. During his eleven years at St. Mark's, the Reverend Allen would march with Dr. Martin Luther King Jr. and travel to Hanoi during the Vietnam War with Joan Baez to visit and bring letters to POWs.

There was little doubt that when Allen took over at St. Mark's, the arts would continue to play a large role in the life of the church. "My father was a great believer in art as a way to promote social justice," remembered his daughter Sarah Allen Wilson. This progressive nature was something he inherited from his own father, Jay Allen, who was a journalist in Spain during that country's civil war, shining a light on the atrocities committed by the right. He was arrested at one point for hiding socialist leaders from the police. Later, while covering the Nazi occupation of France, Jay Allen helped local artists escape to safety.

It's no surprise that his son Michael, as rector of St. Mark's, would open the church to all and embrace new ways of reaching his flock. "The doors of St. Mark's are open to what's happening down here, and the arts are what's happening," he once said. To that end, in 1961 jazz saxophonist

Archie Shepp began organizing free Sunday afternoon concerts in the church's west yard. The summer of 1963, St. Mark's hosted the black literary collective Umbra's arts festival, featuring member painters, sculptors, photographers, poets, and musicians. Allen even pushed the boundaries as to what a church audience might be expected to see. During a Lenten program early in his tenure, he showed Godard's classic film *Breathless*. That cost him one member of the vestry, who got up in the middle of the film and never returned. There would be others.

For most of his time at St. Mark's, Allen had harbored a desire to stage Hemingway's one-act play *Today Is Friday*, but he hadn't found the right people to do so. That changed when he met Ralph Cook.

As Allen recalled, the Village Gate maître d' had attended Mass one Sunday, most likely in the spring of 1964, and appeared depressed and confused. "That day," Allen recalled, "I preached one of my more depressing sermons." Cook claimed to have seen a fellow sufferer in the good reverend and wanted to help. The two men went out for a beer and spent the afternoon together. A friendship quickly developed. Allen told his new friend about the Hemingway one-act he'd always wanted performed at the church. It wasn't long after that Cook pulled a little production together. It cost St. Mark's another congregant, but suddenly the arts at the old church had found yet another outlet. Meanwhile, Allen reported that bringing Cook into his ministry kept his new friend from going "back into the wilderness and death."

Shortly thereafter, some of the children of the parish asked Cook to start an acting workshop. He did so, using the church basement. The kids wanted to stage *A Streetcar Named Desire* of all things. Either the incredulity of such a notion or the fact that Cook had already been contemplating ideas for a theater geared toward adults meant it wasn't long before he began inviting some of his actor friends to the church. Perhaps he had no idea what he was hoping to accomplish, but by July of 1964 he'd renovated the second floor of the parish hall into a theater space, where he staged a play called *Study in Color* by Malcolm Boyd. Dissatisfied for one reason or another with this experience, Cook decided that this new theater would from then on put the emphasis on the playwright and that he would find plays that spoke to the times, no matter where they came from. He wanted something new, a form of "subjective realism" he called it, that spoke to the urgency of the day.

The new theater's name was inspired by Cook's cri de coeur: "Here, now, in Lower Manhattan, the phenomenon is taking place; the beginning, the genesis, of a cultural revolution. Personally I have little hope for the survival of our civilization. But whatever hope we have lies with our artists. For they alone have the ability (if we do not continue to corrupt them) to withstand the onslaught of mass media and the multitude of false gods. They alone have the ability to show us ourselves."

Genesis

Like a lot of people who grow up in a little hick town, you just want out altogether. And at the same time, being out meant you were even more vulnerable. And I wound up in New York, where you couldn't be more vulnerable.

—Sam Shepard

Where would I go, if I could go, who would I be, if I could be, what would I say, if I had a voice, who says this, saying it's me?

—Samuel Beckett

S tanding in the second-story room of the anterior parish hall of St. Mark's Church in-the-Bowery, it's hard to believe that anything of significance happened here. Yet a part of theater history did indeed take place in this square room overlooking East Eleventh Street. For it was here that Sam Shepard's career as a playwright began more than a half century ago, when a double bill of his first one-act plays debuted. In 1964 this room, christened Theatre Genesis, became one of a handful of small performance spaces that had sprung up around the East Village as part of the nascent Off-Off-Broadway scene.

Theatre Genesis was known as a black box theater. Such simple, unadorned spaces had been used to present plays for decades, but they gained popularity around this time due to their suitability for low-cost, experimental productions. Typically the walls were indeed black, but, as in the case of Theatre Genesis, they were repainted based on the needs of the current production. The room also had a high ceiling and tall windows. The chairs were movable, providing multiple seating arrangements, for flexibility was one of the space's key attributes. The theater was a "womblike sweatbox," intimate enough that every sound or facial expression performed onstage made an impression, since even those in the back rows were mere feet from the action. The intimacy ensured that even the meanest of sets and props made an outsized impact, lending even everyday objects a sense of the iconic, according to playwright Murray Mednick, who had many plays produced at Theatre Genesis. "You could use a certain kind of visual symbology . . . to great effect in a small space," he said. The fact that many in the audience were high heightened these effects, Mednick added.

On a winter afternoon in early 2015, touring the space required slipping in between tryouts featuring lots of young girls in tutus. The second floor of St. Mark's parish hall was then home to the New York Theatre Ballet, and the huge stage that once filled most of the room was gone. Theatre Genesis closed its doors in 1978, and other alternative theater companies occupied the space over the ensuing years, including a nearly two-decade residency by Richard Foreman's Ontological-Hysteric Theater. St. Mark's proper is still home to a variety of artistic ventures, including poetry readings, modern dance, musical offerings, lectures, and more.

When Shepard first arrived on the scene, he thrived on the immediacy of it all. Off-Off-Broadway was as close to improvised and freeform jazz as theater could get. As Lee Kissman put it: "Downtown experimental theater was ablaze, writers writing plays faster than they could type them, it seemed, with productions put up wherever space could be found."

Theatre Genesis, from the outset, set itself apart from the other Off-Off-Broadway venues in the Village in at least one way that was noteworthy. "It was sort of like the Hells Angels of Off-Off-Broadway," playwright, director, and Genesis mainstay Tony Barsha said. "It was a very, very macho group, and Ralph Cook had contributed to that when he had announced it was strictly a heterosexual theater." As Barsha had put it to an earlier interviewer: It was "a bunch of guys, and their babes, and their drugs." There were women involved with the theater, of course, including actresses Stephanie Gordon, Barbara Young, and O-Lan Johnson. (The latter would marry Shepard in 1969.) But the writers, at least at the outset, were all heterosexual males, which impacted the plays produced there. In the words of St. Mark's former arts administrator Stephen Facey, "It was pretty male oriented, with a lot of guns. A lot of guns."

As for drugs, it was primarily pot, but Barsha and Shepard were often on speed. Peyote and LSD were also around, meaning some of those coming to Theatre Genesis were wide open to, and probably hoping for, something off the wall, or at least something to jibe nicely with their buzz. Usually they got their wish.

After producing Malcolm Boyd's *Study in Color* as the first Theatre Genesis offering, Cook sought out local playwrights. It turns out he didn't have to look far. Word had spread around the Village Gate that one of the busboys had been doing some writing. Cook asked Shepard if he had anything they might stage over at the church, and the young playwright offered to show him *The Rock Garden*. Facey, who worked side by side with Cook for many years, said Cook told him that he knew about Shepard's writing previous to this, even as far back as when he first discussed with Allen the possibility of staging plays at the church. Either way, Cook visited the run-down apartment where Shepard and Mingus lived and he was bowled over by what he read. The next year, Cook would sum up his take on the burgeoning playwright's gifts: "Sam Shepard's plays are the most totally realized . . . of any writer I have directed," he said. "He has an instinctive sense of what is theatrically right for his plays that goes beyond rules and preconceptions. He is a great poet in both literary and theatrical imagery."

The only problem in staging *The Rock Garden* was that a single one-act was not enough to sustain an entire night, so Cook asked if Shepard had any other plays. He didn't. But give him an hour or two. Literally. Soon enough, Shepard had the other half of his first double bill, *Cowboys*.

"I used to write very fast," Shepard said. "I mean, I wrote *Chicago* (1965) in one day. The stuff would just come out, and I wasn't really trying to shape it or make it into any big thing." A few decades hence, here's how Shepard referred to his writing approach in those days: "[You] threw a lot of shit on the wall and hoped some of it stuck." He said this in 1996 to a reporter for *Time Out*, an alternative magazine in London. In the same interview, Shepard laid out perhaps his most concise description of what he was trying to achieve as a first-time playwright, and the emotions that moved him. "It wasn't a reaction against anything. It was simply that I couldn't understand why, when you go into a bookstore and they have a section called Modern Drama, you'd find Chekhov, Ibsen, Tennessee Williams and Eugene O'Neill, but that was it. Okay—they're great, but there wasn't anything that seemed to relate to now. There's a huge hole there. You have classic drama then you fall off this precipice into a yawning gap. I was interested in this hole. Why don't I write something in that hole? Of course, Vietnam had a big influence on it too, the whole atmosphere of the time. What in the fuck is going on here? We've fallen off the edge of something and there's no response. None. Theatre wasn't looked on as the arena for that kinda thing. There weren't any scripts. How do you relate O'Neill to the psychological atmosphere around Vietnam? It was very palpable, this psychological fire going on. Panic, terror, paranoia, all that shit that was happening—and there wasn't anything that responded to that climate."

These are the intellectualized memories of an older man looking back at his earliest work, but they are illuminating all the same. More simply, Shepard instinctively seemed to know that the theater space he had access to and the audience it would attract cried out for something new, something they could relate to and that spoke to the times.

Whatever the genesis of these early plays, Shepard was a quick study. His characters "spoke" to him with a surprising urgency. "There were so many voices that I didn't know where to start. It was splendid, really. I felt kind of like a weird stenographer. I don't mean to make it sound like hallucination, but there were definitely things there, and I was just putting them down. I was fascinated by how they structured themselves, and it seemed like the natural place to do it was on a stage. A lot of the time when writers talk about their voice they're talking about a narrative voice. For some reason my attempts at narrative turned out really weird. I didn't have that kind of voice, but I had a lot of other ones, so I thought, Well, I'll follow those."

The double bill of *Cowboys* and *The Rock Garden* was cast primarily with actors from the Village Gate. Ralph Cook directed, and Shepard, to hear his own recollection, was a bit of a "pain in the ass." "I was extremely full of myself at that time. I had a feeling, fed by my friendship with Charlie

Mingus, that nobody knew better than you what was good for your work, which in some ways is still true. But there was an arrogance in that," he said. Others mostly remember the newbie playwright as quiet, shy, and funny. "Attentive and helpful," is how Kissman, who was featured in *The Rock Garden*, remembered him.

It was around this time that Shepard, until then known to all as Steve Rogers, changed his name. That he dropped the surname instead of his middle name was perhaps an unconscious attempt to cut free from his past—and his father. However, it's probably simpler than that. "I always thought Rogers was a corny name, because of Roy Rogers and all the association with that," Shepard said. So he dropped it.

Ralph Cook would come to be respected by all involved, thanks in large part to his laissez-faire approach to directing. His method was text-directed, making sure the acting never got in the way of what the playwright was trying to say. Through this, Cook sought to find the truth of the work. "We didn't spend hours theorizing," said Kissman. "We worked to find the truth, the stage reality, what he called the subjective reality. He thought if we worked toward this the play would emerge as it should." Cook was "inclusive," Kissman added, asking the actors questions and including them in the process of figuring out the reality of the play.

The cast and crew had four weeks of rehearsals leading up to the opening night performance of Shepard's double bill. There was no money for sets and props, so Shepard, with help from Mingus, had to "appropriate" from a nearby construction site a sawhorse with a blinking yellow light, which was used during *Cowboys*. (Since no one knew how to turn the light off, the sawhorse was taken outside into the churchyard and covered over when it wasn't being used.)

The printed text of the play includes an opening scene where a man sits reading a magazine at a kitchen table flanked by a boy and girl, each drinking a glass of milk. After a long stretch of silence, the girl drops her glass, which breaks, sending milk and glass all over the place. That scene was either added after the play's initial run or, if it was part of the play all along, it was cut in the earliest days of rehearsal. Kissman does not remember it.

The play, as first presented on October 16, 1964, begins with a woman lying in bed and a boy, dressed in only his underwear, seated next to her in a rocking chair. They are bathed in a blue light, as the woman, after a long pause, begins to reminisce about "angels on horseback," a favorite family treat made of salt crackers and marshmallows toasted over an open flame. She speaks of how Pop likes them burned. She goes on to speak of how Pop had once eaten poison mushrooms, resulting in his falling out of a tree house he was building, breaking his leg, and ultimately living in the attic with a bunch of cats. The boy's responses, no matter how outlandish the mother's story, are disinterested, usually the kind of single-word prompts a bored listener gives for lack of anything better to say. At several points, the woman tells the boy that parts of his body "are a lot like Pop's." When she asks for a glass of water or a blanket, the boy returns from the errand with the body part previously referenced by the woman covered. It was a recurring visual gag, and it worked. Ultimately footsteps are heard and a man passes by a window at the rear of the set, forcing the boy to run offstage. The man enters and sits in the rocking chair abandoned by the boy. After a pause, the man picks up the conversation roughly where the boy and woman had left off. After a long silence, accompanied by only the man's rocking, the lights slowly dim.

The next scene of *The Rock Garden* opens on a man seated on a couch facing the audience and a boy in a chair with his back to him. They are both clad only in underwear. The man drones on about building a rock garden in the yard, while at intervals the boy falls out of his chair, presumably of boredom. There is great humor in what are essentially pratfalls, as they highlight the man's dullness and his utter cluelessness as to how to talk to his son. After several minutes of talk concerning fences and rock gardens, there is an elongated silence. Then the boy has his say, straight-facedly delivering what may be the dirtiest soliloquy in American drama this side of David Mamet. The litany of graphic sexual descriptions begins, "When I come it's like a river. It's all over the bed and the sheets and everything, you know? I mean a short vagina gives me security. I can't help it. I like to feel like I'm really turning a girl on. It's a much better screw is what it amounts to." From there it goes on: sexual positions, oral sex, you name it. The boy is determined to break through the remoteness and tedium of his home life, conjuring what one critic compared to Norman Mailer's much-discussed "apocalyptic orgasm" and almost literally blasting his way out of the doldrums. As a comic finale, after his son concludes his monologue, the father falls off the couch.

The tedium portrayed in *The Rock Garden* brings to mind Shepard's claim that when with his family back in Duarte, he felt like he was "living on Mars." The characters may be disconnected from each other, yet their common actions, vocal tics, and mannerisms indicate that despite it all, heredity persists. Hence they are trapped together in this state of ennui and stasis, and we can imagine they will remain so. It is their fate, biological and otherwise. "Character is something that can't be helped," Shepard said. "It's like destiny. . . . It can be covered up, it can be messed with, it can be screwed around with, but it can't be ultimately changed. It's like the structure of our bones, and the blood that runs through our veins."

The Rock Garden can be counted as the first of Shepard's family plays. Though he would veer away from this territory immediately afterward and stay away, for the most part, for nearly fifteen years, his first "real" play laid a foundation. "If you go back and look at an early play like *The Rock Garden*, you can see the seeds of *Curse of the Starving Class*," Shepard said, citing the first in his later cycle of family plays. Shepard's invocation of the family home as the opposite of an oasis of warmth and comfort is something that would become a hallmark of his writing. At the time, Shepard explained that *The Rock Garden* was about "leaving my mom and dad." Others saw in his early work something larger. Veteran producer Wynn Handman commented, "Albee's *Zoo Story* was a milestone because it dealt with alienation—of an individual. But by the late sixties, it was about alienation of young people in society. That's what Sam was about."

To ensure that the audience for *The Rock Garden* felt as uneasy as the characters onstage appeared to be, during the performances Shepard employed a hidden subsonic oscillator, which emitted a low hum of white noise. It registered in an unconscious yet visceral way, and director Ralph Cook recalled that when the play ended and the machine was turned off, the audience practically slumped with relief. It was a bold intervention for a newcomer.

The play that opened the double bill marking Shepard's debut as a playwright was *Cowboys*. Patti Smith once wrote that Shepard penned this one-act on the back of Tootsie Roll wrappers. This isn't true, but it does speak to the rapidity with which he was turning out new plays back then. The original script of this play has never been published, but there are two mimeographed copies around. Lee Kissman showed me a version with a badly faded cover page in his California home during the summer of 2015. Shepard rewrote the play from memory in 1967, but those familiar with the first version much prefer it. The rewrite is more studied and, in the words of Kissman, "less alive" than the original.

Cowboys begins with two characters, Stu and Chet, on a dimly lit stage. The men appear to be napping, separated by a sawhorse with a blinking yellow light. Construction sounds from offstage are heard; they then give way to nothing but a single chirping cricket. After a moment, an offstage voice announces, "It's going to rain." The men onstage come to and begin talking about how the rain will allow them to clean their clothes. After Chet tells Stu to go look at the clouds, he steps downstage and does so, but he changes into an old man as he tells his friend that the sky is indeed growing dark. At times Chet also changes into an old man in speech and movement, and for the next forty-five minutes they flip back and forth between these personas as they discuss a variety of topics. At one point they adopt the names Clem and Mel and fend off a make-believe Indian attack before returning to their original selves again, trying to outdo each other at every turn. As this is happening, a soundtrack of city noises—consisting of traffic sounds, sirens, voices arguing, and general neighborhood clatter—plays from offstage, and the lights change from a sun-bright yellow to dim and foreboding, in relation to the changing moods onstage. At the end, the characters once again become their cowboy doppelgangers, and Clem and Mel fight over a lost canteen and shoot each other dead.

The play, Shepard has said, was drawn almost directly from experience, how he and Mingus would play cowboys and Indians in the streets of New York City. The way they talked to each other is mirrored throughout the script for *Cowboys*. The play can also be viewed as Shepard's attempt to bring to the stage his version of the western films he'd loved as a boy.

More impressively, in *Cowboys* Shepard felt free and confident enough to toss off many theatrical conventions. There is no plot, barely any props (the guns where mimed), a stark set, and a soundtrack of city noise recorded by Shepard and Mingus in the streets of New York. Once again characters, with no motivation, changed persona back and forth. This last feature was striking but not unprecedented. From absurdists like Eugène Ionesco to Lucky's transformation from silent slave to verbose genius in Act 2 of *Waiting for Godot*, it was accepted that the idea of "character" was unstable and fluid. It's an idea Shepard would keep returning to throughout his career.

Many of Shepard's fellow playwrights recognized his talent from the first. "He was unique; there's no doubt about it," Tony Barsha said. "He was inspired and instinctual, surreal and anarchic. He had no dramatic sense, but his work was very impressionistic and that was good."

Critic Jerry Tallmer of the *New York Post* was not impressed. The critic attended opening night, angering Cook, the director, for not giving the cast and crew a few days' worth of previews to iron things out, which was the custom. Tallmer left after *Cowboys*, not bothering to stay for *The Rock Garden*. As he bluntly summed up the first half of the double bill in his review: Two young men pass the time near a highway, talking to each other in "various dialects from Country Western to Walter Brennan, to Haughty British and Plain American. They wait for rain. It rains. They grovel in the mud. . . . They are attacked by Comanche's." The headline of his review said it all: "Tell Me about the Morons, George." The critic declared *Cowboys* a rip-off of Beckett. Any time there's a sparse stage with two characters that talk, laugh, and argue, comparisons to *Waiting for Godot* are inevitable.

The critic was not the only one unhappy with *Cowboys*. Mingus's father felt his son should have shared the writing credit for the play, given that it was based so heavily on his and Shepard's casual repartee. Regardless, *Cowboys* was funny and strange, striking in its sounds and images. Combined with *The Rock Garden*, it proved an auspicious start for the young playwright.

When Shepard opened up the *Post* on that October morning of Tallmer's review, he thought his career as an upstart playwright was done. Visions of returning home to California and life as a veterinarian filled his head. Then Michael Smith of the *Village Voice* let loose days later with what would become Shepard's Hail Mary pass, issuing the rave that turned things around. Buoyed by Smith's praise and the resultant crowds that showed up at Theatre Genesis for the next two weekends of his debut effort, Shepard canceled his plans to head back home, if he ever really considered doing so. He was on his way.

The obscene nature of the finale of *The Rock Garden* earned the play a bit of notoriety. Some, even in the progressively minded East Village, outright condemned it. They were faced down by none other than the rector of St. Mark's himself, Michael Allen. He said, in essence, that the language was beside the point, that the play "was really an attack on the pornography of American life." In fact, Allen went so far as to tell Shepard, "One day you will be recognized as America's greatest Christian playwright."

Shepard told him he hoped he was right.

"Generally Acknowledged Genius"

He isn't happy with who he is.

—Sam Shepard

Man is least himself when he talks in his own person. Give him a mask, and he will tell you the truth.

—Oscar Wilde

I f there's one word that people who saw Shepard's early plays use to describe them, it's *alive*. Usually it's his use of language that they're talking about. Clearly, from the start he had the voice, the imagination, and the sensibility to reflect upheaval—personal and public—that was part of the early and mid-1960s. The result was that Shepard went in short order from a teenage newcomer to a playwright to watch. He began to write new plays at an astonishing clip and tried to get them in the hands of someone who might be able to help him. "The next thing he did was he stood in front of Albee's house to give him some plays," Lee Kissman recalled. "Once he got going he didn't stop."

Before Ralph Cook had accepted *The Rock Garden*, Shepard was a mere wannabe sharing a dumpy apartment and busing tables three nights a week. He was adrift, but aware that he had something to say and had a desperate hunger to say it. Seeing people respond to his work gave him the confidence he needed to push on. "I don't think he had the idea that he could be a writer until he brought in *The Rock Garden* and Ralph [Cook] liked it," Kissman said.

When Shepard wasn't writing, he was *thinking* about writing, often juggling six or seven ideas in his head at once. "Needless to say, I wasn't very good company. . . . But nothing mattered to me then except to get the stuff down on paper," he said.

Mingus remembers his roommate writing furiously, going at his new-found trade with the dedication and discipline of a master carpenter, but with this kind of crazy abandon. "I just have an image of him sitting down at a small but adequate table with a sturdy typewriter and a pile of papers and then a box—a ream of paper—and a play or two plays. Just neat and simple and clean. Basic, and that's it. From A to Z—the play is done."

Shepard's pantheon of heroes included some of the Beat Generation writers, and from them he inherited the concept of "first idea, best idea" or, as Kerouac and Ginsberg called it, "bop prosody" or "spontaneous prose." The idea was that one's initial impressions were the most authentic. Riffing with words and whipping up plays like Charlie Parker or John Coltrane tossed off solos was how Shepard worked in those days, thanks undoubt-edly to, well, the speed he was taking, and the influence from his nights listening to jazz greats ply their trade at the Village Gate. As he wrote years later in an unpublished fragment: "I used to watch Eric Dolphy, nightly, very close up, front row sometimes. 1963–64; something like that. Watched his listening; ramrod straight spine on a tall oak stool . . . while Mingus mashed away with his meaty fingers, cruel smile."

Shepard was aiming for the same kind of transcendence with language. The critic Clive Barnes didn't compare Shepard's early work to jazz riffs. He said these first plays were "disposable," and Shepard, recalling the remark later in life, didn't disagree. "With the early stuff I never rewrote anything," he said. "It was the arrogance of youth. 'Fuck it. If you don't understand it I'll just write another one.' I was riding those plays like you'd ride a horse. You'd go as hard as you could."

When not writing or debuting new work on a downtown stage, Shepard was living the life of a young man turned loose in New York. His basic diet during this time was "crystal methedrine, crème soda and liverwurst sandwiches." The latter—being merely food—was sometimes optional: Shepard found he could last three straight days without eating. He lived for a time with a well-traveled businesswoman in Spanish Harlem. She'd go to work in the morning and Shepard would check out her place, looking in the drawers and imagining what the rest of her life was like. Then he'd wander back down to the Village where he'd been staying with Mingus and bum around until he found someone he recognized. There was always someone out and about. But more often than not, Shepard could be found alone in a corner, deep in concentration, running his hand through his longish hair and writing out in longhand the one-act plays that would first make his name. Joyce Aaron, his first New York girlfriend, learned one thing quickly: "You just knew he was in another world and you didn't want to interrupt him," she said. "I'd leave a note instead. He wrote all the time, night and morning, and didn't rewrite."

His front-step appeal to Albee evidently worked, or at least somehow the celebrated older playwright got his hands on *Up to Thursday*, a recently penned Shepard one-act. With the success of his 1962 play *Who's Afraid of Virginia Woolf?* Albee and his producers, Richard Barr and Clinton Wilder, formed the Playwrights Unit to encourage emerging dramatists. The one hundred or so plays the organization presented during its eight years in existence included works by Lanford Wilson, Jean-Claude van Itallie, Megan Terry, LeRoi Jones, and John Guare. The team premiered *Up to Thursday* at the Village South Theatre on November 23, 1964, under the direction of Charles Gyns. Never mind disposable, Shepard "didn't even consider it a play at all."

Up to Thursday is supposedly based on Shepard's flunking his draft board physical by pretending to be strung out on heroin. The play focuses on a young man lying in bed under an American flag while four young friends sit around in chairs. There's much talking, sexual and otherwise. "The play is a series of reactions that become combustible," Shepard explained. The playwright is harsher in his retrospective estimation of the one-act than *New York Times* reviewer Richard F. Shepard, who claimed, "The author draws brightness from the banalities of conversation." *Up to Thursday* is perhaps remembered today, if at all, as the stage debut of future film star Harvey Keitel.

During auditions for *Up to Thursday*, a pretty, young actress named Joyce Aaron came in and took her place in front of the producers. As they'd done with all the females who'd paraded through that day, they asked Aaron to read a few lines and then laugh. She did as requested, and as she ended her audition, she noticed a young man standing at the back of the small theater laughing along with her. It was the playwright himself; the more the actress laughed the more he lost it. "Sam got hysterical," Aaron recalled. "I think Sam and I went for coffee after that and he never left my side."

Onstage, Aaron was trying to connect her actions to any sort of motivation in the script. When she failed to find any, she realized that was the key. "The conventional logic and rationale an actor asks for was simply not there," she wrote in a later essay. "The richness lies in the risk taking."

Aaron fell hard for Shepard, becoming his first serious girlfriend since his coming east. "Sam was a very good-looking guy, and he was very funny and sweet, and I loved his play," she said. "I was taken with his whole being." The Mount Vernon, New York, native spent a part of her youth at an all-girls' school in Danville, Virginia. When she realized she wanted to be an actor, she came to New York City. It was the early 1950s, and once in the city Aaron became connected to the Neighborhood Playhouse School of the Theatre. But her real break came through a babysitting job for Richard Gilman and his wife. He was an author and drama critic for *Commonweal* and other publications, and knowing of Aaron's interest in the theater, he gave her some advice that changed her life. "He told me to go down to Spring Street and see Joe Chaikin. Once I saw what was happening there, that was it," Aaron recalled.

What was happening was the inspired magic of the Open Theater, a workshop-based collective of actors, playwrights, and a handful of critics interested in making a new kind of theater. Hence, by the time Aaron stood on the Village South stage and laughed for Shepard and the producers, she was already a regular in avant-garde theater circles. Needless to say, she got the part.

Up to Thursday did well enough to warrant a restaging with the same cast just a few months later as part of a triple bill at the Cherry Lane Theatre. The play remains unpublished, with the only known copy stashed in Shepard's archives at Boston University. Shepard's next plays, a double bill of *Dog* and *Rocking Chair*, are not extant, and little is known about them other than the date and location of their joint premiere, February 10, 1965, at La MaMa ETC. Shepard somewhat recalled the plays but spoke dismissively of them. "*Dog* was about a black guy—which I later found out it was uncool for a white to write about in America. It was about a black guy on a park bench, a sort of *Zoo Story*–type play. I don't remember *Rocking Chair*, except it was about somebody in a rocking chair."

Shepard moved to Second Avenue with Joyce Aaron, and the couple spent their days working on the things that mattered most to them. "We were always doing something to do with theater. We were writing or rehearsing," Aaron recalled. "We were always busy." Aaron had her acting classes, and her nights were often spent at Open Theater workshops. Shepard was usually ensconced someplace quiet with his notebook, writing longhand, one play after another. He finished plays like others finished a grocery list. During the little downtime they had, Shepard and Aaron would meet other scene regulars down at Joe's Dinette, people like Michael Smith and his partner, the lighting genius of Off-Off-Broadway, Johnny Dodd. Shepard was eating more now, ordering scrambled eggs with hot sauce, meatloaf, or a baked BLT along with a milk shake.

Things were not always carefree. Aaron thinks back to her ex-lover's state of mind during this time, and the word she uses to describe him is "paranoid." Indeed, Shepard said as much himself nearly three decades later, while walking the streets of New York once again and reminiscing about the old days. He spent the sixties and part of the seventies, he wrote in a letter to a friend, in a state of chronic paranoia. "It was impossible to enjoy anything back then," he claimed.

Aaron had a little family money that helped them squeak by, but more was sometimes needed, so the couple waited tables together for a while at La MaMa beginning in 1965. They went to the movies, but the most formative experience Aaron remembers was seeing Peter Brook's production of *Marat/Sade*, a play by Peter Weiss (full title: *The Persecution and Assassination of Jean-Paul Marat as Performed by the Inmates of the Asylum of Charenton under the Direction of the Marquis de Sade*). They saw it in late 1965 on Broadway at the Martin Beck Theatre. With its heady mix of

Brecht and Artaud, the play spoke to Shepard's innate sensibilities. "I just think the music and the movements of the insane, the way they interrelated, was really new then," Aaron said. "I think Sam was really impressed." Five years later, Brook would impact Shepard even more when they met in London, but this famous play, set inside an asylum and running for 145 performances on Broadway, was a key influence on Shepard's writing, if only for its ability to create an otherworldly mise-en-scène.

Toward the end of 1964, not long after Shepard's first plays were staged, Aaron took him to a dinner party in the city. Among the guests was Joseph Chaikin, who was almost universally regarded as a brilliant and innovative theater director. "In the early days he was really and truly an original thinker," said playwright and Open Theater member Jean-Claude van Itallie. Chaikin would become Shepard's touchstone for the experimental.

Chaikin was born in Des Moines, Iowa, in 1935 to Russian parents he described as "traumatized, crazy people, who were running away." Struck by rheumatic heart disease at the age of six, he would be plagued with related medical problems all his life. At first Chaikin had tried his hand at acting with the famed avant-garde troupe the Living Theatre. However, at some point he underwent what he termed a "radical change" and decided directing was his life's calling. His former acting teacher, Nola Chilton, who specialized in nonnaturalistic acting techniques, left New York City in 1963 for Israel, and Chaikin began working with her students. After months of trying to find some common ground as a direction for the group, the members coalesced around the freewheeling notion of keeping things open, dedicating themselves to the idea of constant exploration.

All the new collective needed was a name. "I liked the Open Theater because it was an un-confining name, it implied a susceptibility to continue to change. The name would serve to remind us of that early commitment to stay in process, and we called ourselves that," Chaikin said. The influences would range from Brecht to Artaud and the Living Theatre, with the theories and practices of these disparate sources brought together in a workshop format. It was all channeled through the practices of Chilton and Viola Spolin, author of the 1963 book *Improvisation for the Theater*, and her sound and movement exercises, as well as anything else Chaikin and company could come up with. Open Theater cofounder Peter Feldman recalled that he and the other members did not follow the traditional path of new companies. "We did a lot of workshops before we started to perform," he said. "We worked on the body and the breath, and we were very intent on working on that and working on ourselves before we ever thought of performing." Politics, myths, religion, sex, society, and reality itself became the thematic concerns for the members of the Open Theater.

Originally there were seventeen actors and four writers attached to the Open Theater. The latter were Megan Terry, van Itallie, María Irene Fornés, and Michael Smith. The critics affiliated with the group were Richard Gilman, Gordon Rogoff, and Susan Sontag. The Open Theater took up residence on Spring Street in New York, and the members each chipped in three or four dollars a month to cover the rent, remembers Marianne de Pury, a longtime member of the group and its composer. The group came together as a whole one or two nights a week, often with smaller workshops held on other days to work on a specific project, such as Terry Megan's *Viet Rock* or Jean-Claude van Itallie's *Serpent*, both landmark productions for the company. During the regular workshop, after the voice and body work, Chaikin would toss out suggestions for the collective to react to, allowing ample opportunities for improvisation.

When they met at that party in late 1964, Shepard and Chaikin immediately connected. They left early, walking together all the way downtown to the Open Theater's main space. On a return visit, during a regular workshop, Shepard was amazed by what he saw. "I started attending the workshops and I was immediately struck by how unique it was," he said. "The approach to the actor, the questioning. The non-realistic theater demanded a new style of acting. [The old style] didn't work for that."

To a person, members of the group interviewed stress that Shepard never joined the Open Theater but was primarily around due to his relationship with Aaron, an early member, as well as his friendship with Chaikin. "Sam always said to me, 'I'm interested in my own work. I don't want to write with the Open Theater,'" Aaron recalled. "But I think he was influenced by watching the actors and watching Joe ask questions and seeing the actors' responses. I think it was very illuminating for Sam. Joe was a great theater person, and it was all new at the time, and all this really stimulated Sam. The Open Theater made an impact on him."

Shepard participated in some of the exercises, even sometimes took the helm in Chaikin's stead, tossing out suggestions for the troupe to react to, de Pury recalled. "When Sam suggested something, it was always incredibly clear and uncomplicated, like 'walking a dog' for instance. I never forgot that suggestion because of its directness," she said.

Shepard and Chaikin each benefited from their relationship. "I think that Joe gave Sam a kind of legitimacy and a foothold right smack in the center of the avant-garde and that Sam gave Joe an entrée into a larger world and that they were not unaware of that with each other," van Itallie said. "And that does not mean they didn't highly respect each other and that they didn't work well together."

Chaikin's spurning of fame and publicity may also have had a powerful effect on Shepard. The older man renounced "the theater of critics, box office, real estate and the conditioned public" in favor of creating moments onstage that had meaning for himself and his collaborators. Shepard, whose natural shyness made him adverse to stardom and its trappings, now had a role model who gave him permission to spurn the limelight and always put the work before concerns about fame or acceptance.

Joyce Aaron was overjoyed when she got the call in early 1965 telling her she'd captured a role in a Chicago production of a play called *The Knack*. Her lover was less than thrilled. In fact, as Aaron was preparing to leave New York, Shepard had a panic attack. The result was a daylong writing jag that produced his sixth one-act play, *Chicago*. It features a character named Stu, clad only in blue jeans, who spends most of the play in an empty bathtub at center stage. His girlfriend, Joy, has accepted a job out of town and is getting ready to leave, while Stu, marooned on his own, delivers one monologue after another to no one in particular, sometimes in his own voice other times in that of a little old lady. Meanwhile, Joy's friends arrive every few minutes to talk about her job, some of them carrying fishing poles. Stu tells Joy he is glad for her and her new job, yet his soliloquies are loaded with doom-laden scenarios full of death and transgressive sexual practices. He warns of virgins who are devoured by barracudas or, he seems to hint, caught up against their will in some beachside bacchanal. The end of the play clearly dramatizes Shepard's panic attack, as Stu jumps from his tub, steps to the edge of the stage, and breathes deeply in and out—a known remedy for such disorders. The rest of the cast sits alongside Stu "fishing" in the audience and breathing with him as Joy walks offstage pulling a small wagon filled with her suitcases.

Chicago is more or less a guilt trip laid out in script form. Its humor comes from the absurdity of its images and language. The darkness that shoots through it is not accidental: the bathtub that serves as the central image lent a totemic power that Shepard later saw as possessing multiple meanings. "I love the bathtub," he said. "There's something religious about the bathtub. . . . It's like a cleaning, and there's something about death in it. It's like a casket. It's like birth and like death. Certain objects have that power to me. A refrigerator onstage is a very powerful image [laughs]." Shepard was attached to the bathtub in an even more direct way: in the days before the *Chicago* premiere, he and Mingus literally carried it up the street, behind St. Mark's, and up the stairs to place it on the Theatre Genesis stage.

Much has been made of the soliloquies, or arias, that beginning with *Chicago* became a cornerstone of Shepard's plays. These long, lyrical bursts of language date to the days of Elizabethan drama but fell out of favor for centuries until O'Neill revived them. Shepard saw them as his form of jazz soloing, with their alliteration, the repetition of words and key phrases, and the emphasis not on meaning but on rhythm: "Fires! Fires at night. All over the island there's huge fires flaring and they all lie around. They lie there fucking by the fire and picking each other's noses." As another Theatre Genesis playwright and fan of arias, Murray Mednick, saw it, the revived practice stemmed more so from the poetry readings at St. Mark's that predated the theater there. "The reading of the poems became a kind of performance art," he said. "There was a kind of presentational quality to the language which I think we [playwrights] were very influenced by."

Chicago features a handful of arias, or, if you will, one long one that is broken up by bits of action or dialogue. It is in these "incantations," as he called them, that Shepard's reputation as a poet of the theater was initially forged. Shepard has preferred to see them as the literary equivalent of music. "They were just chants, they were incantations, whatever you want to call

them, you just got on and go. To say they were all thought out, they weren't.
. . . They were a pulse." Friend and Off-Off-Broadway director the late
Bill Hart once referred to Shepard's arias in similar fashion. To him they
felt "blazing, youthful, like hearing rhythm and blues for the first time."

Post-1970 readers of *Chicago* may see the play as historically prescient.
Shepard had no way of knowing when he wrote the play in early 1965 the
quagmire the war in Vietnam would become. Stu's dark prophesies conjure
images from the shores and jungles of East Asia that would soon be domi-
nating the nightly news: the "mound of greasy bodies," the recurring talk
of fires flaring, the putrid smells, and the sex that is anything but romantic
but almost violent in its unchained fervor. Toward the end, when Stu lies
down and practically disappears into the tub, Shepard's casket metaphor
becomes all too apparent. Stu's disconnection is that of the soldier in the
jungle, or America on a slow road to ruin.

The play highlights the ways Shepard, in his early work, made use of
elements from his life, in this case Aaron's trip to Chicago. His imagination would take a situation, twist it, and shape it until it reflected the fears,
emotions, and impulses he was feeling. "I never knew where our life—where
my life—was going to turn up on the page, or later on some stage, but inevitably there was always some aspect of our experience together that I would
recognize," Aaron said. "Yet I never felt exposed by Sam—he transformed
whatever he drew on." So impactful was Joyce's influence on Shepard's next
few plays that he signed a copy of his first collection, *Five Plays*, dedicating
it to her because, he wrote, her "loving companionship for more than 3 years
molded the shape and content of these 5 plays. Love, Sam."

Chicago is also an object lesson demonstrating the speed with which
Shepard's plays moved from his imagination to the stage. He wrote it in
a day, and it was onstage at Theatre Genesis less than a month later. The
critics saw the play as a spark that caught fire and burned intensely, if
briefly. Writing of a 1996 revival, the *Times'* Ben Brantley declared: "The
play still glows with the sense of hot, youthful spontaneity, of a mind that
simply opened itself and let the images tumble out. But it's also remarkably of a piece and, if you relax and just give yourself to it, surprisingly
coherent." For *Village Voice* critic Elenore Lester, writing in the *Times
Magazine* shortly after the play's premiere, *Chicago* was characteristic of the

better Off-Off-Broadway plays, with its "forlorn and funny" monologues and image-driven stagecraft.

The play was Shepard's most popular play to date. It opened in April 1965, at Theatre Genesis, as part of a double bill with Lawrence Ferlinghetti's *Customs Collector in Baggy Pants*. The following March it was staged twice at La MaMa. Over the next year, *Chicago* would be performed in Europe and back Off-Broadway.

Not long after Shepard penned *Chicago*, he took a train to join Aaron in the Windy City. By the time she finished her run in *The Knack*, summer was approaching, and she and Shepard left for Philadelphia, where she was engaged to star in *Slow Dance on the Killing Floor*. She spent her days in rehearsals while he stayed in their rented cabin and wrote. Again he turned to his life for inspiration, and the result was *Red Cross*, a play that would debut the following January.

When *Slow Dance* closed its run in Philly and moved on to Milwaukee, Shepard again tagged along with Aaron. The couple was there for the Fourth of July, and while watching the fireworks in a local park, Shepard felt as if he and everyone around him weren't celebrating anything tangible, that they'd all lost touch with the past. It may very well have been drug-induced paranoia (Aaron told me they would smoke pot, drop acid, and even get hold of the occasional blast of cocaine), but this sense of disconnection frightened him. "You can be there celebrating the Fourth of July, but all you know is that things are exploding in the sky," he said. It "creates a kind of terror, you don't know what the fuck's going on." This experience and the strange feelings accompanying it provided the basis for another of his one-act plays, *Icarus's Mother*.

While in Milwaukee, Aaron had a bad experience with LSD that kept her from going onstage one night. To hear her describe the extremis she was in is—far removed from acid's heyday—almost comical. "Sam got me through that. I went back into the womb," Aaron recalled. "He fed me milk from a baby bottle to bring me out." A dozen years later, Shepard would turn the incident into a piece of prose for his second collection of stories, *Motel Chronicles*: "I tried to hold her head as she thrashed back and forth," he wrote. "She moaned in a voice I'd only heard in animals giving birth. Mares moaning. Sheep. It kept rolling out of her as her body unleashed itself."

With 1965 past its halfway point, it was easy to guess that it would become one of the most violent years in U.S. history since the Civil War. The bombing of North Vietnam had increased, and in July President Johnson would increase American forces in Southeast Asia to 125,000. Selma's marchers had been attacked, Malcolm X was dead of an assassin's bullet, and the Klan had killed a man in Michigan. Off-Off-Broadway, home of the radical fringe of American theater, was a perfect place to raise a voice against the ugly zeitgeist. Some playwrights engaged the battle head-on, but Shepard, rarely overtly political, let audiences see the turmoil as reflected in the lives of his characters. He created claustrophobic stage spaces, limned our apocalyptic dread, dotted his work with violent outbursts, and put onstage surrealistic visions that led one to imagine a country coming unmoored. Shepard's output in the mid-sixties seems dated by today's lights, but even the weaker plays had some astonishing image, outburst, or lyrical passage to make them worthwhile. They stood up well against the other plays being staged around the Village at the time, for he racked up several Obie Awards (often described as the Off-Off-Broadway and Off-Broadway equivalent of the Tony Awards).

Shepard couldn't have known upon stepping on a plane one summer day in 1965 that the flight would be transformative. He and Aaron had booked a flight from New York to Mexico in hopes of enjoying a quick and cheap vacation. On the way, they encountered bone-rattling turbulence, leaving Shepard, who was new to flying, terrified. When they landed in Chiapas, he swore he would never fly again. It was a vow he'd keep for the better part of two decades.

Not long after landing, Aaron became desperately ill with a stomach virus. Shepard spent the first part of the vacation hunting for a doctor. The incident would provide the grist for Shepard's first two-act play, *La Turista*, which premiered in March 1967. (In a 1977 interview, he would claim that he was also ill, suffering from "amoebic dysentery.") The pair eventually became well enough to travel the countryside, taking a chicken-filled bus around Chiapas and eventually all the way to Guatemala. The roads were "terrifying," Aaron remembered. When it was time to head home, making good on his vow, Shepard and Aaron left most of their belongings behind and climbed on a bus heading north, riding it for several days until they were back in New York.

Shepard's next one-act plays, *4-H Club*, *Icarus's Mother*, and *Red Cross*, perhaps represent what he had in mind when he wrote in the introduction to a collection of his early works, "For me, these plays are inseparable from the experience of the time out of which they came. A series of impulsive chronicles representing a chaotic, subjective world. Basically, without apologizing, I can see now that I was learning how to write." These plays are most important as stepping-stones to his later and best work. Each has its charms and the spark of originality, as well as all the signs of a bold and ambitious writer working things out for himself.

4-H Club premiered under the auspices of Albee's Playwrights Unit at the Cherry Lane Theatre in September of 1965. It tells the story of three young men living in a filthy apartment, in which they are penned like animals (perhaps the meaning of the title?). The characters are not well delineated, and they talk in chunks of dialogue that are only mildly interesting, relying on one non sequitur after another, until they decide to scare the mice out of hiding so they can squash them.

Better is *Icarus's Mother*, which features an undercurrent of mayhem and frisson of apocalyptic dread, even as the play shoots off in a handful of directions. It premiered at Caffe Cino in November 1965, with a cast drawn from the ranks of Chaikin's Open Theater. The plot, such that it is, involves a group of friends, three men and two women, who have just finished a seaside picnic. The play opens with the group lying on their backs watching a plane circling above; they are unsure whether the pilot is trying to skywrite or if his plan is to simply cough out random streams of exhaust. Two of the men, Bill and Howard, take turns psychologically harassing the others with their words and posturing as they wait for the night's fireworks to begin. The same men, when left alone, run to the barbecue pit and use a rug to try and send smoke signals to someone. In the end, Frank launches into a soliloquy about the plane crashing. The play's finale features the actual crashing of the plane.

The play is often funny, or anyway can be played for laughs. Audiences are left to ponder whether it is an update of *The Lord of the Flies*—albeit an adult version—or if the mendacious behavior of the men is going to lead to actual violence? Or is it trying to say something about life during wartime? A sense of dread pervades the one-act play, embodied, Shepard has said, by the omnipresent airplane and its inexplicable actions in the sky. A few years later, when a fringe theater company in London produced the show under the direction of Nancy Meckler, she recalled how Shepard told the actors the play's origins had to do with "his fear of flying."

Red Cross was written in a Philadelphia cabin while Joyce Aaron was off at a local theater rehearsing. Shepard uses the daily visitations by the real-life maid as the point of departure for an imaginary encounter that goes nowhere particularly interesting yet still manages to be odd and humorous. The set, with intense lighting by Johnny Dodd, presented a striking tableau, but the play is mostly static. It was directed by newcomer Jacques Levy, who'd met Shepard through the playwright's girlfriend, Joyce Aaron. Levy was a trained clinical psychologist who had found his way to the world of New York City's underground theater. His greatest fame was still years in the future, when he'd direct the bawdy Broadway hit *Oh! Calcutta!* Later he would cowrite songs with Bob Dylan for the *Desire* album, including the radio-ready protest song, "Hurricane."

Red Cross opened in January 1966 at Judson Poets' Theatre in Greenwich Village. The play ends with a flash, as a man, dressed all in white against that all-white set, faces the audience with blood running down his forehead. That abrupt ending left some in the audience gasping, recalled director Levy. Using bright lights to make the all-white set nearly blinding, having his actors play some scenes in a highly affected manner, and breaking the fourth wall by having some of the dialogue directed to the audience, Levy tried to highlight the intentions of specific moments in the play. This spoke to the director's belief that Shepard "is more interested in doing something to audiences than in saying something to them." How he managed to strike the right balance with all this was easy, Levy claimed—he had Shepard sitting at the back of the theater during rehearsals giving him "the raspberry" if he thought things got too corny.

While many have described Shepard during this time as quiet, funny, and generally good-natured, this wasn't the case when he felt his writing or his vision was being corrupted or interfered with. Throughout his long career, Shepard has defended his work for the stage with both his words and his fists. It is a recurring motif of his artistic life. On this point, those who have known and worked with Shepard over the years say he does not take criticism well. Michael Smith found this out after penning a less-than-flattering review of *Red Cross* for the *Village Voice*. Smith admitted to liking the play but complained it had no content. "I remember Sam writing me a long letter in response to that review, being really annoyed at me for saying that," Smith recalled. "It really offended him."

The playwright had a right to be a little full of himself. The *New York Times* featured an article on December 5, 1965, headlined "The Pass-the-Hat Theater Circuit," in which Shepard was declared the "generally acknowledged genius" of the scene. The paper of record was actually late in arriving. By the time the article came out, Off-Off-Broadway had produced more than four hundred new plays by two hundred different playwrights. In 1964 the Obie Awards had expanded its categories to include Off-Off-Broadway. For the 1965–1966 season, *Chicago*, *Icarus's Mother*, and *Red Cross* won in the Distinguished Plays category, and Levy earned an Obie for his direction of the latter.

By the end of 1965, Shepard's reputation had already spread, and not only was he attracting attention from journalists and producers from around the city but the Boston Theatre Company invited him up in the fall of 1965 to deliver a reading of a new play. Meanwhile, the next year, Shepard received a fellowship from Yale University and signed on with his first agent, Toby Cole's Actors and Authors Agency. Cole was known as "a lifelong devotee to progressive causes and avant-garde talent." Retaining her services was a sure sign that Shepard was on his way. He no doubt enjoyed the fact that Cole represented one of the poets his father used to read to him, Pablo Neruda, and had links to two playwrights he'd come to admire: Bertolt Brecht and the avant-garde playwright Peter Handke.

However, despite the professional steps Shepard was making, along with the occasional influx of grant money and fellowships, he would remain in relative penury until winning the Pulitzer Prize more than a dozen years later. Even afterward, there would be times when money was tight.

His next play, *Fourteen Hundred Thousand*, would first be presented at Minneapolis's Firehouse Theatre and would be featured on National Education Television. It involves a small family and a few friends who are building a bookcase. Things get rather dissociative very quickly, as Shepard seems intent on filling the stage with dialogue and actions that defy expectations. The young adults argue about whether to vacation before finishing the bookshelves, while the parents add unrelated commentary before opening up books from the surrounding stacks and reading to themselves. Donna, for whom the bookcases are being built, taunts and argues with her friends almost as a Pinter character would, without point or provocation, until a paint fight breaks out. In the end, the whole cast launches into a soliloquy about a "linear" city of the future.

Shepard would never push the limits of coherence this far again. Perhaps he was testing his own theory, as laid out in his 1977 essay "American Experimental Theatre, Then and Now," where he defines experimentation as "taking steps into the unknown with the hope of knowing," as he tries to come to terms with the small-minded attitude that reflexively rejects the new. He writes: "It may be that the territory available to a theatrical event is so vast that it has to be narrowed down to ingredients like plot, character, set, costume, lights, etc., in order to fit it into our idea of what we know."

For now at least, he would not be bound by such narrowing. Shepard's next plays would often confound, but not as aggressively. They have, at minimum, their own inner logic. It was another step in his development as one of the most original and daring playwrights of his time, and as an artist who refused to compromise or kneel at the altar of the box office.

Musical Interlude

Ma's out there switchin' in the kitchen
And Dad's in the living room fussing and a-bitching
And I'm out here kicking the gong for euphoria

—"Euphoria,"
The Holy Modal Rounders

Shepard's restless nature meant that being recognized as one of the leading lights of New York's experimental theater scene wasn't enough. Whether it was boredom or the need to fill some kind of void, it's hard to say, but as the sixties wore on, he was looking for more, and he found it in music. His father had taught him how to play drums back in California, but since leaving home he'd been unable to afford a kit of his own. What he had managed to acquire were hand drums. Often, Shepard could be seen tapping away backstage while a director and actors worked through his latest play. Producer Wynn Handman remembered waiting on Shepard for a rewrite of *La Turista* and finding the playwright playing one of his bongo drums backstage in the middle of an afternoon rehearsal. The veteran producer inquired after the rewrite, and Shepard, never missing a beat, told him, "I write at night."

The affinity that Shepard the writer had for rhythm and music was apparent from the very first. How much this was born of his many hours sitting behind a drum kit during his youth is hard to say. He openly admitted to wanting to be a rock star, and who of his generation didn't in the years after the Beatles landed? He got his chance in 1966. Shepard somehow found time to start a duo with a local guitarist, whose name is lost to history. They called themselves The Heavy Metal Kid, taking the name from the William S. Burroughs novel *The Soft Machine* ("Uranian Willy, the Heavy Metal Kid, also known as Willie the Rat"). Lower East Side folk musician Peter Stampfel heard the duo shortly after his first meeting with Shepard and was not particularly impressed. "Sam wrote songs that were kind of like punk rock–ish basically, but I remember very little about them. My recollections of them was, OK but not great," he said.

Stampfel grew up in Milwaukee and first encountered folk music while a student at the University of Wisconsin. He took up the five-string banjo and found his way to New York City, where he joined a coterie of musicians coalescing around the folk revival. In March 1963, he met a country blues–picking free spirit named Steve Weber, who had grown up in Philadelphia, dropped out of high school, and for years lived on the streets of New York. The pair discovered common ground between them and set out to add their own twist to the acoustic music that was ascendant at the time. "I really hated the seriousness of the people on the folk music scene," Stampfel said in a 2009 National Public Radio interview. He liked instead the "goofy stuff."

After trying a few different names, he and Weber became the Holy Modal Rounders, and their psychedelic folk music soon found a cult audience. However, some people didn't know what to make of the group's highly original and quirky style. An Austin newspaper, years later, headlined a concert review: "Rounders destroy country music in bizarre five-hour concert."

On record, the band could range from technically brilliant to downright disorderly. "Our first album was recorded on speed and pot," Stampfel said. "All our early albums were recorded on . . . well, I was on amphetamine and marijuana and beer. How [the substances] affected it was what you hear when you hear the records."

Yet the first two Holy Modal Rounders records are full of interesting and tuneful tracks. One thing's for sure: it was music unlike anything else being heard around the Village, or anywhere else for that matter. Both Stampfel and Weber eschewed accepted notions about singing, never vying for the sweet harmonies of fellow travelers like the New Christy Minstrels or even pulling off updated imitations of their heroes like Charlie Poole and Uncle Dave Macon. No, they sang unfettered by concerns about tradition or the marketplace or how Peter, Paul, and Mary might be doing it. For these things alone, they deserve their place in music history. Also, the band is credited with the first use of the word *psychedelic*.

After a year or so together, Stampfel and Weber threw in with the Fugs, helping that like-minded rock band cut a few albums, but by the end of 1965 Stampfel had quit that gig and founded a new band, the Moray Eels.

As Stampfel recounted, one day in September 1966 guitarist Carol Hunter informed him that a promoter was willing to pay "a few hundred bucks" for a Holy Modal Rounders reunion at the University of Illinois. "That was a lot of money in those days," Stampfel said. "The only problem was I'd pawned my fiddle to buy speed. That was why I happened to be in the pawnshop un-pawning my fiddle where Sam Shepard happened to be."

Despite the fiddle case in Stampfel's hand, Shepard asked him if he played electric bass. It just so happened that Stampfel, a multi-instrumentalist from way back, did. Shepard was looking to add some bottom to The Heavy Metal Kid's sound. The duo became a trio, but it was clear from the start that the conglomeration wasn't going very far. "The Heavy Metal Kid thing kind of came to an end within three to six months after it started and Sam started playing with us," Stampfel said. "And we started hanging out a lot together and talking. He was a smart and interesting guy, so we became friends."

Shepard was with the Moray Eels when, beginning around 1967, people started to recognize him. "People started asking us if that was the guy who writes plays," Stampfel recalled.

The band didn't tour a lot, primarily staying close to its home base on the Lower East Side, which was useful for Shepard, who had his other life to get back to. "We were mostly rehearsing. . . . Like the basic thing was we'd take a bunch of speed and play music and didn't really do much as far as gigs," Stampfel said.

That changed in early 1968, when the band traveled to California to record. Out west, the band landed some pretty high-profile performances, and people were eager to hire them back then, to hear Shepard tell it. "People were so dumbfounded about the band. They liked something about it because they kept hiring us," he said. "They couldn't figure out where we fit. And we didn't fit anywhere. We certainly didn't fit as the warm-up band for Ike and Tina Turner, or for Pink Floyd. It was just like a renegade . . . insanity. I don't really know how we got into the studio or why anyone would want to record us."

The Rounders cut two albums during Shepard's tenure, *Indian War Whoop* and *The Moray Eels Eat the Holy Modal Rounders*. The band did have two big breaks. "Bird Song" made it onto the soundtrack of the hit 1969 film *Easy Rider*. It plays while stars Dennis Hopper, Peter Fonda, and Jack Nicholson ride their motorcycles down a country road. Stampfel's vocal, "If you wanna be a bird," fits perfectly over the famous sequence where Hopper stands on his motorcycle seat and Nicholson, riding with Fonda, flaps his arms. Hopper, who also directed the film, selected the song for the film and the huge-selling *Easy Rider* soundtrack. "I heard it was Sam Shepard's group is what I was told at the time," Hopper explained simply enough. The song peaked at number five on the pop charts. Shepard's percussion on "Bird Song" is limited to tapping a tambourine.

The other almost-break came in 1968 when the Rounders appeared on the popular television show *Rowan & Martin's Laugh-In*. The Rounders were heralded by the hosts as the "discovery of the week." Ruth Buzzi, in the guise of her well-known horned-up spinster Gladys Ormphby, introduces the band, which launches into a wonderfully reckless version of the old blues tune "Right String but the Wrong Yo-Yo." Buzzi next heads to the bandstand and takes turns flirting with and touching each member of the Rounders as they play, before Arte Johnson's dirty old man comes and hauls her away mid-song and the tune collapses. The clip can be found online. Shepard had no recollection of the appearance when Stampfel mentioned it in the documentary of the band, *Bound to Lose*. "We were on *Laugh-In*? [Laughs] I don't remember any of this," he said. "What kind of drugs were we on? [Laughs] Just to think, we were on the verge of fame."

The Holy Modal Rounders split up in 1972. Stampfel remained a Village regular and over the years has reunited with his old band, but he also played with everyone from Bob Dylan and Mississippi John Hurt to They Might Be Giants. He also occasionally performed again with Shepard over the years and would like to do so more frequently. "Yes, [Sam's] definitely changed in some ways and not in others," he said. "I still see him very sporadically. . . . I don't want to foist myself on him, so I'm not very pushy."

In recent years, Stampfel has played and recorded with Shepard's youngest son, Walker, a fine musician known for his work with the band The Down Hill Strugglers.

New Territory

T he arrival of 1967 found Shepard making music as well as writing plays and somehow maintaining for the most part his prodigious output. The new plays would be longer and more complex, would feature larger casts and busier sets, and would often incorporate live music. They would also be darker, holding up a mirror to an America seemingly disintegrating. Shepard was among those who did this best, according to veteran critic John Lahr. "To be responsible in such a climate, our theater must be visionary," he wrote. "Like the society, the stage must forge new images—not only to revitalize the imaginative life of its audience but to attempt to give form to our incredible fragmentation and despair." Shepard offered "truly contemporary images" that spoke to the times, Lahr claimed. The playwright was only twenty-three, but the accolades, albeit all connected to the rather provincial world of Off-Off-Broadway, were piling up.

Meanwhile, the publisher Bobbs-Merrill issued a collection of his early one-acts. *Five Plays* includes *Chicago, Red Cross, Icarus's Mother, Fourteen Hundred Thousand*, and *Melodrama Play*. With all this going for him, it's no wonder Shepard's name was getting around town and producers and directors from larger theaters were beginning to show an interest in his work.

As the year began, Shepard was still living with Joyce Aaron in her Second Street apartment. His writing was about to enter a new phase. While directing *Red Cross*, Jacques Levy had told Shepard—who he felt was writing what he described as "chamber plays"—to free his imagination even further. "We were sitting and talking about some scene he wanted to do, and he said, 'I don't think that could be done anyway on stage. There's no point in doing it,'" Levy recalled. "I said, 'You should never think that thought when you're a writer. . . . ' I remember saying, 'Look, Sam, if you have the idea that you want an elephant to appear on the stage without walking on from the wings, you should just write it and see what happens from it.'"

He would take this advice. Shepard's next plays were more daring, even a touch psychedelic, even though Shepard was no fan of hippiedom, which was expanding from Haight-Ashbury across the nation. While young people everywhere were grooving to "Lucy in the Sky with Diamonds," after hearing it that summer in a ground-floor apartment on East Houston Street in New York City with his bandmate Peter Stampfel, Shepard thought the Beatles musical acid trip was a dumb song. Still, he wasn't averse to incorporating into his writing a little Age of Aquarius strangeness. His next plays would be even more imaginative—"far out" in the parlance of the day—than those previous.

Veteran producer Wynn Handman was on the receiving end of Shepard's expanded ambitions when he agreed to stage *La Turista*, which would ultimately become Shepard's first two-act play, though originally the piece included a third act. "I thought the writing was superb," Handman said. Levy directed once again, and the play premiered at American Place Theater in New York in March 1967. As producer, Handman did make a suggestion to Shepard: "I said, 'Listen, man, it's too long, let's make it a two-act play.' He didn't even blink an eye. He just said, 'Fine, whatever works.'"

Based on the trip Shepard and Aaron took to Mexico in the summer of 1965 and the ailment that struck them both, the play appropriately begins with a depiction of "la turista," which is Spanish for "tourist" but is more commonly used to signify the traveler's illness or Montezuma's revenge, primarily a stomach ailment marked by intense bouts of diarrhea. Aaron had it bad; evidently, so did Shepard. Add to this the close quarters of the couple's hotel room and the summer heat, and things soon became unbearable, forcing Shepard to leave Aaron to fetch a doctor. That's where in *La Turista* verifiable fact ends. But for Shepard, it was authentic to his experience, and that was his measure. "In that state any writing I could manage seemed valid, no matter how incoherent it might seem to an outside eye," he said.

The play unfolds like a fever dream, as a vacationing couple, Salem and Kent, relax in their Day-Glo Mexican hotel room. They are suffering from sunburns, but the topic changes quickly from the possibility of "fourth-degree burns" once Kent begins to feel the effects of "la turista." Not long after, a "dark-skinned boy" arrives with a shoeshine kit and verbally abuses the couple. When medical help finally arrives, it is in the guise of a witch doctor, who tries to cure Kent by killing two chickens and chanting in a ritualistic ceremony. (As for the "killing" of the fowl, Levy's widow, Claudia, provides a hint as to what really happened: "Jacques was very good at sleight of hand. He figured that one out.")

Act 2 mirrors its predecessor but takes place in a room described as "American," presumably back home, before Kent and Salem had left for Mexico. Shepard's directions stress that much of the set is "plastic," perhaps commenting on the unreality of life in America circa the mid-1960s. The witch doctor now appears as a Civil War–era country doctor, who arrives with his son. The doctor believes Kent is suffering from sleeping sickness and that the key to saving him is to keep him moving and awake. The doctor and Kent begin a circular kind of crazy talk before Ken, feeling threatened by the lunacy of the medicine man, runs through the back wall of the stage.

Shepard attempted to keep reviewers from seeing the play, but when asked about this he questioned the very essence of criticism. "Why should everything be evaluated in terms of success or failure?" he said. "If I ever got wealthy enough to produce my own plays, I'd never have them reviewed." Looking back in 2009 at his younger self, Shepard seemed ashamed of his attitude. "I was a belligerent asshole back then," he said. "Really. I mean I was really not a pleasant person to be around. I was rude and belligerent."

Critic Elizabeth Hardwick found her way into the theater and in her review, which ran in the *New York Review of Books* on April 6, 1967, found much to like about the play, calling it a "dazzling production" of a work of "superlative interest." Hardwick even seems to give Shepard a line he could throw at those disappointed subscribers and walkouts when she writes: "Our new American theater cannot play to the old audience; it must have a new one." Where others saw chaos, she saw a work held together by "tone and style," and while so much of Off-Off-Broadway was inane, Shepard, she wrote, "possesses the most impressive literary talent and dramatic inventiveness."

Audiences didn't agree. Most weren't ready to ride along with Shepard into this murky dream world. "The most hostile audience I faced was up at the American Place Theatre when we were putting on *La Turista*," he said. "They invited all these Puerto Rican kids, street kids, and they were firing at the actors with peashooters." Nonetheless, the play marks a transition in Shepard's writing. Not only was it his longest play to date, for the first time he'd worked hard at rewriting. Gone was the idea of "first idea, best idea" that he believed was the key to authentic expression. *La Turista* was still a stop on the way to greater things, and it proves Shepard was a playwright intent on extending his reach.

Producers had their hands full with the play. "We lost lots of subscribers with *La Turista*, I'm *still* furious," Handman said many years later. Shepard's first trip above Fourteenth Street and a step closer to the "big time" issued a wake-up call. He'd left his people—the more adventurous audiences of the Village—and found that at more established places like the American Place Theater "most of them were geriatric," he said.

Looking back with the wisdom of a sixty-five-year-old, Shepard offered an unkind assessment of *La Turista*. "It's still kind of an odd play, a pretty weird play," he said. "I wouldn't write a play like that now. I was totally arrogant then. I didn't read anybody else's plays, I didn't go to anybody else's plays. I *hated* theater. Everything was in this angry situation, it was Vietnam and everything. I carried a big grudge. I guess—the John Osborne routine. We were all angry young men. But Wynn was very tolerant. *More* than tolerant."

In May *Melodrama Play* premiered at La MaMa ETC. The story of a songwriter being pressured to write a follow-up hit is most notable for its autobiographical reflections and the way it points forward to a better, more fully realized work. Singer-songwriter Duke is locked in a room by his Svengali-like manager, Floyd, until he writes another big song. Floyd sends in Duke's brother, Drake, who actually wrote the first hit, and a friend, Cisco, to help. When it's discovered that Duke didn't even write his first hit but stole it from his brother, Floyd turns to Drake and Cisco and applies the same pressure tactics, placing a large guard named Peter at the door to make sure they get down to work.

Those seeking to read into Shepard's work could find in *Melodrama Play* his feelings concerning the pressure that success was beginning to exert on him. By this time, producers were actively pursuing his work, each hoping to stage a premiere of the latest Shepard play. Meanwhile, the restlessness that led him to write plays at a staggering pace, play drums with a folk-rock band, and (soon) begin dabbling in film work meant he was amassing commitments. Grant money would come and go, but for the most part he'd remain struggling for cash. The pressure being put on the songwriters in *Melodrama Play* reflected what Shepard was feeling as the demands on his time and talent piled up. He'd address the same theme a few years later, but instead of a blocked songwriter, the focus would be a preternaturally gifted handicapper who's kidnapped by mobsters intent on taking advantage of his gifts. That play, *Geography of a Horse Dreamer*, is a more coherent work, more mysterious and darkly humorous, but *Melodrama Play* first set the theme.

The play also marks the beginning of a turning point for Shepard's work, as he begins incorporating rock music, with all the possibilities and complications this presents. It should be said that despite Shepard's lyrical gifts as a playwright, when it comes to penning songs, as exemplified by those in *Melodrama Play* and later works, something is lost in the translation. His lyrics lack any traditional structure and are really just miniature soliloquies set to music. They are too often silly, nonrhyming, and meandering. Still, *Melancholy Play* would be the first of his dramas to include songs written by Shepard and played by members of the Holy Modal Rounders, sometimes with the playwright manning the drums. (In his notes on *Melodrama Play*, Shepard suggests that the band be enclosed in a cage above the audience's heads.)

In the spring of 1967, Shepard took the pillows from the bed of the Second Street apartment he and Joyce Aaron had been sharing, put them in his car, and left with a good-bye honk of the horn. Aaron says that she and Shepard had come close to marrying, so close that she'd already had the mandatory blood test. However, she says she could see he was not the settling-down type. "I was brokenhearted, and he was not very happy either," she recalled. Over the next few months, he'd write to her suggesting reconciliation, she said, but it was not to be. Aaron saw in Shepard the qualities he himself would assign to Kosmo, the lead character in his 1971 play *The Mad Dog Blues*: "Tall, lean, angular, wolflike. Leads with his cock. . . . Lots of dashing images. Taken with himself as a man with the ladies. . . . Moves from spot to spot to spot across the planet hoping to find a home."

Shepard's next move would take him further into the avant-garde scene, where he would meet the woman he would marry and encounter an idea that would soon permeate his work.

Shepard was far from the only playwright pushing the boundaries. Two of his old Theatre Genesis colleagues, Murray Mednick and Tony Barsha, and another director named Eddie Hicks were doing likewise and trying to deglamorize the junkie life. To that end, in April they gathered a musician and nine actors and headed south. Mednick at that time had just two pages comprising an "impressionistic scenario" when the contingent traveled from New York to the Keystone Dairy Farm in the Poconos Mountains of Pennsylvania. What developed on the farm was a creative commune of sorts. The troupe worked and lived together; there was plenty of pot, speed, and some LSD; and no doubt the free love ethos of the time led to romantic entanglements. They spent two months there, calling themselves the Keystone Company. The actors improvised their lines based on Mednick's outline until what emerged was a remarkable play called *The Hawk*.

At one point, Shepard joined the crew at the farm. Barsha respected Shepard's talent but still viewed him as an upstart, albeit one with a natural gift. "He was unique; there's no doubt about it," he said. "I identified right away, because I come from the same area." The main difference between the two writers was that Barsha was academically trained and had worked in theater overseas; Shepard, he said, was "inspired and instinctual." However, personally, Shepard struck Barsha as still green, despite his having been an Off-Off-Broadway regular for a few years at this point. "He was a quiet guy; he didn't have a lot to say. He was almost like a nerdy guy, kind of a gawky kid type. He seemed more childlike than anything. Then I found out he belonged to the Future Farmers of America. I said, 'That figures.'"

It's hard to say how much, if anything, Shepard contributed to *The Hawk*. Nowhere is he credited or officially associated with the play, other than the fact that he was at the farm during its creation and may have acted out a few improvised parts during its development. The play, which turns on the idea of the titular character having two distinct personalities, provided the first inklings of a theme Shepard would turn to over and over again—the idea of man's split or dual nature. In *The Hawk*, the main character is a heroin dealer shadowed by a double. For Shepard, this proved to be a powerful idea, one that would be reinforced in the early 1970s when he fell under the sway of the spiritualist G. I. Gurdjieff, who believed every person contained multiple "I"s. "I mean, it's an old, old tradition that goes way back into an almost religious knowledge that there's this 'other,' that there's this companion," Shepard said. "The obvious one is the brothers, the counterpart, the shadow. There's some sense of another being that accompanies you. Whether that being is for you or against you is up in the air." This idea is what made *The Hawk* such a unique and compelling drama.

The play is important in Shepard's history for another reason. It was at the farm in Pennsylvania that he first spied a young actress named O-Lan Johnson. The petite actress with the pretty, round face had turned seventeen while at the farm and was costarring in *The Hawk* with her mother, Scarlett, a redheaded bombshell herself, then in her mid-thirties.

In 1967 the Johnson family lived on the Lower East Side of the Village on East Eleventh Street. Scarlett Johnson lived with her mother, Pat, and two daughters, O-Lan and Kristy (named for characters in Pearl Buck's *The Good Earth*), along with a cat named Bartley. The Johnsons had a tough go of it: a few years earlier in their native Los Angeles, Scarlett's husband had walked out on the family, leaving them next to penniless. They moved east, first stopping in Chicago, where they were reportedly so broke that O-Lan would have to hurry home from school so her mother could use her shoes to go to work on the late shift. Eventually they made it to the East Coast and the Village.

Enter Johnny Dark, a devotee of the Beats who spent as much time as he could around lower Manhattan and Greenwich Village. Dark had been adopted at the age of two and raised in Jersey City, New Jersey. He began dating Scarlett in 1967, when he was twenty-six, and moved in with the Johnsons just weeks later.

The Keystone Company, including Scarlett and O-Lan Johnson, left the farm in June of that year and premiered *The Hawk* on October 13 at Theatre Genesis to mostly rave reviews. In April, it was revived at the Actors' Playhouse, where audiences were mostly baffled. Despite being at the farm, Shepard had never met Scarlett's boyfriend, Dark. It was only back in New York in late 1967 that the two men met, after Dark had seen Shepard's latest play, *Forensic and the Navigators*, in which O-Lan had a leading role. Dark asked the playwright what drug he was on while writing the play, and the two men hit it off, with Dark inviting Shepard back to his and Scarlett's apartment for spaghetti. Shepard thought his new friend, in his red plaid shirt, looked like Kerouac and that he was different from all the hippies he was meeting around the city. Shepard liked the fact that Dark talked "like a guy without an agenda and no ambition of any kind."

When Dark moved Scarlett to California a few months later, O-Lan and a friend named Lizette moved in with Barsha on First Avenue in New York. Barsha and O-Lan were romantically involved at this point, spending time seeing movies up the block at St. Mark's Cinema or eating and drinking at the L and M Café, the Orchida, Phoebe's, or the Blue and Gold Bar. Barsha must have sensed some connection between his young girlfriend and Shepard, for he was always wary of his fellow playwright and his obvious charms. Hence they never got along well. "He was a tricky guy. He couldn't be entirely trusted. I couldn't trust him with my girlfriend, and he ran off with her," Barsha said.

As the fall of 1967 arrived, Shepard's longtime penury was eased with a Rockefeller Grant. He also premiered a rewrite of his second play, the long-lost *Cowboys*, in Los Angeles at the Mark Taper Forum, under the moniker *Cowboys #2.*

With the arrival several months earlier of what would become known as the Summer of Love, hippiedom was at its apex. It was a social movement that Shepard did not identify with. He did, however, embrace aspects of the lifestyle, including the drugs and rock 'n' roll. While jazz was his defining aesthetic early on, as the sixties rolled along and the times grew more complex and darker, Shepard sought the rawer and more direct sounds of rock. He must have believed, like his father's favorite poet, Lorca, that music held special powers. "Never in poetry will I be able to say as much as I would have said in music," the Spanish writer once said. Similarly, in a few short years, Shepard would declare his own sentiments on the matter: "First of all, let me tell you that I don't want to be a playwright. I want to be a rock 'n' roll star."

These were trippy times: the Doors' first album had been released earlier in the year, the Vietnam protests were ratcheting up, poet Allen Ginsberg famously tried to levitate the Pentagon by chanting, and in June the Beatles released *Sgt. Pepper's Lonely Hearts Club Band*. It was a good time for Shepard to get his freak on. Though 1968 would prove even more troublesome, there was enough paranoia and concern about the war—with its body bags filling the nightly news—that some Americans likely felt as if the end was nigh. Shepard, in turn, was about to enter what could be termed a fantastical phase of his career. Space aliens, modern-day cowboys, giant snakes, ghosts, and interstellar rock stars would populate his next plays, and they would traipse across a more diverse set of locales, from deserts and oceans to roadsides, jungles, and postindustrial wastelands.

To round out 1967, Shepard brought *Forensic and the Navigators*, directed by Ralph Cook, to Theatre Genesis in December. The play opens with a cowboy, Forensic, and an American Indian, Emmet, each seated at the end of a long table in the center of a nondescript room. Two exterminators arrive, but one departs almost immediately to make sure they have come to the right address. The remaining exterminator is quizzed about what appears to be a nearby fortress that holds some threat to Forensic and Emmet. A woman, Oolan, enters and feeds Emmet Rice Krispies in a comical scene. The exterminator being questioned wants to trade any information he may have for Oolan. The other exterminator returns after calling headquarters and is filled with doom-laden prophecies, including that someone is about to gas the building they're in. Before anything is solved, the audience and stage are slowly covered in smoke. "You couldn't see your hand in front of your face," recalled veteran producer Albert Poland, who would soon be working with Shepard. When the smoke dissipates enough to allow the audience to see clearly again, the stage is empty and the play is over.

Not quite empty. Ralph Cook recalled that the Holy Modal Rounders were there with Shepard on drums. The band was fronted by a screaming woman. The sound they made was seemingly composed and performed with the sole intent of driving the audience out of the theater. "The noise was so bad that all you wanted to do was get out," Cook said. "People were just outraged, but Sam wanted it that way." Not everyone was blocking their ears. Shepard on drums was "jolly good," claimed *New York Times* critic Clive Barnes.

In keeping with the times, *Forensic and the Navigators* has an apocalyptic feel to it, with its unseen enemies and strange happenings. Perhaps one too many critics made this observation about this play and subsequent ones, for in Shepard's 1971 *Mad Dog Blues*, a character says, "I'm getting fucking tired of apocalypses. All I ever hear anymore is apocalypse, apocalypse. What about something with some hope?"

Shepard didn't do hope. In his review of *Forensic and the Navigators*, critic Michael Smith said in the *Village Voice* that he saw in it the skewed reality of the 1960s. "It's like real life: you can't tell what's going on. The whole thing may be a smoke dream, but the smoke that fills the theater at the end is real. So are the people, for all their elusiveness as dramatic characters, and so is the paranoia of our times, which Shepard expresses better than anyone else now writing."

One thing Shepard was clearly hopeful about was his prospects with O-Lan Johnson, who'd been featured in *Forensic*. She was still living with Tony Barsha when the play premiered, but when she and Shepard had met that previous summer at that Pennsylvania farm, there must have been some spark. Shepard's naming of a character in *Forensic* after her (Oolan), and writing a comic, attention-drawing scene for her (in which she plays with a bowl of Rice Krispies), was either clairvoyant or supremely confident. They soon became a couple.

Early Film Work
(1968–1970)

*I'm in an incredibly privileged position, and in a way it's acci-
dental. I didn't go out of my way to get into this movie stuff. I
essentially think of myself as a writer. But, there's no reason why
you can't be many different things.*

—Sam Shepard

T he kid who used to imitate Burt Lancaster's large and menacing
grin in the film *Vera Cruz* would eventually grow up to become
a bona fide film star himself. At first, however, he would have
to pay his dues, working sporadically in the margins of the industry as a
cowriter and player of bit parts. Shepard's looks and charisma called to mind
any number of matinee idols, so much so that his first serious girlfriend,
Joyce Aaron, said from the earliest days of their relationship that she knew
he'd go on to become a screen star. Additionally, his restless nature was
always leading him to seek out new ways of expressing himself.

When asked in 2015 to revisit his burgeoning days as an artistic poly-
math, Shepard explained the impulse behind his genre hopping. "Playing
music, as you know, is quite different from writing or acting. . . . I was
looking for something, you know? You're constantly looking for form, for

forms that are synonymous with what you want to project, for lack of a better word," he said.

The place and time in which Shepard found himself set the stage for his move into film. By the early 1960s, Hollywood, as represented by its long-abiding studio system of film production, "had bottomed out," as author Mark Harris puts it. The standard fare was mostly old and tired genre films. After the critical and commercial success of *Bonnie and Clyde*, released in the summer of 1967, Hollywood began looking for young talent on both sides of the camera. The members of the rock 'n' roll generation had strength in numbers and were intent on being heard. Just as on their stages they wanted to see people and situations that reflected their lives and beliefs, they also wanted to see them in movies. In the coming years, young maverick directors and actors would produce what would become known as Hollywood's second golden age.

The spring of 1967 found Italian filmmaker Michelangelo Antonioni driving across America seeking ideas for his next film. What he saw was young America in revolt of one kind or another. The music, the hair, the clothes, the drugs, the demonstrations—he made notes during his tour and took them back to Rome. Eventually he decided to make a film about two young Americans; it would be called *Zabriskie Point*, taking the name from a section of the Amargosa Range, located in California's Death Valley National Park. (Perhaps the erosion that is the topographical hallmark of the site was meant as a metaphor for American society.) A year after his first trip around the United States, Antonioni returned just in time to see the chaos that engulfed the 1968 Democratic National Convention. "My ideas about young Americans were shaped by what happened in Chicago, and I hope that somehow those ideas were expressed in the film," Antonioni said.

To better understand his subject matter, Antonioni also read a number of novels and plays by American writers. Shepard's were the ones that had the most impact on him. In particular, *Icarus's Mother*, with its central metaphor of the airplane and the feeling of dread that pervades the play, likely connected with the director; *Zabriskie Point* involves a young man who takes off in a stolen airplane and whose risk-taking clearly has him on a doomed trajectory.

That Antonioni would see something he liked in the young playwright may also have been due to the inherent similarities of their work. "It is difficult to put into words films composed principally of images, of colour, of movement, of shape, of design more than they are of story, character and event," the critic Sam Rohdie wrote of Antonioni. Others have noted the director's constant search for poetic images through which to tell his story and his disdain for psychological realism. Similar things have been said of Shepard's work, and despite their differences, the playwright himself would eventually come around to seeing how closely his major themes aligned with those of Antonioni.

When *Zabriskie Point* was at the synopsis stage, the director realized he needed help. "I started to look for someone else because I could not write dialogue in Italian," he said. "You can't translate dialogue. An American answers in a different way from an Italian or Frenchman. I wanted to write the dialogue in English." In the fall of 1967, he was back in America and met with Shepard. The pair left New York for Rome during the run of *Forensic and the Navigators*. There, he and Antonioni wrote the first version of the script together. Initially, the legendary director saw the film as dealing with the interior feelings of the characters. However, it slowly turned more political. There were many successive versions of the script; ultimately Fred Gardner, a political activist, was enjoined to write the final version with Antonioni. Additionally, the director was tight-fisted with the screenplay, not even letting Shepard take it home to work on. Later, this stricture was relaxed, but Antonioni remained chary of letting anyone outside his circle see the script.

At one point, a frustrated Shepard asked the picture's studio, MGM, to give him his own camera so he could go out into the desert and shoot something of his own. Antonioni squashed this idea, Shepard recalled, out of fear that Shepard would "go out in the desert and shoot his movie."

No matter how many thematic parallels existed between Antonioni's work and Shepard's, there could have been no meeting of minds concerning the importance of dialogue: for Shepard it was the sine qua non of storytelling; for Antonioni, actors and the things they said were merely elements of a scene, not unlike props and costumes. Perhaps that's why Shepard left the project prematurely and little of what he wrote ended up in the final version of *Zabriskie Point*. Though the film does echo many of the playwright's major concerns, about the overdevelopment of his beloved Southwest and the fact that progress often isn't all it's cracked up to be.

Shepard wrote dialogue for the film, changed some scenes around, and added a section where "a girl goes into a ghost town to find her brother. Her brother's working with . . . welfare kids—and a whole bunch of little Puerto Rican kids hollering and blowing up paper bags and pinching her ass, grabbing her tits, and everything."

Ever helpful, Shepard also recommended for one of the leading roles an actress he'd long had a crush on, Tuesday Weld. But the onetime child actor, who'd turned into a screen siren, was deemed by Antonioni, though only in her mid-twenties, to be "emaciated and worn down," Shepard recalled.

Shepard was also disillusioned during his time in Rome, seeing the ways money infiltrated the creative process. "I like Michelangelo a lot—he is incredible—but to submerge yourself in that world of limousines and hotels and rehashing and pleasing [producer] Carlo Ponti is just . . . forget it," he said. When the production was in L.A. for filming, the prodigality seemed to get ratcheted up. "The whole thing was so fully of Money. It was unbelievable . . . like you'd get a phone call saying: 'He wants to meet ya tomorrow morning, we're sending over a chauffeur to get ya!'" Shepard was staying nearby at his family home in Bradbury, but eventually the limo rides added up and the production moved him to Hollywood's famous Chateau Marmont. Meanwhile, members of the Open Theater were staying in Las Vegas and were brought in by helicopter for the desert orgy scene. (The Justice Department came down on the film's producers, using the Mann Act, which banned the transport of females across state lines for so-called immoral acts. The producers claimed that no actual sex took place before the cameras. Shepard would not have been a very good witness for the defense: "I think people got screwed on the desert, for real, you know.")

Shepard quickly got over any ill will toward Antonioni and company, though in a prerelease interview he would call the film "Hollywood's most expensive flop." And in 2007 he participated in a documentary focusing on Antonioni's body of work. He narrated a small section, provided his take on Antonioni's best films, and bemusedly told stories about the director's demand to clear the set to give him five minutes to think before shooting a scene. Shepard always held out for his angle on the story. Antonioni, he said, "wants it to be some kind of metaphor for the Radical Left, or something like that. . . . I don't think it's going to work that way. It's going to be a love story. . . . I don't think it's going to move all those politico people." Then again, he at that time admitted to having seen only three minutes of the film.

Zabriskie Point was, for the most part, savaged by critics upon its release in February of 1970. Though some saw virtues in its depiction of late-1960s America: *Rolling Stone*'s John Burks called the film highly flawed but urged readers not to miss it. However, time and changing tastes have somewhat redeemed it. With music by Pink Floyd, scenes of angry youth and aggressive cops, and a story of a rebel with a cause who goes down in flames, *Zabriskie Point* is now hailed by some as one of the quintessential films of its time.

While in Rome, Shepard met Rolling Stones guitarist Keith Richards and was enlisted to turn a story by Anthony Foutz into a screenplay. Foutz was the son of a Walt Disney executive and a friend of the band. Shepard spent six weeks at Richards's country house in West Wittering, on the shore of the English Channel across from the Isle of Wight, surrounded, as he tells it, by an alligator-filled moat and barbed wire. With a couple of elderly locals bringing them milk and steaks and stoking the fire, Shepard and Richards worked most days in a hash-fueled haze from morning to about 3 a.m. When things got too "heavy," Shepard hitchhiked into town to escape for a bit. Overall, the situation was "groovy," he recalled, despite the lack of anything ever showing up on-screen.

The resulting script, *Maxagasm*, is billed on its title page as "a distorted Western for soul and psyche," according to an undated second draft of the script. The abandoned project was to feature a character named Cowboy, a handsome "professional hero" with striking blue eyes and long blond hair, matching pistols on his hips, and "reflecting a quiet inner strength."

The film was to feature more than twenty main characters, all bearing archetypical names (Child, Speed, etc.) in service of a plot in which Princess, daughter of the mysterious ruler of the desert, is kidnapped. Cowboy reads in the paper about the incident and sets out to save her. Mercenaries line up against him, and other obstacles stand in his way.

Shepard claims that *Maxagasm*, though unmade, was "a really great movie" and that it was the Stones themselves, particularly Mick Jagger, who killed it. The band's lead singer felt the finished script seemed "dated." Compounding things was the recent death of guitarist Brian Jones.

Back in New York City, Shepard's old friend, the director Bill Hart, decided to make a film and didn't want him to write it but asked the charismatic and handsome playwright to step before the camera. The film they embarked on, tentatively called *Blood*, would never be completed. It was a mostly improvised affair featuring Shepard and Joyce Aaron, as well as their old friend Charles Mingus III. Nearly a half century later, Aaron could recall little of the film's content: "I remember a bar scene and a taxi scene and some apartment scenes," she said. "All pretty cloudy memories." Reputedly influenced by director John Cassavetes's 1968 film *Faces*, with its free-association dialogue and cinema verité style, the film set out to examine an important issue of the day. "It has some extraordinary scenes, mostly about Black Power," Hart said. "We shot it mainly in my apartment, some in Harlem, and some in taxicabs going back and forth on mysterious routes. . . . It's very upsetting material and it was very on time, but we ran out of money and I ran out of discipline." Hart died at age seventy in 2008, and the whereabouts of the unassembled film are unknown.

The best film Shepard worked on in the latter half of the 1960s was *Me and My Brother*, a quasi-documentary directed by Robert Frank. Frank was the Zurich-born photographer behind the groundbreaking book of images *The Americans*, which was published in France in 1958 and in America a year later. With his reputation made, Frank began hanging out with younger artists who worked in other fields. In 1959 he made the short film *Pull My Daisy*, featuring Beat Generation writers, with rambling narration by Jack Kerouac. Later Frank would provide the images and cover concept for the Stones' *Exile on Main Street* album and film the band's 1972 tour for the surreal documentary *Cocksucker Blues*.

Hanging in the hipper circles around New York City, Frank no doubt knew of Shepard's early plays. When he needed help with additional dialogue for *Me and My Brother*, his first full-length feature film, he asked Shepard.

Initially, Frank wanted to make a film centered on Allen Ginsberg's 1961 poem *Kaddish*, about the poet's late mother and her battle with mental illness. Ginsberg came to Frank's office every day trying to come up with a script. The *Kaddish* idea eventually stalled, but about a year later, in 1965, Frank began filming around Ginsberg's Lower East Side apartment and was intrigued by the relationship between the poet's lover, Peter Orlovsky, and Peter's brother Julius, who had recently been released from a mental institution. "So what began as Kaddish, a study of mental family tragedy and mental illness finally became *Me and My Brother*," Ginsberg recalled.

During the three years he shot footage for the project, Frank also captured a 1966 tour of readings by Ginsberg that took him across America with the Orlovsky brothers in tow. Julius, always a distant presence in the camera's glare, disappeared after a reading in San Francisco. To compensate for his subject's understandable reticence and to fill in for Julius while he was missing, Frank hired Shepard's mentor Joseph Chaikin to play the role of Julius in particular scenes, allowing him to give voice to what might be going on in Julius's mind. It's difficult to pin down when Shepard was brought onboard, but it was likely around this time.

Me and My Brother is the closest one can get to a filmic version of an early Shepard play, with its mingling of identities, digressions, non sequiturs, and mysterious interactions. It may also be as close as one can get to being inside the head of a schizophrenic. "It was about that whole world [Julius] was living in, trying to get into that," Shepard said. Frank proved to be a canny filmmaker, working against the standard of realism set by his famous photography work. Here he gives us a black-and-white dream world with Julius as a cipher at its center, allowing the viewer to enter, just as Chaikin the actor does, and inhabit the story he's trying to tell. In the end, Frank finally confronts Julius, where the subject finally speaks. It's the only scene in color, and it takes place outside on a porch. It is cold and rainy, and Julius, in his cryptic answers to simple questions, says more than he could possibly mean. The camera, he says, is "a reflection of disapproval or disgust or disappointment or unhelpfulness or unexplainability to disclose any real truth that might possibly exist," he tells Frank. Neither Frank nor Shepard wrote these lines, but if there was ever a naked statement about the kind of art the two men were intent on making, together or separate, it is here, spoken by the man who has refused to play along in their game. When a few seconds later Julius says he's cold, indicating that he wants to come inside, he becomes all too real. The cipher has given birth to a troubled young man, and we see the whole film in a new light. We may even wonder about the ethics of following him with a camera all this time. For Shepard, working with Frank was "a really nice experience." Working on an underground film like *Me and My Brother* was one thing, but being a gun for hire for big studio productions was something Shepard knew he wasn't cut out for. "You can't be free in it," he said.

Shepard's next film project didn't involve any writing. It was the infamous *Brand X*, ostensibly a spoof of politics and television with plenty of nudity and bathroom humor. The 1970 film was written by New York City–based painter Wynn Chamberlain and financed through donations from friends. It was conceived during a snowbound weekend in 1969 when Chamberlain and his wife, Sally, were left with nothing to do but watch television. The film starred Abbie Hoffman, Sally Kirkland, and Warhol discovery Candy Darling.

Brand X became a cult favorite that, despite its amateurishness, earned good reviews at the time of its release. How Shepard somehow got mixed up in the proceedings is a mystery, other than the fact that a part of the film was shot in the Bowery, where by this time he was a known entity. However, his only scene (based on an extended online trailer; the film is impossible to get on video or DVD) depicts him and a blond woman, both naked and shown from the waist up, making faces and screaming in unison, "U . . . S . . . A."

It was not an auspicious start to Shepard's acting career.

There were other nonstarters during these years, mostly screenplays that were never finished or produced, including a project with his old Theatre

Genesis colleague and playwright Murray Mednick called *Ringaleevie*, which incorporated scenes from Shepard's 1970 play *Operation Sidewinder*.

As his work on *Zabriskie Point* was wrapping up, Shepard was approached by the producers of a film-in-the-works called *Alice's Restaurant*; they wanted him to script the film. He turned them down.

After seeing so much of his writing for the screen come to naught, Shepard swore off movies for the next few years. The next time he'd say yes to a director he would play a major role in what would become a highly regarded film—after which he would never want for film roles again.

Dazed and Confused
(1968 and 1969)

L

I am afraid, Spider Lady. I find myself holding a great power. I have not the wisdom to use it. Speak to me of its secret.
—Sam Shepard, *Operation Sidewinder*

The divorce of Shepard's parents became official in January 1968. By this time, the differences between Samuel and Jane Rogers had become a chasm too wide to be breached. "He thought it was all ridiculous, this idea of being a solid citizen," Shepard said of his father late in life. "And he went further and further off in the direction of being an outsider, mainly, in simple terms, of alcoholism. My mother was the opposite. Very together, figuring out how to get along." Afterward, Jane Rogers stayed in the family home in Bradbury and continued her career as a much-beloved teacher at the Polytechnic School in Pasadena. Sam Rogers continued teaching for more than a year at San Marino High School, but the divorce marked the beginning of his most difficult years. As his son put it, he "went out to Texas for a while [and was] in and out of jail, and then went to New Mexico." Local records indicate that Samuel Rogers began living in Santa Fe in 1975. The only job he's shown as having was in 1978; he is listed as a janitor at the hotel La Fonda, though he evidently also worked in a warehouse for a time. The old man would spend the rest of his life in Santa Fe, living in trailers and cheap apartments until his death.

Shepard spent the first part of 1968 in Rome with Antonioni, and whether it was this experience or the hectic pace he was keeping between the film work, writing plays, and drumming with the Holy Modal Rounders, something led him to recall these days as "the tail end of the worst time in my life."

Things turned around quickly.

Upon returning to New York City from Rome, Shepard learned that he'd earned a Guggenheim Fellowship, and soon after he moved in with O-Lan Johnson. Though feeling spurned at the time, O-Lan's former lover, playwright-director Tony Barsha, admits in hindsight that their breakup "was for the better, for both of us." Shepard remembered that when he got together with O-Lan, "everything began looking up."

In March Shepard traveled to Los Angeles to play drums on the album *The Moray Eels Eat the Holy Modal Rounders*. The band also played in some of the marquee clubs up and down the West Coast and even opened for Pink Floyd at San Francisco's Avalon Ballroom on August 23. While on the road, Shepard wrote his next play, *Operation Sidewinder*. Yale Repertory Company agreed to stage the play beginning on January 23 of the following year, paying $500 to option its premiere. Student protests about the depiction of blacks in the play, however, led Shepard to withdraw it.

Gauging Shepard's feelings about issues of race at this time is difficult. However, it's telling that his best friend and roommate from a few years earlier, Charles Mingus III, was black. Those who knew Shepard's father report that he didn't have a racist bone in his body and that during his later years living in Santa Fe had many Mexican friends and preferred to speak exclusively in Spanish. It's hard to spot any overt racism in Shepard's work or actions. (The playwright's feelings about homosexuals are, however, easier to read. Shepard has a history, in life and in his work, of being rather loose with slurs like "fag," "faggot," "faggot photographers," and "fag makeup man.")

All this suggests that there's little reason to suspect that Shepard was doing anything more than reflecting the times or, at worst, being provocative with his depiction of black characters in *Operation Sidewinder*. Granted, the play does stereotype black revolutionaries and at one point employs the slur *spades*. These would prove the undoing of the play's planned premiere. That being said, one can't assume that a writer's characters reflect his or her beliefs. Regardless, the black students at Yale weren't in the mood for such explanations.

Seemingly with little fight, Shepard withdrew the play on December 20, "convinced it could not be presented amid the dissension the black students' objections caused."

With *Sidewinder* on hold, and movies and music taking up so much of his time, Shepard experienced the longest gap yet between premieres of his plays. *Forensic and the Navigators* debuted during the last days of 1967, and his next, *The Unseen Hand*, wouldn't premiere until December of 1969. Yet his work and name were never totally out of the public eye. In May of 1969, *Esquire* magazine ran the full script of *Operation Sidewinder*, despite the fact that the play itself, thanks to the Yale rejection, was now nearly a year away from being staged. Also around this time, Michael Butler, producer of the Broadway hit *Hair*, approached Shepard about working on a musical version of *Frankenstein* in which the mad doctor in Mary Shelley's classic horror story is depicted as "a very beautiful person." The show never materialized.

Shepard received some help in mid-September of 1968 when he was notified that he'd earned a Guggenheim Fellowship that would support him for the next year. A regular paycheck, albeit small, would soon find its way to him as well. In June of 1969, Kenneth Tynan's comic revue *Oh! Calcutta!* debuted at New York's Eden Theatre. The show began Off-Broadway and was controversial due to its many scenes of full nudity. This guaranteed it would be the must-see show of the season. Among its many sketches, the revue incorporated the final scene from *The Rock Garden*, featuring a boy's X-rated diatribe about his sexual appetites. Tynan decided to transform Shepard's father and son into hicks in rocking chairs, seemingly whiling away the hours of a hot afternoon with idle chatter. The scene is not nearly as funny, discomfiting, or powerful as it is as part of *The Rock Garden*, but the playwright received $68 a week in royalties while the show ran. And boy, did it run. *Oh! Calcutta!* made it into the *Guinness Book of World Records* as the longest-running revue in history.

Shepard would need the money, for on November 9, 1969, he married O-Lan Johnson. The marriage ceremony was performed at St. Mark's Church in-the-Bowery, the place where his first plays were presented. It was a double ceremony: Shepard and O-Lan were joined at the altar by playwright-actor Walter Hadler and Georgia Lee Phillips. Director Bill Hart served as best man, and the Reverend Michael Allen, who years earlier had provided the space in his church hall for Theatre Genesis, presided. Shepard's favorite director, Ralph Cook, gave a reading from the Book of Ruth, and playwright Murray Mednick read a poem. Befitting a theatrical wedding, those in attendance wore antique clothing, likely lifted from the wardrobe room next door, where Theatre Genesis was still very active.

After he asked the couples to join hands, Allen intoned: "In a broken world and a polluted land, nothing could be more beautiful than a marriage." When it came time to ask the traditional, "Who gives these people to be married to each other?" the whole congregation answered, "We do!" Allen's daughter Sarah Allen Wilson recalled, "My dad's favorite story about Sam and O-Lan's wedding was that before he could proclaim them husband and wife, Sam picked O-Lan up and ran down the aisle, with my dad yelling the proclamation after them."

The wedding was more of a party, really, with purple tabs of LSD being passed around by members of the Holy Modal Rounders and plenty to eat, drink, and smoke. Shepard and his new bride moved to a place on Sixth Street.

Around the time of the marriage, O-Lan was rehearsing on the stage at La MaMa a play titled *Sprintorgasmics*, while Shepard was in the basement working on what would become his next play, *The Unseen Hand*. The production was to be his debut as a director. However, another new play, *Back Bog Beast*, was in the audition phase, with Albert Poland set to produce. Poland didn't much care for *Beast* but was eager to work with Shepard. Hearing the auditioning actors read his lines aloud, it turns out Shepard himself wasn't very happy with the play. Poland recalls how the playwright was pacing about, saying things like, "I don't know about this play," and "This sounds like bad Tennessee Williams." Ultimately, Shepard pulled *Back Bog Beast* and invited Poland and director Jeff Bleckner down to the basement at La MaMa to check out *The Unseen Hand*. "It was like an acid trip," Poland said. Shepard, who, Poland observed, liked playing poker during rehearsals, eventually surrendered the role of director to Bleckner.

The Unseen Hand premiered at La MaMa in December 1969. Shepard admits he had the title before he had any notion of what the play would be about. It tells the story of a 120-year-old man named Blue Morphan who wears some semblance of a cowboy outfit, swigs from a bottle, and lives in an abandoned car somewhere in Azusa, the real-life California town not far from Duarte that Shepard once described as "a collection of junk." When Willie the Space Freak appears, he has a wild story about the place he comes from and the High Commission that rules the land. The commissioners control people like Willie by placing an unseen hand on his brain, which squeezes when he "moves beyond a certain circumference of a circle."

Amid all this, Willie is able to bring back Blue's two long-dead brothers and partners in crime, Cisco and Sycamore. They talk of helping Willie by staging a revolt against the High Commission. Sycamore, however, would rather get his brothers back together and ride like the gang of outlaws they used to be. At one point, a whacked-out male cheerleader appears and advises the brothers on the ins and outs of guerrilla warfare.

Not much else happens, but with its spacey goings-on and talk of revolution, the play likely registered with contemporaneous audiences. Stephen Rea, an Irish actor who would work with Shepard on several later projects, could have had *The Unseen Hand* in mind when he said: "The people are all dislocated and strange in Sam's plays. It's all about this kind of terror, the horror that's outside, that undefined, outside world. The unseen terror suddenly striking."

Robert Redford was interested at one point in optioning *The Unseen Hand* for the big screen. Playwright and Theatre Genesis stalwart

Tony Barsha was involved in the talks and recalls: "Sam came to [Redford] and said he wanted me to direct it." But ultimately Shepard "blew it off."

There is a little-known episode connected to *The Unseen Hand* after it transferred as part of a double bill with *Forensic and the Navigators* to the Astor Place Theater in April of 1970. Believing the publicity that Shepard had been getting was going to his head, a few fellow playwrights and artists decided to "rescue him." Barsha and artist Joey Skaggs were the head pranksters, leading a handful of coconspirators to the theater on opening night. The plan was to kidnap Shepard and take him to the Port Authority, where they'd hand him a ticket saying "Azusa," the setting of the play. "We didn't give a shit about consequences," Skaggs said.

Dressed like gangsters (Skaggs even carried a violin case like the ones Al Capone's men used to hide their tommy guns), they pulled up outside the theater in a car from the 1930s and rushed in. Shepard was playing drums in the lobby with the Holy Modal Rounders before the show. When the would-be pranksters made their move, all hell broke loose. "As we went to grab him, Sam started throwing fists, swinging wildly and yelling," Skaggs recalled. "The crowd erupted. We decided this isn't working, we'd better get out of here. So, we made a hasty retreat, jumped into the waiting car and took off, laughing our asses off."

Shepard's new wife, O-Lan, was present. That fact that she'd been Barsha's girlfriend may have led to her husband's overreaction. "He thought I was coming to revenge myself for him for running off with O-Lan," Barsha said.

A month after Shepard's marriage, one of the most tumultuous decades in American history came to an end. During these years, he'd gone from college dropout and Future Farmer of America to "the most prolific and prominent playwright in the underground theater." Meanwhile, *Village Voice* critic Ross Wetzsteon wrote, "There is not the slightest doubt in my mind that Sam Shepard is the most important living American playwright."

As for the praise, Shepard certainly welcomed it but felt it was unnecessarily qualified: "The main theme of the press in reaction to my own work has been, 'It's fine if you like that kind of thing and he certainly has a way with words but when is he going to stop playing around and give us a really MAJOR NEW AMERICAN PLAY,'" Shepard wrote in the pages of *Performing Arts Journal*.

Shepard was twenty-six at decade's end. It would be another two years before he'd write his first major play. His restless spirit would lead to a few detours along the way.

New Directions

In art one must kill one's father.

—Pablo Picasso

Whether it was his new status as a married man, the fact that O-Lan was expecting, his parents' divorce the previous year, or just the inevitability that he'd eventually have to move into this fraught territory, Shepard would next take on the subject of his father. *The Holy Ghostly* first appeared in Europe as part of a tour put together by La MaMa ETC. Director Tom O'Horgan brought the U.S. premiere to Princeton's McCarter Theater in January 1970, with the actor-dancer Ben Vereen playing the lead.

The Holy Ghostly is Shepard's second attempt to bring to the stage aspects of his home life and to deal, at least indirectly, with his feelings about his father. Ice is a young man who has left home, traveled cross-country, changed his name, and become somewhat famous. (Sound familiar?) He has been called home from New York City by his father, who goes by the name Pop but whose full name is Stanley Hewitt Moss VI. The pair sits near a desert campfire, the father looking to his son for comfort. Evil spirits are about, telling the old man that he's dead. The father and son bicker about their shared past, and it becomes clear there's fault and acrimony on both sides. The father recounts his life, as if it is passing before his eyes. The old man's soliloquy contains elements of the real Samuel Rogers's life story, including his return from fighting in World War II and being happy to come home to find his wife and son waiting for him. Part of the long speech includes an apology, perhaps something Shepard had hoped in real life to hear from his father.

> POP: I know ya' probably think I was rough on ya' and the truth is I was. But I tried to show ya' the ropes. Tried to give ya' some breaks, too. Me, I never had no real breaks.

This hints at the mixed emotions Shepard harbored toward his real-life father—hating him for his drinking and violent temper but understanding where it all stemmed from. However, there is no forgiveness. This attitude toward the old man would later soften as Shepard matured both as a person and an artist.

Ice tells his father that he stands by the decision he made to leave home and make his way in the world. As the play nears its climax, Chindi, a white witch, appears, bearing Pop's corpse on her back. When after some additional bickering, Pop tells Ice, "Well, now you can pay me back," the son shoots him and walks away. The play concludes in an inferno, as Pop throws his corpse on the fire and burns everything down.

Though it's usually given scant attention by scholars and critics, *The Holy Ghostly* is Shepard's strongest, most emotionally honest play to date. It's more than just the story of a prodigal son gone awry. In the one-act play, Shepard brings his personal vision into sharper focus as he draws from his life its most difficult and dramatic elements and pushes past reality into a land of symbolism, Oedipal revenge, and perhaps wishful thinking, with the father character, despite being dead throughout the play, still being shot by the son.

In *The Holy Ghostly*, Shepard conjures onstage many dark and compelling images through which to tell his tale, as well as an unusual set design.

The audience was made to sit in a circle around a real campfire. Shepard saves the best for last, illustrating the self-destructive nature of the father through the fire that consumes him and everything in sight.

Shepard would later tell a writer from *Playboy* magazine, "As far as I'm concerned, Broadway just does not exist." However, there's no way he forgot his first experience above Fourteenth Street and into what critic and author John Lahr termed "enemy territory" for the playwright. It was in March 1970, with the long-delayed premiere of *Operation Sidewinder.* Withdrawn from Yale after the protestations of black students, the play found a home at the Vivian Beaumont Theater at Lincoln Center, under the direction of Michael Schultz. Shepard's far-out and somewhat paranoid fantasy play was not the fare typically put on for subscribers of the uptown theater, which at that time rarely staged world premieres.

Operation Sidewinder, written for the most part in the summer of 1968 while Shepard was on the road with the Holy Modal Rounders, is notable for many reasons beyond its structure, which owes a debt to Hollywood. "My idea was to write a movie for the stage," Shepard said. His increasing experiences working with filmmakers had freed him to move beyond the type of short plays featuring a single set that he'd up to this point made his name on. Nearly every scene in *Sidewinder* changes locale, and with a cast of more than three dozen, new characters come and go throughout the play's two acts. As if he had the money and space of a feature film, Shepard had written into the script a handful of outsized props, including the giant snake of the title, an automobile on a hydraulic lift, and a desert cave full of Native Americans. His set directions include things that sound more like movie special effects than the typical lighting cues and sound directions meant for the stage, including the giant snake's ability to rise "ten feet off the ground" with eyes that flash different colors, shooting stars overhead, sonic booms, winds that blow hot and cold, and a sky that "lights up." It was clear he was no longer interested in the restrictions in sets and props imposed by Off-Off-Broadway's mean budgets. Though he would continue to work for the most part on smaller stages, with *Operation Sidewinder* Shepard was eager to see what size and heft could do for his vision. The Holy Modal Rounders once again supplied music during the play, featuring

Shepard on drums, though none of the songs are really tied to the play's themes or action. The one standout tune in the play, "Euphoria," predates it, being the fourth track on the Holy Modal Rounders' 1964 debut album.

The play features Shepard's first real attempt at a coherent plot. Things do get murky, of course; after all, this is a Shepard play. But *Sidewinder* is a story that mixes adventure and espionage, as a secret government computer in the shape of a giant snake breaks free and roams the Mojave Desert. As the government, represented by a group of *Dr. Strangelove*–like buffoons and drunkards, tries to locate the missing computer, a group of black revolutionaries develops a plot to take down a local military base with the help of a tribe of Native Americans who are sick of the jets—or "silver birds"—filling the skies. In the end, the sidewinder/computer ends up in the hands of the Native Americans, who place it at the center of a Hopi ritual. As in many of Shepard's plays, the final scene has echoes of a mini-apocalypse, as desert tactical troops enter and begin shooting the tribe members to get the computer back. The Native Americans continue with their ritual, and the troops quickly find themselves engulfed by smoke, flashing lights, and the ever-increasing sounds of the Indian chants. When the smoke clears, the Natives are gone, leaving just the military men, holding their ears and confused over what's happened.

This is the clearest expression to date of Shepard's belief in the deleterious effects of progress. The military with its jets and giant computers wreaks havoc upon the land, with the Native Americans playing the victims who have at stake their homeland, heritage, and sense of identity. One need not be a biblical scholar to see the symbolism in the military computer taking the form of a giant snake. And Shepard makes clear in his stage directions that the Native Americans' ritualistic dancing is to be treated with great seriousness ("spiritual and sincere," not "cartooned"). Only in *Curse of the Starving Class* (1977) will Shepard so directly examine the clash between progress and nature.

The other theme that one finds often in Shepard's earlier work is the idea that myths are necessary to sustain us, providing important links to an idealized past. Nowhere can one find a better symbol for this than Native Americans and their culture. Critic George Stambolian includes Shepard in a group of contemporary artists and writers, such as Warhol,

Lichtenstein, Barth, and Barthelme, believing that "our country's identity is largely determined by the figures, images and myths out of popular culture." He said this of another Shepard play, *Mad Dog Blues*, but it applies here as well: the mythic impulse clearly shapes the characters and action of *Operation Sidewinder*.

The play is a product of its troubled times, reflecting the anxiety felt by Americans during the latter half of the 1960s. The decade featured its share of assassinations, war, conspiracy theories, racial strife, and social upheavals. Distrust of the government—even in these pre-Watergate years—was practically reflexive for any artist of the time, and audiences were receptive to such ideas. Darkness was also infringing on the Age of Aquarius, as the drugs once thought to be fun and mind freeing were turning more deadly, and rock music quickly moved on from the Summer of Love to embrace the chaos in the mud of Woodstock, a deadly stabbing when the Stones played Altamont, and the bleaker sounds of bands like the Velvet Underground. *Operation Sidewinder* nods toward many of these developments, however obscurely, once again securing Shepard's place as a writer able to capture the zeitgeist.

Comparing the published script of *Sidewinder* with the version that ran in *Esquire* magazine ten months earlier (which it is safe to assume, given the months of lead time major magazines require, was the same or very close to the script Yale's black students objected to), it appears Shepard cut a not insignificant amount of text from the opening of Act 2, when the black revolutionaries show up on the scene. None of what was cut seems inflammatory, though in the magazine the script contains the term *Negro*, where in the final published form the characters are referred to as *blacks*. A line that included the racial slur "the spades," however, remained in the magazine and was delivered on the stage at Lincoln Center and survives in the published script.

The reviews for *Operation Sidewinder* were a mixed bag, and in retrospect it is considered to have been a flop—"deservedly so," Shepard would later say, claiming it as a victim of too large a budget and the wrong theater. Plus, he wrote it like a movie, which was a mistake. "That single frame editing kind of thing doesn't work on stage," he said. "It was very static." Two *New York Times* critics used their reviews of the play to take aim at the theatrical wunderkind. Clive Barnes found the symbolism too much and the points Shepard was trying to make too obvious, yet he still called *Sidewinder* a "possibly significant play." The following week, writing in the same pages, Walter Kerr found the play uninteresting and sought to instruct Shepard on the waywardness of his plotting and character development. Kerr was nearing sixty when he reviewed *Operation Sidewinder*, disliked Beckett, and had more of an affinity for the age of traditional musicals. In other words, if there was a generation gap, he was clearly on the other side. Not that he was totally wrong about the play, but holding avant-garde theater to standards of the spoon-fed rationality that so permeated Broadway at the time missed the point. Regardless, Kerr was another dose of reality greeting Shepard on the playwright's arrival uptown.

There were certainly good notices. NBC called the play "a glorious piece of pop art" and "the wildest and most ambitious show yet at Lincoln Center." The biggest rave came from John Lahr, who was instrumental in bringing the play to Lincoln Center. He saw the work as a necessary salvo. "The theater needs distinct, ruthless visions like those of Shepard to shock its audiences from their life-sleep," he wrote.

Lincoln Center attempted to prepare its audiences for what they were about to see in *Operation Sidewinder* with ads in the *Times* promising, "The world premiere of a startling new drama charged with the beat of hard rock." To that end, a lavish program contained an explanation of the origins and meaning of the Hopi snake dance, general articles about Native Americans and the "Hopi Prophecy," and a feature on the Holy Modal Rounders, replete with the lyrics to the show's songs. Still, many in attendance were unhappy with the show, or failed to get it. There was laughter during the Hopi dance scene, and subscribers' comments ran along the lines of "Terrible, terrible, terrible" and calls for all involved to be fired. Perhaps Shepard realized he was pitching his tent in the wrong place when he and his wife arrived for the first preview and the bartender thought they were too scruffy for the uptown environs and tried to shoo them away as if they were street people. Lahr recalls how Shepard looked gloomy before curtain one night, saying, "I'm not worried about the old people, I'm worried about the young ones." Then he went to the bar and got a beer, which he hid in his shirt before going back into the theater. According to Lahr, when all was said and done, "We lost about 10,000 subscribers."

After closing, *Operation Sidewinder* was staged again at the Williamstown Theater Festival, where it was given an X rating in the press to keep the kiddies away and it racked up better reviews.

In May of 1970, Shepard and O-Lan became parents with the arrival of Jesse Mojo Shepard, whom they named for the outlaw Jesse James rather than making the boy the sixth Samuel Shepard Rogers in the line. This decision precipitated another break with the past. "That blew it entirely," Shepard later said with a laugh. "Now in a way, I kind of regret it. But it was, you know, one of those reactions to your background."

Eventually that background would prove to be rich territory for the playwright to mine. But first, his restlessness would get the best of him once more, first leading him into the arms of another woman, then across the Atlantic. Both experiences would change him as a playwright for the better.

Patti

Sam Shepard is an awesomely talented writer with a freedom
fixation.

—Marilyn Stasio

It was an early fall night in 1970 at the Café au Go Go, a basement club on Bleecker Street in the heart of the Village. On this night, the members of the Holy Modal Rounders were playing the usual mix of psychedelic blues and folk. The vibe suddenly changed when the drummer took over for a rare vocal. The music became harsh and the singing urgent. Sam Shepard was thrashing his way through a tune he'd just written called "Blind Rage." The song was a blast of edgy, proto-punk energy, featuring Shepard's near-out-of-control vocal. "He was actually embodying blind rage as he's singing this song and pounding the shit out of his drums," remembered fellow Rounder Peter Stampfel. The song itself is now lost to history, as this was its only performance, but in trying to convey its essence, Stampfel yell-sang these lyrics to me over the phone one night: "Get my gun/Shoot 'em and run/Blind rage."

A spindly young woman with a shock of longish black hair approached the stage that evening when the set was over. Her name was Patricia Lee Smith. Pretty in a nontraditional way, she introduced herself as a poet. She was there as a guest of rocker Todd Rundgren, who wanted to check out the band. The connection between her and Shepard was instantaneous, and off they went. The affair would last the better part of seven months.

Shepard had an infant son and a young wife at home. What would make him up and run off with a burgeoning poetess? Stampfel thinks it may have been his bandmate's status as a new father. He saw a connection between the violent new song Shepard debuted that night and his new responsibilities at home. "Apparently the blind rage had something to do with . . . I don't know, Sam was speaking about suddenly being a father. It's a very throws-you-for-a-loop situation."

Joyce Aaron, Shepard's ex-girlfriend, had recognized this wandering spirit in her ex and understood it to mean that Shepard wasn't the marrying type. She seems to have been right. When Smith arrived on the scene, married or not, just like that Shepard was gone.

At least he didn't go far.

Patricia Lee Smith was born in Chicago on December 30, 1946, the daughter of a waitress and a factory worker. She was raised primarily in Woodbury, New Jersey, but dropped out of college in 1967 to move to New York City. While trying to make her name as a poet, Smith lived for a time at the famed Chelsea Hotel with photographer Robert Mapplethorpe.

The Chelsea was as famous as some of its residents. Located at 222 West Twenty-Third Street and built in 1884, the redbrick building was the largest residential structure in New York City at that time, with room for eighty families. The top floor was home to artist studios and gardens, with room for performances, which may help explain why the Chelsea from the start attracted the cream of America's creative class. Later, by the time Smith arrived, word was that the owners would take artwork in lieu of rent. Those who had passed through its halls included Bob Dylan, Thomas Wolfe, Jackson Pollock, Mary McCarthy, Terry Southern, Dennis Hopper, and Arthur Miller, who wrote *After the Fall* here. It was designated an architectural and cultural landmark by the city in 1966.

By the end of summer 1970, Smith had been forced to move out of the Chelsea and was living in a loft a few doors down on Twenty-Third Street. She was still living there the night she heard the Holy Modal Rounders, which she later compared to "being at an Arabian hoedown with a band of psychedelic hillbillies." Her attention went right to the good-looking guy behind the kit. "I fixed on the drummer, who seemed as if he was on the lam and had slid behind the drums while the cops looked elsewhere."

Smith was captivated by Shepard's new song, "Blind Rage," and believed the handsome musician embodied "the heart and soul of rock and roll. He had beauty, energy, animal magnetism." Backstage, Shepard told his new fan that his name was Slim Shadow. "Rock and roll needs you," Smith told him. Shepard's easygoing reply was, "Well, I never really thought about that."

She came to think of Shepard as the "fellow with the cowboy mouth," taking a phrase from Bob Dylan's "Sad Eyed Lady of the Lowlands." Her new lover was a good talker, a storyteller, she recalled in her memoir *Just Kids*. She told him she wanted to write a profile about him for *Crawdaddy* magazine. Shepard came back to Smith's place on subsequent nights, and she recalled their walking around the neighborhood together. One evening after Shepard saw that she'd shoplifted a couple of steaks, he took her to Max's Kansas City, the famed music club, for some lobster. It was on this night that a friend tipped off Smith that the man she was with was not simply a drummer named Slim Shadow. "What are you doing with Sam Shepard?" her friend asked. The name didn't ring a bell with Smith; her friend explained he was an award-winning playwright.

It's not hard to figure out what Shepard and Smith saw in each other. As James Wolcott wrote in an early review of Smith performing at the Village punk club CBGB, "Patti possesses . . . a genius for phrasing. She's a poet of steely rhythms—her work demands to be read aloud—so language is her narcotic, her lover, her mustang." Which sounds like a good description of Shepard's work. Wolcott goes on to state that Smith's great early theme could be summed up by the phrase "penetration draws blood." Her new man knew this from his own experience. Shepard was guarded, wary of attachment, then as now. Somehow, they fell in love.

Shepard soon got a room with a balcony at the Chelsea, and the pair became inseparable, often spending time reading—she about Crazy Horse; he the plays and prose of Samuel Beckett.

It seems at first Shepard did not tell his new paramour that he was married and the father of an infant. In *Just Kids*, Smith seems to indicate it was something that didn't come up right away. But she loved being with Shepard and back at the Chelsea, for which she had a mysterious affinity. Her former lover and now friend Mapplethorpe never took to Smith's new man and openly disparaged Shepard in front of her.

During their time together, Shepard and Smith lived the bohemian lifestyle to the hilt—art, music, poetry, and general chicanery comprised their days. "We'd have a lot of rum and get into trouble," Smith said. To her, he was the bad boy, the man in hiding, her own Rimbaudian enfant terrible. For Shepard, Smith ignited his interest in international literature and poetry, something that survives to this day. She encouraged him to write poetry, some of which would be featured in his 1973 book *Hawk Moon*. Both were determined to stay true to themselves and not submit to the so-called star-making machinery; if genuine fame came, which it would for both, it had to be on their terms.

Shepard split his time between Smith and rehearsals at Theatre Genesis for his next play, *Mad Dog Blues*. At his urging, Smith contributed lyrics to a couple of the play's songs. (She also wrote two poems for Shepard around this time.) The fact that Shepard's wife, O-Lan, was featured in *Mad Dog Blues* would seem to be a serious complication regarding both his new life and the mounting of his latest play. Evidently not. Which is evidence that the ethos of the free love era was going strong as late as the early 1970s. "Me and his wife still even liked each other," Smith said. "I mean, it wasn't like we were committing adultery in the suburbs or something." (In fact, by 1972, after Shepard and his wife had reunited and moved with their child to London, Smith and O-Lan were nearly pen pals, and Smith would visit the couple there that same year.)

Smith credits Shepard for not only encouraging her poetry but also pushing her to sing it. It would seem only natural for Smith, always a lively spoken word performer, to take the next step and add music to her work. But it didn't actually happen until Shepard helped her make that leap, as he explained in a 2008 interview: "Essentially Patti was a poet back then. She hadn't really broken into music. I'm certainly not responsible for it, but I kept tellin' her, you know, that she should *sing* this stuff. She was doin' poetry readings and stuff at St. Mark's Church, and she was kind of performing these poetry readings as though they were songs, and I said, 'Why don't you sing 'em?' So I got her a guitar, and she learned a couple chords, and she started singin'."

A handful of famous incidents occurred during Shepard's time with Smith. Inspired by her reading about Crazy Horse, who is said to have tattooed lightning bolts on the ears of his horse, Smith wanted a similar tattoo. She cajoled a former artist named Vali to do it and, with Shepard in tow, visited the room of another Chelsea denizen, Sandy Daley, with plans for the avant-garde filmmaker to capture the event. Using a large sewing needle, Vali "stabbed the lightning bolt into my knee," Smith recalled. Next Shepard wanted a "hawk moon" tattooed on his left hand, in the tender space between his thumb and forefinger. Both marks remain.

The first guitar Shepard gave to Smith, she in turn gave to her younger sister. When he learned of this, he took Smith to a Village guitar shop and had her pick out another. She took from the wall a beat-up-looking 1931 Gibson acoustic, and Shepard plunked down the $200 for it. Smith named the guitar Bo, and over the years she wrote many of her most famous songs on it. To this day it remains one of her prized possessions.

Their relationship, like many in Shepard's life with the opposite sex, was at times tumultuous. "I remember a terrible scene when he destroyed some of her drawings, and she was absolutely crushed about it," recalled Ann Powell, a friend of Smith's. However, the reason for their parting wasn't a final blowout but something more mundane. Smith claims their consciences simply caught up with them. By the early months of 1971, the relationship began to fall apart.

One night as the affair was winding down, Shepard broke the silence in the room by saying, "Let's write a play." Smith said she didn't know how, but he said, "It's easy." Shepard began typing up the description of a set, based on Smith's room, then pushed the typewriter across to her. "You're on, Patti Lee," he said. She was worried she might screw up the rhythm of what Shepard had already laid down, but he told her that was impossible.

"It's like drumming," he told her. "If you miss a beat, you create another." In *Just Kids*, Smith writes, "In this simple exchange, Sam taught me the secret of improvisation, one that I have accessed my whole life."

The play was finished quickly; "it just kind of spewed itself out there," Shepard would later recall. "No craftsmanship at all. Just pure emotion." They called it Cowboy Mouth.

When on February 12, 1971, Smith gave her first real poetry reading at St. Mark's Church—the same place Shepard's artistic life began—he was in the audience, despite the fact that their relationship was winding down by that point.

In April 1971, *Cowboy Mouth* premiered in Edinburgh, Scotland. Later in the month, at the American Place Theatre, the production featured Shepard and Smith playing the leads—though this arrangement wouldn't last: Shepard bolted after opening night. This also brought down the curtain on his affair with Smith. He first went to New Hampshire to hang out with the Holy Modal Rounders who were gigging up north, before returning to New York and his family.

By all accounts, Smith was desperately in love with Shepard. "Patti was devastated by Sam's departure. It completely ripped her apart," her friend Powell said. Another friend recalls an inebriated Smith being carried out of Max's Kansas City, at one point screaming Shepard's name.

In a diary entry from February of that year, Smith proclaimed her continued love for Shepard and remarked how much she missed him. She remembers how in bed she'd throw her leg around him, while other times they'd wait together at their room in the Chelsea for the sun to come up. Other men, she wrote, were boring compared to Shepard. "Your [*sic*] something else again," Smith writes. "Like any snake, you've rattled your way into my heart."

After Shepard went back to his family, he and Smith would not spend any appreciable time together for more than three decades. In 2006 he'd confide to his notebook how, according to Smith's memory, he'd left $1,000 on the bureau when he departed, which she used to go to Veracruz. There she was bitten by a stingray.

In early 2005, Smith reentered Shepard's life. She called him out of the blue and wanted to get together. They met at Café Dante in the West

Village, one of Dylan's old haunts, near where the Village Gate once stood. Shepard found her "as sweet as ever, somewhat haggard around the edges like all of us."

Their time as lovers was relatively short, yet Shepard and Smith had a marked impact on each other. "She had a tremendous influence on me, because I was unaware, at that time, of any of these French poets, the symbolist poets and all that stuff, and she kind of turned me on to Baudelaire and Rimbaud and all those poets that I never paid any attention to, bein' a dumb-ass American out in the middle of nowhere," Shepard said.

After reuniting as friends in 2005, Shepard and Smith have only grown closer. He's performed with her onstage and on record, and she dedicated her 2015 memoir to him. In an interview that same year, Shepard called her his "best friend." "She's precious to me," he said.

Smith said it was while acting in *Cowboy Mouth* that she began to feel at home onstage. She'd told Shepard, both in life and in the lines she wrote in the play, that he was the rock 'n' roll Jesus with greatness lying in wait for him. As he was leaving her life, Shepard provided the perfect coda to their love affair. As Smith tells it: "He looked at me, my cowboy with Indian ways. 'You know, the dreams you had for me weren't my dreams,' he said. 'Maybe those dreams are meant for you.'"

Mad Dogs, Splits, and More
(1971 continued)

I'm not doing this in order to vent demons. I want to shake hands
with them.

—Sam Shepard

Conspiracies, paranoia, political upheaval, bad drug trips, and
violence were the order of the day during the first few years of
the 1970s. Shepard watched these developments and naturally
reflected in his plays the tension felt across his homeland. Soon, combined
with the pressures of his life, it would all become too much and he'd flee
the country, seeking personal and creative respite in England.

Despite how busy his life continued to be, Shepard's dramatic output
picked up again in these first years of the new decade. During his time
with Patti Smith, two more of his plays premiered, *Shaved Splits* and *Mad
Dog Blues*. Much of what one needs to know about the former is that it
first appeared in the pages of the July 21, 1971, issue of *Screw* magazine.
A prefatory note from the editors of *Screw* claimed that "*Esquire* wouldn't
print it because of its 'obscene' language'" and went on to call the play "an

imaginative excursion to the far frontiers of American consciousness and beyond, a representation of contemporary feelings and attitudes that tells us more about what it's like to be alive today than all the platitudes and middlebrow theorizing of the mass media put together."

The opening of *Shaved Splits* features a barely dressed woman named Cherry splayed on her bed reading aloud from a pornographic novel, her voice filling the theater as she intones the smutty lines over a public address system. For what it's worth, Shepard's writing here is a dead-on impression of cheesy erotica. Cherry's afternoon is interrupted in turn by her servant, Wong; a salesman named Chunky Puke, who hawks the porno paperbacks she reads; a mute masseuse; and finally an armed felon named Geez, who's running from the cops. Those cops are firing at him from down in the street. Geez holds Cherry hostage and the two of them argue. At one point Cherry runs to the window to tell the cops to stop shooting, but they blast her in the face. When her husband, D.T., comes home after six weeks away, he is wounded in the shoulder. Cherry begs Geez to take her away in her husband's helicopter, which is parked on the roof of the building, but instead he launches into a rambling yet no less poetic soliloquy that includes the line "But now the war was over. Peace was the hard part."

The premiere of *Shaved Splits* took place in July 1970 at La MaMa; it ran for four midnight performances and was helmed by Shepard pal Bill Hart. Often dismissed, the play offers at least a few things worth pondering, albeit it's most compelling when viewed from the perspective of those coming of age in the early 1970s. Juxtaposing Cherry's fantasies with the violence in the streets may be Shepard's commentary on the disparate but contemporaneous movements of the sexual revolution, antiwar protests, and civil rights struggle that were eating away at the country's soul. The cops outside Cherry's window are hot for blood, and given that the shootings at Kent State took place just a few months before *Shaved Splits* premiered, there's no way audience members could have missed the point. Especially when Geez decries those who "shoot down their own kind."

As in much of Shepard's early work, things move so quickly that it's hard to fully parse his ideas; the works are best enjoyed for their humor, energy, and stagecraft and best absorbed as a holistic experience. Or, as Mark Fisher of the *Herald* put it when he reviewed a rare 1998 revival of

Shaved Splits, "Ideas spring to life, burn momentarily, then disappear as quickly and as inexplicably as they arrived."

Albert Poland wanted to move *Shaved Splits* to an Off-Broadway venue but was told by Shepard's agent, Toby Cole, that Shepard wasn't interested. The producer felt that recent events, including the consensus that *Shaved Splits* was not up to par, may have influenced this decision. "He had a triple-whammy at the time because *Operation Sidewinder* had opened to a not good response at Lincoln Center, *Zabriskie Point* opened to bad reviews, and he was devastated," Poland said.

Nevertheless, Shepard was already on to the next thing. *Mad Dog Blues* premiered in March 1971 at Theatre Genesis. Like *Operation Sidewinder* before it, the play, structurally at least, feels more like a film. Indeed, the printed script reads like a screenplay, with scenes alternating between locales and groups of characters. Shepard even uses screenwriting terminology in the stage directions, such as, "cut to Mae and Kosmo." Meanwhile, the characters are mostly drawn from popular culture or America's western mythos: a rock star, a drug dealer, Mae West, a cowboy, Paul Bunyan, Marlene Dietrich, Captain Kidd, Jesse James, and a "Ghost Girl." They travel constantly around the set, which is meant to convey a number of locales but is comprised of literally nothing. "All the places the characters move through are imagined and mimed," the set directions read, as if the play were written as an old-time radio show. A few minor props, music, and lighting are all the director and cast have to work with. As critic Jack Gelber noted, "The abstract quality of the open stage lends credibility to the mythical figures" Shepard puts on stage. It gives them the effect of being suspended in time and space, making the characters seem universal, as the best mythical creations are. In the published script, Shepard indicates that the pianist of the band should closely follow the action "like they did with the old silent movies."

Mad Dog Blues begins with a rock star named Kosmo and his drug dealer, Yahoodi, deciding to collaborate on a story based on a vision Kosmo has had. Presaging Shepard's real-life impending abdication to London, Kosmo tells his friend, "The city's getting me down. Too many tangents." The pair split up. Yahoodi goes to the jungle and Kosmo to San Francisco. Eventually they meet some friends and head out separately to recover a large treasure that Captain Kidd knows of. The two gangs move about the bare stage, and as the yarn unfolds, they cover plains, oceans, jungles, and deserts. Ultimately, Yahoodi and Captain Kidd get all the treasure, but the guilt of his actions in trying to secure the cache causes Yahoodi to commit suicide. However, when Kosmo comes upon his body, he tells his friend to get up, which he does. As the second act proceeds, the characters are all adrift and wander the stage calling after each other, except for Jesse James and Mae West, who have ended up with the treasure, which turns out to be nothing but bags of bottle caps. In the end, the pair leads a sing-along as they head home; the other characters fall in line, and for once Shepard gives us a clear and definite happy ending.

Mad Dog Blues marks the first, but not the last, time that suicide plays a role in Shepard's work. Director George Ferencz, one of the most respected interpreters of Shepard's work, believes that in addition to his exposure to symbolist poetry, Shepard also inherited from his time with Patti Smith ideas about suicide as a dramatic device. In the play the pair wrote together, *Cowboy Mouth*, the Smith doppelganger, Cavale, speaks often of the French poet Nerval, who, she says, "hung himself on my birthday." There is also the suggestion at the end of *Cowboy Mouth* that one of the characters, Lobster Man, kills himself as the lights fade.

"Before Patti, you don't see that suicidal bent, that self-destructiveness" in Shepard's work, Ferencz says. *Mad Dog Blues* is where it is first manifest. Four years later, Shepard would write a play titled *Suicide in B♭*, and suicide, or its handmaidens—reckless or self-destructive behavior—becomes a not uncommon theme in his work. In fact, in a 2008 letter to a friend enthusing about Beckett's famous line "I can't go on—I'll go on," Shepard approvingly recalls how his old flame Patti Smith "said to me once, 'Aw hell let's just all go kill ourselves'—I like that one too."

Shaved Splits and *Mad Dog Blues* seem farcical, but Shepard treated them with great seriousness. To wit, during the rehearsals for *Mad Dog Blues*, Shepard punched Beeson Carroll and broke his jaw. For some reason, the playwright was unhappy with the popular actor, who was playing Paul Bunyan.

The play that Shepard and Smith had written together in the waning days of their relationship, *Cowboy Mouth*, had its American premiere, featuring

Shepard and Smith as the leads, ostensibly playing themselves, in April 1971 at the American Place Theatre. She is Cavale, a crow-like woman who lives in a past full of romantic notions about suicide, poetry, and rock 'n' roll; Shepard's character, Slim, is described as being like a coyote. Each looks like ten miles of bad road. This mad rush of a play takes place in a run-down apartment. Their messy bed sits center stage; the walls are adorned with graffiti and posters. In this tight, cluttered space, Shepard and Smith act out their urgent last gasps as a couple. They talk, they sing, they cajole, they accuse, they embrace. It's a dance they know will be their last. She wants to be loved and famous; he's not sure what he wants, but he knows he's not where he should be and accuses her of tempting him away from his wife and child. As Smith said at the time, guilt played a large part in driving her and Shepard apart. Hence Slim throughout delivers the cry of a guilty man torn between what he wants to do and what he knows he should do. "You led me on. You tempted me into sin," he proclaims. And later, Slim's torn emotions are on full display: "I don't want! I do want! I don't want! I want you!" When Cavale tells him if this is the case, he should stay, he retorts: "I want her too." To this point, Shepard had never written as close to the bone as this, with the possible exception of the father–son relationship in *The Holy Ghostly*. Further demonstrating his split allegiance, in the *News of the American Place* from that month, printed to coincide with the run of *Cowboy Mouth*, in an autobiographical sketch Shepard listed the things he loved, ending with his wife, son, *and* Patti Smith.

Ultimately, saying onstage the lines he'd written with Smith proved too much for Shepard. "The thing was too emotionally packed," he said at the time. "I suddenly realized I didn't want to exhibit myself like that, playing my life onstage. It was like being in an aquarium." And so he left after a few previews and exactly one performance, heading north to New Hampshire, where the Holy Modal Rounders were playing at Franconia College. "He came up with us for that gig just to hang out, as a way of bailing from the play," Peter Stampfel recalled.

Cowboy Mouth is important because it showed Shepard how to write a true rock 'n' roll play, which he would build upon in the coming years. It also presaged one of Shepard's most popular plays, 1983's *Fool for Love*, which was nominated for a Pulitzer and revived on Broadway in 2015. That play gives us another pair of fighting lovers trapped in a confined space, only this couple is linked by genetics—they share the same father. In *Cowboy Mouth*, the lovers are related not by blood but by their separate struggles for fame and meaning. He wants to be a rock star but is an underpaid playwright; she wants to be a poet, but the world has yet to notice. The obstacles in their professional lives come to be equated with the obstacles between them: the pair slowly come to the realization that they are doomed if they remain together.

A June 2012 production of *Cowboy Mouth* staged in a Greenwich Village apartment proved the play has held up relatively well over the decades. At the immersive event—with the small audience seated on chairs at one end of a cramped bedroom—one experienced the claustrophobic feel Shepard and Smith were striving to convey in their script. The youthful actors were typical of the performers who gravitate toward this play. In Slim and Cavale they see themselves—hungry for more but unsure if fate will ever deliver. Shepard, however, has noted that in his eyes, *Cowboy Mouth* has not aged well. Seeing a rehearsal of the play in early 1980, he "felt embarrassed by its adolescent rantings."

For its U.S. premiere, *Cowboy Mouth* was paired with another Shepard short play, *Back Bog Beast Bait*, directed by Tony Barsha. Set in a shack in bayou swamp country, the play tells the story of a group of people in hiding from a "beast" that has been roaming the area. Slim and Shadow, guns for hire, have been retained by Maria, the lady of the house, to protect her and her son. A preacher enters spewing biblical verse, followed by Gris-Gris, a mix between a voodoo witch and a gypsy, playing a "death song" on her fiddle. The beast puts in a brief cameo, and we learn it may have killed Maria's son. The three-scene play, which includes songs written by Shepard, his Holy Modal Rounders compatriot Peter Stampfel, and Lou Reed, ends in a fugue of black magic chanting, animalistic behavior, and rising music. More than story or character, the play offers a sense of atmosphere that is disorienting and a little spooky. The Reed song "Wrap Your Troubles in Dreams" was recorded by Nico on her 1967 album *Chelsea Girl* and was sung in Shepard's premiere by a character known as Ghost Girl, who comes on just for this song and an opening number.

Back Bog Beast Bait was neither an achievement nor a stepping-stone, but it did mark the close of a chapter in Shepard's life. The next premiere of a Sam Shepard play would not take place for more than a year. It would happen an ocean away from his adopted home turf of New York City, and it would be his best work to date.

On September 10, 1971, an admirer wrote a letter to Shepard, hoping they could get together at some time in the near future. Weeks earlier, Shepard had already left the United States for England. The correspondent, a fellow playwright named Tennessee Williams, would never meet the young man whose work he so admired.

Gurdjieff

Personality is not the man. Personality is the opposite of man.
—Sam Shepard

I really think that we are not just one person. We are a multiplicity of beings, if you want to call it that. . . . Characters are ever changing. I'm more interested in this shifting of character.
—Sam Shepard

Someone who's known Shepard for a long time once told me that to fully comprehend him, as both man and artist, one needs to understand the teachings of George Ivanovich Gurdjieff, a Russian-born mystic and spiritual leader. Shepard has throughout his life turned time and again to the Work, as Gurdjieff's program is called, seeking inspiration, answers, and solace. Gurdjieff's main beliefs have also provided the animating ideas central to some of Shepard's best plays. The connection is something fans, scholars, and critics have neglected, or at most mentioned in passing. Close examination of Shepard's letters, journals, interviews, and writing reveal a deep commitment to the ideas of the Russian mystic beginning around 1971 and lasting nearly four decades.

Central to Gurdjieff's system is the belief that people sleepwalk through their lives, and he endeavored to find a way to wake them up, to bring them into full consciousness so they could be fully present in their lives. Once introduced, Shepard dove headfirst into the Work.

Which is why on a Wednesday evening in early June 2015, I sat in the small baptistery of the First Parish Church of Cambridge for the monthly meeting of the Gurdjieff Society of Massachusetts. When the 7:30 start time arrived, thirteen men and two women arranged themselves next to me in the lushly padded chairs as three speakers prepared to digress on the evening's topic, "Observation and Attention."

The talk served as a jumping-off point about the belief system founded by Gurdjieff, who was born around 1866 and died in 1949, first coming to notice in Moscow in 1912. Hailed as a "messenger of the spirit" by some, a charlatan by others, Gurdjieff fundamentally aimed to "help human beings awaken to the meaning of our existence." Before his death, an event Gurdjieff predicted would never happen, he entrusted his teachings to a small group of followers. Centers dedicated to the spreading of the Work sprung up in major cities around the globe. As of this writing, there are sixty-two sanctioned Gurdjieff groups, like the one I attended in Cambridge, across thirty-eight states.

Two influential people in Shepard's life introduced him to the Work. One was his then father-in-law and lifelong friend Johnny Dark, who in 1970 attended Gurdjieff meetings when he lived in San Francisco. He, in turn, had most likely been introduced to the Work by his wife, Scarlett Johnson, mother of Shepard's wife, O-Lan. Shepard and his wife visited her mother and stepfather in the Haight-Ashbury section of the city in 1970. Shepard may have gotten a taste of Gurdjieff then. Shepard has also mentioned, while in London the following year, encountering director Peter Brook, who was so devoted to the Work that he made a biopic of Gurdjieff called *Meetings with Remarkable Men*. Brook convinced Shepard that the Work might represent a viable alternative to the hectic life of working and partying he'd left behind in New York City.

The Work incorporates various strains from other religious and philosophical systems. Gurdjieff's primary claim that man is asleep in his daily life is similar to ideas found in everything from Scientology to existentialism to Zen and meditation practices of various stripes. Seymour B. Ginsburg, in his book *Gurdjieff Unveiled*, traces the roots of the Work to a mix of belief systems, including Western esotericism, Sufism, Kabbalistic teaching, mindfulness/Buddhism, Hinduism, and the modern occult movement, particularly the work of Helena Petrovna Blavatsky, founder of modern Theosophy.

Two questions constantly arise in the Work, and they seem to guide all that follows: Who am I? and the related question, What is the purpose of human life? Only those with a sufficiently raised consciousness (those who are awake) or those who reach what Gurdjieff calls "objective consciousness" can hope to gain answers to these questions.

Gurdjieff teaches that man is put to sleep from tuning into outside stimuli from a variety of sources, including the media, other people, and daily experiences. Thus we consume and engage without thinking. At its simplest, the Work can be seen as a series of exercises in self-observation meant to address this problem, so that one can live in the moment or, as Gurdjieff would have it, be awake. Most people are fine with being asleep, but for those who wish to be beneficially self-conscious, it takes effort and long years of practice to learn how to be watchful of these outside stimuli and to limit their deleterious effects.

Also central to Gurdjieff's teachings is the idea of the personality as being merely what or who we mistakenly believe we are. Each person, in fact, possesses many "I"s. Thus personality, he taught, is transient, like a mask we don and shed as necessary. What really matters is one's essence, that which he or she enters the world with, the permanent "I" or soul. Gurdjieff believes that human beings are qualitatively the same as god, whom he also calls "the universal" or most often "Endlessness," and that as we become more our true selves—that is to say, get closer and closer to our individual essence—the more we can know this supreme being.

Gurdjieff's teaching is most commonly referred to as the Work, but he sometimes considered it a "Fourth Way." Unlike the seeking of enlightenment undertaken by the fakir, the monk, or the yogi, which demanded a monastic life, the Work takes into account modernity's busy and urbanized ways. Thus it is designed so that it can be practiced "in the midst of life." The optimal way to practice the Work is in groups led by a teacher or teachers well versed in Gurdjieff's program. The monthly event I attended in Cambridge in the summer of 2015 was merely informational.

Those who were interested in pursuing the Work further were referred to weekly group meetings where they could join others in the lectures, readings, exercises, meditation, and dance movements that delve deeper into Gurdjieff's teachings.

(The above description of Gurdjieff's program barely scratches the surface of all that he wrote and taught. Go deeper into the Work and things get murkier, with talk of "transforming energies" and a doctrinal diagram known as the "Ray of Creation" that "provides one of the conceptual keys to approaching [the] interconnection between humanity and the universal order." Shepard never mentions or writes of these aspects of Gurdjieff's schema, dealing instead with just the basics, having to do with being in the moment, the idea of the personality/mask we all wear, and notions about the multitudinous nature of personality. Nonetheless, the Work is a very complicated belief system, and it's unfair to claim that what I've written above is a full depiction of it.)

It's easy to see how an inveterate seeker like Shepard would be drawn to the idea that he might expand his consciousness to the point where answers might be found to age-old questions such as "Who am I?" "What is our purpose?" and "What is the nature of reality?" Additionally, when he first encountered the Work it was the early 1970s. Hippiedom may have begun its slow retreat, but things like est (Erhard Seminars Training), the New Age movement, and all sorts of mind-expanding and spiritual programs were being promulgated across the United States and beyond. Also, given that Shepard was already predisposed to some of Gurdjieff's ideas, such as the masklike and multiple nature of personality, and that people he admired, like his in-laws and Peter Brook, were involved in the Work, it's no wonder he embraced it.

Though in his letters and notebooks Shepard is very open about his involvement in the Work, he rarely speaks about it in public, even as he allows that Gurdjieff's teachings were responsible for allowing him to appreciate "another approach, another attitude," an alternative to "arbitrary mindlessness." It was, he said, "the most informative stuff that I'd ever come across." Shepard also said that this "stuff," as he put it, along with Peter Brook's suggestion that he focus more on character, "shifted the direction of his work." Shepard learned in his post-1975 plays to write characters who don't behave arbitrarily but instead honor the reality of the moment—ideas that echo some of what's found in Gurdjieff.

While in London, between the summers of 1971 and 1974, Shepard was deep into the Work, attending meetings on a regular basis. He said he felt out of place among the faithful, suspecting he was the "bad boy trying to shape up to his imagination of the 'Conscious Ones—the real adults.'" Indeed, a couple of times commitments to the Work meetings left him agitated. In October of 1972, the local Gurdjieff group was practicing Movements, the sacred dances developed by the spiritual leader himself. Shepard groused that he and his wife had to travel to London's Charing Cross to buy some "dumb ballet shoes at some fruity ballet store." At the meeting, they joined the others in moving like "little, wooden soldiers all in lines to some morbid piano music being dictated by some fat, little tank of a woman." During the same meeting, "the English twerps" got on his nerves, and worst of all, he finds out there's a meeting the next day in Bray, which means he'll have to miss the running of the Anglo-Irish Challenge Cup at the dog track in White City. However, after all this, Shepard writes of the Work as saving his life. "Still there's something that keeps me hanging onto all this like a drowning man. I know that without it I got no chance for anything in life."

That the Work filled some void in Shepard's life isn't difficult to imagine. After spending a mid-December day in 1972 with his London Gurdjieff group, led by Basil Tilley (always "Mr. Tilley" in Shepard's letters), he admits to feeling "like a little kid," safely ensconced with this adoptive family. Tilley read to the group and drinks were poured, Merry Christmas wishes exchanged, and Shepard proclaims, "At last I'd found a father" in Mr. Tilley. O-Lan was crying as they drove back to their home in London; Shepard felt like he was driving on another planet. "Now it almost seems miraculous that we find ourselves under this kind of influence," he wrote to his friend Dark, thanking him for introducing him to the Work.

In 1972 Shepard wrote a letter to Joseph Chaikin from London that contains a handful of overt references to the Work. Shepard tells his friend and mentor how he wasted so much time when he was with Chaikin, "never feeling really there," and confesses that all he'd accomplished "has been in sleep." He ends the letter feeling amazed and sad that he "was never present" during the times they spent together.

After he left London to return to California, Shepard and his wife lived with her mother and stepfather and joined them at Gurdjieff meetings; the Work was a regular topic of conversation around the home the couples shared. The household's weekly schedule was "totally mapped out" around meetings. Shepard also took to his notebooks to hash out his thoughts about Gurdjieff. In an entry from 1975, he seems to be chiding himself for giving in to distraction. When he's not self-observing, he writes of feeling as if his life is going on without him being present. In a notebook entry from 1980, Shepard diagrammed some of the steps featured in Gurdjieff's "sacred dances."

In his plays dating from the mid-1970s on, aspects of the Work turn up repeatedly. There are "dreamwalkers" in *Geography of a Horse Dreamer*; the four characters in *Action* seem to be going through life "hypnotized." Meanwhile, the idea of a dual nature is central to Shepard's most popular play, *True West*. Multiple identities, characters not knowing who they are, and talk of people being hypnotized or in some sort of trance would permeate his plays in the coming years. In the early 1990s, while talking to a writer about his film project *Silent Tongue*, which he wrote and directed, Shepard sounded like he was quoting directly from Gurdjieff: "Don't you have the feeling that we all develop masks, layers of masks, and these masks make up a personality, a persona, and if you stripped these away what you come down to would be something completely different? An essence. Something more pure—or nothing at all."

Shepard never overdoes it or beats his audiences over the head with these ideas, but subtle references show up in his work right up to and including his most recent play, 2014's *A Particle of Dread*. His letters to Dark continually reference Gurdjieff or books inspired by his teachings, and in at least one interview, included as part of the 2000 documentary *This So-Called Disaster*, Shepard practically repeats the hallmarks of Gurdjieff's program, chapter and verse: "It's an amazing dilemma when one begins to discover that you are living your life as a somnambulist. That you are living your life in a trance, in a dream, to be corny about it. When that occurs there's a kind of amazing thing that takes place. One is despair. The other is a sudden awakening. There's another way of seeing." Shepard's letters to his friend and former father-in-law Johnny Dark continued into the new century to feature references to the Work or its late founder.

In 1983 he wrote, "I know the Work point of view is the only true one." The following year he would attend the funeral of Henry John Sinclair, also known as John Pentland, who'd been appointed by Gurdjieff upon his death to spread the Work in North America. That same year, Shepard told a *New York Times* reporter that "personality is everything that is false in a human being. . . . Everything that has been added onto him and contrived. It seems to me that the struggle all the time is between this sense of falseness and the other haunting sense of what's true—an essential thing that we're born with and tend to lose track of."

Fast forward to 1997, and in a letter to Dark, Shepard is still pondering the Work, admitting he still doesn't "comprendo." Two years later, he was still returning to Pentland's writings "on an almost daily basis" and reading him again in 2000 and 2002. In early 2005, Shepard writes to Dark of once again attending Gurdjieff meetings in New York City and leaving one of these feeling as if he'd finally transcended thought and desire. "It lasted about four blocks," he writes of the sensation.

The end of Shepard's fascination with all this seems to arrive in the summer of 2008, when everything he saw in the Work seems to "have gone up in smoke." Thus falls away nearly four decades of looking for answers in the writings and teachings of G. I. Gurdjieff.

It's interesting, and perhaps not unrelated, that beginning in 2007, mentions of his drinking increase in Shepard's letters, culminating in his 2009 and 2015 arrests for DUI.

London

I think that he did some of his best writing here.

—Stephen Rea

A number of London theatergoers knew the name Sam Shepard in the summer of 1971 before he'd ever hit town. Two years earlier, the Royal Court's Theatre Upstairs had produced *La Turista* as its third offering, and shortly thereafter, the King's Head staged *Chicago*, *Red Cross*, and *The Holy Ghostly*. But it wasn't the theater that brought Shepard across the Atlantic; it was music: He really did want to be a rock star. "I had this fantasy that I'd come over here and somehow fall into a rock 'n' roll band," he said. Evidently, the dream didn't last long. "I was just a backbeat drummer. It just didn't happen," Shepard said. He saw the competition, people like Ginger Baker, who "drummed circles around me," and thereafter he returned to his original calling. Despite these rock 'n' roll dreams, the impulse to write for the stage never left him, and after less than six months in London, Shepard was working on *The Tooth of*

Crime, a new play that at the time existed only in his notebooks, in his "nutty, juvenile scrawl."

Shepard's fear of flying meant that his trips back and forth across the Atlantic had to be made by ship. Upon arriving in London, Shepard, his wife, and his son found it hard to locate a decent place to live, due to landlords at the time holding a prejudice against small families. They made do with a small apartment in Shepherd's Bush. Money was so tight that Shepard remembered "trying to find shillings to put into the heater." In early 1972, theater director and expat Charles Marowitz found the family a basement flat in Hampstead, about five miles north of London, at the foot of the leafy and posh Pilgrim's Lane. The flat was typical for a young family and had the benefit of being close to Hampstead Heath, a nearly eight-hundred-acre park. Quickly the place filled up with toys, diapers, Shepard's guitar, and signs of his growing fascination with greyhounds.

Just as Shepard's work had preceded him, so had his reputation, and it seems he immediately lived up to it. He possessed "a laconic, dry, very laid-back very masculine Gary Cooper-ish kind of style; certainly very direct, capable of being quite rude," remembered Nicholas Wright, who in 1971 was artistic director of the Theatre Upstairs. But he also sensed something else about the recent transplant. "My sense was that he was in recovery from something," Wright said. Upon landing in London in the summer of 1971, Shepard was heralded by some as the great voice of the American West. Still, he kept a low profile once he settled in. When he did go out, true to form, he didn't mingle much and avoided small talk. A reporter for the *Observer* seeing him at parties described Shepard as "detached" and the "most unostentatiously glamorous person" in the room. Meanwhile, Jennie Stoller, an actress who appeared in the London incarnations of *Icarus's Mother* and *Action*, remembered the playwright as "long, lanky and quiet. We'd go on very long walks and when he did talk it was quite often about Gurdjieff," she said.

Shepard may have come to England to try his hand at music, but he was also escaping from a life grown too hectic in New York. Some of this was personal—too many drugs, a complicated love life, and the new demands put upon him by fatherhood. "A lot of stuff was just frayed. I needed to get into another environment. It was kind of an escape," he said. Other reasons for his self-exile were purely professional: "I left [New York] for the same reasons I don't hang out there now, the commercial parts of theater were just not interesting," he told an interviewer in 2014. "I went to London because the fringe theater was happening at that time. It was very eclectic and very exciting, in the way that the original Off-Off Broadway was, and that's exactly what I was looking for."

Though in later life Shepard would refer to this time as "three years in stagnant London," his time overseas affected him in many ways and made him a better playwright. In retrospect, he claimed that in England he learned "how much work it takes to make good theater, and that it might mean something to be an American." It was here that he turned himself into a disciplined writer, one who worked on character development and who spent time rewriting, paring away any excess.

Also in London, Patti Smith's enduring impact on his life was made manifest in the reading he was doing. Shepard inherited her love of books, specifically of European poets, and he also began investigating the dramas of the ancient Greeks. "They're all about destiny! That's the most powerful thing. Everything is foreseen, and we just play it out," he said. This belief in fate, especially as it pertains to heredity, would be an important theme in the family plays he would begin writing in a few years.

London's theater scene in the first half of the 1970s featured parallels to what Shepard had left behind in the United States. There was the West End, which, then as now, was London's version of Broadway. Next were the three state-supported institutional theaters, the Royal Court, the Royal Shakespeare Company, and the National Theater. Lastly there was the place where Shepard would find a home away from home—the fringe theaters. Taking its name from an annual Edinburgh festival known as Beyond the Fringe, this string of theaters was analogous to New York's Off- and Off-Off-Broadway. These lower rungs even had their own *Village Voice*–like publication called *Time Out*. From the fringe emerged such well-known playwrights as David Hare, Howard Brenton, and Trevor Griffiths, as well as filmmaker Mike Figgis.

Shepard made important connections during his first months in London, including with the director Charles Marowitz.

Viewed as progressive, even by members of London's avant-garde theater scene, Marowitz was a cofounder of the experimental Open Space Theatre, where he remained as artistic director. Once he helped Shepard and his young family settle into their new flat, talk turned to Shepard's work in progress, the play that would become *The Tooth of Crime*. The manifestation of Shepard's dashed rock 'n' roll dreams, the two-act play would turn out to be a high-water mark in the career of the twenty-eight-year-old playwright. Marowitz read the nascent work in Shepard's notebooks and was ready to stage it as soon as possible.

Shepard also met like-minded souls Nancy Meckler and Stephen Rea, both members of the experimental theater group Freehold. The trio would continue as friends and collaborators into the next century. (And in 2012 Meckler's son Daniel Aukin would direct Shepard's play *Heartless* and four years later would take a revival of *Fool for Love* to Broadway.)

Meckler was born on Long Island and studied for her master's degree in performance theory at New York University between 1966 and 1968. For a time, she was a member of La MaMa Plexus, a resident company of the famous Off-Off-Broadway venue, where she served as an assistant director and did some acting. By 1971 Meckler had married producer David Aukin and was living in his native London. During her New York years, Meckler had only read Shepard's plays and never seen one. By a stroke of luck, she soon entered the playwright's circle. O-Lan Shepard was taking a physical theater workshop that Meckler was leading, and once when she was giving the American actress a ride home to Hampstead, O-Lan surprised her by mentioning that her husband was Sam Shepard. From there, invitations for tea, tennis matches, and more followed. Meckler's memories of Shepard from those days are consistent with those who knew him in America. "I found him friendly, although very laid-back and not prone to small talk," she said. "They were living a very domestic life." Shepard was working his way through a gourmet cookbook at the time, trying the various recipes, she recalled. There was also secretive talk about Gurdjieff—Shepard had already joined a local group studying the spiritual leader's teachings. "I got the feeling Sam and O-Lan were trying to get away from their New York life," Meckler said.

Shepard always had an affinity for minimalist staging and expressionistic theater, for which Meckler had gained experience through her time at La MaMa and her studying of theorists like Jerzy Grotowski. It also didn't hurt that Meckler's work owed a debt to the Open Theater, run by Shepard's friend Joseph Chaikin. The result was a simpatico relationship with Shepard and his work. "It was meat and drink for our actors to tackle his texts, whereas others might have been defeated by the obscurity," Meckler said.

In time, Meckler asked Shepard if Freehold could stage his 1965 play *Icarus's Mother* at the Roxy, a swingingly named theater that belied its real existence as a garage in Kentish Town. He said yes and ultimately was pleased with the results. "Sam came to a few rehearsals and the show and loved the work," Meckler said.

The Freehold connection also introduced Shepard to actress Dinah Stabb, who was pregnant during this time and was thus the inspiration behind one of Shepard's next plays, *Little Ocean*, which premiered in London in 1974 and also featured O-Lan and Caroline Hutchinson. Hutchinson had a boyfriend named Stephen Rea, who would become a lifelong friend of Shepard's. The Belfast-born actor is most familiar to American audiences through his lead roles in such films as *The Crying Game* (1992), for which he was nominated for an Oscar, and *Interview with a Vampire* (1994). However, his theater work is perhaps his greatest accomplishment. In 1980 with Brian Friel he was a founding member of Ireland's Field Day Theatre Company and has been featured to date in four Shepard plays, beginning with 1974's *Geography of a Horse Dreamer*.

Rea admitted that hitting it off with Shepard took some time. "One didn't approach him warily," he said, "but you approached him, you know, with some respect for his self-containment." It wasn't long before the two were drinking together, spending hours talking about the difficult situations in Vietnam and Northern Ireland. They also talked about Beckett, a shared favorite.

The other important relationship formed during Shepard's time in London was with the legendary director Peter Brook. Though Shepard describes it as less a relationship and more a few instances when the older man passed on some important advice. "I had a conversation with him once about character, and he simply posed the question, 'What is the nature of character?' For a long time it caused me to investigate that," Shepard said. There's no doubt that after his time in England, Shepard's plays were more often peopled with multidimensional characters. He continued to omit any backstory or obvious motivation for his characters, which is part of Shepard's long-held belief that each individual harbors many different "I"s, an idea omnipresent in the Work. But his time with Brook definitely paid dividends; the veteran director shared one other piece of advice with Shepard: "[He] once said that everything is, in a certain way, storytelling." Ironically, this veteran of the avant-garde theater advised Shepard to adopt practices more closely associated with mainstream dramas. It was winning advice.

Another discovery Shepard made in England was greyhound racing. Well before he brought a new play to a London stage, he was a racetrack devotee. He'd always loved animals and as a youth had raised a prize-winning German shepherd. Even during his days in the Village, when his own living quarters weren't the best, Shepard kept a canine companion. He owned two greyhounds before marking his first anniversary in London. He also shared ownership of another with actor Tony Milner.

Dog racing's popularity peaked in London in the 1950s, when up to 100,000 people would spend the night gambling at places like White City Stadium, one of the tracks where Shepard raced his dogs. Visitors to Shepard's flat on Pilgrim's Road around this time could expect to see a large black, spotted, Irish-bred greyhound named Keywall Spectre sleeping on the divan. Shepard would brag how the greyhound was practically unbeatable in the three-hundred-yard sprint. He might have preferred horses, but dogs were a lot less expensive and could live in the house. "Greyhound racing is great because you can breed your own dog, raise it, take it to the track, and race it, which is unheard of in horse racing because it's too expensive," he said.

The purse winnings came in handy, as there was still little money being derived from his plays, here or in America. Even beyond the extra money, greyhound racing was a serious part of his life; Shepard even named a character in one of his plays after a greyhound (Sara D in *Geography of a Horse Dreamer*). Missing a big race at White City, even for a Gurdjieff meeting, pained him. Shepard admitted there was a "romantic impulse" behind his love of the sport. Something about a man and his dog facing off against the competition and bringing home a day's wages, perhaps. Just before he left

England to head back to the United States, Shepard even tried his hand as a sportswriter for a day, contributing an article to *Time Out*, covering the 1974 Greyhound Derby. He ended the piece in typical Shepard fashion, with a short soliloquy about the final sprint for the finish line that proves he saw nothing less than romance in the sport. "So those few seconds are what it's all about. Less than half a minute and all that money, all that feeling, all that pounding energy has been pushed out into the night. And at the heart of it is this strange event of six dogs doing something that comes natural to them. Chasing something small, something moving, something that isn't even what they think it is."

During his first full summer in England, Shepard had to change hats from dog trainer to playwright, as the premiere of *The Tooth of Crime* was scheduled for July 1972. The play has a spontaneity to it onstage that belies its long gestation period. A few years earlier in New York, Shepard had been toying with the idea of a war or duel where the weapons weren't guns and knives but language. Just before he'd arrived in London, *AC/DC*, a play by Heathcote Williams, had premiered at the Royal Court's Theatre Upstairs. The play would influence Shepard's work in progress. "[It] struck me as opening in that direction," Shepard said. "Not only was the language uncanny but it also had the aura of assault about it." *AC/DC* featured two characters, Maurice and Perowne, who fight back against the controlling media that surround them. Language is their weapon, and just as Shepard would, Williams coined many hip words and phrases for his characters to speak in the heat of battle.

There was another key influence that shaped *The Tooth of Crime*. At some point, either influenced by his mentor Joseph Chaikin or by the reading binge Patti Smith had set him on, Shepard fell further under the sway of Bertolt Brecht. *The Tooth of Crime* clearly bears the influence of the German playwright's *In the Jungle of Cities*. That play, written circa 1924, tells the story of a battle between a book clerk and a lumber merchant that, Shepard observed, "is never defined as being anything but metaphysical."

It took a while for these influences to coalesce into *The Tooth of Crime*. First Shepard had tried to write a three-act play set in a jail. "At the end it was a complete piece of shit, so I put it in the sink and burnt it, and then an hour later I started to write this," he said. Hearing a voice in his head,

Shepard grabbed one of his notebooks and began quickly jotting down the words. He imagined a black throne at center stage, and the language he was imagining turned hipper and darker. Believing that music communicated emotion better than any words, Shepard decided this had to be his true rock 'n' roll play.

Shepard reports that writing *The Tooth of Crime* was a long, difficult process. Even when it was finished and ready for production, the playwright had his doubts about the second act. (In 1997, in fact, Shepard would undertake a drastic rewrite of *Tooth*, attempting to address the problems he saw.) Marowitz believed it to be "the finest American play I had read since Mike Weller's *Moonchildren*." What really captivated the veteran director was the way the characters spoke. By the same token, Marowitz believed the play to be the most "American" work he'd read in a while, and while that was a good thing, he feared it was too much of a good thing—British audiences might fail to connect with it. He beat back his reservations and those of his assistant director, Walter Donohue, and decided to take a gamble. Marowitz told Shepard he'd stage the play at the Open Space Theatre as soon as possible.

It wasn't as easy as all that. Marowitz and Shepard did not see eye to eye on everything—mostly the amount of "flash" and artifice Marowitz envisioned bringing to the production. Fortunately, there was enough common ground to proceed. However, the financing took some time to fall into place, and Shepard's patience wore thin.

The Open Space Theatre was a 128-seat venue located in a basement at 32 Tottenham Court Road in London, and most of its productions played to full houses, said Thelma Holt, who cofounded the theater with Marowitz. The producer and former actress first saw Shepard in New York City behind a drum kit. "I didn't know he was a writer," Holt said. "He was very seriously handsome." When she met him during the run-up to the premiere of *Tooth*, she was impressed. "Shepard was enchanting and [*The Tooth of Crime*] was way ahead of its time," she recalled.

In Act 1 of *The Tooth of Crime*, an aging rock star, Hoss, comes to grips with the knowledge that he is losing his "turf" to an aggressive upstart named Crow. Shepard employs a handful of overarching metaphors throughout the play: at times the backdrop for the battle is the world of rock 'n' roll, at other times it's gangland or the Old West, while at others it's some sort of high-stakes game or auto race. This would seemingly lead to confusion. However, Shepard so adroitly mixes elements of each of these, while allowing Hoss's regal attitude to gloss over any muddling, that it works terrifically. "It wound up somewhere between the old classic Western and rock nihilism," Shepard said.

Whereas the first half of the play deals with the corrosive effects of fame, in the second act, when Hoss and Crow actually face off, the focus shifts and sharpens, and the primary theme of the play becomes one of Shepard's favorites—authenticity. Crow has the style of the new, while Hoss has tradition on his side and a definitive link to the blues and early rock that Shepard posits as a state of innocence. Hoss emerges as the rock 'n' roll savoir that Patti Smith saw in Shepard himself the night the two met, and to prove it, when it's clear that Crow and all he stands for will triumph, Hoss takes his own life—a martyr to the tradition. Shepard's Hoss flirts with the idea of selling out to the latest fad but in the end decides he'd rather burn out and fade away.

When the characters are locked in the second-act duel, Shepard ups his game, and the writing has the poetry and energy unseen in his work thus far, maybe even since. Hearing good actors spin these lines out is a transfixing experience; even the songs register—for the first time Shepard managed to align his lyrics with the themes of what was happening onstage, and for the most part, each tune stands on its own as well. Sadly, there is no recording of the rock band Blunderpuss's performance during the London production.

The Tooth of Crime also contains bits of autobiography, including some of Shepard's memories of growing up in Southern California, as well as the names of a couple of friends from his teenage years. There's even some dog-racing lingo tossed in, such as *front-runner.* Meanwhile, the whole play deals with the idea of tradition (in the play it's known as "upholding the code") versus the new and novel, with Shepard coming down solidly on the side of the former. "In 1972, it seemed to me that rock and roll, as we had known it up till then, was being transformed into a river of sameness," Shepard said. "It was beginning to lose its original fire and brass balls." His intent was to reclaim the music's glorious, more authentic past.

The Tooth of Crime didn't have an easy launch. It was contracted to open at the Open Space Theatre on July 1, 1972, but for a variety of reasons, angering Shepard, it did not premiere until July 17. Still, *Time Out* gave the play a rave and championed it, while a handful of other London critics praised it. However, Marowitz believed his fears were realized, that the play went "uncomprehended" by London theatergoers. "It not only belongs in America, it actually looks exotic and unreal in England," he wrote in the *Village Voice*. "Only a public that has been conditioned by the assault course which *is* contemporary American life can fully appreciate its psychic implications." In the United States, as Marowitz predicted, the play went on to earn many excellent reviews, and scholars have held it up as an important work in Shepard's oeuvre. Writer Florence Falk viewed the metaphorical changing of the guards and the battle between Hoss and Crow to be "as classically rendered as any Elizabethan tragedy."

Around this time came news from California that Shepard's mother had sold the family home. His parents having divorced a couple years earlier, and with at least one sister, the eldest of the two, Sandy, done with college and moved on, his mother put the house up for sale. She'd spend most of her remaining years up north, near Santa Rosa.

When Shepard returned across the Atlantic for vacations in the summers of 1972 and 1973, he headed for a small waterfront cottage in West Advocate, Nova Scotia, located on a strip of land extending into the Bay of Fundy. His friend Rudy Wurlitzer, who also had (and still has) a place in Cape Breton, said the rural setting suited Shepard well. "Sam's always had a need and a longing for country places, and Nova Scotia represents a way to get completely off the U.S. grid," he said. Up north, Shepard relaxed along with O-Lan's mother and stepfather. When he came back to London after that first trip, Shepard divided his time between Gurd-jieff meetings, dog racing, writing, and, of all things, helping a friend build cabinets.

During his time in England, Shepard also reconnected via a series of letters with his old friend and mentor Joseph Chaikin, who was still in New York City. Chaikin had drastically changed the Open Theater, reducing it to just six members, down from more than a dozen, and had created two new pieces, *The Mutation Show* and *Nightwalk*. The latter, produced in New York in 1973, featured contributions from Shepard, albeit long distance, as well as from Megan Terry and Jean-Claude van Itallie. The play had its U.S. premiere in May, along with *The Mutation Show* and a revival of *Terminal*, all Open Theater projects. After taking the triple bill to Europe in late spring and early summer of that year, Chaikin disbanded the Open Theater, though the decision to do so had nothing to do with the latest productions. He simply felt the troupe had "run its course."

It was about this time Shepard got involved with Tony Richardson, the English film and theater director, who commissioned him to write a version of the classic Jacobean tragedy *The Changeling* set in the American West. The completed script was titled *The Bodyguard*; it was never produced or published.

Shepard was tiring of London by the start of 1973. "It's only dog racing and consciousness (the promise of) that keeps me here," he said. Consciousness, of course, refers to Gurdjieff and the Work. The weather certainly wasn't keeping him on. That winter, as during the previous ones, Shepard and his wife kept their flat warm by using both an electric and a paraffin heater. Multiple sweaters were necessary on top of this. The days in London were slushy and frosty, with plenty of the fog the city is famous for. Money was tighter than ever; in fact, Shepard sold a play, *Blue Bitch*, to BBC Television to stay afloat another month or so.

Finished during the first half of 1973, *Blue Bitch* features a couple from Wyoming named Cody and Dixie who, like Shepard and his wife, are living in England. Cody has put an ad in *Sporting Life*, seeking to sell one of his greyhounds, and the results are odd and occasionally humorous. There are obvious autobiographical details in *Blue Bitch*, not the least being a need for extra heaters, as well as Shepard's love of greyhounds. Overall, the play feels like an extended gag. Perhaps Shepard was watching *Monty Python* while he was in the United Kingdom.

Blue Bitch aired on the BBC in July and was shortly thereafter performed at Theatre Genesis back in New York. It remains unpublished. Despite the bit of money the short play brought in, it did not alleviate Shepard's thoughts about moving back to the States.

No matter how dreary he was beginning to find London, Shepard must have been heartened by the publication of his first book of prose and poetry. *Hawk Moon: Short Stories, Poems, Monologues* was published by Black Sparrow Press in 1973. Its contents date to at least 1971, based on Shepard's archived notebooks, and it is dedicated to Smith ("For Patti Lee"), who first encouraged Shepard to branch out into other forms of writing. If the ninety-three-page book failed to rank Shepard with the greats of American letters, it at least planted a stake in the ground indicating that this was territory he was planning to return to and that his inventiveness and gift with language could transcend the stage.

Hawk Moon is rife with descriptions of both people and places, as Shepard creates both compelling characters and sharply realized scenes. He portrays the more rugged aspects of life, serving up visions of small-town America that would have scared the life out of Norman Rockwell, as well as desert scenes where mayhem seems to be just around the next corner.

Throughout *Hawk Moon*, Shepard mixes ersatz western scenes with magical realism and Beat poetry to create something closer to a literary collage than a sustained statement of any kind. That being said, there are many pleasures to be found in these pages. "Montana" tells the story of a man who covers the body of a naked woman on a motel bed in hundred-dollar bills before going down to the bar for a drink, where he gets a tip on how to cremate a corpse. He then returns to his room, brushes aside the money, and puts the woman's body in the tub, where he pours gasoline on the corpse and ignites it. Then there's the burned-out rocker of "Wipe Out," who wakes up on the floor of the recording studio and rolls over to have intercourse of a sort with his Les Paul guitar. "The harder he pumped the more she screamed," Shepard writes. The territory where *Hawk Moon* unfolds was already familiar to Shepard fans: a place marked by deserts, cheap motels, tar shacks, and the netherworlds of his darkest imaginings. Throughout, his power of description rarely fails him. It is gritty and poetic at the same time, and the result is a book full of humor, dread, and mystery.

At the same time, *Hawk Moon* has the shortcomings found in the early efforts of many writers. The vignettes are static, with little plotting and hardly anything akin to character development. Meanwhile, at times Shepard tries too hard to shock, sometimes relying on these jolts as opposed to crafting suitable endings for his narratives—for instance the prostitute who ends up with a stick shift in her vagina, and a gun that ends up in a similar place during a bizarre game of Russian roulette. As he would later admit, his poetry was not very good, often comprised of rambling paragraphs sans punctuation, disconnected images, or mere lists of things he liked. All this aside, *Hawk Moon* was an interesting start to a side career that would eventually blossom into something substantial.

While Shepard was continuing to eke out a living in London, back in the United States *The Tooth of Crime* was receiving its U.S. premiere. It took place in November 1972 at Princeton University's McCarter Theater, with Frank Langella in the role of Hoss. It earned mixed reviews—from "brilliant" to criticisms such as, "[Langella] has no idea what to do with the rock songs Shepard has given him." Shepard knew the play deserved better and began corresponding with Richard Schechner about bringing *Tooth* to New York. Schechner's avant-garde The Performance Group staged the play the following year at its Performance Garage on Wooster Street in the city, with Spalding Gray in the role of Hoss.

Part of Schechner's modus operandi was to "open the space between performance and theater," and he did this with *The Tooth of Crime* from the start, beginning with the design of the set. A large central construction was employed as the stage, which made it impossible for an audience member to see everything going on from a single vantage point. The meant the audience had to move with the actors to fully see the play. This division of the space into "spatial-emotional areas," Schechner wrote, "strongly contributed to opening the performance-theater seam." The director also made changes to the cast of characters, from seven males and one female to four males and two females, which necessitated the combining of four roles into two. Hoss's theme song ("So here's another illusion to add to your confusion/Of the way things are"), meant as a kickoff to the play's action, was split between other characters, who sang parts of the tune at various times in the play. The character Crow appears not at the start of Act 2 but at the end of Act 1, and the rock band Shepard wrote into the play was not used; instead the characters made their own music.

These changes and the set design reflect Schechner's emphasis—not on character or the "demands" of the drama but rather on "patterns of movement, arrangements of bodies, 'iconography,' sonics and the flow of the audience throughout the environment." Shepard did not see the final production (a filmed version can be found in the digital video library of the Hemispheric Institute's website), and he caught only a single rehearsal when The Performance Group was readying the production in Vancouver. He didn't interfere, but he wrote Schechner to let his feelings be known, after hearing from friends and reading reviews. The playwright claimed the production was "far from what I had in mind." Shepard believed that if directors were drawn to his vision, they "should respect the form that vision takes place in and not merely extrapolate its language and invent another form which isn't the play. It may be interesting theater, but it's not the play and can never be the play."

Schechner proudly stands by his production of *Tooth* and has used it as a model in his writing and teaching. His version of the play had its share of fans as well. Garry Hynes, director of the Druid Theatre and its coproductions with Lincoln Center Festival, DruidShakespeare, saw The Performance Group's version of *The Tooth of Crime* and not only raved about it but was inspired. "It was so extraordinarily different from any sort of experience I'd had until then," he said.

Schechner's production of *The Tooth of Crime* would not be the last time Shepard was to openly do battle with a director or producer. The next time would be more vitriolic and very public.

Shepard's time in London was winding down, though he remained as busy as ever. Perhaps it was the pressure of producing new work and making money that led him to write *Geography of a Horse Dreamer*, his two-act play about a man named Cody who successfully dreams the next day's thoroughbred winners, until a couple of greedy gangsters kidnap him in hopes of putting his special gifts to work for their benefit. After being under the gun to produce more winners, the horse dreamer can no longer turn the trick. Eventually he begins dreaming the winners of greyhound races, though not as effectively. The gamblers, fearing Cody's powers will continue to fade, bring in a so-called doctor, who plans to inject Cody to try and make him once again infallible. The denouement arrives when Cody's brothers arrive to save him, with a shoot-'em-up ending seemingly ripped from the pages of an old western. The play premiered at the Royal Court Theatre in February 1974, marking Shepard's directorial debut and featuring a cast that included Stephen Rea as Cody and Bob Hoskins as Beauo.

To make sure audiences didn't miss the parallels Shepard intended between the dreamer being pressured to produce winners and an artist relying on the marketplace for his living, Cody is at times referred to as "Mr. Artistic," while his captors remark how his dreaming is akin to an "art form." Another of Shepard's favorite themes is on display here, though more subtly than usual. Cody evidently needs to be connected to the land in some way to have his winning dreams. Locked in a hotel room, not knowing where the kidnappers have taken him, only exacerbates his dry spell. In much of his work, Shepard holds up land and man's connection to or disconnection from it as central to the characters' fate.

The play's kidnappers speak like gangsters, though not to the degree seen in *The Tooth of Crime*. Shepard says he was "using language from Raymond Chandler, from Dashiell Hammett—from the thirties, which to me is a beautiful kind of language, and very idiomatic of a period in America which was really strong." For example, one of the kidnappers waves his pistol at Cody and says, "Just remember the old iron here. She gets very ticklish in a nervous situation." The rhythm and lingo come directly from the alleys and backrooms of 1920s Chicago. For good measure, or perhaps to please his young son, Shepard name-checks the family dog, Banjo, near the end of the first act.

Shepard's decision to direct *Geography* was born out of dissatisfaction to this point with the ways in which his plays had been realized onstage. He claimed at the time that only five out of the hundreds of productions of his plays that he'd seen actually worked. Shepard would ultimately say that directing "opened up lots of new doors" for him, but he wasn't afraid to admit to being terrified at first. Before diving in, he conferred with the two directors he had the highest regard for, Peter Brook and Joseph Chaikin. One thing that came through that would always guide Shepard's direction was the idea of "the actor being the actor first and the character second. It's not about dissolving into the character, which we do in movies, where it's no longer Clint Eastwood, it's the Pale Rider. In theater, the most interesting thing is to sustain the actor, not get rid of him. Keep the actor moving in and out of character. This is one of the most interesting things in theater.

. . . Because it's so true to the performance aspect of theater, and we can't get away from that." This is a very Brechtian idea, and it fit well with the Gurdjieff notion of every individual containing multiple "I"s.

Whatever advice Brook and Chaikin provided, Shepard's manner of directing perhaps most resembled that of Ralph Cook, who'd helmed the playwright's earliest work back in his Theatre Genesis days. In other words, Shepard was a hands-off director, allowing actors to find the truth of their characters, drawing not only from the script but from aspects of their own lives and personalities. "When I first worked with [Sam] some years ago I used to ask him to give me a clue: 'What is this all about?' And he would just look at me, straight in the face, and say, 'That's for you to understand, mate. This is our secret,'" remembered Bob Hoskins from his time starring in *Geography of a Horse Dreamer*. "He gave you just enough to relate to the audience with truth and intimacy." For his part, Rea said Shepard the director was "very good at letting people do what they could do . . . it felt like a very easy experience," with everybody "in tune with everybody else." Things came together quickly in rehearsal, which left time for playing poker and going to the dog track. The cast actually spent very little rehearsal time on the stage. But there was a method to this seeming madness, Hoskins said. "Sam said: 'Practicing saying words is nothing. Look here. Here is the feeling. You can touch it. You can know it. This is really better than rehearsing with words.'" To give his actors some insights into their characters, Shepard often brought in records from his own collection. "For my character it was Hank Williams," Rea said.

Shepard liked working at the Court Theatre, finding the actors "very willing to explore, much more so than American actors, who are paranoid about their technique." The actors in London were less concerned with the style of Method acting, and to Shepard they were well-rounded, able to act, sing, dance, and even tackle Brecht and Beckett with seeming ease. Directing these actors made Shepard an even better playwright, forcing him to see his work from the inside out. The visceral experience of standing onstage with actors and seeing what they needed, watching how they moved, and understanding the limitations and possibilities of the stage would be inculcated into his future work. "It was a great experience, which changed the way I approached writing, because I started writing for the actors. I'd shape things and move them around and realize what was possible or not possible. You understand the rhythmic structures much better when you work directly with actors. It's like a piece of music, it shifts and changes."

Geography of a Horse Dreamer ran for three weeks at the Royal Court but soon after had its American premiere at Yale, where it received good reviews.

Shortly after *Geography*'s run, *Little Ocean* opened at the Hempstead Theater, very close to where Shepard and his wife were living. O-Lan was featured in the production, which ran as a late-night show. The play stars three women in a handful of sketches containing "a haunting series of poetic images" concerning the women's attitudes toward pregnancy and childbirth. Actress Dinah Stabb recalled that Shepard wrote the play for her, O-Lan, and Stephen Rea's girlfriend, Caroline Hutchinson. Stabb was seven months pregnant, and Shepard's wife had been through childbirth just a few years earlier and was dealing with being a young mother. "One day [Shepard] said, 'I'll write something for you,'" Stabb recalled. "So we all held our breath, crossed our fingers, and waited. It was extraordinary: it was written by a man, but it didn't feel like that." *Little Ocean* received at least one rave review, but the play remains unpublished.

Meanwhile back in the States, *Blue Bitch* made its debut and would be the last Shepard play produced at Theatre Genesis. It was directed by Murray Mednick and featured none other than Patti Smith. The theater where Shepard's work had made its debut more than a decade earlier would continue on for several seasons and continue to feature important work by Michael McClure, Michael Smith, and Megan Terry.

As the summer of 1974 approached, Shepard was growing homesick for the American West. Looking back, Rea said he understood his new friend's desire to head home. "He's an American," he said. "He had to be close to his source." Shepard had spent three years in London, written his greatest play to date in *The Tooth of Crime*, and forged connections that would impact his work for decades to come. The benefits went both ways. One critic said Shepard's tenure overseas had had "a revivifying influence on the English fringe." He'd gotten more into the Work and met Peter Brook, directed his first play, and—thanks to the enduring influence of

Patti Smith—buried himself in books, studying the plays of the ancient Greeks, Shakespeare, Marlowe, and many others. The impact of all this was that Shepard began to see himself as part of a vital tradition and realized he had the opportunity to be more than just a young man with a nifty turn of phrase and a boundless imagination. He was thirty years old and knew there could be greater things ahead. "I'd been writing for ten years in an experimental maze—poking around, fishing in the dark. I wasn't going anywhere," he said. "I felt I needed an aim in the work versus just the instinctive stuff."

Before returning to the States, the family stopped by its summer cottage in Nova Scotia. There, in August, Shepard opened up a brown notebook and began working on a play called *The Last American Gas Station*. As is to be expected with first drafts, it wasn't very good—there were too many sections where nothing of import happened, too many characters and loads of exposition. The half-written play would pass unremarked upon except for the fact that it contains the seeds of *Buried Child*. (An actual first draft of a play by that name is dated December 19, 1977, more than three years in the future.) *The Last American Gas Station* features a married couple named Dodge and Halie and a son named Eamon who is missing a leg. Dodge is emasculated by life and the federal government, whom he claims is taking his land; he has the same cough as the father in *Buried Child*. The eighty-five handwritten pages show that Shepard was starting to turn away from what had always worked for him before. Back in the American West, he would find the key to combining his ability to create fractured and disorienting worlds with the thing he knew best but had managed to avoid for so long—his own family. In effect, he was going home in more ways than one.

Mill Valley Days

I do miss those amazing days where we'd get stoned and just
wander around through shopping markets or ride bikes or just stare
at life and go on mental journeys. There was something so great
about that time but I guess it's gone. Hard to believe things just pass
like that but I guess you just go on to the next saga.

—Sam Shepard

I n a letter dated January 25, 1973, written more than a year before
moving home from London, Shepard shares with his father-in-law
and friend Johnny Dark back in California his feelings of homesickness. He longs to go cruising together in his friend's white Chevy Nova,
pretending to be detectives and spinning the kind of philosophical musings
(also known as bullshit) common to old friends. Then Shepard imagines the
"Darks and Sheps" sharing a home, a ranch in fact. Visions of domesticity
mixed with farm life fill the rest of the letter.

Eventually, this all came to pass. Shepard and his family left London
for good in the summer of 1974. They would live with his in-laws in three
different places in Mill Valley, California, over the course of the next nine
years. The Marin County city was surrounded by Mount Tamalpais on
one side and Richardson Bay on the other. When Shepard arrived, it was a

tight-knit community where the arts thrived. "Back then, Mill Valley was a small artistic town that actually had working-class people, two hardware stores, a 76 gas station. Lots of blue-collar types," recalled actor Peter Coyote, who lived there for decades. "It's now like a little Beverly Hills."

The city was home to art galleries, open-air coffee shops, musicians, art festivals, and more. Jack Kerouac had shared a cabin in town with poet Gary Snyder in the mid-1950s. At first, Shepard, O-Lan, and son Jesse moved in with O-Lan's mother Scarlett, stepfather Johnny Dark, and sister, Kristy. Money was tight in the household even before the Shepard clan arrived, and things didn't improve with the addition of the penurious playwright and his family. Throughout the rest of the decade, Shepard would struggle to make ends meet with meager royalty payments. Even when the film work began to arrive around the middle of the decade, it was barely enough. Yet the two families would scrape together enough by the fall of 1975 to lease a twenty-acre ranch at 420 Bayview Drive. Shepard named it the Flying Y Ranch. The property overlooked San Francisco Bay in the distance and the tall redwoods of the Golden Gate Recreational Area. It was the realization of what Shepard had imagined and written to Dark about during that cold London winter of the previous year, yet now that it had arrived, he felt the weight of responsibility. "I'm filled with a mixture of the past and all this new life happening to me now," he mused. The Flying Y was a fixer-upper, and Shepard and Dark installed wood-burning stoves and repaired the roof and fences. At one point, Shepard planned to expand the house and update his agreement with the landlord to a longer lease or possibly a lease-to-own deal.

Shepard had already earned a reputation as "the cowboy playwright," and now, with his own ranch, he was living up to it. He had a few Appaloosas and began in earnest what would become a lifelong pursuit of buying, selling, breeding, and riding horses. He and Dark would take turns feeding the animals (including one named Vallejo, after the great Peruvian poet). Shepard must have felt like he was reliving his high school years, specifically those summer days when he worked at Santa Anita Park.

As for the rest of the time in Mill Valley, Shepard sums it up thusly: "Cycles, weed, convoluted conversations." He and Dark went for long walks, rode motorcycles, talked about books and writers, and even tried to collaborate on a play called *Two Prospectors*. Typical of their friendship, the pair invented a club that only they belonged to called the Garcia Y Vega Club, which gave them license to spend even more time away from the women of the house, smoking cigars and generally goofing off. Shepard had been drug-free since leaving New York in 1971, but he and Dark began getting high together, which only added to the screwball fun the two engaged in. They played cops and robbers in the streets of nearby San Rafael or just hung out and discussed the most off-the-wall things. Years later, after Shepard had moved on to a new life with actress Jessica Lange, he often wrote to Dark, reminiscing about these carefree days.

Around this time, Shepard and his father-in-law had an experience they'd speak of often. It's worth sharing here, as it speaks to the friendship between the two men and the ways they spent their time together while living under the same roof in Mill Valley. The story goes that a mutual friend, Dennis Crews, brought back some mescal from Oaxaca, Mexico. Shepard and Dark drank from the brown bottle all day, finally becoming so impaired that they were having auditory hallucinations, or at least believed they were. Eventually, after watching a Brian De Palma film, they began to discuss who was the greatest writer in America. Deciding it was Charles Portis—best known as the author of *True Grit*—Shepard and Dark began frantically calling every bookstore and library in the area to see if they had a copy of the Portis novel *Dog of the South*. When they tracked down a copy at the nearby San Rafael Public Library, they jumped in Dark's white Nova and raced, still stoned, down Highway 101 to try and make it before the library closed its doors. "I remembered the stunned look on the librarian's face as we stood outside bashing on the glass doors demanding entry—we were out of our minds," Shepard recalled. The librarian let them in and the two madmen checked out the book, neither ever reading more than five pages of it. As Shepard remembered: "Those were indeed rare and cherished days full of a wild sense of being alive but not having a clue why or what or how." Such was Shepard's life in Mill Valley, broke for the most part, but simple enough. The lackadaisical lifestyle luckily left him time to write.

Time spent with Dark and the picaresque stories the older man told wound up being filtered by Shepard into his writing. "Thin Skin," a story in his 1996 prose collection *Cruising Paradise*, is based on the pair's time together, and in Shepard's 1993 play *Simpatico*, the character of Vinnie, who pretends to be a detective to impress strange women, is based on Dark.

The lease for the Flying Y ran out in the fall of 1977, and the two families moved together once again that December. This time it was down the mountain to 33 Evergreen Avenue and a white Spanish-style bungalow built in 1935 on a quiet, residential street in Mill Valley. The house was small, with no basement and with a second floor where the bedrooms were located. The place, from its neat and orderly interior to its unkempt backyard, reminded Shepard's then-publisher Michael Roloff of "a set for *Buried Child*." There was a noisy parakeet and several dogs. Fortunately, across the highway there was a strip comprised of restaurants, and closer to the downtown area were some better eateries, as little to no cooking was done at the Shepard–Dark household.

Roloff, who visited in May of 1979, noticed how good Shepard was with his son. "It was darling to see how they got along," he said. "Mystically—as it should be between a father and a son." As for marriage, Roloff noticed the playwright was less devoted. O-Lan was in Los Angeles at the time of his visit, working on a project of her own, and Shepard said that "works for me." The impression was that the couple was, by this time, living two separate lives and pursuing their own careers.

Shepard's own career was not waiting for him in America where he had left off before heading to London in the summer of 1971. It took him a while to hit his stride again. Respected though he was, American theater hadn't been biding its time readying to welcome him back with open arms. Yet he continued to write like a man possessed. He had many irons in the fire as soon as he settled back in California, including a just-completed screenplay and new poems and plays. He reported to Chaikin that his moods swung from feeling "alive" to "some kind of self-pitying despair." Yet there was also the sense of "starting a 'new' life" in California and being absorbed by the Work.

Shepard's new plays did eventually find willing producers both back in London and in New York City. Early in 1974 he'd written *Action*, about four young people stuck in an apartment, apparently after some catastrophe in the outside world. The playwright was high on it—"It's very special to me," Shepard wrote to Chaikin that February. Scholars like Stephen J. Bottoms have noted that *Action* is the closest to date that Shepard came to replicating the effects he so admired in the work of Beckett. Shepard honed the play carefully, to create a world replete with four lost souls slowly coming to grips with the fact that there is nothing left for them to cling to. *Action* was directed in London by Nancy Meckler, who was becoming an old hand at putting Shepard's work onstage. It premiered at the Royal Court Theatre Upstairs in October.

Action is an odd name for a play that is so consumed with stasis. Its meaning was also difficult to pin down. "Sam . . . helpfully talked about where it was coming from—basically a fear of time passing. This was hugely helpful," Meckler said. The play takes place in a room split precisely in half—dark upstage but for the lights of a small Christmas tree; pale yellow and white lighting downstage. A table downstage is set for dinner, with a chair on each of the four sides. Overhead, running left to right, is a clothesline attached to pulleys at each end. At curtain, two men, Shooter and Jeep, and two women, Liza and Lupe, all early twenties to early thirties, are sitting at the table drinking coffee. Jeep opens the play with a line typical of the play's dialogue, delivered as he rocks back and forth in his chair: "I'm looking forward to my life. I'm looking forward to uh—me. The way I picture me." Moments later, Shooter pulls a book from his lap, and throughout the play, each character tries in vain to find the place where they'd left off reading the time before—a hint from the playwright that their lives are unconnected to any sense of time, hence their sense of lostness. Lupe serves a turkey dinner, and everyone eats but Shooter, who says he's "too scared to eat," though he doesn't show the corresponding actions one would expect. None of the characters do. They speak and act without ever really connecting with their words, actions, or each other. If they are fighting an extreme case of shared existential dread, this disconnection saves them from ever dealing with their reality.

It is the mix of dread and levity that keeps the play moving. As in most of his work, Shepard's humor works in a subtle way. He doesn't write jokes like Neil Simon. His humor is born of the strangeness or absurdity of the situation onstage, similar to Pinter. Characters underreact or react ironically, state the blatantly obvious, or spout non sequiturs so abstruse that they compel the audience to laugh in surprise at their foolishness or the general folly of mankind. At one point, Shooter plops down in a living room chair and keeps announcing that he will never get up again. Each time he says this it is apropos of nothing else going on around him. Finally, he says, "I could conduct all my business from here. I'll need a bedpan and some magazines," and the absurdity of this notion brings the biggest laugh yet.

If there is more to *Action* than the creation of a tense and troubling atmosphere, it's hard to find, though it is successful in doing this. Those familiar with Gurdjieff and the Work will notice Shepard slips in several references to sleepwalking, being hypnotized, and people seeing other sides of themselves, all key themes in the Russian mystic's teachings. After hypnotically pouring water over his hand for several minutes, Jeep says, "I can't figure out what I've been doing here all this time." None of the characters can, leaving one to wonder if the zombie-like behavior on display is derived from the Work and is expressing Shepard's belief that modern man is indeed asleep in his daily life.

To help the members of her cast explore the play, Meckler had them improvise several situations where they had to survive by remaining positive amid frightening circumstances. "The improvs eventually took the four actors into a space where they felt so terrified and disoriented that they overreacted to things and no longer knew who they were or where they were," she said. "The comedy comes from them living in terror but trying to ride it out, survive, keep going, normalize."

Action was a hit in London and soon after moved to the Mickery Theatre in Amsterdam. It had its American premiere in New York at the American Place Theatre in April 1975 and eventually landed at San Francisco's Magic Theatre, where Shepard himself directed it. To this day, Shepard remains fond of *Action*, citing it as one of the plays he's most proud of. On his writing desk he still keeps a photo of his friend Stephen Rea in the role of Jeep.

To accompany the play's early performances, Shepard wrote a ten-minute solo piece called *Killer's Head*. It's a strange but very affecting play. When the lights come up, the audience faces a man tied and blindfolded in an electric chair. He speaks not of regrets or final wishes but in a "clipped, southwestern rodeo accent" talks about his horses and the new truck he's going to buy. He stops speaking after a while and sits quietly for a full minute before resuming. Again, he talks of the truck and how well it will pull his horse trailer around California. He stops suddenly and stays silent as the lights begin to dim. When the stage is black, an electrical charge lights up his entire body.

Reading this short play, one finds humor in the incongruity of the man's situation and his soliloquy. However, in person, Meckler, who directed its first productions, said *Killer's Head* is anything but funny. "It is so upsetting to see someone blindfolded in an electric chair," she told me.

Notably, the short play's U.S. premiere starred a young struggling actor named Richard Gere as the killer, Mazon. The actor recalled *Killer's Head* as "bizarre" but also claimed the role spoke to him. "It was the first part in which I felt I really connected," he said. "As a prisoner strapped to an electric chair and blindfolded, I couldn't move my body, and so it had to be a total manifestation of energy. No narcissism, no wondering how I looked."

Critics noted Gere's performance, and Wynn Handman, then director of the American Place Theatre, agreed that his acolyte triumphed in the role. After *Killer's Head* and *Action* closed, job offers for Gere increased, and shortly thereafter he was cast in his first film, *Report to the Commissioner.*

Shepard had been back in California for several months and, ready to settle down artistically, was looking for a theater to serve as a home base. He'd had little difficulty finding homes for his work before moving to London, and he wanted to know this would continue to be the case, even if he was now three thousand miles away from the stages in Greenwich Village he'd first conquered. Plus, he needed money and was sick of relying on grants and foundations to make ends meet.

The Magic Theatre was founded in San Francisco in 1967 by John Lion, a graduate student at the University of California–Berkeley. He and his mentor, Professor Jan Kott, were looking for a space to stage Ionesco's *The Lesson* and settled on the Steppenwolf Bar in Berkeley. It was a tiny space with hard bleacher seats with no backs, but in 1977 the theater moved into larger digs at Fort Mason Center in San Francisco, where it remains today. The first major playwright to put down stakes at the Magic was Michael McClure, who, beginning in 1969, enjoyed an eleven-year relationship with the theater. In 1971 the Magic staged the West Coast premiere of

Shepard's *La Turista*. Four years later, once Shepard had settled back in California, McClure introduced him to Lion, who invited Shepard to be the playwright-in-residence and to direct his own work at the Magic.

Shepard loved the local scene: it reminded him of his early days back in New York, but with "an even more positive sense of community." The Bay Area actors were talented and unafraid to take chances, and in the coming years his new theatrical home would greatly inspire him: "I started to catch fire and write my ass off," he said. In the spring of 1975 he directed the double bill of *Action* and *Killer's Head*, beginning a relationship with the Magic Theatre that would see him create his best work for the stage. For a time in 1978, Shepard at least occasionally even used the theater as a mailing address.

By the fall of 1975, Shepard was ready to chase bigger game and had begun to consider what would become his great subject—the American family. The first of the so-called family plays, *Curse of the Starving Class*, would not premiere until April of 1977, but while on tour with Bob Dylan as part of the extended entourage with the so-called Rolling Thunder Revue, he took time out to commit to one of his ubiquitous notebooks a rough outline of the play. There's also evidence that he was pondering a different title for the three-act drama, *Poison Lamb*. From the start, it seems the play's famous ending, featuring the image of an eagle carrying off a screaming cat, was already in place. So too were its theme about the destructive aspects of progress and the explosive denouement. Shepard by this time was ready to turn to his own past for material. It was clear that after years of avoiding the subject of his father and all the accompanying baggage, Shepard was about to live up to his credo: "Theater is a place to bring stuff from your life experience. You bring it and you send this telegraph and then you get out."

Dylan

I don't know him because I don't think there is any him. I don't think he has a self!

—Allen Ginsberg

Rolling Thunder is searching for something too. Trying to make connections. To find some kind of landmarks along the way. It's not just another concert tour but more like a pilgrimage. We're looking for ourselves in everything.

—Sam Shepard

One day in October 1975, Shepard came in from cruising around with his father-in-law Johnny Dark in his Chevy Nova to find a phone message. It said simply, "Dylan called." Dylan? Shepard and Dark had just been talking about the singer as they rolled through downtown San Anselmo. The friends, driving back from a hardware store with roofing supplies to do some patching up at the farm they'd just leased, had in fact been talking about Dylan as a has-been. "It's a long way back to the mid-sixties and dancing naked to 'How does it feel?' in the bedroom of an older woman," Shepard had just been thinking. Now the man himself was calling.

Thus began Shepard's involvement with Dylan's Rolling Thunder Revue, a concert tour-cum-caravan that wandered the East Coast and into Canada from late October to early December 1975, forgoing stadiums in favor of midsized venues. A second leg set out the following spring.

Dylan was all the rage around Greenwich Village when Shepard arrived from California in 1963. It was, in fact, the singer's home base. Dylan lived at the time on West Fourth Street, and the photo adorning the cover of his album *The Freewheelin' Bob Dylan* was shot nearby. Songs like "Blowin' in the Wind" and "A Hard Rain's a-Gonna Fall" were written in Village nightspots. All this to say that as a new arrival in Greenwich Village in the fall of 1963, Shepard no doubt felt the presence of the songwriter everywhere. Though Dylan was primarily writing protest songs at this point, having not yet moved into the more symbolist lyrics of his later work, his songs were still full of striking images and wordplay. There was also a sense of spontaneity about them, and quite often a lack of concrete meaning. No doubt, Shepard picked up on these things and they influenced his own writing. If Beckett freed him from traditional ideas about form, and jazz gave him inspired ideas about rhythm, Dylan's daring verbal dexterity and allusive imagery also helped shape Shepard's writing.

The playwright was no less impressed with Dylan the man. Shepard learned the importance of cultivating a sense of mystique and a fierce suspicion of the media in part from watching Dylan. Shepard wrote that Dylan needed "protection from intellectual probes, which are a constant threat to any artist." Words Crow speaks in *The Tooth of Crime*—"I believe in my mask/The man I made up is me"—could have been Dylan's credo, just as it became Shepard's. What critic Jon Landau wrote of Dylan in 1963, "He was better at playing the rebel than the citizen, the outsider than the insider and the outlaw than the sheriff," could likewise apply to Shepard.

His fascination with the songwriter and the love of his music would last into his later years. In a scene in the 2012 documentary *Shepard & Dark*, Shepard walks out of a hotel singing to himself "Buckets of Rain," a track from Dylan's 1975 album *Blood on the Tracks*. In the parking lot, Shepard turns to a friend and, after marveling at Dylan's lyric, smiles and says, "He's OK for a little guy."

The call from Dylan on that day in 1975 was a summons: He needed someone to script scenes for a film to be shot as the Rolling Thunder Revue made its way around the Northeast. The songwriter had heard about Shepard from Jacques Levy, who'd directed Shepard's *Red Cross* nearly a decade earlier and who had been brought in to give the revue some shape, to "make it appear like it was a spontaneous evening . . . like a traveling vaudeville show or a traveling circus." Claudia Carr Levy said her late husband didn't want to be involved with the movie; "That's why he brought Sam in." Patti Smith may have also mentioned Shepard, as she and Dylan had previously hung out at CBGB when she was just starting to perform with a band. When one considers what Dylan's ideas about the film revolved around—"the duality between illusion and reality, and about a search for our real selves under the varying masks of appearances"—it's no wonder he called on Shepard. Much of the playwright's work focused on these very ideas.

Despite his reservations, Shepard soon left by train for New York, where Dylan and his musical entourage were holding final rehearsals in preparation for the tour. Arriving in the city, Shepard recognized some old friends, or at least people he'd known from his former life in New York, among them Levy, Allen Ginsberg, and Bobby Neuwirth, who had put the band together. When Shepard finally met Dylan, the singer began discussing the screenplay Shepard was to pen: "We don't have to make any connections," he said. "None of this has to connect. In fact, it's better if it doesn't connect." If this was some sort of job interview, it was a strange one. It got even stranger: The only question Dylan asked was if Shepard had seen the films *Children of Paradise* and *Shoot the Piano Player*. These were evidently the touchstones Dylan had in mind for his epic in the making. Elsewhere the singer went into more detail. "My lawyer used to tell me there was a future in movies," Dylan said. "So I said, 'What kind of future?' He said, 'Well, if you can come up with a script, and outline and get money from a big distributor.' But I knew I couldn't work that way. I can't betray my vision on a little piece of paper in hopes of getting some money from somebody. In the final analysis, it turned out that I had to make the movie all by myself, with people who would work with me, who trusted me. I went on the road . . . to make money for this movie."

The revue was loaded with talent: Joan Baez, Ramblin' Jack Elliott, Roger McGuinn, Ronee Blakely, Mick Ronson, and a host of top session players. Also making cameos were Phil Ochs and Joni Mitchell. Shepard would make connections on the tour that would prove important years later. He met T Bone Burnett and cemented his friendship with Rudy Wurlitzer. The former would become a collaborator; the latter a connection that would help turn Shepard into a film star.

The entourage and musicians filled two buses—Shepard rode on an old Delmonico with Ginsberg, Levy, and various guests of the tour. At each stop there was the usual hotel and backstage shenanigans. Mitchell would later memorialize it in song, referencing the "pills and powders" and "temporary lovers." Shepard writes of Valiums being delivered to the tour hotel, while Mitchell would later recall how "everybody was strung out on cocaine."

Shepard was dazzled seeing Dylan up close on stage and off. He fell for and fed into the artist's singular mystique. "Dylan has invented himself. He's made himself up from scratch," he'd later write. "Dylan is an invention of his own mind. The point isn't to figure him out but to take him in." Offstage, the enigma became exposed quickly as being all too human, and Shepard became disillusioned early on. Before the tour departed Plymouth, Massachusetts, where it opened, he realized the musicians were not going to be memorizing lines from any script he'd be writing and that the film would be improvised. This didn't stop Shepard from trying to fulfill his role. He spent at least the earliest part of the tour in the van with the film crew, busily scribbling pages, a bit lost as to what was going on.

In addition to his role being ill defined or nonexistent, there was the money situation, which only a handful of stops into the tour had Shepard ready to quit and go home. "I'm pissed off, I've been lied to," he snarled during a stopover in Stockbridge, Massachusetts. "They made some assurances to me in terms of money that they didn't follow through on. There's like this reverse Dylan generosity syndrome here," Shepard said. "They say that because Bob is so generous and this tour is making a sort of antimoney, antiestablishment position in terms of money and large halls therefore they can rip you off and it's all right 'cause it's an antimaterialist thing." Claudia Carr Levy, who was on part of the tour with her husband, Jacques, sensed the problem. "Ultimately I think it was a clash of egos," she said. "Sam once said to me that he was losing his mind."

Shepard stuck it out. The tour wound around New England, and by Thanksgiving homesickness came close to sending him back west. He stayed on and made himself useful as the filming of the movie shambled on. He wrote a bit, including a scene involving a turkey bone, and played a mechanic in another scene. As anyone who has seen the resulting film, *Renaldo and Clara*, can attest, things did not go smoothly. At one point, Shepard lost his wits and tried to explain to the filmmaking crew that making movies isn't as easy as writing a song, that a little planning and scripting go a long way. They answered that Dylan was a genius and disregarded the playwright's wisdom. A few years later, in an interview with the *Times* about the finished film, Dylan said most of Shepard's dialogue was not used due to a "conflict in ideas."

As for the temporary lovers Mitchell sang about, for Shepard there appear to have been two during his Rolling Thunder days. In her 2009 autobiography, hanger-on Chris O'Dell claims she and Shepard would meet in the post-concert hospitality suite and "spend the rest of the evening together." Things got a bit complicated in November when Mitchell joined the tour. O'Dell recalls how she'd failed to connect with Shepard one night, only to subsequently overhear someone say that he and Mitchell had been together. A few days later on the bus, Bob Neuwirth remarked to O'Dell, "You know Sam's having it on with Joni." All this could be chalked up to gossip or ancient history but for the fact that the supposed fling between Shepard and Mitchell resulted in one of her finest songs, "Coyote." From the "No regrets" Mitchell repeatedly sings, to the lyrics about a woman "up all night in the studio" and a man "up early on your ranch," the latter with "a woman at home and one down the hall," the tune would seem to be a pseudo-record of her fling with Shepard. Mitchell wrote the song on November 25, 1975, and performed it the next night as part of the revue in Augusta, Maine. "Coyote" became the opening track of her 1976 album *Hejira*.

Shepard left the tour and returned at least once. When all was said and done, he was credited as cowriter and as having a small role in *Renaldo and Clara* when it came out in 1978. Part concert film, part backstage peek, and part surreal trip through the back roads of America, the film was blasted by critics. Its original running time of five hours didn't help matters. Dylan told the *New York Times'* John Rockwell, "My film is truer than reality."

During the tour, Shepard kept a small notebook that had little or nothing to do with the occasional scriptwriting he was doing for Dylan's film. From those reflections and observations he assembled *The Rolling Thunder Logbook*, which chronicles the tour as only Shepard could. Hip, insightful, funny, and sad, the *Logbook* captures the joy and rush of being on a rock 'n' roll tour as well as the unavoidable chaos and tedium. Shepard divides the book by tour stops, occasionally dropping in bits of the unused dialogue he wrote for the film, real-life scenes from hotel rooms, backstage discussions, portraits of the musicians, and musings on Dylan and his music. It's a diary not of Shepard's life while on the road but of the tour and the people who rolled with it from town to town.

The book ends with Dylan and his wife, Sara, attending the U.S. premiere of Shepard's play *Geography of a Horse Dreamer*. Shepard's stomach did backflips as he waited in the lobby of a New York hotel for the singer to arrive for their departure to the Manhattan Theatre Club. "The idea of him sitting in the audience is more like a nightmare than a blessing," Shepard wrote. To avoid riding in the same car, Shepard sneaked past a distracted Dylan in the lobby and grabbed a cab downtown.

It happened to be press night, and Shepard felt the weight of "Judgment Day" upon him. Before curtain, he nervously gulped brandy after brandy. Dylan was late and the theater was holding the curtain for him. When he arrived, he was "plastered" and had in tow, along with Sara, three members of the tour. They took up an entire row, and when the play started the silence was deafening—"cadaver city," is how Shepard would later describe it. In Act 2, when one of the characters takes out a hypodermic needle and prepares to stick another character, Dylan stood up and loudly said, "Wait a minute! Wait a second. Why's he get the shot? He shouldn't get the shot! The other guy should get it! Give it to the other guy!" The singer was momentarily quieted, but when the final shootout began, Dylan leapt to his feet once more and yelled, "I don't have to watch this! I didn't come here to watch his!" Eventually Dylan was convinced to leave, climbing through the seats toward the exit as the critics were "desperately clicking their ball-point pens and scribbling in the dark like crazy."

Claudia Carr Levy was there that night. "Bob was genuinely upset. He really was," she said. "He had a very visceral response to that play."

The Rolling Thunder Logbook was published in 1977 and has gone through several printings. Talking with Shepard a decade later, Dylan admitted, "That tour wiped me out."

It was the mid-1980s before Shepard and Dylan spent any serious time together again. The two would join forces for two disparate projects around this time: a song that unreels like a mysterious western and an article for *Esquire* magazine.

Many fans and critics of Bob Dylan consider the song "Brownsville Girl" a mid-career masterpiece. The 1986 album on which the song appears, *Knocked Out Loaded*, was trashed by critics, save for this eleven-minute epic he cowrote with Shepard. When the album first appeared, listing Shepard as a cowriter on "Brownsville Girl," a critic asked Dylan about the collaboration. He gave a typically cryptic answer: "Well, in the course of life you find yourself with different people in different rooms. Working with Sam was not necessarily easier, but it was certainly less meaningless. In every case writing a song is done faster when you got someone like Sam and you are not on your own."

Shepard's notebooks indicate that he met with Dylan at the singer's Malibu home on October 21, 1984, to begin work on the song. At some point—Shepard dates it to the spring of 1985—he and Dylan spent two more days together working on the track. By that time, Dylan already had the melody for the song.

The singer's first attempt to record "Brownsville Girl" took place at Cherokee Studios in Hollywood between December 6 and December 11 of 1984, during the sessions for his album *Empire Burlesque*. That album took some of its cues from Hollywood movies like *The Maltese Falcon*. "Brownsville Girl" follows suit with its references to the 1950 Gregory Peck film *The Gunfighter*; the opening stanza encapsulates that movie's plot. Elements of *Duel in the Sun* may have also influenced the lyrics.

At this time, the song was known as "New Danville Girl" (perhaps inspired by Woody Guthrie's tune "Danville Girl"). In place already were the song's most memorable lines: "Your memory keeps callin' after me like a rollin' train" and "She said 'Even the swap meets around here are getting pretty corrupt,'" to name just two. The most drastic lyric changes between this version and the final one that appeared on *Knocked Out Loaded* take place after the third chorus, which comprises the final section. Neither the early version nor the final one marks a clear-cut narrative. But the mixing of the film's actions and the narrator's tale is the most intriguing aspect of the song. The tune's central conceit is of a kind with Shepard's writing for the stage, of which fluid identities and dual natures are hallmarks. "It has to do with a guy standing on line and waiting to see an old Gregory Peck movie that he can't quite remember—only pieces of it—and then this whole memory thing happens, unfolding before his very eyes," Shepard said. "He starts speaking internally to a woman . . . reliving the whole journey they'd gone on."

Those present in the studio during the 1984 recording session recall running down the song until Dylan stopped it cold. He'd run out of verses to sing. No matter. He pulled out his pen and a tiny slip of paper and went to the corner of the studio for a few minutes and returned with what he needed. The new verses worked perfectly, recalled Ira Ingber, guitarist on the session. From the outset, the band had a feeling that this song was different from the other few dozen Dylan was recording at this time. "We felt this was an important song because there was a sense that this was a return to form," Ingber said. The band later shared this opinion with Dylan, but for some reason the songwriter decided not to include the track on *Empire Burlesque*. The basic tracks laid down during those sessions would be used more than eighteen months later when Dylan took up the song again.

When Dylan assembled "a shitload of musicians" at Skyline Studios in May of 1986, according to recording engineer Britt Bacon, the singer seemed to lack a clear idea of what kind of record he was hoping to make. *Knocked Out Loaded*, the resulting album, would be slayed by critics for lacking direction, among other things. The band recorded roughly forty songs, including adding to the basic tracks of the Dylan–Shepard composition, now renamed "Brownsville Girl." Why the new name? Ingber asked Dylan, who said, "There're too many Danville songs."

As the sessions neared an end, Bacon cornered Dylan with the list of songs they'd recorded, hoping to narrow it from about forty down to a suitable number for the record. "Brownsville Girl" was on the list. "I asked him where to start," Bacon recalled. "But I knew that was *the* song." Dylan ultimately picked the track to kick off side two of the album. "I love that song," Bacon said. "I could just follow along in my mind. It's like a movie."

There was no producer on *Knocked Out Loaded*, so Bacon and Ingber mixed "Brownsville Girl" and then played it for Dylan. "He said, 'It's too clean. I can hear everything. It sounds like a Lionel Richie record,'" Ingber recalled. The singer evidently wanted to reproduce Phil Spector's Wall of Sound, which is essentially what he got on the final version of the track. "I find it just noisy," Ingber said. "It felt artificial." Any sense of intimacy he and Bacon had created with their mix was gone.

Still, the song was included on Dylan's third greatest hits album and was a favorite with critics and ardent fans. For Shepard's part, he learned a lot from working with Dylan. "I think the most surprising thing is his phrasing," he said. "I'd say, 'But how the hell are you going to fit this into the melody?' He said, 'Don't worry about it. It'll work.' And inevitably it did. The way he squashes phrasing and stretches it out is quite remarkable."

At some point someone thought "Brownsville Girl" not only played like a film but would indeed make a good one. An eight-page treatment from 2010 sits in Shepard's archives, but it was never produced. Meanwhile, Shepard suggested to Dylan that they extend the song and turn it into a ninety-minute opera.

The other thing Shepard learned from working so closely with Dylan was the importance of being true to one's self and always being open to even the wildest ideas. He has this "total disregard for whether or not it's going to fit into an existing idea of what is a good song. He doesn't give a shit," Shepard said.

Shepard hadn't flown in more than two decades, but he made an exception for Dylan in the summer of 1986, when he met the singer in California. *Esquire* magazine wanted Shepard to interview Dylan, imagining a meeting of minds between two accomplished artists. It had all the makings of a great article, maybe even a great event—Dylan and Shepard exchanging ideas, talking shop, looking back over their eventful and singular careers, discussing current events, and maybe chatting about future projects. It was nothing like that. The tapes reveal a petulant Dylan noodling ceaselessly on an acoustic guitar while Shepard tries time and again to break through and engage him.

> SHEPARD: It seems like things are on the verge of something. It's almost happened, but it hasn't quite happened . . .
> DYLAN: Something public?
> SHEPARD: Everything's public.
> DYLAN: Like an earthquake?
> SHEPARD: For the most part, I think the dark side is getting more publicity. And everyone starts thinking that the dark side is winning.
> DYLAN: [No response; continues noodling on acoustic guitar.]

And so it went. Shepard sounds like a little brother trying to get the attention of his older sibling. The insecurity Shepard often confesses to in private is on full display. By this time Shepard had won the Pulitzer and had been nominated for an Oscar, but still Dylan commands the room, distracted as he was. On Shepard's part, the tapes reveal a lot of nervous laughter and jittery prompts, like, "OK, moving right along." But Dylan strums away, giving short answers and only occasionally opening up. At one point, Shepard even floats a little Gurdjieff-speak his way.

> SHEPARD: Like every once in a while I get this thing where everything falls away, you know, and all of a sudden you're just . . . essentially there. You know? And everything's OK. You know what I mean? The trees and the dog and the place. And everything's fine. . . . And then it seems like life makes sense in a kind of a simple way, instead of it being something on the way to the next gig or the next thing you're going to do.
> DYLAN: [Strumming] Yeah, doesn't it.
> SHEPARD: I'm just wondering about like some kind of . . . why you have to dote on other things then? You do it anyway. It seems like the important thing is moving toward this other

thing you're going to do, and in the course of that you pass over the act of living. Just living, moment by moment.

DYLAN: Yeah, if everyone would do that it would be a perfect world. There would be no need for Picasso. There would be no need for Stravinsky. There'd be no need for Houdini.

Once in a while, Dylan does offer something insightful.

SHEPARD: What about home? Do you feel like you have a home?
DYLAN: Well, my real home is on the stage.

Shepard would take bits and pieces of the afternoon's conversation and arrange them into what he called a one-act "playlet." *Esquire* ran the piece in its July 1987 issue under the title "True Dylan." The subhead "A one-act play, as it really happened one California afternoon" stretched the bounds of poetic license. Shepard added the intrusion of mysterious phone calls for Dylan in an attempt to bring some much-needed structure to the piece. Given what he had to work with, Shepard did an admirable job salvaging it.

Being close to Dylan and seeing him work, and even occasionally collaborating with him on the road, forced Shepard to think hard about his own writing. "I once showed him a piece of writing I was working on for a sequence in the film—he read it through, slowly and silently," Shepard wrote. Dylan's right foot tapped, as if trying to find the rhythm of the language. After a moment, the singer stopped reading. "Is your thought clear on this line?" he asked. Shepard took the page. "I stared at the line and questioned it in a way I hadn't when I wrote it. Right then I was faced with the dimension he works in and I couldn't help seeing the space between his world and mine."

Shepard now saw that any writer has "a responsibility toward the whole line. The position of each word. The words themselves. The rhythm, the color, the tone of it. The whole thing had to resonate with intention. There was nothing purely accidental about it."

This may be Dylan's most enduring impact on Shepard. If Peter Brook told him to concentrate more on character, from Dylan he learned about writing with honesty and precision. It wouldn't happen overnight, but Shepard's upcoming plays would bear the imprint of the lesson Dylan imparted. Rewriting and paring away excess would help turn some of Shepard's next plays into major and enduring works. Not long after arriving back home, Shepard seemed to be reminding himself of the incident with Dylan when he wrote in one of his notebooks: "I need more head—I need to bring my head into it more."

Heavenward
(1976)

Acting is "sanctioned vanity."

—Terrence Malick

S hepard tells a story about his father working in a book warehouse a few years after his parents divorced. When Sam Rogers came upon a copy of his son's first collection of plays, "He saw it and he didn't believe it was me: 'This is an imposter,'" Shepard recalled. Such was the distance that had continued to grow between father and son.

Sam Rogers, after years of traveling around Texas, settled in 1975 in Santa Fe, New Mexico. He would live in various apartments and even a trailer home at one point, spending his military retirement checks on rent and alcohol; he rarely worked.

Late that year, already broker than broke, Rogers slipped on some ice and gashed his elbow. The wound became infected, and to avoid blood poisoning, he finally went to the hospital. On January 4, 1976, he wrote a letter to his son asking for money to cover the bill, as well as his back rent.

This wasn't the first time the father had turned to him for help. Shepard sent the money, and on February 24, the father finally sent a thank-you. He began his letter by addressing his son by his old family nickname, but then wrote, "I guess the 'Steve' bit is passé. I'll call you 'Sam' now, how's that?"

The letter provides a portrait of the father's desolation as it recounts in heartbreaking fashion how Rogers had recently taken in a twenty-three-year-old man who had been sleeping in an old Toyota. He invited this "young kid" to sleep on the floor of the motel he was staying at, and for six months they were the best of friends. One day the kid took off. The father wrote to Shepard that he was now "desolate." "This caused a great 'loneliness' in my life which I will never really be able to explain."

The letter ends with the father recalling the recent visit of his daughters, Shepard's sisters, Roxanne and Sandy. The old man imagines them still at the table talking with him, but all that's there now is an empty chair. "When they leave it's sad, an emptiness that a guy suddenly says to himself, I wish they would have never come here because now I'm miserable," he writes. Sam Rogers admits to crying in their absence. Shepard's father ends the letter proclaiming that the only thing he did that "was worth a shit" was raise "three great kids." He closes with a dig at his ex-wife, saying that "damn, selfish Jane will take all the credit for that."

During the next eight years of Sam Rogers's life, Shepard would occasionally visit. However, the gulf between them would never fully close. These visits and the years he spent living under the old man's roof fed the playwright's imagination. The father figure of Shepard's greatest work, often indistinguishable from the real thing, would soon come alive on stages around the world, when Shepard began turning out the plays that would cement his reputation.

The seeds for Shepard's first major film role were sown in 1975, when film producer Bert Schneider met director Terrence Malick. The film that would result from this partnership, *Days of Heaven*, would not hit theaters for nearly three years. Shepard was far from being on anyone's radar as an actor at this point. In fact, the role Shepard would eventually fill, a Texas farmer and landowner, was originally imagined as an older man, since his impending death figures in the plot. At some point, the character was changed to a younger man who receives a fatal diagnosis. Early in the film's planning stages, executive producer Jacob Brackman was having lunch with Rudy Wurlitzer. Wurlitzer was an author and screenwriter whom Shepard first met during his early days in New York. He wrote the screenplay for the 1972 film *Pat Garrett and Billy the Kid*, and through that project, he'd met Bob Dylan, who invited Wurlitzer along for part of the Rolling Thunder Revue, during which he reconnected with Shepard. Wurlitzer saw something in Shepard he felt would translate well to the screen. "Sam has a presence on many different levels," Wurlitzer recalled. During lunch with Brackman, when the role of the former came up he said, "You should see Sam Shepard."

Brackman visited Shepard to discuss the film. "I got off on the wrong foot with Sam," he said. "I would say both of us brought our prejudices into the discussion. . . . I was a suit to Sam so he had a real attitude." Brackman was a Harvard-educated writer who had by this time cowritten the screenplay for the 1972 Jack Nicholson film *The King of Marvin Gardens*. He worked hard at writing and didn't subscribe to the more spontaneous, "intuitive" style Shepard was known for. That's where their differences started.

Eventually, it fell to Malick himself to recruit Shepard. What ensued was a strange form of wooing as the devastatingly shy director began visiting Shepard at his Mill Valley ranch to discuss the role of the farmer. On at least one occasion, Shepard and his friend Johnny Dark took the director out for a stoned ride around Mill Valley; on another, Malick had to wait while Shepard and Dark hustled around in the mud to feed a friend's forty horses. "Terry was very shy, you know, which enamored me to him immediately," Shepard said. "He was almost embarrassed about asking me about the possibility of acting. And I hadn't really considered it. I mean, I was totally devoted to writing at that point. And then he started talking about the script. He didn't even show me the script. . . . Then one day I got a phone call and he said, 'You want to do this movie?' I said, 'Why not?' I rented a Ford Mustang and drove to Alberta, Canada. That was it."

Filming was set to begin in the fall of 1976.

Shepard's archives from around this time contain many unfinished plays, screenplays for films that were never made, and at least one unpublished novel. One of the most remarked upon is a play called *Man Fly*, written in 1974–1975. It's a modern take on Marlowe's famous tragedy *Doctor Faustus*, about a man who sells his soul to the devil to have the devil's servant at his command. Shepard has often cited Marlowe as one of his favorite writers. His version begins promisingly enough, with hip dialogue reminiscent of *The Tooth of Crime*. However, the script verges too often on the cartoonish, despite the fact that Shepard is mostly faithful to Marlowe's version, with a finale that's taken from the original nearly verbatim. There were plans to produce *Man Fly* at La MaMa, with Lee Kissman directing. Ellen Stewart wanted Shepard to make some cuts that he disagreed with, and he withdrew the play. Shepard also submitted the play to Joe Papp at the Public Theater. Papp had two of his people read it and write up their thoughts; neither was impressed. "I don't understand why Shepard wrote this play," one commented. The other reader was "disappointed" by the play and felt it was "too little, too soon, too fast." The Public passed on the work, and it has never been produced.

Kissman read into Shepard's Faust rewrite the playwright's fear that he was selling his soul to Hollywood. The observation echoes concerns Shepard himself had expressed in interviews, that his becoming a movie star might adversely affect his writing. When Shepard agreed to Malick's overtures to star in *Days of Heaven*, it was clearly with mixed feelings. On the one hand he said, "The movies! I can make lots of money and I won't have to ever again apply for a Guggenheim Grant or a Rockefeller Grant or a Ford Grant or a National Endowment Grant or write a play on commission for Joe Papp just to get a crumby five thousand so I can pay the fucking rent to some whacked out landlord." Then came second thoughts: "I remember also the feeling that I was about to enter a whole new world and that world was somewhat scary in its connectedness to the public and the fear of becoming maybe 'famous,' and how I might lose something of myself as a writer and all kinds of confusing psychological frictions—all based on some notion of 'self,' without really realizing that I had no sense of 'self,' that I had absolutely no clue who I really was or what I was trying to accomplish," he said.

The money turned out not to be much of a worry, as Shepard made only $6,000 for his work on *Days of Heaven*. Still, he sensed it might represent a "monumental turning point" in his life. He was right.

Shepard's next play, *Angel City*, premiered in July 1976 at the Magic Theatre under Shepard's direction. Earlier drafts were titled *Terror in the City of Angels* and *City of Angels*, with a subtitle of "A Moving Picture Show." In it, Shepard gets to parse some of his conflicted emotions about the movie business. The play begins as an ersatz companion piece to *Geography of a Horse Dreamer*. Two studio executives bring in a man named Rabbit Brown to save their upcoming movie. They have a plot and stars for this film but know that something is missing. Rabbit is an "artist," who "dream[s] things up." They turn to him to create "something beyond the imagination, something impossible." From here, the play spins off in multiple directions, as Rabbit is held like a prisoner by the film studio along with a drummer and a wannabe actress. Meanwhile, outside, Los Angeles is being swallowed by some atmospheric irregularity that makes people's skin turn green and is slowly killing one of the studio heads. In *Angel City* things are never dull, despite the fact that it's impossible to locate a fully realized idea. Shepard at least feints in the direction of a few of his signature concerns: the instability of personality, western mythology, Native American mysticism, and suspicion of money. *Angel City* also features music, characters that speak in non sequiturs, and a Day-Glo ending. There are Gurdjieff-derived bits as well, such as people in trances, characters who don't know who they are, and talk of mass hypnosis. In directions that precede the published text of *Angel City*, Shepard famously instructs the actors to forgo the idea of a "whole character." Instead, characters should be considered "fractured," "with bits and pieces of character flying off the [play's] central theme." Actors, in other words, should view the characters they're playing as collages or jazz improvisations, Shepard insists. What does this mean? It could clearly reflect his long-held belief in the Brechtian idea that each actor should let aspects of himself shine through his performance. Either this, or it is the ultimate expression of the fluidity of personality. If nothing else, it demonstrates Shepard's continued commitment to the experimental, his refusal to bow to the expected, and his utter fearlessness as an artist.

When *Angel City* moved in April 1977 to L.A.'s Mark Taper Forum, a critic from *Variety* noted: "Only two-thirds of the audience came back after intermission, and when one of the characters said, 'Let's get out of here and go to a movie,' a number of people in the audience shouted back that that was a good idea, starting an exodus of the audience that continued until the final curtain." However, a 1998 production in San Diego garnered an excellent notice in the *Los Angeles Times*.

October of 1977 saw the world premiere of two Shepard plays. The first, *Suicide in B♭*, which opened at Yale Repertory Theater on October 15, begins with a mystery and grows increasingly more mysterious and murky. The play may seem like a whodunit, but Shepard's advice to a director who later took on the play was: "Don't try to solve it, just trust the characters."

In the early stages of writing *Suicide* in his notebook, Shepard indicated that he was after a form of theater possessing the same "emotional impact" as music, with an ultimate goal of producing a "sensation of deep mystery."

The play begins as two detectives arrive on the scene to investigate the murder of Niles, a well-known composer. After some initial bumbling, the detectives are joined by two musicians who'd worked with Niles, and they may or may not have any knowledge pertaining to the murder. While they reveal what they know, Niles and a woman named Paulette appear and act out the words spoken by the other characters. It's a nifty bit of stagecraft, but the play devolves into some truly confounding cases of swapped identities, and the two worlds presented on stage intermingle in strange ways. There's some Gurdjieff-influenced dialogue about the characters having multiple identities and at least one character who claims not to know himself. One of the characters speaks of the need to find "a new dimension" for the music, possibly reflecting Shepard's own push to find the next plateau as a playwright. Like *Angel City*, *Suicide in B♭* is amusing in parts, but overall it's a bit too confusing to be counted as fully successful. It finds Shepard running through his usual themes and theatrical maneuverings as if to cleanse the palate for what lay just up ahead in his greatest work.

Agreeing with such an assessment would no doubt be playwright David Mamet, who came to Yale to meet *Suicide in B♭* director Walt Jones after an evening performance. Directly after the play there was a question-and-answer period featuring the director and the cast, during which someone in the sixth row of the theater spoke up, making his opinions clear. He "kept cutting people off and asking if this wasn't a schizophrenic writer who was writing only to be produced and that all the pieces do not connect," as author Ira Nadel recounts the story. "The aggressive manner of the speaker offended the actors and Jones; this guy seemed to be redirecting their production. When it was over, the figure approached [Jones]; it was Mamet, affable and pleased with his own aggressiveness."

That same month also saw the premiere of a forty-five-minute piece, an operetta to be exact, called *The Sad Lament of Pecos Bill on the Eve of Killing His Wife*, written by Shepard (with music by Shepard and Catherine Stone). It had been commissioned as part of San Francisco's bicentennial project and premiered during the inaugural Bay Area Playwrights Festival. Robert Woodruff had been working at the Eureka Theatre, not far from Shepard's stamping grounds, for three years and had gotten to know him. The director, like Shepard himself, had fled New York City for the other coast. "I didn't feel New York needed me," Woodruff said. "They had a lot of people and it was real crowded. I just went where it was a little less crowded." What he responded to in Shepard's work was the musicality of the language—he heard jazz in Shepard's plays—as well as an open-endedness. Woodruff found "holes" as well but says he knew better than to try and "solve them." "You just have to leave them there and allow them," he said. "They're for the audience."

With the Bay Area Playwright's Festival, which he was helping organize, approaching, Woodruff asked Shepard for a piece. He handed him *Pecos Bill*, an eight-page manuscript with words and sheet music. On October 22, 1976, it was first produced at the Palace of the Legion of Honor with Woodruff directing.

The play begins with the titular hero and his wife, Sluefoot Sue, riding into view on a giant catfish. One day Pecos Bill accidently shoots his wife, and at the end he must face the realization that he was "born a legend, he'll die just a man." Critics found the operetta an amusing diversion, but more important was the fact that it brought Shepard and Woodruff together. The director would become instrumental to Shepard's work in the coming years, being the playwright's director of choice, along with Nancy Meckler, for his most accomplished work.

Fall arrived and Shepard was on the set of *Days of Heaven* in Alberta, where he'd spend eleven weeks acting the role of the Texas farmer. To prepare for his first film, Shepard read books and talked to various actors. Ultimately, he learned that just like his first time directing for the stage, the only way to really learn was by doing. His long-term prospects were helped by Malick's decision to make the farmer a man of few words. This played to Shepard's strengths. It was a practice that was continued in his next film, *Resurrection*. Soon, the die would be cast. Directors realized that Shepard's expressive eyes and finely chiseled features could say more with a close-up than five pages of dialogue. Not long after began talk of Shepard as "the new Gary Cooper." The suit fit and Shepard wore it well, and he would continue to do so for the better part of the next four decades.

The road to movie stardom began as a bumpy ride for Shepard. He was used to being the toast of Off-Off-Broadway, but on a movie set he was a stranger in a strange land. "On this movie shoot he was with people who barely knew who he was, and who had no respect for him," said *Days of Heaven* executive producer Jacob Brackman. This fed on Shepard's insecurities and gave him something of an attitude.

It was only his first film shoot, but Shepard was already bored by all the waiting around—"so much spare time," he wrote in a letter home. He indulged in "orgies of reading," and Brooke Adams, who played Abby, said some of her downtime was spent talking with Shepard about writing. The spare time was spent in other ways, with sex and drinking being favorite pastimes. Both raised tension on the set. "Sam really has a mean streak, especially when he's drunk," Brackman said. "He could be a mean drunk, as could [costar] Richard [Gere], and both of them in that old macho way when people break furniture and break glass or take a swing at someone."

Not helping matters was the fact that there were many long days on set, thanks in part to Malick's desire to shoot at only particular hours of the day when the light was best. The schedule stretched on, week after week, in the frigid nowheresville of the Alberta countryside. Malick also got sick from inhaling smoke from the large fire sequences he was shooting, which further held things up. Shepard hoped the filming would wrap up by early November, allowing him to get home for his birthday. In fact, when the film did wrap, Shepard left in the middle of the night and said good-bye to no one.

Little did he or anyone else know, Malick would take two years to edit the film, postponing the rave reviews and additional film offers that would come Shepard's way once *Days of Heaven* hit theaters. But Shepard had given himself over to the movies. He'd come to hate Hollywood, but the camera loved him, and soon the fame the big screen delivered meant his life was "forever, irrevocably changed."

Family Matters

There is nothing but a voice murmuring a trace. A trace, it wants to leave a trace, yes, like air leaves among the leaves, among the grass, among the sand, it's with that it would make a life, but soon it will be the end.

—Samuel Beckett

As the New Year arrived, Shepard had acted in the film that would make him an in-demand screen actor and had already committed to paper the beginnings of two of his greatest plays. Instead of building upon this momentum, he took a sharp turn back toward the experimental. Indeed, no one could have guessed that Shepard's next project would be an improvisational jazz piece about a current event involving a young woman in a coma. "I've had this idea bobbing up in my mind for several years, this image of a body in a coma in a hospital bed, but I didn't know what to do with it," Shepard recalled. "So finally I put together this group of actors and musicians I've worked with before and we went to work."

Karen Ann Quinlan was twenty-one on April 15, 1975, when a mix of gin and tonics and Valium left her feeling faint. She was taken home and put to bed. Fifteen minutes later, when friends checked on her, Quinlan was not breathing. She was already in a coma when admitted to a New Jersey hospital. Ultimately, she was diagnosed as having suffered irreversible brain damage and entered a persistent vegetative state. It became one of the biggest stories of the year.

Shepard was intrigued by the Quinlan case and the myriad issues her condition raised. Questions about identity and destiny, long-held interests for the playwright, played a role in his desire to explore the situation and the larger issue of the right to die.

Shepard gathered a smattering of reference material before embarking on the idea of dramatizing the situation, including a February 2, 1977, *San Francisco Chronicle* article, "Living Wills—Directives to Doctors for Right to Die," and a *New York* magazine piece titled "The Girl in the Coma," which was heavily underlined by the playwright. One of the lines highlighted by Shepard asks: "What is life and what is death?"

"I'm very interested in writing some material around this impulse of an inner voice," Shepard wrote to his friend Joe Chaikin. Chaikin, in fact, can be viewed as the spiritual godfather of the play, for *Inacoma* was Shepard's attempt to produce an Open Theater–like piece, full of chanted refrains, movement, and improvisation.

Initially, Shepard tried to tackle the issue in a more traditional manner. For a few years, he'd tried to script something that fit into a "fluid written structure." "All I could visualize was a hospital bed, the coma victim and creature-characters," he said. "Then various scenes would start popping up, all out of context and wandering in and out of different realities. The scenes were joined by sounds of breathing, then music, then back to sounds. I kept abandoning the idea of even starting to write something because the subject became too vast and uncontrollable."

The best approach, Shepard decided, was a collaborative one. With just six weeks to work out a way to tackle this difficult material, Shepard was careful to warn audiences at the newly opened Fort Mason stage of the Magic Theatre that the play was a work in progress. A group of eight local actors, including Shepard's wife, O-Lan, along with eight musicians calling themselves the San Francisco Theatre Jazz Ensemble, brought the piece to life. It premiered in March 1977; Shepard directed and wrote the lyrics for the songs. Taking a page from the Open Theater workshops he used to watch a decade earlier, Shepard led the actors and musicians in a series of sound and movement exercises and then primed their improvisational impulses with various ideas and readings. The improvisations became the de facto script for the production.

In the play, Amy Renfrow lies comatose in a hospital bed after falling from scaffolding at a rock concert. Meanwhile, her parents, doctors, lawyers, experts, a faith healer, and priests gather around her and selfishly pursue their own ends. At one point, members of the cast chant together, "Who is the person/Who is the person when the person's gone/When the body's left alone/Where is the person when the person's gone." These are the central questions Shepard is trying to address. Ultimately, Amy's parents pull the plug, leaving her to proclaim, "Without seeing my being, they decide my fate."

Critics thought the production was a mixed bag, with its share of compelling sections but too often falling back on easy satire. At three hours, it was too long. One critic complained that *Inacoma* lacked the things that made other Shepard productions stand out, namely his singular use of language and images. The short life of *Inacoma* ended with its final performance at the Magic. If nothing else, Shepard's experience taught him that he could effectively embroider true events with touches of the gothic and magical. Put another way, he could mix realism with the imaginative flights that marked his best early work.

While Shepard was on tour with Dylan late in 1975, he got a phone call that would change the direction of his work. The legendary producer of New York's Public Theater, Joseph Papp, was on the line. He had taken some time to come around on Shepard's writing. In February of 1971, Shepard's agent, Toby Cole, had sent the producer a book of his plays. That August Cole wrote to Papp, asking for the book back because, she wrote, she now knew that Papp didn't "cotton to" her client. Later, Papp had members of his staff review three Shepard plays (one of which was *Man Fly*) for possible staging at the Public Theater; none made the cut.

Papp evidently must have felt the playwright had some unexplored territory where a rich vein of material was hiding. As Shepard recounted the story, he was a bit flip with the veteran producer when he called: "I said, 'Hi, why don't you ever do any of my plays?' In ten years he's never done one of my plays. And he said, 'I'd like to do one of your plays, why don't you write one for me?' 'And I said, "How much money will you give me?"' And he said $200. Two-hundred dollars?!!? Sheesh! I got him up to $500. So I asked Joe, 'What kind of play do you like?' And he said, 'Oh, a family, two sons, one stays home, one goes off to Vietnam, or anyway to war, and gets fucked up.' So I said, 'OK.'"

Shepard would never write *that* play exactly, but he would turn in a new direction and its focus would be an American family that was similar in many ways to his own. But even after the breakthrough that was 1977's *Curse of the Starving Class*, Shepard did not foresee himself writing a string of plays dealing with the family. As he wrote to Chaikin in September of that year: "I'm not sure what new direction to take."

In retrospect, Shepard gave several reasons for his move into the family drama. One was his meeting in England with the famed director Peter Brook, who told him to focus more on character. The more Shepard took this to heart, the more he turned to those he knew best for models. Another was simply the need to overcome his trepidation. "It suddenly occurred to me that I was maybe avoiding a territory I needed to investigate, which is the family. And I'd avoided it for quite a while because to me there was a danger. . . . I was a little afraid of it. Particularly around my old man and all that emotional territory. I didn't really want to tiptoe in there then I said, maybe I better."

At age seventy-two, perhaps thinking of posterity, for the first time Shepard spoke of a larger aim in writing about the family. "What I wanted to do was to destroy the idea of the American family drama," he said. "It's too psychological. Because this and that happened, you wet the bed? Who cares? Who cares when there's a dead baby in the backyard?" This was a new expression of intent. Shepard had never before spoken of himself as a disrupter or a destroyer of traditions.

It may be that the real reason Shepard began writing family plays was money, pure and simple. He needed it and Joe Papp had it. Hence it appears that a commission triggered the writing of his first family play. Consider that before he started earning six figures for his film acting, beginning about 1980, Shepard and his extended family were barely scraping by. An examination of Shepard's financial papers for the years before he won the 1979 Pulitzer Prize for drama, limited though they may be, reveals letters where he claims that his financial situation is "severe" and pleas to his publisher along the lines of: send royalty checks as soon as possible. A snapshot of his royalty earnings from all his plays during the year 1977 totaled just $5,126.07.

On December 18, 1975, Papp sent Shepard $500 to secure the right to have the first look at his next play. This indeed turned out to be a play about the family—*Curse of the Starving Class*. Shepard needed the money so badly at this point that four months later, having submitted the finished work, he asked Papp's office to make a copy of the script and send it to him, as he couldn't spare the "small fortune" to copy it himself.

There are many themes running through *Curse of the Starving Class*, the most prominent being the linked ideas of progress and heredity. Ideally, the two move toward a general betterment, but in Shepard's world the opposite happens. Heredity becomes the carrier of ruinous habits, the "curse" that "comes upon us like nighttime," the thing one can never escape. Meanwhile progress, in terms of the development of the open land, translates in *Curse* to the bulldozing of everything: "So it means more than the losing of a house. It means losing a country," as the play's son Wesley says.

Despite evidence in the text that supports an emphasis on these ideas, when Shepard handed the play to one of his favorite directors, Nancy Meckler, for the premiere in London, he mentioned nothing of the sort. "People often want to think he is writing about the state of the nation, but Sam was clear it was a 'family play,' and I assumed it had lots of autobiographical detail," Meckler said.

Shepard wasn't around to help much with the premiere of *Curse* because in 1977 Meckler was still in England, where she remains to this day. She evidently had made a deep impression on Shepard during the times they'd spent together in England working on his plays. "I like to think he felt we 'got' him," Meckler said. Shepard wanted her to be the first to direct the new play. "She's very much oriented towards the actor and doesn't worry about The Concept, you know?" he said. "Nancy leaves herself open to the play, she says, 'Let's find out what sort of thing this is as we work it out in rehearsal.' Nancy approaches the play through the actors she's hired. So when this chance to do the show in England came, Joe [Papp] said, 'go ahead.'"

Indeed, despite the fact that Papp had given Shepard a $500 commission for the work, he allowed Meckler to stage the world premiere of *Curse of the Starving Class* at the Royal Court Theatre in April of that year.

The play opens on Wesley Tate fixing the door to the family farmhouse that his father had kicked in during a drunken rage the night before. While Wesley works away, we meet his mother, Ella, and sister, Emma—both firebrands. Ella is trying to sell the family farm "for development" with the help of a lawyer friend named Taylor so she and the kids can move to Europe. Emma is working on her 4-H project and dreaming of escaping the scene all together and heading on horseback to Mexico. The only problem with the mother's plan, we learn later, is that her husband, Weston, has his mind set on selling the farm for money he needs to pay off his debts. As Act 1 nears its conclusion, Wesley brings into the kitchen a maggot-infested lamb and puts the animal in a small pen. The lamb onstage is a source of comic relief at several points in the play, but of course it also symbolizes something hidden that's eating away at the Tate family.

Ella then goes off with the lawyer, Taylor, for a lunch meeting about the selling of the farm, and while she's gone Weston stumbles back home, drunk, with all his dirty laundry, which he dumps on the kitchen table. Weston also has a bag of artichokes with which to feed his family, and he tosses them into the empty refrigerator. After talking with his children, Weston passes out on top of the kitchen table, amid his strewn laundry. Ella stays out overnight with Taylor, and when she returns home she finds Weston still sprawled on the table unconscious. She learns from Wesley that her husband is going to sell the farm. Eventually a man named Ellis arrives. He owns the Alibi Club, where Weston spends time drinking. He has in hand the $1,500 he says Weston accepted for the farm and is ready to close the deal. He also warns that the money should be used to pay off Weston's debts to avoid problems with dangerous people.

The third act begins with a cleaned-up Weston at the kitchen table, sober and folding the clean laundry he's washed. He's cooking breakfast and appears to have turned over a new leaf. When Wesley arrives, his father explains how he was walking around the farm and came to the realization that all this land was his. This registers with Weston as never before, he says, and during an almost out-of-body experience: "I started wondering who this was walking around in the orchard at six-thirty in the morning. It didn't feel like me. It was some character in a dark overcoat and tennis shoes and a baseball cap. . . . It didn't feel like the owner of a piece a' property as nice as this."

Weston tells of how he emerged from this experience and went back in the house, stripped naked, and took a bath, first in hot water, then in cold. He was, in a sense, now fully reborn. In a Gurdjieff-influenced line, Weston says the effect was "like peeling off a whole person."

Later, in Act 3, Wesley mimics the father's actions offstage. Thus does Shepard put a fine point on the theme of heredity and its inescapability. While the reborn Weston finishes cooking a full breakfast for the family, the freshly bathed Wesley walks naked into the kitchen, picks up the lamb, and carries it off. He slaughters it offstage.

We learn that Taylor, the lawyer, is a real estate huckster who'd years earlier sold worthless desert land to Weston. He argues on behalf of "building this country up," countering one of Shepard's main themes in the play, before being driven off. The play ends with Emma taking her mother's keys and heading out to the car so she can flee to Mexico. Offstage, an explosion is heard. Two men enter, laughing about the money Weston owes and the message they've just sent. The implication is that the daughter was killed in the explosion.

Despite what would appear to be a tragic ending, *Curse of the Starving Class* is full of Shepard's dark humor. It helps save the play from its slight but not insignificant flaws. Those flaws include a script overly packed with a few too many ideas and a denouement that can feel comically ironic rather than tragic. "With *Curse* people criticized the ending as being too arbitrary," director Robert Woodruff said. "If it seems arbitrary, maybe it's just because it's challenging in its expectation. [Shepard] doesn't satisfy his audience in any conventional way. . . . He doesn't give it to them and it bothers people. If everything is as expected then you don't have theater, you don't have tension, you don't have anything."

The ideas that resonate in the play are powerful ones. Shepard's time in England spent reading the dramas of ancient Greece had served him well. His depictions of a doomed family and the accompanying treachery that exacerbates its problems have their roots deep in the soil of both the Athens of Sophocles and his own Southern California. The most effective metaphor yet employed by Shepard is the idea of blood: blood that passes on the curse of heredity and blood that has "nitroglycerin" flowing through it, adding to the explosions—inner and outer.

The kind of heredity Shepard has in mind is blameless, just a fact of nature. Which is perhaps why he lets the father in *Curse* somewhat off the hook. Weston says in the play's final minutes: "It all turned on me somehow." In this line, one senses Shepard softening his opinion of his own father, beginning to see him not as an abusive alcoholic but as a victim himself.

Curse also mirrors many of the ideas Shepard was heavily invested in at this time through the Work. The concepts of Gurdjieff's teachings— multiple personalities, the feeling of becoming aware and awake that strikes Weston after he reconnects with his land—work well within the context of the play. They add a mysterious dimension and at the very least keep us off balance with regard to who these characters really are and who or what's to blame for their collective fate.

Most critics when reviewing *Curse* focus on the theme of hunger and the capitalist system that creates haves and have-nots. Indeed, class is something that comes up over and over in the play and jumps out of the title. The Tate family members insist at several points that they are *not* members of the starving class. Yet these ideas are secondary to that of heredity as a curse and may even be the reason some critics see the play as a bit unfocused or even self-indulgent.

Regardless, with *Curse of the Starving Class*, Shepard's writing took a dramatic step forward. Critics took notice of the new direction. When *Curse* made its New York premiere at the Public Theater as part of the New York Shakespeare Festival on March 2, 1978, under Woodruff's direction, *New York Times* critic Richard Eder wrote: "Mr. Shepard has worked out the message in images of considerable power, and in a style that oscillates between realism and savage fantasy. A violent humor predominates, slipping into plain violence."

One problem with the play concerned bringing a live lamb onstage night after night. This is something that has surely given fits to countless directors over the years. In London, Meckler recalled that the lamb situation was "disastrous." "The lamb had to be driven to the theater each day by van from a farm, and the little lambs kept dying. Finally, we had to have a dummy lamb towards the end of the run," she said.

After seemingly discovering his forte, Shepard characteristically struck out in a different direction. That summer, Jacques Levy tried to bring to the stage of the Public Theater in New York a project that had been gestating since 1972 called *Jackson's Dance*. It had moved along far enough by 1977 that discussions about actually staging it had begun. Jeremiah Burnham and Raun MacKinnon composed the music, with Levy providing most of the lyrics and Shepard contributing words for at least one section of the piece. Described as both a "musical score in ten parts" and "a play about Jackson Pollock," the work never saw the light of day, as the painter's widow, Lee Krasner, refused to grant the necessary legal permissions.

Not everything Shepard wrote during this time panned out. His archives are full of unfinished or unproduced work from these years. "Writing, for me, has become more and more difficult, and I tear up four plays for every one that I turn out," he wrote to Chaikin. "I'm still as uncertain about my motives for writing as I was when I started. I guess it's mainly an obsession or, at worst, a habit I can't get rid of."

The Shepard and Dark families were still sharing the house on Evergreen Avenue. Shepard was busy cutting down blackberry bushes and erecting fences for his animals. He'd even taken up bird-watching, which gave him something to do on those long walks in the marshes with his dogs. Feeling like he was lacking in some important ways due to his avoidance of serious reading while growing up, Shepard was doing as he did back in England, taking in some of the classics, including the novels of Joyce, Conrad, and Faulkner. In November he took part in a two-week laboratory workshop with Polish theater director and theorist Jerzy Grotowski. It's clear he was going in a hundred directions, and perhaps he was speaking more than geographically when he claimed, "I like living out here a lot, although I'm always returning to a feeling of dissatisfaction no matter where I am."

The year 1978 began with the release of Dylan's movie *Renaldo and Clara*. Janet Maslin of the *New York Times* said the singer "has seen fit to produce a film that no one is likely to find altogether comprehensible." Ultimately, few saw it; fewer still grasped what Dylan was after or were much entertained. Eventually, Dylan cut the running time down by half, to two hours, and focused more on the live concert footage. As for Dylan's response to the negative reviews for his film, he said, "Contemporary 'critics' write from coffins."

Shepard's next play, *Seduced*, was written in early 1977 and made its world premiere in April 1978 at of all places Trinity Repertory Company in Providence, Rhode Island. Director Adrian Hall was a fan of bare-bones writing, especially that of Shepard and Harold Pinter. All the same, the best that can be said for *Seduced* is that it's two acts and not three. Shepard seems to have been working quickly, and the overall feeling is of a playwright throwing a lot of things at the wall to see if anything would stick, in hopes of stumbling upon some semblance of a compelling narrative or sense of meaning. *Seduced* tells the story of the dying Henry Hackamore, a Howard Hughes–like character stuck in a barren Caribbean hotel room fetishizing his past. He has a servant named Raul who cares for him and fulfills his wishes. Henry's ultimate wish is to fly home.

Henry has Hughes's well-known tics and germophobia, and by playing these up, Shepard manages to wring some humor from his situation. Henry has had Raul fly in two women from his past. In the end, Raul tries and fails to shoot him dead. No consistent themes or ideas arise from the dialogue, and it's impossible to construct from the play's words or actions any sense of narrative movement. Does the main character represent the cost of isolation? Of fame? Of untrammeled desire and wealth? Looking to the title of the play, are we to conclude that Hackamore's condition—his paranoia, intermittent bouts of terror, and failing health—is due to his seduction by money and power? Maybe the point is that for all his money and precautions, not even the great Henry Hackamore can escape the fate of Everyman.

Wynn Handman, producer at American Place Theater in New York, caught the play in Providence and saw something deeper in it. "It's not attempting to be an accurate biography of Howard Hughes," he said. "It's a mythology. It's also about how power that feeds on itself can finally destroy itself. The key line in the play is, 'I was taken by the world, and all the time I thought I was taking it.'" Handman told Shepard he'd stage *Seduced* in New York if he could get Rip Torn to play Henry. The playwright was excited: He'd hoped years earlier that Torn would play the lead in *The Tooth of Crime*'s American premiere. That didn't work out, but Handman successfully got Torn for *Seduced*'s New York debut.

There are two ways to look at these lesser works that Shepard would continue to write during these years. One is that he was still unafraid of experimenting in public even as his star was rising at an ever faster pace. Or one can wonder about his judgment, to be writing these one-act plays of little consequence while his great subject—the American family—was before him. It's slightly unsettling to imagine Shepard setting aside a play like *Buried Child* to spend time, energy, and imagination on plays like *Seduced*. What-ever the reason, Shepard would continue to split his time thusly, at one point telling a reporter: "I've been following two streams. One is the outside play, more improvisatory; the kind of writing that writes itself. I'm not ashamed to share those experiments. Beethoven and Mozart also improvised. The other is the inside play, the family play, much more structured."

Joseph Papp, in March of 1978, decided to strengthen his ties to Shepard. "I think Joe responded strongly to the family relationships in Sam Shepard's plays," said his widow, Gail Papp. The founder of New York's Public Theater sent the playwright $5,000, on top of the $500 he'd previously sent. The deal was for five plays. The money was much needed. Despite the investment, Papp evidently didn't mind if some of Shepard's next plays made their premieres in San Francisco at the Magic Theatre. However, ultimately he would not get all five of the plays he paid for; he and Shepard would have a major falling-out in 1980 when *True West* transferred from the Magic to Papp's Public Theater in New York.

In the fall of 1977, letters between Shepard and Chaikin nailed down their first real collaborative effort. It would become the short piece *Tongues*. The two men were on different coasts, and Shepard felt that the "geographical gap" between them made working together problematic. He floated the idea of Chaikin flying west to work for a few weeks, with the help of a Rockefeller grant obtained through the Magic Theatre. It could be, Shepard felt, "a very exciting time, where we could exchange lots of information and explore some new kind of territory." If nothing else, reaching out to his mentor showed that Shepard continued to hew more closely to the experimental side of things, even if he'd begun writing three-act plays that were more naturalistic in style. Chaikin had helped shape the writer Shepard had become, and he would continue to provide a connection to the new and the daring.

In his dealings with Chaikin, we see yet another side of Shepard. Not the inward, taciturn man-of-the-West persona he presented in the media; nor the playwright with a chip on his shoulder ready to do battle with any director or producer he felt did him or his work harm. With Chaikin, Shepard is openhearted and generous, treating the stalwart of American experimental theater like a surrogate father. Shepard feels free enough to confide to Chaikin things like, "I never felt it was easy to talk—that's one reason I write, I guess." Every letter to Chaikin is signed, "Love, Sam," and after Chaikin sounds weak from health problems during a phone conversation, Shepard admits to breaking down and crying.

The correspondence leading up to Chaikin's mid-May visit in 1978 features one word time and again—*discovery*. With only a handful of vague ideas to begin with, the pair planned to develop a short work for the theater involving music. Chaikin's free-thinking approach was contagious. "He would say things like, 'It doesn't have to be a play. . . . We don't have to call it a play,'" said Shepard, who at the time didn't want the collaboration to produce just another work for the stage. "[This] all of a sudden liberates something. It could be just words."

And so it was.

The plans were almost derailed in early December when Chaikin's recurring medical issues once again landed him in a New York hospital. Endocarditis was the diagnosis this time, an inflammation of the inner layer of the heart, and even after he left the hospital there would be the risk of complications. Chaikin said he would still plan to be in California by the middle of May to work with Shepard. As usual, his outlook in the face of serious illness bordered on the heroic. As he wrote to Shepard on January 8, 1978, "What funny, always unexpected, turns life takes. I have never found living so wonderful as in the last couple of years or so. And I have never understood so little."

When Chaikin arrived in California, he and Shepard worked over the course of three weeks in different places, from a beach to restaurants, a hotel room, and even Shepard's truck. The result of their collaboration, *Tongues*, was performed at the Magic Theatre in June 1978. As the play began, Chaikin sat on a bare stage facing the audience, while Shepard sat with his back against Chaikin's with an array of percussion instruments in front of him. When Shepard's arms moved to strike the various drums they appeared to the audience like an extension of Chaikin's body. The mélange of voices that Chaikin brought to life onstage, accompanied by Shepard's precisely calibrated percussion, resulted in a piece of performance art of the highest order. Chaikin loved Beckett even more than Shepard did, and this piece comes as close to capturing the Irish master's tone and perspective as anything Shepard would produce on his own.

> *This night.*
> *He goes to sleep in*
> *his same bed.*
> *This night.*
> *He falls to sleep in*
> *his same way.*
> *This night.*
> *This dream he dreams*
> *he's dreaming.*
> *This night.*
>
> *A voice.*
> *A voice comes.*
> *A voice speaks.*
> *A voice he's never heard.*

Tongues is about mortality and the ways we manage to live with the terrible knowledge of our limited time on earth. To read these words does not do the piece justice. But combined with Shepard's percussive highlights, the result proved powerful.

In August of 1979, Chaikin again came west, and this time the collaboration with Shepard resulted in *Savage/Love*. It was paired with *Tongues* at the Magic, and in November it moved back to New York, where the double bill was performed at the Public Theater. A *Times* critic commended the text, almost all of it written by Shepard, but lavished praise on Chaikin's performance. *Tongues*, as a stand-alone piece, would be performed by Chaikin throughout Europe beginning in summer 1980.

Savage/Love addresses the joys and fears of romance, investigating particular moments in a relationship that most in the audience could identify with. Once these moments were found, Chaikin improvised and Shepard wrote the monologue until they agreed upon the final script. Though still effective, the concreteness of the text doesn't mesh as well with Chaikin's performance. There are points where the words the actor speaks come close to treacle. The joys and pitfalls of relationships would be treated by Shepard with greater results in a few years with his play *Fool for Love*.

Shepard and Chaikin had a bond from the first. Working together in the late 1970s only strengthened it, said actress Joyce Aaron. "Sam looked up to Joe as almost a father figure," she said. "He certainly respected Joe as a theater person, and Joe respected Sam's writing. They really came together with those projects." The pair would come together in the ensuing decades for two more highly original pieces.

Shepard also stepped into the role of teacher in 1978. Fellow Theatre Genesis playwright Murray Mednick, along with five other playwrights, including Shepard and María Irene Fornés, held a workshop on the old Padua Hills estate in the foothills of the San Gabriel Mountains, not far from where Shepard grew up. The Padua Hills Festival and Workshop focused not so much on becoming a successful playwright but on craft and creativity. It had more in common with the Off-Off-Broadway aesthetic than with the world's commercial stages. The students were comprised of writers and actors, and they looked at different approaches to creativity and ways to sharpen their skills. Mednick served as artistic director of what would become a veritable institution in the region. In its second year, the festival featured *Curse of the Starving Class*, directed by Shepard.

You Can't Go Home Again

That play was never intended to be a piece of realism, I just used elements of the family to fabricate this thing, you know. There are elements of the truth in it, but I didn't give a shit about the truth and I still don't. [Laughs]

—Sam Shepard

*T*he Last American Gas Station resides in one of Shepard's note-books dating to August 1974, and in it are the seeds for what would become *Buried Child*. The key element missing in that first pass is the child buried in the backyard. That bit of inspiration came from a relatively mundane source, as Shepard recalled four decades later. "It came from a newspaper article, actually. It had to do with an accidental exhuming of a body, a child, in a backyard," he said. The other missing component was the notion of a young man returning home to his dysfunctional family. For that, Shepard thought back to an actual trip he'd taken around 1966, when he and then-girlfriend Joyce Aaron drove from New York to California for a visit to the house he grew up in in Bradbury. The strange goings-on that made *Buried Child* such a memorable play did not take place exactly, but it wasn't a run-of-the-mill homecoming. "It was a very odd, weird visit, just the feelings around the house," Aaron recalled.

In the play, Joyce became the character of Shelly, and by the end of 1977, Shepard had completed a first draft. A major difference between this version and the finished play is the father Dodge's explanation for the titular buried child. In the 1977 draft, the patriarch admits to killing the baby but claims God told him to do it, recalling perhaps the biblical story of Abraham, who was ready to make just such a sacrifice. After ranting about how jealous he was that others had heard the voice of God but he hadn't, Dodge stops short. Shelly asks why he stopped. "I heard myself lying," he tells her. "That was all a lie?" she asks. "Every bit," Dodge says. No such religious justification for Dodge's actions, real or fabricated, made it to the final version of *Buried Child*.

Robert Woodruff had done such a fine job directing the New York premiere of *Curse of the Starving Class* at the Public Theater that when Shepard realized the new play was too complex for him to helm himself, he called his friend "Woody." The director saw 650 actors during the audition process for the world premiere of *Buried Child* in San Francisco.

The play premiered at the Magic Theatre in June 1978. From the first, the audience is left trying to figure out what's wrong with this family. Shepard maintains this effect throughout the three acts thanks to the unsettling actions his characters engage in. Throughout, the playwright takes the cliché that you can't go home again to a new level.

The play unfolds, or better to say unravels, in three acts. The opening presents Dodge and Halie living out their so-called golden years in the Illinois countryside. Dodge is a drunkard who spends his days wasting away on the couch, his menacing cough a metaphor for the decay eating at him and his family. His wife is a blowsy flirt who's probably done her share to drive him to such a state. Their home, their lives, the way they talk to each other—it's clear that life has ground them down. Whatever is left, they're intent on sapping from each other. The couple's shared remoteness is expressed in the staging of the play's first scene: Halie is out of sight in the upstairs bedroom and forced to yell down to her husband in the living room. They rehash some of their past and also discuss a grown son named Ansel, who died on his honeymoon after marrying "a Catholic." For Halie, at least, Ansel is the idealization of everything that might have been. This character recalls Shepard's real-life Uncle Bill, who also died on his honeymoon.

We next meet Tilden, an adult son who is back home after some sort of trouble in New Mexico. It's clear he's mentally challenged to some degree. He emerges from the backyard with an armful of corn, even though the field has been barren for more than thirty years. The crop is treated by Halie as mysterious, if not miraculous. She soon departs for an engagement with the local priest, Father Dewis, who, we are led to suspect, may not be so priestly after all. The house now quiet, Dodge falls asleep on the couch, and Tilden covers him in the cornhusks he's just removed from his armful of corn. Once Tilden exits, the couple's other son, Bradley, enters with his fake leg and proceeds to cut the hair of his sleeping father using a pair of horse clippers. This tableau merely sets the scene for the real strangeness that next descends.

The second act begins with the arrival of Tilden's adult son Vince and his girlfriend, Shelly. Neither Dodge nor Tilden recognizes Vince, who is visiting the old homestead for the first time in many years. Unable to convince his grandfather Dodge that he is who he says he is, Vince acquiesces to the old man's demand and agrees to go to the liquor store to get him a bottle, leaving Shelly at the house.

Shelly's interactions with Dodge and his two sons recall those of the wife, Ruth, in Pinter's *The Homecoming* and are disconcerting to say the least. As Dodge becomes absorbed in watching the television, Tilden draws Shelly into a conversation while together they peel carrots that he's also brought in from the "barren" backyard. He asks about Vince, but she is unable to tell much about him, due to the fact that they've only been dating a short while. But this leads to a key bit of dialogue:

> TILDEN: There's certain things I can't tell you either.
> SHELLY: How come?
> TILDEN: I don't know. Nobody's supposed to hear it.
> SHELLY: Well, you can tell me anything you want to.
> TILDEN: I can?
> SHELLY: Sure.
> TILDEN: It might not be very nice.
> SHELLY: That's all right. I've been around.

TILDEN: It might be awful.

SHELLY: Well, can't you tell me anything nice?

After a few minutes, Tilden opens up.

TILDEN: We had a baby. [Motioning to DODGE] He did. Dodge did. Could pick it up with one hand. Put it in the other. Little baby. Dodge killed it.

With the first secret out, we now wonder about the rest of the story, what led to this horrible act—and whether it's even true.

The third act finds Shelly getting to know Dodge, and when she talks about seeing a photo upstairs of Halie holding a baby that looks "like it didn't even belong to her," Dodge responds with: "That's about enough outa' you! You got some funny ideas. Some damn funny ideas. You think just because people propagate they have to love their offspring. You never seen a bitch eat her puppies? Where are you from anyway?"

After Halie comes home with Father Dewis, Dodge is pressured into letting loose with more of the story, how his wife got pregnant out of the blue, despite the fact that they hadn't shared a bed in six years. Finally, the whole truth emerges.

DODGE: Tilden was the one who knew. Better than any of us. He'd walk for miles with that kid in his arms. Halie let him take it. All night sometimes. He'd walk all night out there in the pasture with it. Talkin' to it. Singing to it. Used to hear him singing to it. He'd make up stories. He'd tell that kid all kinds of stories. . . . We couldn't let a thing like that continue. We couldn't allow that to grow up right in the middle of our lives. It made everything we'd accomplished look like it was nothin'. Everything was cancelled out by this one mistake. This one weakness.

SHELLY: So you killed him?

DODGE: I killed it. I drowned it. Just like the runt of a litter. Just drowned it.

The silence that this truth brings is interrupted by Vince, who has arrived back at the house. He stays on the porch, throwing empty bottles against the wall, smashing them to bits. His return at this moment and the revelation about the dead child are synchronized to demonstrate the fact that heredity cannot be denied. Dodge has tried to deny both the dead infant and Vince, yet before the final curtain both will have returned. As the play nears its end, Dodge speaks his last will and testament and then quietly dies, seated on the floor in front of the old couch. Vince, having been told he's inherited the house, sits on the couch, taking Dodge's place, and delivers the play's most famous speech, about driving the night before and watching his reflection in the windshield as his face became that of his father, then of his grandfather and right on back through the line. "Clear on back to faces I'd never seen before but still recognized. Still recognized the bones underneath. The eyes. The breath. The mouth."

This speech, along with the family's failure to recognize their own flesh and blood in Vince, and with the dead baby who not only will never leave their thoughts but who is carried in from the backyard at the end of the play by Tilden, shows that the march of heredity is an unstoppable force, biological destiny if you will. It can't be denied or buried out back.

Buried Child is a dark, complicated play, but Shepard believes it is imperative to find the humor in it, especially with the character of Dodge. "They have to laugh at this character, even though he's killed a child. Otherwise it's deadly," he said.

Richard Eder, writing in the *New York Times*, gave the play one of its many raves, saying "it manages to be vividly alive even as it is putting together a surreal presentation of American intimacy withered by rootlessness." *Buried Child* performs an autopsy on this Midwestern family right before our eyes, even before it enters its final throes. The inherited defects have piled up, leaving something rotten at the core. Despite Halie's somewhat hopeful coda about a "good hard rain" taking everything down to the roots and the subsequent "tiny little white shoot" that breaks through the earth to find sunlight, the fate and destiny of this family had long ago been cast.

Days of Heaven was released in September 1978 and it made a film star out of Sam Shepard. This is despite the fact that by his own measure he was not particularly good in it. "I didn't know what the hell I was doing," as he himself has said. Lee Kissman, a friend of Shepard who was featured in some of his earliest plays and who has remained close to his family, watched the film with Shepard's mother. "After the movie, she was really kind of upset," Kissman recalled. "First of all, she said he looked so much like her husband used to. Plus, she didn't think he was quite good enough and wished he could have been a little better." Shepard's father was less critical, though not at first. The old man's first impression upon seeing his son on the screen was that he was merely watching his kid up there. However, when Shepard's farmer gets angry at the conniving of Richard Gere's character, "then I saw a real actor," Sam Rogers wrote in a letter to his son. After seeing Shepard's second film, *Resurrection*, his father was sold: "You are a damned good ACTOR."

The filmmakers adapted the script to let the camera hang on Shepard's good looks instead of having him say much. Given too much dialogue, Shepard showed his lack of training and experience, almost to comic effect. The producers shared some laughs at Shepard's expense when he'd appear less convincing and almost amateurish onscreen. "We'd watch these scenes in the rushes and we'd call them 'Sammys'—but not to Sam's face," said Jacob Brackman, executive producer of *Days of Heaven*. "Most of those scenes wound up on the cutting-room floor. So Terry [Malick, the director] went with Sam's silence and the way he looked when he had a big sky or a wheat field behind him, or tall in the saddle. He really was a rider and looked great on a horse."

Days of Heaven is set in Texas circa 1916 and involves a manual laborer named Bill (Richard Gere) who kills his boss at the Chicago steel mill, forcing him to flee with his lover, Abby (Brooke Adams), and her younger sister, Linda (Linda Manz). They find their way to the Texas panhandle, where they join a large seasonal work crew on the farm owned by Shepard's character. Bill and Abby tell everyone they are sister and brother to avoid complications, only to have the farmer fall for Abby. Bill learns that the farmer is dying and convinces Abby to encourage his affections. She goes so far as to marry him, with the plan being that when he dies, she will inherit the farm. The love triangle understandably becomes complicated, resulting in friction between Bill and the farmer. When Bill sees that Abby is truly in love with the farmer and that he may not be dying after all, Bill kills him, forcing himself, Abby, and her sister to flee once again.

The critics were torn over the film to some extent. Some raved about it while others claimed the cinematography stole the show ("scenery porn," some called it). Today it is considered a great American film. The reviews for Shepard's performance were mostly positive. "He has a tall, rangy figure, a broodingly intense quality, and his work comes as a welcome surprise," wrote Harold Schonberg in the *New York Times*.

It's true that Shepard may have benefited from low expectations, but he is more than serviceable as the doomed farmer.

Shepard didn't find the work much fun. Still, he'd made his mark on the big screen and his agent's phone began ringing. In a letter dated November 7, 1978, Lois Berman asked her client if he could be "romanced away from [his] writing to be a film star." Someone from a major film studio had called her praising Shepard's performance in *Days of Heaven*. Another call was from actor-director Warren Beatty, who wanted Shepard to play the role of Eugene O'Neill in his upcoming film *Reds*. Shepard demurred, and Beatty cast Jack Nicholson instead. Over the years, Shepard would turn down roles in such hits as *Urban Cowboy*, *Field of Dreams*, and *Brubaker*. After his first blush of cinematic success, he continued to worry about the effect his newfound movie fame might have on his writing. Years later, he'd recall: "There was this feeling that my credibility as a writer would go in the toilet if I suddenly became Robert Redford. I didn't want to be a movie star. I didn't want to have that thing of being an icon. It scared the shit out of me." But then there was the money. Money that would sustain him, his family, and his hobbies for decades. "It's like having a little oil well back there in the backyard—you go and dip into it."

One role Shepard did entertain in the wake of his big-screen debut was that of the writer Dashiell Hammett in a semi-fictional portrait being made by German filmmaker Wim Wenders. "Not only was he tall and slender and remarkably looking like the legendary novelist who had single-handedly invented the genre of the hard-boiled detective story, Sam was also a great writer himself. And he had just proven that he could act," Wenders said. Plus, Shepard could actually type, he added. However, the studio making *Hammett*, American Zoetrope, was looking for a bigger name to play the lead. (Shepard would eventually play Hammett in a TV movie called *Dash and Lily*, earning an Emmy nomination.) Wenders continues: "Sam and I had to drop our hopes for collaborating, with a lot of regret, but with the clear understanding that we were meant to do something together one day." At the time, Wenders suggested maybe something in the science fiction vein, having seen and liked Shepard's play *Angel City*.

Shepard treated acting very differently from writing. As demonstrated multiple times in the past, he would fight—with both words and fists—over the way his plays were produced. With acting, he was able to compartmentalize things; the movie roles Shepard would take on in the coming years would fall into one of two categories: ones that held personal meaning for him or at least involved a subject he was interested in, and ones that were done strictly for a paycheck. In the beginning at least, the scripts Shepard was eager to do typically featured rural backdrops, or dealt with horses, cowboys, or American myths of one kind or another. These scripts, as found in his archives, are heavily marked by Shepard with suggestions to himself about how to approach a scene, reminders about what his character stands for, and esoteric jottings that likely had meaning only to him. The scripts from the so-called paycheck movies are free of any such notations. This isn't to say that in the paycheck movies Shepard isn't convincing. He learned his lines, did his job well, and likely forgot about these movies before they came out. There would be dozens of these performances, and they indeed paid the bills. "You can't make a living as a playwright," he said. "One movie, and I don't have to work for a year—then I can feed some horses."

Shepard's life at this time was full of distractions that kept him from overcommitting to films or even writing plays. He had become a rodeo enthusiast and on many a weekend could be found loading up his sorrel quarter horse and heading over from Mill Valley to Santa Rosa in his custom Ford pickup and matching trailer. The horses would come to play an ever-larger role in his life as the years and decades wore on. "I don't go to the theater—I go to the rodeo, go to the track a lot, too—I guess you could say my cultural appetites are kinda narrow," he said. Anyone needing to be convinced that Shepard was serious about the cowboy life need only check Shepard's notebooks beginning around this time. Most of the end pages and back covers are filled with lists of his current horses, noting which ones he intends to breed, which ones he intends to sell, along with related expenses and other details. Spending time on a movie set was definitely less appealing for him than sitting in a saddle. Meanwhile, at home there were four dogs to run around with, and occasionally Shepard sat in on the drums with a local jazz group. This constant flurry of activity speaks to his restless nature. Although someone who has known him for many years suggested that Shepard also bores quickly and is always eager for what's next.

One person who saw Shepard in *Days of Heaven* took note of the powerful presence he projected. Actress Ellen Burstyn figured she'd discovered the new "Gary Cooper." As for Shepard, he thought she was "a genius." At that time, the actress was busy with director Lewis John Carlino casting her next movie, *Resurrection*, which told the story of a woman who, after surviving a terrible accident, finds she has amazing healing powers. They asked Shepard to play the role of Cal, a man who becomes her troubled lover. "To me, he was the sexiest man alive. I was very attracted to him," Burstyn said of her future costar. She hoped that in the film, "the sexuality would be real." The thirteen weeks of filming for *Resurrection* would begin in Texas and Los Angeles early the next year.

Meanwhile, in the theater, his stock continued to rise. However, the money still wasn't rolling in. *Buried Child*, his best play to date, had moved from San Francisco's Magic Theatre to New York's Theater for the New City. It next transferred to the Theater de Lys in Greenwich Village but closed once ticket sales grew tepid. Financially, things got to the point where his wife joked with him that she and her mother could start taking in ironing to help make ends meet.

Things would soon change.

True Brothers

I mean, it's an old, old tradition that goes way back into an almost religious knowledge that there's this "other," that there's this companion. The obvious one is the brothers, the counterpart, the shadow, there's some sense of another being that accompanies you. Whether that being is for you or against you is up in the air.

—Sam Shepard

Driving back from Texas and the set of *Resurrection* in mid-April of 1979, Shepard arrived home to a pleasant surprise. It was a telegram telling him he'd won the Pulitzer Prize for *Buried Child*. The news did not have him jumping for joy: He famously said that he'd rather win a roping contest at the local rodeo. Actually, he said far worse: Winning the Pulitzer was "like news of a terminal illness . . . something to get through so you can move on." Glib? Sure. Echoing the obstinacy of his hero Beckett, who famously tried to hide out from the press after he won the Nobel Prize? No doubt. Regardless, the Pulitzer Prize placed Shepard as close to the mainstream of American theater as he could stand. Of course, he would do all he could to back away as quickly as possible. His next piece written for the stage would not be a play at all.

It was called *Jacaranda*, and it comprised the libretto for a thirty-minute dance piece, which was performed solo by Daniel Nagrin. Shepard's text was heard live as spoken by the dancer and also on tape, allowing Nagrin to have "a kind-of conversation with himself." The piece marked the first time the dancer had commissioned a libretto. "I always liked Sam Shepard's writing," Nagrin said. When he got a grant, he wrote to the playwright about possibly collaborating and two days later got a positive response. They collaborated by letter, and the result was a story of a man who awakens alone in the bed of his lover, torn whether or not he wants the union to continue. Musically, Shepard suggested something by Jelly Roll Morton for his text be read to, but Nagrin opted to use Shepard's words themselves as "music." When he wanted to make a change to the text and asked for approval, Shepard answered with what has become a favorite quote among his fans and scholars: "My work is not written in granite. It goes out into the air and dissolves forever."

Jacaranda was performed in the first half of June 1979 at New York's St. Clement's Church. While at first blush, modern dance may seem an odd place to stray, even for someone as artistically restless as Shepard, the relationship to music and rhythm he and others have noted in his writing provides all the connection one needs. Nagrin saw this immediately and choreographed his movements to the beats of Shepard's language.

Saturday, September 29, 1979, was a nice day in Mill Valley. The members of the Shepard and Dark household headed out that afternoon for a bike ride, all except for Scarlett, Shepard's mother-in-law, who stayed at home. On their way back, Shepard and his wife, son, and father-in-law, Johnny Dark, were passed by an ambulance. When they arrived at the house they couldn't find Scarlett: she'd been taken to the emergency room. It took a while for doctors to figure out what was causing her symptoms, and for some time it was touch and go whether she was going to pull through. Shepard remembered feeling a need to pray, but "realized I'd never learned how." They moved her to another hospital, where she endured six hours of surgery, followed by a long recovery.

Ultimately, Scarlett was diagnosed as having suffered an aneurism in her brain's basilar artery. Shepard took the news hard—the entire last section of his next book of prose would be dedicated to chronicling her illness and slow recovery. Scarlett had to relearn everything, from walking and general muscle control to speaking. She also suffered from aphasia, which affected her ability to comprehend language. "She turned into a child really," Shepard recalled, citing the frantic screaming and crying that marked periods of Scarlett's recovery. Instead of placing Scarlett in an institution, the family took her home. They set up a special bed for her in the dining room and kept her wheelchair nearby. The members of the household took care of her in shifts, Shepard doing his part with the others. "It was a really arduous time," he said. "She lost language, dexterity, and a fundamental idea of who she was. So we built this thing around her where she began to reidentify herself."

Shepard and his mother-in-law had a special connection. Scarlett, by all accounts, was a life force, an actress who lived for years as a single mom before marrying Johnny Dark. Important to Shepard was the fact that she was, like him, a seeker. It was she who helped him and the others in the household get deeply into the teachings of G. I. Gurdjieff. Just as he would years later with Chaikin after his stroke, Shepard was there for his mother-in-law when she needed him, and the two would remain close throughout the rest of her life, even after he was divorced from her daughter. "Scarlett and Sam were great to watch together, absolutely great," Dark said. "He just softened and melted, and he was so concerned with her. And she was so glad to see him after not seeing him for so long, and he would look at her and laugh and say, 'How are you doing? Look at you.' They were really tender with each other. It was really nice." Shepard said, Scarlett's life was "one of the greatest examples of courage I've ever come across."

Seeing his mother-in-law struggle to regain control over her sense of identity registered keenly with Shepard, whose work for the stage often dealt with the fragile hold each of us has on the sense of who we are. It likewise spoke to his ongoing belief in Gurdjieff's ideas about the multitudinous nature of personality. These ideas would play a role in *True West*, the play he was developing around this time, as well as his 1985 play *A Lie of the Mind*.

During the summer of 1980 Shepard did something for the second time that he would rarely devote time to—teaching. He spent four weeks at the

San Francisco Theological Seminary in San Anselmo, California, leading a workshop in late June and July. His intent, he told the students at the start of the first day, was to pursue the mystery of character. "Voice is the nut of it," he said. In the shade of the redwood trees, Shepard led the students through writing exercises, beginning with just that, the first thing that turned him on as a writer—voice. The need to embrace accidents in one's writing and the importance of having a rhythmic structure were also covered. Shepard told the students that writing is an art form often practiced in the dark. "It's a great mistake to assume that just because writers are involved in making pieces of work, they know what they're doing," he told the students. "They know to a certain extent, but to a large extent, they don't, and that's the reason they are doing it—to find out."

The workshop was held a mere twenty minutes from Shepard's home in Mill Valley and less than an hour from San Francisco, where concurrent with the workshop, rehearsals for the premiere of *True West* were taking place at the Magic Theatre under the direction of Robert Woodruff.

When casting the brothers at the heart of *True West*, Shepard and Woodruff first turned to an alumnus of the San Francisco Mime Troupe, a collective of musicians and political satirists who staged experimental theater pieces in local parks. Peter Coyote was someone Shepard and O-Lan had known from around Mill Valley, and when it came time to cast the part of Austin, Shepard called him up.

Jim Haynie had run into Shepard around the Magic Theatre and had wanted to play Tilden in *Buried Child* two years earlier. That part had already been cast, so Shepard offered him the part of Bradley, the other son, with the wooden leg. "I didn't want to walk around with that thing tied to me," Haynie said. Later, when auditions were being held for the character of Lee in *True West*, stage director Linda Koulisis called Haynie. "She said, 'Get down here. This part is perfect for you,'" the actor recalled. Thus the play's two leads were cast for its premiere.

Upon completion of *True West*, Shepard said he "knew it was going to work." This may have been due to the fact that he gave full rein to his long-held notion (and a chief Gurdjieff-ian precept) that within each individual reside many personalities. This, combined with another one of his primary themes—the bad things that happen to men who are alienated from the land—gave Shepard plenty to work with in this play about two brothers on the edge of the desert locked in a battle of wills. It didn't hurt that he also knew a few things about Hollywood—a place he would come to hate, referring to it at one point as a "sprawling, demented snake . . . its fanged mouth wide open, eyes blazing."

Then again, Shepard simply worked hard on *True West*, "to peel it back until I got the language exactly the way I wanted it to sound," he said. No tangents, no digressions or unrelated flights of fancy. Shepard confessed at this point to being impetuous in some of his earlier work: "I wanted to get on to the next thing and I was compulsive. And a lot of things just weren't worth rewriting," he said. The discipline Shepard was now showing in his writing reflected the encounter with Dylan years earlier on the Rolling Thunder Revue, when the singer pointedly questioned a line Shepard had written for the film they were shooting.

Austin is a successful screenwriter holed up in his mother's house while she's away in Alaska. His brother Lee, a drifter prone to drink and burglary, among other things, arrives out of the blue. The tension is immediately apparent. Each man represents a different way of life. Austin is successful, controlled, and seemingly happy with his life, his work, and his family. Lee is the restless criminal who can live on the land and spurns his brother's success and anything remotely associated with the so-called American Dream. The brothers also represent disparate reactions to their father, a drunkard who does not appear on stage but hangs over the play like a reckless specter. Austin has written the old man off and dedicated himself to being as unlike him as possible (just as Shepard had done with his own father); Lee is a chip off the old block, and his brother's disdain for their father adds to the tension between them. Shepard dedicated the play to his father, Sam Rogers, who at this time was still living in Santa Fe on his military benefits and the occasional bit of money from his son. "I never intended the play to be a documentary of my personal life. It's always a mixture," Shepard said. "But you can't get away from certain personal elements that you use as hooks in a certain way. The further you get away from those personal things the more in the dark I am."

Lee wants to show his brother that there's nothing to this screenwriting business of his and tells him of an idea he has for a movie about two horsemen chasing each other across Texas. It's a bad idea. However, Austin's producer stops by the house that afternoon, and Lee arranges a tee time for them the next morning, during which he pitches his idea. The producer likes it, and suddenly Austin's project is in danger of being dropped in favor of Lee's crazy scenario.

There's fine comedy found in the way the brothers slowly trade places, and this was Shepard's driving impulse at first. "I wanted to write a play about double nature," he said. "It's a real thing. I think we're split in a much more devastating way than psychology can ever reveal. It's not so cute. Not some little thing we can get over. It's something we've got to live with." Yet Shepard would never write a play where the drama turned on so simplistic an idea as a simple swapping of places. Disney had produced a film in 1976 called *Freaky Friday*, where a mother and daughter trade personalities for a day, and three years after *True West* debuted, Eddie Murphy's breakout film, *Trading Places*, used the same conceit to winning effect. No, Shepard's brothers have fluctuating or multiple personalities inside—or as the Gurdjieff literature would have it, many "I"s. Austin gets as drunk as his ne'er-do-well brother once he believes his producer is passing him over. He even tries his hand at burglary and prowls the neighborhood one night stealing toasters, but he never becomes as reckless or unthinking as Lee. Meanwhile, Lee tries his hand at screenwriting, but as the play's finale nears, he takes a golf club and beats the bejesus out of the typewriter, his film script unrealized. Here, Shepard's other great theme, destiny, takes over. Neither brother can totally escape what fate has in store for him.

Shepard had had a taste of the film world by this time, and his experiences likely fueled some of the humor and frustration that permeates *True West*. However, it is the sense of menace that pervades the piece and the violence that may break out at any moment that drives the plot. The denouncement finds the warring brothers toe to toe, and the overriding feeling is that they can't go back from here. The lights fade, but the battle will surely go on.

Some of this friction onstage during the premier run was real, especially between the two leads. Coyote was turned off by the way he saw Shepard, fresh from winning the Pulitzer, being fussed over. "I got my first taste of how people behave when someone with status is in the room," he said. Also, Coyote felt slighted in others ways, including the fact that his photo wasn't in the lobby with those of the rest of the cast. When asked if he'd continue playing Austin when the play moved to a bigger theater, Coyote demurred. "I said, 'Are you fucking crazy? You guys have treated me terribly. Why would I do that?'" The actor soon after got an agent and went to Hollywood, where he's since starred in dozens of films and television shows, including *E.T.: The Extraterrestrial*. He's also written two acclaimed memoirs.

For others, the initial run of *True West* was a great experience. "It was riveting theater," Woodruff said. "These two actors, although they didn't see eye to eye on a lot of things, were brilliant together."

Shepard was very happy with the production. "[It] was a real thrill," he said. "It was the only production I kept feeling actively involved with all the way through the run. I just kept coming back night after night. The play had a certain fascination about it—I don't know what it was, in the performance of it—that just never died for me." It was so good that he wanted to share it. Plus, he owed Joseph Papp and the Public Theater the opportunity to stage the play next, due to their 1978 agreement. He excitedly called the producer and told him that *True West* was his best play. Haynie was willing to stay on for the New York production, which was quickly slated for that December, but it wasn't to be. In one of the more public skirmishes Shepard has ever had with a producer or director, *True West*'s transfer to the Public was by all accounts disastrous. The playwright had much to say about the production, though he never saw it—he was in Texas filming his third feature film, *Raggedy Man*.

Things started out auspiciously. "This [play] reminded me of David Rabe," Papp said. "It had elements of *Goose and Tomtom*, where the author splits himself into two brothers and examines the internal violence that's inherent in that situation." Papp suggested JoAnne Akalaitis as director. "Sam called her but he said, 'No, no, a woman can't understand this play.'" It was agreed upon that Woodruff would direct the play in New York as he had at the Magic. The next issue, casting, would quickly become divisive, and in a very public way.

Shepard didn't fly at this time, so dropping in on the rehearsal process in New York from the film set in Texas didn't seem to be an option. According to Papp, that's where the problems began. "If I ever do a Sam Shepard play, Sam will have to be here," he told the *New York Times*. "I won't let what happened stop me from producing him, but he'd have to be here." Shepard's retort from the Lone Star State was to the point: "He'll never see another play of mine." Shepard and Woodruff wanted Haynie to reprise his role as Lee. Haynie came to New York and read twice for the part. "Papp said I 'just wouldn't do,'" Haynie recalled—this despite the fact that the actor had received raves for his performance at the Magic. (Papp told the *New York Times* that after the second reading there was "widespread agreement that Haynie wouldn't do.")

Meanwhile, Papp's people had been talking to Peter Boyle and Tommy Lee Jones. The producer said he left the final casting decision to Shepard and Woodruff, the latter saying, "I cast the play, with whatever Joe's influence was in steering me in that direction. I listened to him, I considered what he had to say, and then I cast the play. . . . He didn't cast the play. I try to get that very clear. I cast the play. Nobody twisted my arm. It was fine." Shepard maintained that the two actors were forced upon him and Woodruff. Years later, Papp would say, "We ended up with two marvelous actors. Woody went along with it. He was playing both sides to stay alive. Sam was against it, but I convinced him. I said, 'No, they'll be very good.' There was a little pressure, a kind of resistance and fighting, and I finally got my way."

Either way, the production wasn't working, and Woodruff was having problems with the actors, according to Gail Papp, the producer's widow. "The actors weren't doing the things that he wanted them to do," she said. "He was not satisfied with what he was getting. But what they were doing was specifically what he'd asked them to do." There were fears that Boyle and Jones were going to come to blows onstage. Meanwhile, Boyle was threatening to quit all the time. Gail Papp recalls Woodruff spending lots of time out at a pay phone, long distance to Texas, discussing the problematic production with Shepard.

Papp also spent time on the phone with Shepard, begging him to come to New York to help get the play on track. "He was angry as hell," Papp said. "Sam was furious he didn't have his own people on it and was making some kind of threats to withdraw the play." Papp told him that wasn't an option and again begged the playwright to come east. Days passed and things didn't improve. "I got Sam on the phone again and I said, 'Sam, you better come here.' And he started to shout at me, 'I'm not gonna come!' I never heard a more hysterical voice in my life," Papp said.

Years later, Tommy Lee Jones would detail what he saw as the problem. "I wasn't really delicate enough to play Austin, and Peter wasn't insidious enough to play Lee," he said. He doesn't blame Woodruff but says there was a disconnection in their communication. The director himself said, "I had difficulty creating a situation in which they were going to grow, in which they were going to learn to trust each other and delve into the material."

A few days before previews began, Woodruff resigned, telling the *Times* that the production "isn't my vision of the play or Sam's" and accusing Papp of "acting high-handedly." When the previews began, Papp said the audience liked the play. He committed to staying with it, with Boyle and Jones onboard, through the January 11, 1981, closing date. Frank Rich, of the *New York Times*, in his review of the play, began with an open indictment: "Some day, when the warring parties get around to writing their memoirs, we may actually discover who killed 'True West.'" He went on to say that the play seemed to be a good one, only in this incarnation it appeared as though no one took the time to direct it. "We had a rudderless production," Gail Papp said.

Shepard released a statement to the press in the midst of all this. The full text claimed that Papp was holding over the playwright's head the commission money he'd paid him back in 1978: "I would like it to be known that the 'production' of my play, *True West*, at the Public Theatre is in no way a representation of my intentions or of Robert Woodruff's." He went on to say that Papp would produce no more of his work, citing what he saw as the producer's arrogance.

For his part, Papp claimed that he was careful with what he said to Shepard for fear of losing the play.

The question remains: Why didn't Shepard simply slip away from the Texas set of *Raggedy Man* and get to New York to make sure this play, one he was truly fond of and would remain fond of, received the best possible production? The character he plays in *Raggedy Man* is seen onscreen only a handful of times, meaning his shooting schedule could not have been prohibitively onerous. Gail Papp said that even after this battle with Shepard, her husband "continued to have the highest regard for his work."

Despite all this, *True West* has stood the test of time, even for its hard-to-please author. "I'm not proud of any of [my plays], but the one I feel least embarrassed by is *True West*," he later said.

John Lion, founder of the Magic Theatre, had traveled to New York to see the Public Theater's production of *True West*. He didn't like what he saw, and when he got back to San Francisco, he contacted Shepard to see about staging the play once again. The playwright was still upset about the New York production but agreed to give it another go. They settled on using San Francisco's Marines Memorial Theatre, this time with Haynie and Ebbe Roe Smith, no stranger to Shepard's work, replacing Peter Coyote, and that March the team got to work. Things went well, but it would be another year before a production of *True West* once again matched the brilliance of its premiere. The Steppenwolf Theatre Company in 1982 had a hit with the play in Chicago with Gary Sinise (who also directed) and John Malkovich. It transferred to the Cherry Lane Theatre in New York, where it ran for more than 760 performances and was filmed for PBS. The play would also mark the second time a Shepard play made it to Broadway proper when another revival opened in February 2000 at the Circle on the Square Theatre, with Philip Seymour Hoffman and John C. Reilly taking the leads (and actually switching roles each night). That year it was nominated for a handful of Tony Awards, including Best Play.

That September, the second feature film Shepard appeared in had its premiere. He may have felt like an outsider, or at the very least a newcomer, on the set of *Days of Heaven*, but by his second film he understood more clearly the process of acting and the things he needed to do to prepare for his time before the cameras. *Resurrection* stars Ellen Burstyn as Edna Mae Macaulay, a woman who experiences clinical death after a car accident that kills her husband. When she emerges from her coma, she has the power to heal. She goes back to her family home to recuperate and there begins healing others, including a young farmer named Cal, played by Shepard. They fall in love, but the fundamentalist streak in his family and in himself will not allow him to accept Edna Mae's special abilities, especially since she attributes them to simple human love and empathy and not a higher power.

Shepard does a fine job throughout the film, whether acting the brooding lover or the out-of-control zealot. He looked every bit the heart-throb Burstyn wanted to play opposite her. In fact, O-Lan said that she found her husband so "magnetic" onscreen that she felt like sending him "a filthy fan letter."

Shepard's script for the film is heavily marked. There are reminders about what's going on in the plot at various points, as well as his character's motivation for particular scenes. After Burstyn's character saves Cal's life, Shepard prepared for the next scene, where the two have a drink, making copious notes. He writes, "To talk to her. He's curious about her." Then he mentions a knife, a fight he had back in Duarte High School, and how his character wants to "prove his superiority," with a reminder that Burstyn's character may have this mysterious power, "but she's still just a woman."

Later in the script, Shepard lists on the back of a page a column that includes items such as:

> Smells her power
> Want to hold her
> Protect her
> Loves her little girl
> Sees her sacredness
> Smells her room
> Sees her pain
> Smells her dog
> Sees her aloneness.

The senses and emotions listed here show Shepard, when playing the role of Cal, trying to follow the advice of his mentor, Chaikin, and be fully present in the moment. Shepard also wrote a complete workup of his character, including his home life, religious experience, and sense of grief. He also read a small pamphlet titled *How I Became a Christian* that featured a picture of the Shroud of Turin on the cover, and more. "I went to a lot of charismatic churches where they lay on hands and everything . . . and boy, you'd be hard pressed to argue with somebody and say that he or she hadn't *really* found Jesus! They'd certainly found something . . . whether it was Jesus Christ or an emotional truth or whatever. Whether it was true or not."

Resurrection did poorly at the box office, and its fortunes were not helped by Universal's decision to open the film in the South and Midwest, marketing it as if it were a religious picture. When the film finally opened in New York, slow ticket sales during the first days led Universal to scale back the advertising. "It's a self-fulfilling prophecy. They don't spend any money on advertising and promotion and they wonder why the box office falls off," an angry Burstyn told the *New York Times*.

Shepard's reaction to seeing the film in a theater was disappointment. He felt the editing was much improved over a rough cut he'd seen but that it "still smacks of soap opera." He also didn't like the film's musical score. If the film had one benefit for Shepard, it was that he befriended costar Lois Smith, who would be featured in his later plays, and was reunited with actor Ebbe Roe Smith, who'd been featured in several of his more recent plays. Longtime Shepard fans watching the film may have also gotten a laugh when, in the final scene, the parents of a sick child stop at a small service station and are invited to peruse the "rock garden" out back.

The actress Jessica Lange had a strong reaction to Shepard's performance in *Resurrection*: "I immediately felt I knew something about him—the typically American wildness, a no-restraints outlaw quality." The start of his relationship with the actress was still more than a year in the future, but seeing Shepard onscreen was the catalyst that would eventually bring them together, first as costars, then as lovers.

Shepard may have been feeling the need for change about this time. He confided to his notebook in December of 1980, upon returning to his family in Mill Valley, how conflicted he felt. The place still felt like home, and he had a deep sense of belonging, but at the same time he admits that he "didn't know exactly what to do here. How to be. What my potentials are." His restless nature was getting ready to emerge again.

The notebook entries during this year reflect a troubled state of mind beyond these questions. Shepard writes that by 10 a.m. each day, he's "in a state of panic." Or, in another entry from earlier that year, he notes how he's "hallucinating earthquakes all thru the body," looking for "premonitions of panic," and is concerned over his "persistent shaking." He concludes: "Maybe I'm just plain spooked for no reason." On the brink of greater fame, his old insecurities were surfacing. They might have caused him to stumble and even doubt himself, but Shepard would not allow them to stop him.

Judging by outward appearances anyway, Shepard's life was good. For starters, he was the second most produced American playwright in the country at this time, right behind Tennessee Williams. Meanwhile, across the Atlantic, contemporary American drama meant one thing— Sam Shepard. Europe couldn't get enough of his work. And thanks to his growing film career, he was no longer teetering on the edge of bankruptcy. He had enough money and freedom to buy horses and take them around to local rodeos in his custom pickup and trailer. People like Diane Keaton were calling him on the phone, looking to work with him. Yet, as busy as all this kept him, there was still one primary focus. As he wrote in his notebook, he was surrounded by opportunities, but "all I wanna do is write."

In October of 1979, Shepard turned once again to his prose and poetry. The notebooks dating to this time are labeled "Transfixion," which was the working title for a collection that would be published in 1982 by City Lights called *Motel Chronicles*. (An early typescript of the book suggests that Shepard wanted to employ both titles; editor Lawrence Ferlinghetti advised against this.) Throughout the last days of 1979 and the following year, Shepard would craft in his notebooks various scenarios, reminiscences, and poems with the aim of compiling the collection.

Meanwhile, Shepard's wife, O-Lan, discovered in these short pieces the basis for something of her own. In 1980 she'd founded a theater troupe called Overtone Industries; she continues to serve as the theater's artistic director. During its second year, the theater staged the premiere of a piece called *Superstitions*, written by "Walker Hayes." The piece was actually created by O-Lan from bits of text from the book that would become *Motel*

Chronicles. Walker Hayes was Shepard's pseudonym. "Sam didn't want the hoopla," his wife said. In September of 1983, *Superstitions* moved to New York, where it was paired at La MaMa with Shepard's strange and brief musical *The Sad Lament of Pecos Bill on the Eve of Killing His Wife.* Two reviewers critiqued *Superstitions*: Frank Rich seemed to be bored by the piece, while Benedict Nightingale found it strange but enjoyed "glimpses of the unsettled furniture of Mr. Shepard's mind."

After *True West*, Shepard wrote eight plays and threw them all away. Perhaps to touch base with the more experimental side of things, he reached out in the summer of 1981 to his friend Joseph Chaikin, suggesting they once again collaborate. Shepard said his schedule was in flux and difficult, but he definitely wanted to meet and work someplace other than home—his or Chaikin's. When that fall the possibility of visiting Harvard for this collaboration was on offer, Shepard said he was open to this. "I'm ready for a little East Coast at this point," he tells Chaikin. It can be dangerous to intuit too much from someone's reading. However, it's at least intriguing to consider that this summer Shepard had taken on *The Brothers Karamazov*, Dostoevsky's great novel of ethics and free will. An interesting choice given the big step he was about to take in his personal life.

The arrival of 1981 was marked by Shepard's desire to broaden his palette as a dramatist. Critics and feminists had long found a streak of misogyny in his work, a charge the playwright has outright dismissed. One can certainly point to aspects of his earlier work that gratuitously featured naked or half-dressed women and less-than-enlightened perspectives (at least by today's standards), but by mid-career he was interested in creating realistic, fully rounded female characters. For his next play he set himself the goal of creating and "sustain[ing] a female character and hav[ing] her remain absolutely true to herself, not only as a social being, but also as an emotional being." The resulting play would be *Fool for Love.* A notebook dating to 1981 contains Shepard's initial thinking about this play, which involves a torrid but furtive love affair between Eddie and May, who turn out to be related by blood. Mixed among the plot notes and points of emphasis on one page is Shepard's brief outline of a story by the Brothers Grimm called "Brother and Sister." The story deals with a brother and sister who run away from home to escape their wicked stepmother. The plot takes many twists and turns, but the main point of the story concerns the wishes of girls for the return of their brothers—many of whom were at that time sent off to war.

When asked more than fifteen years later about *Fool for Love*, Shepard mentioned not a fable nor his hopes of creating a three-dimensional female character, saying instead: "The play came out of falling in love. It's such a dumbfounding experience. In one way you wouldn't trade it for the world. In another way it's absolute hell. More than anything, falling in love causes a certain female thing in a man to manifest, oddly enough." He could have just said that the play was ultimately shaped by his affair with Lange.

Before heading off to the set of the film *Frances*, where he and Lange would meet, Shepard was featured that September in his third film. *Raggedy Man* was the kind of "rural" picture Shepard favored back then. The film deals with a small-town divorcée, Nita Longley, played by Sissy Spacek, who is struggling to make ends meet during World War II as she raises her two young boys. The film moves along two tracks, one involving a young sailor (Eric Roberts) who stops in town long enough to begin romancing Nita and developing a fondness for her sons. This brings a swift denunciation from Nita's neighbors. The other track features a strange man with a facial deformity known around town as Bailey, who Nita sees sneaking around her property. After pressure from the townsfolk causes Nita to send her new lover away, two local thugs attempt to break into her house to rape her. Bailey, the deformed mystery man, stops them and saves her life but is killed in the struggle. The end of the movie brings the realization that Bailey was Nita's ex-husband, who after their divorce was badly wounded in the war and came home to live as a stranger in town, watching over his ex-wife and sons. Shepard starred as Bailey, though the heavy makeup and lack of any dialogue meant that it could have been anyone in the role. He merely limps about, works as a landscaper, and then silently comes to the rescue of the film's heroine.

Spacek knew Shepard and told William Wittliff, the film's writer, about him. However, Wittliff already knew Shepard, having met him on the set of his previous film, *Resurrection*. To him, Shepard was a perfect western type. "In my view, Sam is exactly what you see. He's *that* guy. And he's totally authentic. . . . And I think that's his great attraction in both his work and his acting. He is totally authentic. There's not a whiff of the fake or the counterfeit."

When it came time to cast his next film, *Country*, Wittliff would look to Shepard to bring that very authenticity to bear.

"Stuff"

Well, that's not exactly how it happened, but I know you fellas have to flower it up.

—Chuck Yeager

The year 1982 saw the publication of Shepard's second collection of prose and poetry. *Motel Chronicles* is similar to *Hawk Moon* in style and substance, again painting well-detailed scenes of the Southwest and its many oddball characters. There are bits of biography as well, including a story about running away from home as a boy with two friends, only to be caught by the police and brought back. The pieces of memoir tell of the men on his father's side and their oddball deaths and afflictions—his grandfather with his spittoon full of bloody discharge and his racist comments. The book contains tales of lawlessness, such as stealing cars, underage drinking, sex with teenage girls, and other troubles a young man often strays into. There are also vignettes from Shepard's time spent on movie sets, still a relatively new experience for him.

ABOVE LEFT: Samuel Rogers, Shepard's father, circa 1960. *Courtesy San Marino High School Yearbook.* ABOVE RIGHT AND BELOW: Shepard, age 1, with mother at Bailey's Harbor, Wisconsin, 1945.

Buddy Saffrhan, Steve Rogers, Mike Chase, Rick Swain.

SAM SHEPPARD

ABOVE LEFT: "Steve Rogers," as he was then known, as a high school junior. ABOVE RIGHT: Shepard as a high school yell leader. *Both images courtesy Duarte High School Yearbook.*

CENTER: The house Sam grew up in, Bradbury, California. *Courtesy Jack Tarlton.*
BOTTOM: Shepard, seated second from left, in *Harvey* at Mount San Antonio College. *Courtesy of the college.*

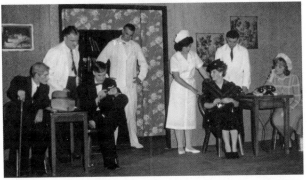

ABOVE: Shepard with the Bishop's Company (front, second from left) circa 1962.

CENTER LEFT AND RIGHT: The Rev. Michael Allen, left, and Director Ralph Cook and his wife Pat. *Courtesy of The JC Michael Allen Papers.*

BOTTOM: Judith Malina with Shepard's friend and mentor Joseph Chaikin in early 1960s production of Brecht's *Man is Man.*

TOP: Shepard, second from left, with the Holy Modal Rounders, circa 1968. *Alamy Photos.* CENTER: A contemplative Shepard, circa 1965. *Credit Martha Swope, New York Public Library/Billy Rose Collection.* BOTTOM: Shepard at La MaMa in 1971 during the run of Melodrama Play. *Photo by Jens Heilmeyer, courtesy of The La MaMa Archive.*

ABOVE LEFT: Shepard and Patti Smith, New York City, May 7, 1971. *The Estate of David Gahr.* ABOVE RIGHT: Shepard with his wife, O-Lan, in Nova Scotia in the summer of 1973. *Courtesy of Michael Smith.*

CENTER: Shepard, left, directs a scene from Renaldo and Clara during the 1975 Rolling Thunder Revue with Bob Dylan. The singer is at center. *Credit Ken Regan/Camera 5.* RIGHT: Shepard relaxing in his trailer home during a break in shooting the 1980 film, *Resurrection. Photo by Joanie Blum. From the Sam Shepard Collection, Howard Gotlieb Archival Research Center at Boston University.*

TOP: John Malkovich, left, and Gary Sinise in a 1982 revival of *True West*. *Credit Photofest*. CENTER: Shepard as Chuch Yeager in *The Right Stuff*, from 1983. *Credit Photofest*. BOTTOM: Jessica Lange with Shepard in the 1984 film *Country*. *Photofest*.

RIGHT: Harry Dean Stanton as Travis in *Paris, Texas*, 1984. *Credit Photofest.* CENTER: Shepard with director Robert Altman on the set of the 1985 film *Fool for Love. Credit Collection Christophel Alamy.*

RIGHT: Shepard in *Steel Magnolias*, 1989, *Photofest.*

LEFT: Shepard in the 1991 film *Voyager. Credit Gregorio Binuya/Everett Collection, Alamy.*

CENTER: Actor Sam Shepard and actress Jessica Lange (center)—with family members Shura Baryshnikov (second from left), her husband Bruce Bryan (left), and Hanna Shepard and Walker Shepard (right)—attend a ceremony honoring Lange at the Film Society of Lincoln Center at Avery Fisher Hall on April 17, 2006, in New York City. *Credit Paul Hawthorne/Getty Images Entertainment.*

RIGHT: Shepard in early 2016. *Credit Chad Batka/The New York Times/Redux.*

Shepard ends the book with a long story about the day of his mother-in-law's aneurism and the year it took her to recover. It's a story so painful that his publisher at City Lights, Lawrence Ferlinghetti, suggested not putting it last. It left "no time for the reader to recover," he said. Shepard acquiesced and added a short poem on the final page.

The pieces in *Motel Chronicles* date to between 1979 and 1982. They had already provided the basis for O-Lan's short play *Superstitions* and would be the initial inspiration for a storyline that would become the film *Paris, Texas*. The reviews were positive overall, with most critics noting that these were plotless snippets but ones that managed to conjure such feelings as restlessness, solitude, and danger through the threat of potential violence. Some make even larger claims for the collection. David Thomson, author of *The New Biographical Dictionary of Film*, said *Motel Chronicles* "is one of those books movie people seem to have read. Its influence on the urge to road pictures, loneliness and a fateful wildness is very large."

Shepard gave a series of readings in support of *Motel Chronicles*. At one of these appearances in San Francisco, the audience included the film director Philip Kaufman and his wife, Rose. Kaufman had been looking for an actor to play nerves-of-steel test pilot Chuck Yeager in a film he was making about the space program. "I was looking everywhere for somebody who had the Yeager-esque quality," Kaufman said. "Chuck is, you know, tough and a very energetic guy." At the reading, Rose Kaufman nudged her husband after Shepard took the stage and said, "There's your guy." Years later, she recalled thinking how Shepard had "a cowboy quality about him. He was Gary Cooper."

Kaufman approached Shepard several times about playing Yeager. "I refused," Shepard recalled. "I felt like it was ridiculous to play a living person. I knew Chuck and I didn't feel like I was him at all."

Eventually, Kaufman tracked Shepard down at the famous L.A. hotel the Chateau Marmont and slid the script under his door. After Shepard said yes, Kaufman's producers expressed some reservations. Kaufman came back to them a day or two later with a new draft of the script, rewriting parts of it with Shepard's strengths in mind. "He'd excised much of Sam's dialogue and added . . . a dimension of his physicality," producer Robert Chartoff recalled. "And in fact it turned out to improve the character a great deal."

If anyone was still concerned as to whether Shepard had the right stuff to play legendary tough guy Chuck Yeager, when he arrived on set in jeans and leather jacket, all doubt was removed. He didn't exactly look like a young Yeager, but he looked every bit the cool-under-pressure character the role called for.

The story of *The Right Stuff* began in 1979, when producers Irwin Winkler and Robert Chartoff, flush with success after producing *Rocky* and *Raging Bull*, bought the rights to a just-completed book by that name, written by their friend Tom Wolfe, for $350,000. Thus began the story's long and winding road to the big screen.

Wolfe had wanted to write about America's space program, but he found it more compelling that while the astronauts got all the attention and adoration, the men doing the really dangerous work that cleared the way for space travel were so far from the spotlight. "Tom Wolfe started writing a book about the astronauts' early days. Through that, he discovered the Air Force test pilots who were doing the nitty-gritty work," said Yeager, who was not only one of those test pilots but was the one who, in October 1947, first broke the sound barrier. "We weren't getting free houses or notoriety. We were working our tails off for $250 a month. Many of us were dying in the process."

The Right Stuff ultimately became a divided film, one part focused on Yeager, who spent his days at Edwards Air Force Base pushing the limits of flight, while the other part followed the astronauts into orbit and the history books. As for the phrase that Wolfe and Kaufman both took as their title, it defined that ineffable quality that both men felt Yeager personified. "This isn't the tale of one man. It's the tale of a spirit called 'the right stuff,'" Kaufman said. Ultimately, he decided that the phrase meant having "grace under pressure."

Decades later, Shepard said he took the role due to the famous opening scene. "One of the main reasons I did it was that there was this great chase scene at the beginning on horseback. Galloping," he said. "And the character I was playing was chasing his wife on horseback across the desert, figure eight-ing through the cactus and stuff. I figured, 'Wow, I'll do that.'"

Shooting took place in the Mojave Desert between March and October 1982, with additional filming in January of 1983. Shepard prepared for the role of Yeager by reading the pilot's autobiography, and in his notebooks he sketched some ideas he wanted to bear in mind while portraying him. "Be present in every second," is written across the top of one page, bringing to mind not only the Zen aspects of flying a fighter jet but also the primary tenet of Gurdjieff's teachings. He also notes that Yeager, or at least his conception of him, had no use for the "parasites," meaning the suits at NASA, the press, and cadets. Shepard also reminds himself that Yeager is a man who embodies the fun-loving outdoorsman, as well as a man who understands the complex science of flight. His final note to himself is written across the bottom of the page: "SIMPLICITY FIRST."

Once filming began, Shepard took to the role of Yeager both on *and* off the set, much like the other actors did with their own parts, Kaufman recalled, making like the space cowboys they were portraying. The cast and crew stayed at the Lancaster Hotel, located in the next town over from Edwards. They spent their nights at a nearby restaurant called Tosca, where much drinking went on, accompanied by the occasional piano pounding by Shepard. "Eddie [Harris] and me were big buddies and we liked liquor a little bit more than we should have," Shepard said. "And yeah, we got into some fights in that bar."

Dennis Quaid remembered the shoot as a very special time. "It was a real sense of community, unlike anything I have ever experienced on a movie set, and no one wanted it to be over," he said. Even Shepard, the usual loner, said, "You can't get that many great guys together and not have a little bit of fun."

Jessica:
The Beginning

The proper response to love is to accept it. There is nothing to do.
                                            —Archbishop Anthony Bloom

S hepard was so nervous on this morning in late 1981 that he tried on three different sets of clothes in his Hollywood motel room before settling on an old pair of black corduroys, a brown-and-white-checked shirt, and western boots. Even deciding whether to leave his shirt open at the top or snap the button took some thought. He didn't want to appear "too Hollywood." He went unsnapped. When he pulled onto Santa Monica Boulevard a short time later, he drove around for a while, to be sure he was casually late. That plan failed, and instead he found himself in a nondescript office killing time, sitting on a couch and flipping blankly through copies of *People* and *US* magazines. He was there to meet the actress Jessica Lange and talk to Graeme Clifford, who was to direct her in a film based on the life of the late actress Frances Farmer. Shepard was being considered for the role of Farmer's lover and confidante, a quasi-fictional character named Harry York.

Lange had already been in four films, and her fifth, *Tootsie*, was due soon; it would be a smash and earn the actress the first of her two Oscars. Shepard had seen only two of her films and hoped there would not be a quiz or that he'd be expected to discuss her work. He hadn't studied her movies, despite the fact that she reminded him of Tuesday Weld, a Hollywood starlet who was one of his boyhood crushes. The resemblance was centered on that smile. And Lange was "definitely sexy," Shepard thought.

As if to defy her image as a blond bombshell, when Lange arrived she was pushing a baby carriage, wearing a loose blue sweater, white skirt, penny loafers with white socks, and horn-rimmed glasses. Was she trying to give him the impression that "she was more than just another great piece of ass?" He thought so, and he couldn't help himself: He began to look down on her, regarding this acclaimed actress as "a college girl. One of those dumb sorority chicks" who chased not men but good grades.

Maybe Lange sensed this. She barely met his eyes and spent much of their first minutes together fiddling with her infant daughter and the carriage. They made small talk, basic stuff. Lange seemed more animated when talking about the character this film was based on, Frances Farmer. Even before she got the lead role, she'd been studying the life and career of the late actress. When there was more silence than talk, Shepard decided he'd had enough. They exchanged farewells and shook hands.

Director Graham Clifford's memory of this first encounter between Shepard and Lange is a bit different. The director had called the meeting to bring the pair together to see if she liked him and if there was any chemistry between them. The trio spent a few minutes together in the office, but at one point Clifford excused himself to make a phone call, purposely leaving the pair alone for a short while to see how they got on. When he came back, things were looking up. "They were getting along like a house on fire, so Jessica subsequently told me that she really liked him and would be really happy if he played Harry York, so we made that happen," Clifford said.

The next time Shepard and Lange met was in mid-October of that year in Seattle, where portions of the film would be shot. Shepard and the rest of the cast were booked into a fancy hotel overlooking Puget Sound. He checked into his third-floor room on Saturday, October 18, 1981. It was nice, facing the water, and right next to Lange's room. Feeling trapped already, Shepard went to the front desk, where he found a message from Clifford, inviting him to dinner with some of his fellow cast members.

Shepard walked to the restaurant and found their table out back. Soon after he sat down, Lange got up to use the restroom, wearing a green silk dress that was semi-transparent. "Astonishing" was the word that leapt to Shepard's mind as he watched her disappear around the corner. Or, more accurately, as he followed her ass as she left the room. She was gone for only a moment, and he was surprised to realize he was missing her. Five minutes into this thing and already he had these strong feelings for her. When Lange returned, she'd fixed her hair and put on some makeup. When she used her finger to stir the ice in her drink, he "realized she wanted [me]."

They walked back to the hotel with another cast member and the director. The next morning, Shepard arrived at a remote beach and joined the cast and crew shivering on the shore in the shadow of a lighthouse. After the director had the crew shoot Lange walking along the beach, he called for Shepard to join her. The pair was to walk for a few moments then stop and kiss. They were tense, and in his nervousness Shepard concentrated on the mark in the sand where they were to pause. When the first kiss happened, he was "surprised how open her mouth was." Whether it was the forwardness of this or the tension finally breaking, something caused Shepard to lose his balance. He fell on top of Lange, and they laughed, as did the crew.

That night, Shepard called his wife, who told him how lonely she was and how much she missed him. Then he took a shower. He "felt a sinking lostness" and a loneliness that often hit him in hotel rooms like this one, feelings he sometimes welcomed, other times not. But with Lange right next door, albeit with her baby and the baby's nanny, he was tempted to "go wild like he used to," dropping his restraint.

Shepard left the hotel and drove downtown for a drink. When he got back to his room after midnight, he lay in bed and tried not to think about the woman on the other side of the wall. Perhaps she was lying there thinking of him. Shepard told himself to put these thoughts out of his head before "they became obsessive." Instead, he tried to convince himself that she wasn't that special. But soon his thoughts turned to the idea of sleeping with her. Just a few times. No big deal. "Just for the hell of it." Then he'd get back in his truck and drive the thirteen hours south to Mill Valley and back to his real life.

On the set the next morning, Shepard saw Lange's large trailer and "walked past it without knocking."

Of course, soon enough he would come knocking, and the two would begin a relationship that would last nearly three decades.

Jessica Phyllis Lange was born on April 20, 1949, in Cloquet, Minnesota, a lumber town with a population of 7,865. She was the third of four children born to Al and Dorothy Lange. Her mother was the consummate midwestern homemaker and wife. Her father was a restless soul and a drinker prone to fluctuating moods. Al Lange's tendency to move from job to job meant the family was uprooted many times during Jessica's youth.

When Lange was eight, she escaped into reading and drawing. A favorite book was Margaret Mitchell's *Gone With the Wind*, and when Lange saw the film, she was further smitten, acting out scenes in her bedroom. When she entered Detroit Lakes High School in 1963, she was "shy and withdrawn" and preferred to focus on getting good grades, said her first drama teacher, Terry Knutson. However, after a friend persuaded her to try out for the school play, *Love Rides the Rails*, Lange seemed to find her calling. "Jess came kicking and screaming into the play. She took to acting very, very fast," Knutson recalled.

Upon graduation, Lange earned an art scholarship to the University of Minnesota, and in 1967 she moved a few hours away to campus. It wasn't long before she met a handsome fellow student, a Spanish photographer named Francisco "Paco" Grande. A few months later, at age nineteen, she dropped out of school and began traveling with Grande.

They went to New York and then London, before returning to the United States and traveling around the country for the next two years. When Grande was busted for possession of marijuana in 1970, his lawyer suggested that he and Lange marry to help his case, which they did the following year. Eventually, they moved to the SoHo section of Manhattan, where Lange began to settle into her new life, which included painting and participating in a modern dance troupe. Then she saw Marcel Carné's 1945 film *Children of Paradise*, and despite being only twenty-one, having $300 to her name, and being newly married, she left for France to learn the art of mime. "She was a nonconformist and a very free spirit," said Arnold Baskin, a professor at New York University's film school who knew Lange at the time.

In France, Lange trained and even worked on the streets of Paris as a mime. But after two years, in 1973, she returned to New York, broke up with Grande for good, and got a fifth-floor walkup in Greenwich Village, supporting herself by waitressing at the Lion's Head Tavern in Sheridan Square. There, she made about $30 in tips on a good night. The other members of the waitstaff nicknamed her "the beautiful one," recalled Claudia Carr Levy, widow of director Jacques Levy, who was fresh from California herself at the time and also worked at the Lion's Head. "She told me, 'Don't worry, you'll get used to the city,'" Levy said. "She was so sweet."

The dream of being an actress had never left Lange. She enrolled at the famed Herbert Berghof Studio, where she was a determined student. "From the beginning, Jessica was going to be an actress," remembered her acting coach Warren Robertson. "I mean, she was attentive, she studied, she really applied herself. She had that focus."

Opportunity knocked soon after when the Italian-born film producer and director Dino De Laurentiis spotted Lange while seeking an actress for his remake of *King Kong*. One day Lange got a call from a modeling agency, asking if she'd be interested in flying out to Hollywood to audition for the film. "That sounds good because I don't have money for a subway uptown," she later recalled thinking. It was her first audition, and she got the job. De Laurentiis actually offered her a six-figure, seven-year contract, and soon Lange was off to Hawaii, at age twenty-six, to make her first movie. Young, beautiful, and free-spirited, she struck *King Kong* costar Jeff Bridges as "a beatnik."

Lange figured prominently in Paramount's heavy promotion of the film, which was released just before Christmas 1976. (The advertising tag line was "The most exciting *original* motion picture event of all time." An odd claim for a remake.) Yet *King Kong* was a failure, and Lange felt as if the critics were too quick to judge her. "[When] she first hit the public consciousness it was almost precisely the same time that Farrah Fawcett did and a number of other beautiful young blond women. Jessica did not want to be thought of in that light," said film historian Douglas Brode.

Lange decided to make sure this would be the last time she'd be taken as just another pretty face. She went back to New York to continue her studies. "I hated being lumped into that category of model-turned-actress," Lange told the London *Independent*. After *King Kong*, she would seek out challenging roles, winning accolades for her performance opposite Jack Nicholson in the remake of *The Postman Always Rings Twice*. With the money she made from that film, Lange bought 120 acres in her home state of Minnesota, in a town called Holyoke.

While at a party thrown by De Laurentiis, she met the famed dancer, choreographer, soon-to-be-actor, and Russian émigré Mikhail Baryshnikov. They became a couple, and on March 5, 1981, Lange gave birth to their daughter, Aleksandra, known to all by her nickname, Shura. Lange was thirty-one, a mother, and a successful actress with a new home in Minnesota. It appeared she was well on her way to settling down.

Then she met another restless soul, Sam Shepard.

When the role of Frances Farmer became available, Lange already knew the doomed actress's story: her acting coach used to have her perform scenes out of Farmer's autobiography. The role allowed Lange to explore a long-held interest of hers. "I've always been fascinated by madness. I'm drawn to it," she said. "From an acting point of view, I think what it does is it frees your imagination in a way that other roles that are more constrained . . . don't allow. The idea that you can imagine that character anyway you want."

She and Shepard were similar in many ways. Both grew up with difficult fathers for whom alcohol was a serious problem. They shared an artistic restlessness coupled with a drive to succeed. And they both were willing to fight for what they believed in as artists. As Jeff Bridges said of Lange, "She runs the show, she doesn't let the show run her." Jack Nicholson was more blunt, calling his former costar "a cross between a fawn and a Buick."

She and Shepard fell in love while filming *Frances* but had to keep their relationship a secret. Once it transcended the film set, this was no easy feat. On January 27, 1982, Shepard and Lange were spotted by photographers exiting The Port restaurant in West Hollywood. The image of an angry Shepard throwing his rolled-up jacket at the paparazzi was carried by newspapers around the world.

But it would be more than a year before Shepard would leave his wife and move in with Lange. He'd had flings on movie sets before, but this was different, and it clearly troubled him. Here he was, the father of a preteen with a wife back home.

Oddly enough, one of those he confided in was Johnny Dark, who had the dual role of being O-Lan's stepfather and also Shepard's close friend. Dark described one of their many discussions about the situation. "It's just two guys sitting on a wall, and one of them says, 'I've got this blond. I'm, like, insane mad for her and I want to run off, you know?' And I'm sitting there saying, 'Yeah, you should run off with her. It sounds great. . . . You stay here you're going to tear yourself to pieces. Go for it.' I mean, this went on for a year where he said, 'I want to leave but I can't abandon my family, I can't leave my son, I can't do it. But I can't live without her. I just can't live without her. But I can't leave my family. What am I going to do? Maybe I should just kill myself. I don't have any idea what to do.' And I'm saying, 'You don't have to do anything. One day it's just gonna happen. You're gonna go one way or the other. Something's going to happen. But in the meantime you're going to have this terrible suffering, of being pulled in two different directions.'"

Lange was less open with her friends, but they sensed early on that something was going on. "I could just tell the way her voice would change a little bit when she would discuss that 'very interesting playwright,'" recalled friend Dorothy Pearl. "Past the organic, physical attraction, I think that there was a very deep attraction to who the other person was."

Shepard, in his anguish, turned to music and poetry. He reports how one early spring day he was sitting alone at his Mill Valley house, playing over and over on the stereo Bob Dylan's "Simple Twist of Fate"—a song that dealt with both the discovery and the loss of love. With lines like "He felt an emptiness inside to which he just could not relate," the tune must have seemed like the perfect soundtrack for his predicament. Shepard also immersed himself in poetry around this time, specifically that of Rainer Maria Rilke and Wallace Stevens. He may have also dug into the work of a poet he'd delved deeply into the year before, César Vallejo. The Peruvian writer was known as "the poet of absence," and his downcast vision of life would no doubt have fit well with someone in Shepard's frame of mind.

The fact of Shepard's burgeoning relationship with Lange still being a secret, and the excitement and frustration it entailed, affected the final version of his next play, *Fool for Love*, which he was writing at the time. In fact, in March of 1982 he committed to his notebook a synopsis for the play, and it reads like slightly disguised autobiography and a result of the tumult his new relationship introduced into his life. Eddie and May, the main characters in the play, fall victim to a sort of love that dare not speak its name—incest. It was a form of forbidden love. Forbidden love of a different kind was slowly engulfing him and Lange. Relations between men and women, Shepard would concede, were often "terrible and impossible."

Shepard's life was living proof of that statement. The evidence can be found in a page of his notebook dating from that time, where he imprinted his emotions on a single page in all capital letters. The phrases flow into each other, a reflection of his state of mind and the issues he must have been churning over and over. "BEING IN LOVE . . . SEEING YOU CAN'T RUN FROM THE HEART." He goes on in this way for another seventeen lines, saying he has no choice concerning this love and that he's in a real fix. He concludes by stating how much liquor he can consume, it perhaps being the only cure, and how he can "DRINK ALL DAY."

A more philosophical entry begins with him trying to reassure himself: "If she truly loves you and you truly love her then this love will endure any hardship." He ends this entry by assigning their coming together a mystical inevitability.

By February 18, 1983, Shepard was already transitioning, at least in his heart and mind, to his new life, or so he wrote to his friend Joseph Chaikin. Shepard admitted to a "sadness I can't even name." In addition to the old standby Dylan, Shepard was listening to a lot of Vivaldi at this time, because the music seemed to have the capacity to "celebrate a victory where man is the loser." It's clear that as Shepard and Lange grew closer he was plagued by the self-doubt and insecurities he'd dealt with throughout his life. He moved not like a conquering Lothario but as any man might, afraid of rejection and tortured over the pain he was leaving in his wake.

Fools for Love

I would have been down the river if I hadn't met Jessica. There was salvation for me.

—Sam Shepard

The relationship between Shepard and Lange blossomed during the filming of *Frances,* which continued production into the early part of 1982. The story of the real-life actress Frances Farmer, who was deemed mentally ill and institutionalized against her will, allowed Lange to showcase the full range of her talents. She later admitted that playing Farmer over the course of the five-month shoot was "a nervous breakdown a day, I lost a lot of weight and had huge black circles under my eyes." Yet those who knew Lange said it was a role she was born to play. "I think there's a lot of the rebel in Jessica Lange and that part of Frances Farmer appealed to her. There was a kind of anti-Hollywood animus in Frances Farmer, as there has been in Jessica Lange. She wanted to do things her own way," said film critic Molly Haskell.

Lange's portrayal of Farmer earned her an Oscar nomination. (That same year saw her win the Best Supporting Actress Award for her role in *Tootsie.*)

Shepard said he was drawn to the screenplay of *Frances* "because it is like a Greek tragedy." Always concerned with notions of fate and identity, Shepard saw in the material ideas he would continue to deal with in his own work. Farmer could be a poster child for some of Shepard's main themes, chief among them the effects of a dysfunctional family and the broken promises of life. Meanwhile, director Graeme Clifford said he cast Shepard for his "enigmatic sexuality." Clifford said that since the character of Harry York is only intermittently onscreen, he was looking for an actor who made an immediate impression and "someone Jessica would personally respond to as well as respond to as the character of Frances. But I felt it needed to go beyond that, I felt it needed to be someone she personally liked."

From their first moments on screen together, when Shepard's York shares with Lange's character a sly wink across a crowded room, the chemistry between them is apparent. Harry York alternately plays lover, attempted savior, and shoulder to cry on for Farmer and in the end walks her off into the night talking about the darkness of the past and looking toward a better future.

Frances premiered in the United States on December 3, 1982. Reviews for the film ran the gamut, but the critics were universal in their praise of Lange's performance. "It was uncanny. It was as though Frances' spirit had come into her," said Farmer's nephew David Farmer.

Fool for Love opened in February 1983 at the Magic Theatre in San Francisco. It was another installment in the playwright's canon of family plays. Eddie and May are troubled lovers holed up in a low-rent motel room with faded green walls. As the drama moves along, it slowly becomes clear that these two feverish lovers are related by blood. They share the same father, who appears as a ghost sitting on the sidelines of the action and sharing the backstory that ultimately puts all the story's missing pieces in place.

Shepard writes in the directions of the printed text: "This play is to be performed relentlessly without a break." Actors love this directive, for it's an open invitation to chew up the scenery. Most do so.

By turns, Eddie and May teeter on the edge of making love and tearing each other to shreds. It's a cycle that is emblematic of their years together. Now that he's back on the scene, Eddie tries to convince May to come live with him in Wyoming. He's a stuntman, a pretend cowboy, who tries to evince authenticity by lassoing the bedpost as he makes his pitch to May. She has already moved on, however, believing she's found a new life apart from her onetime love. When Martin, her unwitting date for the night, arrives, the complications increase. Eddie becomes more menacing and the overall temperature of the play jumps by degrees. In fact, in the original production, Ed Harris, as Eddie, dragged Dennis Ludlow, playing Martin, right off the edge of the stage. The four-and-a-half-foot drop to the cement floor meant the actors landed right in front of the first row. It happened spontaneously in previews, and Shepard kept it in as part of the production. (The playwright admitted loving this cast's performance, feeling they were "carriers of my emotions.")

The character of the father, an apparition seen only by Eddie, not only reveals the lovers' true connection, he seems to be tempting his son to follow his footsteps. As in many of Shepard's family plays, the mother has a role in the resulting mess at the play's center. In *Fool for Love*, Shepard mingles past and present, letting the audience witness the cause and effect of illicit love. The moral of the play, as demonstrated by the father's infidelity and Eddie and May's attraction to each other, is that true love has a destiny of its own and will not be denied. This insight likely came to Shepard as he and Lange slowly entered their new relationship.

The playwright admits that the addition of the ghostly father hanging at the perimeter of the play was almost an afterthought—basically a way to get to the final curtain. "I was desperately looking for an ending when he came into the story," Shepard said. "That play baffles me. I love the opening, in the sense that I couldn't get enough of this thing between Eddie and May, I just wanted that to go on and on and on. But I knew that was impossible. One way out was to bring the father in."

Fool for Love was a finalist for the 1983 Pulitzer Prize and moved to New York City's Circle Repertory Company in May of 1983, with the same cast. It later transferred to the Douglas Fairbanks Theatre. Shepard was, for the most part, an absentee director when the play moved to New York. He was off with Lange beginning his new life by this time and admitted that he would have to "force myself" to spend ten days working on the transferred production. He even asked Chaikin to look in on things in his stead. The production still did well, despite the absence of the writer-director.

Though it's often revived, including a Broadway run in 2016, *Fool for Love* has not aged well in Shepard's eyes. At best, he was torn over it: "I had mixed feelings about it when I finished. Part of me looks at *Fool for Love* and says, 'This is great,' and part of me says, 'This is really corny. This is a quasi-realistic melodrama. It's still not satisfying'; I don't think the play really found itself."

Shepard would take some comfort perhaps from the fact that his idol Samuel Beckett became familiar with him and his work around this time. *New York Times* critic Mel Gussow brought Shepard's name up while interviewing the Nobel Laureate in Ireland, and Beckett proclaimed his astonishment that one man could be both a successful playwright and a movie star at the same time.

Shepard would have been less pleased, though he often told the story, with a chuckle to boot, with his father's reaction to seeing a production of *Buried Child* in Santa Fe around this time. "My Dad took it upon himself to go, and he was rolling drunk and started talking to the characters and stood up and made all this noise," Shepard recalled. "He definitely struck up a relationship with the production. When the audience finally found out he was my old man, everyone stood up and gave him a standing ovation. He was in a state of shock." Other versions of the story as told by Shepard have the old man being escorted out of the theater by the ushers, only to be readmitted when they learn he is the father of the playwright.

One the morning of March 17, 1983, Shepard sat alone at a Pancake House in San Rafael, "completely strung out" about whether to leave his family and go live with Jessica Lange or stay put. He decided to leave. He drove the eight miles back to Mill Valley and, finding his wife, mother-in-law, and son not at home, quickly packed. "Where's my fucking bag?" he shouted to no one in particular. Shepard tossed his guitar into the trunk of his car, let his father-in-law, Johnny Dark, snap one last photo of him at the house, jumped behind the wheel, put in a Hank Williams tape, and drove south on rainy Highway 5 for L.A. There he met Lange, and they headed off together for their new life in northern Minnesota, living in a log cabin with five acres of surrounding woods and a barn.

Afterward, when Shepard's wife and mother-in-law came home, they were in a good mood. In fact, they were singing goofy songs in French. It was left to O-Lan's stepfather, Dark, to break the news. "I'm thinking, 'Oh, my God, this is unbelievable.' And then the phone rang and it was Sam on the phone. [O-Lan] says, 'Where are you?' And he was being kind of vague and he's not coming out and saying anything. And she's saying, 'When are you coming back?' And he said, 'Ah, I don't know.' And she said, 'Well, how 'bout if I meet you halfway?' And his thing was, 'No, I don't want to get together; I just want to leave everything completely. I'm left. I'm gone already. This is just a courtesy call. I'm outta here.' And he went off and started this new life."

Shepard seems to have found time to type out some thoughts that morning of his departure. In all caps, double-spaced text, he again spills out a wide range of thoughts and feelings. "ME—I'M IN THE EYE OF MY OWN HURRICANE," he writes. He also shares his thoughts about the surprise many people would feel when they learn of the break with his wife. He continues, writing how close he felt to Hank Williams at that moment, how he would finally like to be his own friend, and how he figuratively shot himself in the head on this day. He concludes with: "SOMETHING IS TAKING ME SOMEWHERE." Again, with that last statement, Shepard seems to feel a mysterious force is carrying him to his new life and the fate awaiting him.

In his wake, Shepard left a thirteen-year-old son who idolized him and a "pissed-off" wife. The damage done was not limited to them: Shepard would be racked with guilt for decades. "I think the main pain of it is leaving my son at a time when I realized that he was most vulnerable and making the transition, of course, between boyhood and manhood and then having his dad up and virtually abandon him was the toughest part," Shepard told an interviewer nearly three decades on. "I mean, that's what really made me delay so much in running off with Jessica, you know. It's because I realized the damage that I was causing."

Shepard may have been miserable during the past year, being torn over the decision whether to leave his family for Lange, but the time he spent living in Mill Valley with his wife, son, and in-laws would come to represent the happiest days of his life. In the coming decades, he would often look back upon those years with an aching nostalgia. Even at his most successful, Shepard would long for these simpler times.

Meanwhile, things were not going smoothly in his new life. After Shepard made the break and he and Lange became a couple, things soon fell apart. "When we started it, it was never with the intention that we were going to run off, live together, have a family, do all these . . . regular things," Lange said. "He was married and I had a little year-old baby. It was just this unbelievably passionate love affair. But then we just couldn't give it up. When we were together we were so wild—drinking, getting into fights, walking down the freeway trying to get away—I mean, just really wild stuff. I didn't want to keep going in that direction. So we quit talking. Then through the works of some good friends, we got back in touch and that was it."

Five months after moving on, Shepard wrote to his friend Joe Chaikin about the seesaw effects of his new life. "I'm still in a strange time of transition. This whole change has been full of all kinds of powerful emotions from the most violent to the most tender. I feel very exhausted from it all and at the same time exhilarated. It's as though I was swept up in a hurricane and landed in a foreign land."

The scene Shepard left behind remained, as expected, one full of pain and disappointment. O-Lan suffered "heavily," and his teenaged son was quiet. Dark missed Shepard but recalled how he'd seen his friend moping about the house over the past year, seemingly pondering "something dark," and in some ways, Dark realized, Shepard was already gone.

Shepard settled into that log cabin in the woods near Duluth with Lange and her daughter, Shura. They spent their days there in front of the fireplace, trying to come to grips with the fact that their lives had been "suddenly and irrevocably changed." At one point, Shepard and Lange were able to visit downtown Duluth—or as Shepard now viewed it, the hometown of his new lover—walking side by side down the streets that she'd known since childhood. Still he was tortured by the thoughts of those he left behind, but he couldn't help but feel there was "a rightness" to this new direction he'd embarked upon. He fought his guilt and worry, leaning hard on Gurdjieff and the Work and "the life inside." Less than a month in his new city, Shepard began contacting a local Gurdjieff group.

He came to the conclusion through this period of soul searching that guilt had been "the most powerful influence in his life," something that had ruled him since childhood.

The trio moved south to Santa Fe at the beginning of April 1983. Upon arrival, they lived in a rented condominium while they looked for a place to buy. *Fool for Love* was moving to New York, where it would open in late May. Shepard would not be present and looked for someone to take care of things in his absence. A trip was already in the works for Dark and Shepard's son, Jesse, to visit him at his new home.

With his new living situation, Shepard would come to guard his privacy more than ever. The few interviews he gave during these years came with a plea to not reveal where he and Lange lived. He may have found a new home and family, but Shepard was far from ready to settle down, despite facing his fortieth birthday just months away. As a writer, he had two of his most successful projects, both on stage and on screen, under way. His popularity as an actor would reach its apex the following February when *The Right Stuff* went into wide distribution, earning him an Academy Award nomination. More accolades awaited the new work. During these boom years, however, he would also face personal tragedies unlike any he'd yet encountered. Shepard in midlife would have much to balance and plenty to get through.

"Paris"

WALT: *I thought you were afraid of heights.*
TRAVIS: *I'm not afraid of heights. I'm afraid of fallin'.*
—from *Paris, Texas*

G erman film director Wim Wenders spent two months in 1983 traveling around the American Southwest in preparation for his next film. He was alone, except for his Plaubel Makina 6 × 7 camera, as he traveled the dusty roads of Texas, Arizona, New Mexico, and California. He wasn't so much looking for specific locations as falling in love with the light in that part of the country. He already had in mind a partner for his next project, which would come to be the film *Paris, Texas*. Wenders had wanted Shepard to play Dashiell Hammett back in 1978 in his biopic about the famed mystery writer, but he couldn't sell his producers on such a relative newcomer to the movies. Their chance to work together finally arrived in early 1983, while Shepard was getting *Fool for Love* ready for its premiere in San Francisco. The two men would retire many an afternoon after Shepard was done at the theater to the local hangout,

Tosca, playing pool and telling each other stories, hoping to find "what territory we had in common," as Wenders put it.

Motel Chronicles, the collection of prose and poetry that Shepard had published the previous year, was their jumping-off point. The director said he wanted to make a film based on its loosely affiliated stories. Shepard's idea was to instead "take some of the essence of the stories." Thus *Motel Chronicles* wasn't adapted directly but rather informed the overarching aesthetic for *Paris, Texas*. Nevertheless, Shepard's book did provide Wenders with a starting point for the film. "It was a sentence in *Motel Chronicles*: the image of somebody leaving the freeway and walking straight into the desert," he said. "Another feeling that came from *Motel Chronicles*—more an image than a feeling—was just one of someone looking at a roadmap of the United States, ready to leave at any moment for some place he has found on the map. The film really began with that sentence."

Shepard wrote in his notes a list of nine things the film was to be about, and it included memory, time, family, and one of his recurring themes, lostness.

Paris, Texas came to life once the idea of a mute character named Travis walked out of the desert. Purposely forging ahead without a plot or even an outline, Shepard and Wenders thought about the story scene by scene. At night Shepard would go home and turn their ideas into pages of dialogue. They never wrote an ending, for fear they might "rush it [or] go beyond our knowledge of the truth of our story," Wenders said. The director hoped that Shepard would take on the role of Travis. "He adamantly insisted that being the writer precluded him from acting in the film," a disappointed Wenders recalled.

When in mid-March, Shepard left his family in Northern California to live with Lange, the script was put on hold. By the end of April, Wenders was at Shepard's new condo in Santa Fe, where the collaboration continued. Filming was delayed, pushing the start date to the beginning of October 1983. This meant Shepard would not be available to work on the last part of the script, as he was scheduled at that time to be in Iowa with Lange to shoot the film *Country*. It would take some begging on Wenders's part and a marathon late-night phone call to get *Paris, Texas* across the finish line.

The second half of 1983 found Shepard making plans for his next collaboration with Joseph Chaikin. Writing from the set of *Country* in Waterloo,

Iowa, while sipping a glass of brandy, he wrote to his friend about the dread and excitement of working without a set plan. Chaikin was suggesting an interview format, but Shepard was afraid that path might lead to comedy—intended or unintended. They eventually agreed that a theme to tie the work together might be helpful. They settled on one of Shepard's favorites, lostness. They made plans to meet in February of 1984 at the American Repertory Theater in Cambridge, Massachusetts.

Shepard's schedule for the rest of the year was busy. He did find time to finalize his divorce from O-Lan in July. Writing and acting filled his time, with the shooting of *Country* occupying him through the fall and winter. The film tells the story of Jewell and Gil Ivy, a couple trying to keep the farm that's been in her family for generations. The bureaucracy, bad weather, and worsening luck contrive to threaten their livelihood and eventually force them to sell their land. Gil gets lost on a few days' drunk, leaving it to Jewell to tough it out.

Shepard was already beginning to sour on acting, with all the waiting around and the feeling he had of once again being "sort of in the mouth of the mad-movie-machine." He confesses during the filming of *Country* to "holing up like a woodchuck" on the set in his trailer. Yet he took his role as seriously as any he'd previously had. He filled the title page of his script in his tight scrawl with all sorts of questions about his character's backstory, as well as things he wanted to be constantly mindful of ("WALK, TALK, RHYTHM, VOICE, EYES") and various emotional triggers. "Allow emotions from the physical," "Make even the toes aware," he wrote, along with reminders about using physical sensations and ways to stay in the moment. Shepard also prepared for the role by reading up on the crisis then facing America's farmers. His archives contain no fewer than eight articles about the situation.

The shoot was harder work than either Shepard or Lange expected. She coproduced the film with screenwriter William Wittliff, who'd known Shepard from the set of *Resurrection* and who'd also written *Raggedy Man*. Wittliff started out as director on *Country* but was replaced two weeks in. This must have led to further shakeups on the set, as Shepard wrote to a friend that "the shit has hit the fan," noting that the cinematographer had been fired, the director was gone, and he himself had quit until a replacement had been found. Actor Jim Haynie, who'd been in the premiere of *True West*, had a small role in *Country*, and he remembered Shepard getting very angry at one point. "Sam got all pissed off and spun his pickup truck, leaving really big scars in the ground," he said. Richard Pearce stepped in relatively quickly to take over from Wittliff, and the shoot went on.

The Iowa weather in the final months of 1983 would have been enough to make anyone touchy. Two months into the shoot, Shepard was tired of the subfreezing temperatures and long days on the set but was "finally starting to feel a whole new territory of freedom in this form of acting." Others took notice. As his costar Wilford Brimley put it, "Jessica's great, and Sam, hey, he's one hell of an actor. It's funny in this business," he added, "I guess now it's Sam's time."

That December, Shepard tried to introduce a little warmth into his and Lange's time in Iowa when he proposed to her. He'd bought an antique sapphire ring set in gold, and when Lange entered the hotel where they watched the dailies from *Country*, Shepard took her outside in the freezing cold and popped the question. Lange said yes, and they jumped up and down like two little kids. They would never officially marry.

Meanwhile, in the sweltering heat of the Southwest, the filming of *Paris, Texas* ground to a halt after just two and a half weeks while Wenders waited for more of the pledged funding to arrive from his Europe-based financers. It was a "fucking nightmare," he wrote, to always be waiting for money. The director was also worried that the ending they'd conceived for the film wouldn't work. "It is not ONE PIECE," Wenders wrote. Watching the dailies, the director was put off by what he saw as disruptive changes in attitude and storytelling. The director also feared that the part they envisioned at this point for Nastassja Kinski was too insubstantial for an actress of her fame and caliber. The film had hit a serious crisis point.

The director sat for a couple days during the break in filming and outlined a new ending for the film. It included the idea for a final scene at a peep show. Most of what would become the final section of *Paris, Texas* was laid out in seventeen typed pages. But they needed to be turned into a shootable script. Shepard was still in Iowa. "I sent it to Sam and told him, 'Sam, you have to deliver it, no matter how occupied you are up there,'" Wenders recalled. "'Please, you have to write this.' And he replied, 'I can't, but I'll do something, if you can shoot up to the peep show. . . . I promise to write that scene, but until then you're on your own.'" Kit Carson, the father of the young actor who played the boy in the film, filled in the gap with scenes and dialogue, and shooting continued.

In Iowa, Shepard took the outline and the few scraps of dialogue Wenders had provided and scripted the bravura finale of *Paris, Texas*. He wrote it out longhand on his usual yellow legal pads and called it in over the phone to Wenders one night long-distance. The call lasted from midnight to 6 a.m. "He wrote it in one night and passed it on to me the following night," Wenders said. Shepard "delivered gloriously," he added. Indeed, the most pivotal scene of the film had to be perfect in content and tone, and the collaboration between Shepard and Wenders made it happen.

The satisfaction of helping create something as good as he and Wenders both knew *Paris, Texas* was got Shepard thinking about his own future in film. He found himself wanting to write and direct a movie but without "the executives and businessmen who control it." He liked the fluidity and flexibility that film allowed over theater and the ability to "go into many different states." During 1984, he concocted a synopsis for a film called *Machine Dreams*, which featured a father chasing his wife with a burning pitchfork. The mother and her daughter have the father put away, ending the story with the women laughing together in relief. Another potential film, titled *Denial*, told the story of two brothers, Jake and Frankie, and the woman who comes between them. The names and some of the plot points are similar to Shepard's then-in-the-works play *A Lie of the Mind*. The 1985 play may at one point have been imagined by Shepard as a potential film.

A Lie of the Mind is often cited as Shepard's greatest work for the stage. The playwright himself has claimed it is better than even *Buried Child*, which won the Pulitzer, and he's right. *Lie* is Shepard's densest, funniest, and most dramatic play. It's also his bravest, as he cuts closer to the bone than he previously dared. As usual, the play's ending doesn't offer closure, but its final scene is one of Shepard's most touching and poetic.

The first inklings of the characters and plot of *Lie* date to October 1979, when Shepard started contemplating a woman left with brain damage at the hands of her violent husband, who believes he didn't just injure her but killed her. Originally, it may have been called *Imaginary Suffering*; at least that phrase is written across the top of the page in Shepard's notebook where the first outlines of the story appear. "Imaginary Prisoners" appears halfway down the page; it's unclear whether these are themes the playwright wanted to bear in mind as he developed the story or potential titles.

Shepard continued working on *A Lie of the Mind* throughout 1983 and 1984. It would not come into complete focus until a real-life event provided its climax. This would be the death of his father, an incident that would not only be replicated in the play but would be intriguingly altered so as to place the blame for the father's fate directly on the son. It would be Shepard's most disturbing, albeit effective, use of autobiography in any of his work.

As 1983 moved toward its end, Shepard's relationship with Lange, at a mere seven months in, was already proving tumultuous. "I go through such inner dramas over Jessica," he wrote to a friend from the set of *Country* in Iowa. "The whole spectrum of emotions from teen-age jealousies right up to the most tender love I've ever known." Already there were "confrontations" that had him fleeing the house they'd rented near the set and getting a motel for the night.

In Lange, Shepard had found someone as restless as himself, maybe more so. Indeed, it even got to the point where he missed his life at Mill Valley, where the entire household followed a schedule dictated primarily by Gurdjieff meetings and related activities. Now, with Lange, who was well traveled and willing to drop everything at a moment's notice and head to the Himalayas or Europe, Shepard was free to go anywhere. When he left O-Lan, he figured he was heading into a new life where there would be a stable home and eventually more children. However, six months after Lange and Shepard moved to Santa Fe, she was ready for a change. He wasn't sure he wanted such a nomadic life anymore, admitting to feeling a knot in his stomach whenever his new lover began making extravagant plans to hit the road again.

Another growing area of difference between the new couple was Shepard's disdain for Hollywood. The fact that his new paramour was a full-fledged movie star certainly made this an issue. "It's just not my game," he said. It was something he knew he'd have to learn to live with, though he wasn't sure at this point that he could.

"Between Two Deaths"

Our lives are rivers
Flowing on to the sea
The sea of dying.

—Antonio Machado

I am the enormous shadow of my tears.

—Federico García Lorca

The location filming of *Country* went into mid-December, but Shepard had to travel to L.A. for some finishing work. Once the project wrapped for good in early January, he drove across country to meet Chaikin in Boston. They set up shop across the river at the American Repertory Theater (ART) in Cambridge. The two eventually settled on an idea that would take the format of an interview with a captured angel, to be played by Chaikin. Author Don Shewey relates several stories from the two-week session. There was talk of having Lange participate in the finished work, but that plan was nixed in favor of bringing in actress Michelle Collison George, who was familiar with Shepard's previous work. Lange did visit Boston, and she and Shepard took in a performance of *Mother Courage*. When a local paper reported spotting the glamorous couple at a Beacon Hill coffee shop, things began to get out of hand as far as Shepard was concerned. Even at the ART, having a celebrity in-house was causing a stir. "All the women in the company are out of their minds," said Robert Brustein, founder and artistic director of the theater. "He has some special charisma." Shepard also found time for the students of Harvard, the ART's supporting institution, speaking at seminars and the like.

The project that would become *The War in Heaven* went unfinished at this time but would eventually draw Shepard and Chaikin back together to complete it, though under very different circumstances. Chaikin soon after left for Israel for a workshop he was leading, and he couldn't have known that yet another traumatic health scare was on the horizon.

The Right Stuff appeared in theaters in February 1984 to much critical acclaim. (The previous October it had gone into limited release, appearing at 229 theaters around the United States.) Both Gene Siskel and Roger Ebert included the film in their lists of the top three films of the 1980s. Nonetheless, it would take years for Philip Kaufman's film about the space program to find its audience; the box office receipts were initially disappointing. The film was deemed in 2013 to be "culturally, historically, or aesthetically significant," the qualifications for preservation according to the U.S. National Film Registry and the Library of Congress.

The opening of *The Right Stuff* gives us Shepard at his most iconic. At about the five-minute mark, he appears as the pilot Chuck Yeager, riding a horse through the desert in his leather jacket. He comes upon a large jet being refueled and steers his mount around the big orange plane, eyeing it as if he knows his destiny will be tied to it. The look on Shepard's face is a mix of determination and anticipation. He speaks nary a word but conveys cool confidence and nerves of steel. These opening scenes forever cemented for film lovers everywhere Shepard's reputation as a living, breathing western archetype. If the famous door frame shot of John Wayne at the end of *The Searchers* was that film hero's most iconic moment, Shepard on horseback staring down a large jet on the floor of the Mojave Desert is his. These opening scenes confirm what director Philip Kaufman said: "Sam's got the persona of Gary Cooper, the tall solitary American on horseback." With the film's release, *Newsweek* said of Shepard, "If he wants it, he stands on the brink of an extraordinary new career in the movies."

The producers of the film had pushed Shepard to take part in a cover story *Newsweek* wanted to do on *The Right Stuff* and his star turn as Yeager. He refused. In fact, his contract stipulated he did not have to do press in support of the film. There would be even more attention when that year's Academy Award nominations were announced and among the famous names appeared Shepard's for a Best Supporting Actor nod. He skipped the ceremony and missed seeing Jack Nicholson take home the Oscar for his role in *Terms of Endearment*.

Shepard and Lange were living in Santa Fe during their first years together, but it's unclear how much time he spent with his father, who lived nearby at 1200 Camino San Consuelo in Apartment 68 (now the location of Villa Consuelo Senior Center). The sixty-seven-year-old World War II vet and onetime Spanish teacher had come to New Mexico more than a decade earlier, after being divorced by his wife and roaming the Southwest for a time.

Shepard recalls the last time he saw his father. In interviews he's dated it variously as sometime in 1983 or early March 1984. It's most likely the former, as Shepard indicates that he was still living in Mill Valley at the time. As he relates this visit: "It's one of those meetings you never forget, but it was horrible because he was absolutely smashed and I should have known better [than] to try and sit down with him when he was in that state because he was a madman, he was crazy, you know, he was totally crazy. You know this Dr. Jekyll and Mr. Hyde personality thing that happens with true alcoholics. I made the mistake of trying to sit down with him and having a normal conversation but he was ranting and raving, you know, and carrying on. And I remember his main thing was he wanted me to take him with me back to this little ranch I had in Northern California to work as a hand. . . . But he was in no condition to. . . . You know, he'd burn the fucking place down. And I was trying to find a sort of diplomatic way of refusing him. . . . Anyway, once he got wind of the fact that I didn't want to do that, that I wasn't going to do that, he just had a fit. And he started screaming and yelling and telling me to get out of the place. So I was backing out the door and I remember the last thought I had was 'don't retaliate. Whatever you do in this moment, don't retaliate because you'll regret it for the rest of your life.' I don't know why I had that thought in my head. But he was just gone, you know, frothing at the mouth, screaming, throwing shit at me . . . . And I thought if I retaliate in any way, you know, verbally or any kind of way, it would be a bad deal. So I just kind of walked away. And that was the last I saw of him."

Sam Rogers must have had a little money heading into his final weekend in March 1984. A Mexican man named Esteban, who lived in the same complex and looked after his father, told Shepard the old man had gotten an unexpected check from the government, some kind of veteran's benefit. For, as his son would eventually learn, Sam Rogers spent his last days on earth getting a haircut and a fishing license and then heading off to the Pecos River to go fishing with a female companion. At some point, Rogers took a cab to nearby Bernalillo, where he hit the bars. It's a safe bet that he spent most of the afternoon and early evening of Saturday, March 24, drinking. At 7:45 p.m. he stumbled out of a bar and into Camino del Pueblo, a busy street known for its high sidewalks that were originally designed to guard against the effects of flooding. According to the New Mexico Office of the Medical Investigator, the driver of the car that hit Shepard's father did not see him until the moment of impact. Rogers was struck on his right side while attempting to cross the northbound lane. Shepard tells of how his father's last words while conscious were spoken to an ambulance driver: "My name is Sam," he said. He was taken to the University of New Mexico Hospital in Albuquerque with multiple injuries. Shepard recalls that his father died in the ambulance, but officially he was pronounced dead the next day at 1:15 p.m. His blood alcohol level was measured at .334, more than three times the legal limit.

A notebook entry of Shepard's titled "Between Two Deaths," committed just weeks after his father's accident, finds him cursing the old man, referring to his "miserable contemptible death," and surprised to find himself loathing him, "as if he had purposely gone out of his way to lay a curse on me and all those left in his wake."

Yet the son also saw the other side of his father's life. Shepard had spent a lifetime running from the old man, trying not to follow in his footsteps, and alternately putting him front and center in his greatest plays. If he cast his father in a sympathetic light at times, it was because he knew of his pain. "He had a tough life," Shepard would say nearly two decades later.

"[He] had to support his mother and brother at a very young age when his dad's farm collapsed. You could see his suffering, his terrible suffering, living a life that was disappointing and looking for another one. My father was full of terrifying anger." Perhaps Shepard feared that he might be caught in the same trap. His own beliefs about heredity, as manifest in *Buried Child* and *Curse of the Starving Class*, tell us he feared there was no escaping the curse of the Rogers clan. His father was the fourth in a long line of alcoholics. Shepard himself had long fought the so-called battle of the bottle, and as the decades progressed he would seemingly lose more and more ground to it.

The facts of Samuel Rogers's death beg the question whether it was an accident at all. His blood alcohol level of 0.334 means he was not far from drinking himself into a coma or risking respiratory failure and death, which can occur at 0.4. To reach this level of intoxication itself is dangerous, but to head toward a busy roadway in that condition was courting almost certain death. Could it have been something closer to suicide? Certainly Sam Rogers's life had not turned out as he planned, and he'd endured the emotional pain of losing a beloved brother, leaving behind a life he may have envisioned in Colombia, and the dashing of his own writerly dreams. Additionally, he was haunted by nightmares from his time flying bombers during World War II. Estranged for the most part from his family, living alone with no money and a serious drinking problem in a small apartment in Santa Fe, who could blame him for seeking a way to end it all? Shepard himself seemed to consider this a distinct possibility when he told a writer for *American Film* magazine just a few months after his father's death, "He was sort of looking to get out, you know?" Meanwhile, in *The Late Henry Moss*, a play Shepard would struggle with for years before bringing it to the stage in 2000, in which the father's death is central to the plot, a character claims the old man was "wishing for death. Wishing for some way out."

Shepard visited his father's apartment after he died and found nothing but a rocking chair and a refrigerator filled with jalapeno peppers. When the old man had money, the fridge would hold booze and not much else. "It was not the place for food," Shepard said.

Samuel Rogers's body was cremated and his ashes were deposited into a small pine box and buried at the National Cemetery in Santa Fe. While going through his father's sad apartment, Shepard found an unmailed letter addressed to him. It read in part: "You may think this great calamity that happened, way back when—this so-called disaster between me and your mother—you might actually think that it had something to do with you, but you're dead wrong. Whatever took place between me and her was strictly personal. See you in my dreams."

Shepard also found in the apartment evidence that his father was also a writer—not the poet he perhaps once dreamed of becoming but a contributor to the local newspaper. "There were all these little columns in his room about life in Santa Fe, and they were quite astounding, vignettes about things like a double rainbow he had seen," Shepard said. At the funeral, he and one of his sisters read from Lorca's poems, the old man's favorite; Shepard tried to read a Bible passage but broke down halfway through.

Perhaps the life of Samuel Rogers, war hero, esteemed teacher, whose life took a darkly sad turn, would be better summed up by another Latin American poet, one his son had recently discovered, César Vallejo. In one of his most famous poems, "The Black Heralds," the Peruvian writer depicted the utter starkness of life and the impossibility of finding happiness:

> *There are blows in life, so powerful . . . I don't know!*
> *Blows as from the hatred of God; as if, facing them,*
> *the undertow of everything suffered*
> *welled up in the soul . . . I don't know!*

Shepard's dark muse was gone. The wound, of course, would remain. There would be a new family play, his greatest, *A Lie of the Mind*, staged in the coming months. In it, the father would die just as Sam Rogers had, only Shepard would place the character of the son—his surrogate in the play—not only present at the scene but responsible for the father's death.

There was more bad news for Shepard just six weeks later. His friend and mentor Joseph Chaikin had completed a workshop he was leading in Israel, and he next headed to Ontario, where he was working on *Waiting for Godot* as part of the city's Shakespeare Festival. He felt ill and knew it would be best for him to be near his doctors in New York. Chaikin had a long history of heart problems and was right to be cautious. There may have been some advance warning: on March 16, 1984, Chaikin wrote to Shepard that he was going into the hospital for new tests. "My heart again," he wrote. Closing the letter, Chaikin demonstrated his courage and the resiliency of his spirit. Saying he didn't care if he lived to be fifty or eighty, he was convinced that what mattered in the end were the "quality of the moments and the possibility in the endeavors."

This time Chaikin was diagnosed with heart failure. During open-heart surgery on May 7, he suffered a stroke that impaired his speech. It was a type of left-hemisphere aphasia, similar to what Shepard's mother-in-law, Scarlett, had suffered after her aneurism. In other words, it was a problem Shepard was familiar with. He sent his ailing friend a telegram from Los Angeles, saying his heart was with him and that he'd soon be by his side. He signed it, "I love you. Sam." They would speak on the phone in the coming weeks, Shepard checking in on Chaikin's health and making plans for an upcoming visit.

Chaikin spent time recovering at the Rusk Institute of Rehabilitation Medicine on East Thirty-Eighth Street in New York. Shepard drove from Minnesota to be with his friend that August, and they continued to work on *The War in Heaven*. "Sam was there and he stuck with [Joe]. Not everybody did," said Eileen Blumenthal, author of *Joseph Chaikin: Exploring at the Boundaries of Theater*.

Shepard taught his old friend some of the speaking exercises he'd learned while working with his former mother-in-law. "We were doing like word therapy stuff, where he was repeating patterns and rhythms like that," Shepard recalled. "I think he probably believed for quite a while he would regain all of his faculties. He went at it—you know how Joe was—he went at it like a warrior." That September, Shepard sent his friend a handwritten note about their current collaboration but included a reminder to "keep working on the sound cards," and urging Chaikin not to worry when he encountered difficulty, for with every hurdle he overcame, his speaking "grows stronger."

The two men continued working on the material they'd developed in Cambridge, and after Shepard left they worked separately, communicating by mail. Part of Chaikin's task was to master the clarity and diction that would be necessary for him to one day perform the new piece. It was perhaps the best rehab Chaikin could have hoped for, said Barry Daniels, editor of *Joseph Chaikin and Sam Shepard: Letters and Texts, 1972–1984*. "It was a very important element in the process of recovery for him," Daniels writes. "It gave him a sense of stability through work and a revived hope for the future."

Shepard at this time was also working on his next play, *A Lie of the Mind*, reading Stephen Crane, and, when possible, slipping off with a couple of his horses into the Minnesota mountains for a three-day fishing excursion while Lange was filming in Los Angeles. Late in October 1984, Shepard returned to New York to work with Chaikin to shape *The War in Heaven* into its final form. Shepard composed and performed the music for the initial productions.

Chaikin's first official performance of the twenty-five-minute piece was in a recording studio; New York radio station WBAI presented the work in January. It would not be until December 1985 that Chaikin would take the show on the road, performing *The War in Heaven* in San Diego, San Francisco, Toronto, Italy, Poland, Los Angeles, and elsewhere.

The War in Heaven presents Chaikin as an angel who has crashed to earth. He has a mission, orders to carry out, but seems to have forgotten them. Speaking in short phrases and repeating key words that drive the rhythm of the monologue, Chaikin's angel conveys confusion, fear, and "lostness," that theme that he and Shepard had once hoped to build upon. To wit, the piece ends:

> I died
> the day I was born
> and became an Angel
> on that day
>
> Since then
> There are no days
> There is no time
> I am here
> By mistake

Chaikin's angel breaks off his musings at several points to plea for release and a return to heaven.

To read the text gives one the idea of the power lurking in *The War in Heaven*. However, Chaikin's inflection, his occasional struggles with some of the words (he read the text from a music stand during performances), and his expressive facial gestures are the key to the piece's potency.

Reviewers were touched by the performance, viewing the piece as a metaphor for Chaikin's own return to some semblance of normalcy. Bernard Weiner in the *San Francisco Chronicle* said that *The War in Heaven* was "extremely moving." A reviewer in Toronto also captured Chaikin's post-performance interview, where the actor struggled to speak due to his aphasia. The critic wrote that it made the piece even more poignant.

September 1984 saw two of Shepard's best performances arrive in movie theaters. One was as an actor; the other as a screenwriter. His performance in *Country* as Gil Ivy, the farmer whose fortunes have taken a turn for the worse, was well received. Some critics quibbled, feeling his character's temporary detour into drink and depression felt forced. Still, most reviews depicted the film as a heartfelt attempt to explore the dilemma facing America's small farms and the people who relied on them.

Not everyone was as kind. President Ronald Reagan in his published diaries saw *Country* as "a blatant propaganda message against our agri programs." Lange was, as usual, pitch perfect in her portrayal of Jewell Ivy, who doggedly works to save the farm that has been in the family for a century. So realistic was her performance that Congress called her to testify about the importance of the family farm.

Shepard's other triumph at this time was as screenwriter of *Paris, Texas*. (Kit Carson, for his work on the script, was credited with adapting the story.) The film swept the top three awards at the 1984 Cannes Film Festival. Set to Ry Cooder's dust-dry slide guitar and filmed against the gorgeous light of the American Southwest and the desperate neon of the tiny Texas towns encountered along the way, *Paris, Texas* is a road movie for the ages. The film follows the travails of a man named Travis (Harry Dean Stanton), who spends the first part of the film mysteriously wandering through the South Texas desert. After being discovered by his brother Walt

(Dean Stockwell) and taken to his Los Angeles home, Travis slowly begins to open up. Walt and his wife have been raising Travis's son, Hunter, for the past four years, since Travis disappeared. Father and son reconnect and eventually depart on a road trip to find the boy's mother (Nastassja Kinski). Travis finds her in Houston working in a peep show. After he confronts her and she explains the pain he put her through when he abandoned her, Travis makes a decision. Knowing he is not a family man, he leaves again, despite his love for his son. His last act before hitting the road is bringing mother and son together, paving the way for their happiness.

Those aware of what was happening in Shepard's life as he and Wenders came up with the story can be forgiven for reading into it. In the film, a man who walked away from his family returns to help make at least partial amends. Meanwhile, when the forsaken wife tells her side of things near the end of the film, it's as if Shepard is channeling what he may have imagined to be O-Lan's feelings of hurt and abandonment. As Jane, Kinski recalls how after Travis left, she heard his voice and felt his presence everywhere. Finally, it's not much of a stretch to imagine that with the scene where Travis records a good-bye message to leave with his son, Shepard's script could serve as a note to his own son, still back in Mill Valley. The note ends, "I love you more than my life."

Paris, Texas works on many levels, but as an expression of one man's guilt over breaking up his family it couldn't be clearer. Shepard has always included elements of autobiography in his art, and his work on this under-stated masterpiece is no exception. He has often shared, at least with his closest friends, the guilt he felt over abandoning his young family. Despite being fully invested in his new life by this time, Shepard felt that his departure from O-Lan and his son was nothing short of tragic, and something he was still trying to get over. He worried about the effect his leaving was having on Jesse, who was then fifteen. *Paris, Texas* is his plea for forgiveness, or at least understanding.

Between Two Families

L

You know, in a lot of ways I feel like it was given to the wrong play.
Buried Child *is a clumsy, cumbersome play. I think* A Lie of the
Mind *is a much better piece of work. It's denser, more intricate,
better constructed.*

—Sam Shepard

Whether it was the fact of their engagement or just finally getting used to being together, by early 1985, Shepard felt that he,
Lange, and her daughter, Shura, had entered "some brand new
territory of togetherness." More likely this new familial feeling was due to
the fact that Lange was pregnant. Meanwhile, she told a journalist for the
International Herald Tribune that she had made a lifelong commitment to
"taking care of Sam." As for the new arrival, Shepard seemed more than
ready, writing to Chaikin the month before Hannah was born: "I think
I'm at the right age for it now."

Shepard was, at the same time, having a difficult time with Lange's
regular absences. As an A-list actress, even one successfully balancing
work and family, she was often flying off to film sets around the world.
Her mate's feelings of abandonment are made clear in a notebook entry.

Shepard complains of the "unbearable loneliness" he feels when she is away and admonishes himself for suffering like a "dumb animal." The last line of this single-page outcry claims that the only cure is alcohol.

Otherwise, Shepard's days were filled with reading Gurdjieff-related material and even doing some painting. Writing kept him busier than ever. At this time he was expanding his play *Fool for Love* into a screenplay for a movie version that Robert Altman was attached to direct (though afterward, Shepard would claim Altman wrote most of the script). In the film, Shepard was cast in the lead role of Eddie, with Lange originally pegged to star as May. Her pregnancy caused her to drop out.

Altman had a fondness for turning plays into movies and had done so previously with *Streamers* (1983) and *Come Back to the Five & Dime, Jimmy Dean, Jimmy Dean* (1982). Altman liked *Fool for Love* and saw its filmic potential, but he had a caveat. "I read this and I thought, 'Wow, this would be great, but if Sam Shepard played the part then I would find it irresistible," Altman said. Things between the director and writer didn't get off on the most auspicious note: Altman asked Shepard early on what the play was about, and he wouldn't answer.

Shepard was also consumed with writing his latest play. An outline in one of Shepard's notebooks dating to October 1979 contains many of the elements that would come together in *A Lie of the Mind*. The play seems to have stalled over the years, until Shepard once again inserted the character of the dissolute father—as in *Fool for Love*—as a ghost or specter that hangs over the action and is remembered for the harm he caused during his lifetime. "Looks like it wants to be a long one this time," Shepard said of the play while it was in development. He was right. At one point, *A Lie of the Mind* was running an estimated seven-plus hours. Even as late as March of 1985, Shepard was still struggling with the play.

Shepard had set his sights high for *A Lie of the Mind*, hoping to get to "some kind of final, definitive piece" on the ideas that had fueled his writing to this point, specifically about the family. After more than two decades as a dramatist, he felt he was at last able to get down to the "real essence" of it all.

The initial impulse behind the play was "the incredible schism between a man and a woman, in which something is broken in a way that almost kills the thing that was causing them to be together. The devastating break."

Couple this with the fact of two people close to Shepard suffering from aphasia, and there lies a key element of the play. Beth, a central character who has been beaten by her husband, Jake, suffers from brain damage and must relearn how to speak.

A Lie of the Mind premiered at the Promenade Theatre in New York on December 5, 1985. The cast featured Harvey Keitel, Amanda Plummer, Aidan Quinn, Geraldine Page, Will Patton, and Karen Young. The three-act play was a hit with both audiences and critics. The play depicts two families and their reactions to a near-fatal incident of domestic abuse.

Lie opens in mid–phone call, as a desperate Jake tells his brother Frankie that he's not only beaten his wife, Beth, but likely killed her. Jake hangs up abruptly, giving neither his brother nor the audience further details. However, in the next scene we see that Beth is alive but suffering from some sort of brain damage that's affected her ability to walk and talk.

Jake arrives at his mother's house and is a wreck, physically and mentally, still believing he's killed his wife. His mother, Lorraine, cares for him, as brother Frankie slips away to visit Beth's parents' house to find out the truth. Meanwhile, Beth's family struggles with her medical problems, even though she's beginning to show progress. When Frankie shows up at their home, Beth's brother Mike shoots him, mistaking him for a deer. Frankie is brought into the house, where he convalesces, and Beth, confused, begins to mistake him for Jake.

In Act 3, Jake has left his mother's home to find Beth. His mother, Lorraine, and sister Sally are left behind and they start to talk. The subject turns to Jake's and Sally's father, Lorraine's husband, who ran off to Mexico years earlier and was killed, like Shepard's real-life father, when he was run down in the street after a day of drinking. It's at this point that Sally divulges the full account of what happened that night. How she and Jake visited the old man down in Mexico and took him out for a drink. As Jake and his father begin tossing them back, a visible change overtakes each of them.

> SALLY: There was a meanness that started to come outa both
> of them like these hidden snakes. A terrible meanness that was
> like—murder almost. It was murder.

Once they're both good and drunk, Sally relates, Jake comes up with the idea to drink in every bar from there to the U.S. border, a mile away. The competitive streak shared by father and son turns this into a race. At one point, the father falls flat on his face in the street. Suddenly Sally, plain as day, sees something malicious in her brother's plan.

> SALLY: Jake had decided to kill him.
> [Pause]
> LORRAINE: What in the world are you talking about?
> SALLY: It was just the same—it was just the same as if he'd had a gun. He knew what was going to happen. Dad couldn't even walk anymore. He couldn't stand. His knees were all bloody. Jake knew that all he had to do was push him over the edge. Just a few more drinks and he'd be gone.

The plan works. Sally reports seeing her father "splattered all over the road like some lost piece of livestock." Meanwhile, Jake was in the next bar having a drink. "He never even got up when he heard the sirens," his sister says.

The mother doesn't believe Sally, but on the other hand she questions her daughter about her complicity in the incident. The outing of the story seems to clear the way forward for both women. When we next see them, they have a trip to Ireland planned and are sorting through old papers, letters, photographs, and other mementos of the past and tossing them into a large bucket. The scene ends with Lorraine tossing in a match.

Soon after Jake arrives at Beth's house, her brother Mike hauls him inside to make him apologize to his sister. Jake, so wrecked from lack of sleep and the guilt he feels, now speaks like Beth did when she was first injured, in halting and incomplete thoughts. He tells his wife, "I-I-I-I love you more than this earth." He tells her about the voices in his head that lie to him and cause his misbehavior. "You are true," he says. He tells Beth to stay with his brother Frankie and asks for a final kiss. She steps closer and he kisses her on the forehead and walks off.

Jake's actions mirror those of Travis in *Paris, Texas*, who leaves for the good of his reunited son and daughter. Here, Jake does what's best for his wife and absents himself from her life. The play's final scene finds Beth's mother, Meg, looking out the window, seeing "a fire in the snow," referring to Jake's mother and sister burning up their past. The finale involves a touch of magical realism, as many miles separate the two households. Still, it proved a potent metaphor and a poetic end to the play.

A Lie of the Mind is Shepard's best play for many reasons. It's the most consistently entertaining and there are scenes full of real tension, from the opening phone call to the many moments of confrontation. It is a sprawling epic that, with the live Americana music Shepard requires in the script (he had the Red Clay Ramblers on board for the run at the Promenade), can last nearly four hours. Structurally it represents the height of Shepard's dramatic art. Most scenes end on a powerful note—such as Beth screaming out for her husband at the end of Act 2 as the stage goes dark, or when Jake dips into his father's urn and blows a handful of ashes into the air, allowing them to glitter in the spotlight above.

Throughout the play, Shepard juxtaposes his scenes so that images within speak to each other or mirror what came just before. This makes for some interesting parallels that the audience is forced to consider. He does this to great effect when using it to draw distinctions between the two families that inhabit the play.

Shepard's old theme of heredity is expressed more subtly but is still present. Lorraine predicts her son will follow in his father's footsteps. When Jake has run off in search of Beth early in Act 3, she says, "I know what's gonna happen. I can see it plain as day. They'll find him by the highway. That's what'll happen. Crumpled up. Busted open like a road dog. Then maybe you'll be satisfied." Here, Shepard was mirroring in his fictional work a fear he had for himself. Two decades later, he committed to his notebook an entry headlined "recurring terror," and beneath it wrote about his fear that he would be hit by a car and killed, "just like my father . . . blind sided."

If in *Lie* Jake does indeed kill his father, perhaps it is an attempt to kill inside himself all that he fears he inherited from his father. Once his sin has been exposed by his sister, it not only allows the women in the family to move on, it allows Jake to demonstrate an act of pure love toward Beth by letting her go. Then again, Jake may have believed there was no way to stop himself from following in his father's footsteps and therefore mercifully lets Beth go before he does to her what his old man put his mother through.

A Lie of the Mind in some ways also gives Shepard the opportunity to present his mother's side of things. If Lorraine is indeed a surrogate for Jane Rogers, we hear from her perspective how awful the marriage and its dissolution was: "You know a man your whole life. You grow up with him. You're almost raised together. You go to school on the same bus together. And then one day he just up and disappears into thin air." As for how she feels about her late husband after all this, Lorraine says: "I'll condemn him right up to my last breath. He shaped my whole life. Vengeance is the only thing that keeps me goin'."

The play earned the best reviews Shepard had ever received, with *New York Times* critic Frank Rich saying that *Lie* proved that Shepard was "a major writer at the height of his powers." Meanwhile, *Variety* reported that the opening weekend of the initial run brought in $100,000 in ticket sales, breaking a record for Off-Broadway—twice. When tickets went on sale the month before the December opening, it set a one-day record. The Saturday of its opening weekend, it broke that record, with $44,385 in tickets being sold.

Despite all this, by late March 1986, sales had slowed to the point where the producers planned to end the run. They had lost $10,000 in the four weeks between late March and May 22. A letter to Shepard from producer Lewis Allen laid it out for the playwright. It's clear that Shepard was unhappy with many aspects of the production: Allen concedes that Shepard has "a considerable amount of criticism and questions." One thing Shepard was unhappy with was the amount of money, or lack thereof, spent to advertise the run. Hurting the play's continued prospects was the fact that *A Lie of the Mind* was an expensive show to mount. Shepard told Allen from the first that he wanted the play done "right," and "screw the cost." The result was an outlay of about $56,000 a week, an astronomical amount for an Off-Broadway production. (*Fool for Love* had been staged two years earlier for about $15,000 per week by comparison, though that play is minimalist compared to *Lie*.) Allen had spent an additional $16,000 the previous week and saw only minimum return for that investment. He concluded that everyone knew the play was at the Promenade but that everyone had either seen it or wasn't planning to. The good news was that producers from London to Los Angeles to Rome were waiting to get their hands on Shepard's latest.

All the same, Shepard would never again reach these heights as a playwright, critically or commercially. *A Lie of the Mind* won the Drama Desk Award for Outstanding Play, the New York Drama Critics Circle Award for Best Play, and the Outer Critics Circle Award for Best Off-Broadway Play. *Lie* received no attention from the Pulitzer committee, but it is in many respects better than Shepard's play that won the award, *Buried Child*, as well as the two that were finalists, *True West* and *Fool for Love*. *A Lie of the Mind* is more complex and represents Shepard's maturation in the areas of structure and dynamics. It is equal parts brutal and poetic, and it delivers what Shepard hoped it would—his ultimate statement about families in extremis.

Around the same time *A Lie of the Mind* was being prepped for its premiere, Robert Altman's vision of *Fool for Love* arrived in theaters around the country. It landed with a thud. Just who's to blame for this is hard to say. However, it brings to light something about Shepard's plays, and later his screenplays: his stories are small. This is not a criticism, but it does speak to the difficulty in transferring Shepard's material to the big screen, either in his hands or another's. His stories contain few scenes or plot points and are devoid of labyrinthine designs. Most of his stories, for the stage or screen, stick closely to the Aristotelian idea of the dramatic unities—a single action, taking place in one location, usually over a set duration. Shepard has admitted freely that narrative is not his strong suit. He, of course, makes up for this with his other gifts—humor, the ability to create tension, setting moods, and the ineffable aspects of his work, the mystery at the core that, in his best work, is never less than compelling. Shepard's plays are deep in that they are built in layers; narratives fit for mass consumption in film typically stick to traditional storytelling tropes and feature a beginning, middle, and end, adhering at least nominally to some form of logic. In his plays, Shepard relies on his gifts for language and image making, and the creation of worlds or emotional territories where the stakes are personal and "a sense of bafflement and loss prevail." The large strokes of any Shepard play can be stated in a sentence or two: *Buried Child* is about a young man returning to his family home, provoking the airing of an old and terrible secret. Even *A Lie of the Mind*, which sprawls to over three hours on stage, is a simple story with not a lot of dramatic movement.

This is the case with *Fool for Love*. It is a bare-boned story of two old lovers meeting again in a hotel room, where the difficult secret of their relationship is revealed. On the big screen, Shepard's story was a victim of two problems. One of the keys to the play was that it was, as Shepard himself put it, to be performed "relentlessly." Onstage, it comes at you in a burst of energy, Eddie and May's relationship becomes combustible before our very eyes, and its revelations are dispensed in dreamy exposition. In the end, it flares out, albeit with an offstage explosion that somewhat strains credulity. The film version, stretching to 106 minutes, loses all of these effects as it tries to fill the big screen, a long running time, and a large set with the same simple story. Altman fleshed things out with odd flashbacks and additional characters that fit the play's mood and tone but that make the story seem flabby and far less concentrated.

Shepard's feelings about the outcome of *Fool for Love* the movie are similar. "Onstage it was huge," he said. "It had a frightening physical reality to it. . . . On film it comes across as kind of a quaint little Western tale of two people lost in a motel room."

The other problem with the film version of *Fool for Love* is a lack of contextualization at the outset, resulting in confusion and frustration among viewers. Shepard's Eddie pulls up to the desert motel with his truck and horse trailer and begins searching the grounds. When he locates the room he's looking for, he doesn't knock or call out for anyone. He lunges at the door and breaks through. Anyone not familiar with the play would assume he was a rapist or a murderer. Kim Basinger, who plays May, has locked herself in the bathroom, and her reaction isn't one of terror, as one might expect given the circumstances. She simply appears confused as to what to do next. When she comes out of the bathroom, Shepard is sitting on the bed, and they begin to talk as if none of what we've just seen has taken place. The juxtaposition of Shepard's breaking the door down and this quiet discussion, followed a few moments later by the couple's sharing a knowing and sly smile, is too odd to accept without foregrounding. The film continues this way for some time, and the effect isn't mysterious but baffling. The audience has been dumped into the middle of this lovers' battle without an inkling about why Eddie and May are fighting one minute and the next ready to jump into bed.

The source material begins differently and with great effect. Onstage, *Fool for Love* starts with a touch of mystery, of course, but coherently presents what is clearly a love–hate relationship. We know this couple aches to be together but simply can't. Later, we find out they're related by blood, and this fact and its accompanying baggage is the gulf they know they'll never breach. Not that they don't want to and haven't enjoyed doing so in the past. The play has its problems, most notably that forced and incredulous ending, but it works on stage like a powder keg with an ever-shortening fuse.

The film version of *Fool for Love* was also laden with excess baggage. Harry Dean Stanton plays the father of Eddie and May, who simply hangs around the motel, playing harmonica, laughing, and ultimately trying to defend his actions near the end of the film, when it is revealed that his infidelity means he's father to both Eddie and May, and thus the root of their problem. Altman added to the film a confounding recurring bit where Stanton's character appears as his younger self with a family in tow, including a baby who we are led to believe is May as a child. And, it's worth adding, any film that has to use fifteen minutes of flashbacks to explain what's going on in the present has most likely gotten away from the writer and director. Altman saw this intermingling of the past and present as "kind of a thing inside of a thing. It was very incestuous, which is what the play was about. . . . Everything was incestuous, that was the idea, to make this play kind of spiral back into itself and out."

Shepard hated acting in the film. "I felt very uncomfortable," he said. "I was *not* having a good time. I didn't get off on that. [Laughs] First of all, this was a situation I tried to avoid for a long, long time—acting in my own stuff—because I always felt it was silly and pretentious. You know, 'acted and written by' and all that crap. Appearing in! Jesus. . . . I didn't feel comfortable with that at all. And I don't think I'll ever do it again if I can help it." Yet even with more lines than most "strong, silent types" should be given, and the need for some sentimental emoting, Shepard does a fine job in *Fool for Love*. His best scenes are when he's toying with the hapless Martin (Dennis Quaid), who comes to pick May up for a date. Shepard's good-natured joshing has an edge that could cut metal. *Newsweek* magazine's Jack Kroll felt Shepard's acting took a "giant stride forward" on *Fool*. The critic recalled something Altman had told him about a day when Lange visited the set. "We shot the scene and he did it in an entirely unexpected way," Altman said. "It was aggressive, it was hostile, and really shocked me. And then I thought, 'He's doing this for [Lange].'"

Not everyone raved about Shepard's performance. *Fool for Love* premiered in May of 1986, and for the most part critics trashed the film. David Denby went so far as to say it would end all talk of Shepard as a movie superstar: "Sam Shepard isn't really an actor," he wrote. It was the first time Shepard took such a hit for an onscreen performance. He was really just a victim of a project that was ill conceived from the start. In fact, Shepard was against the idea of transporting *Fool for Love* from the stage to the screen. If it were to be done, he said, the one to play Eddie should have been the actor who created the role in the first place—Ed Harris. "Bob kept insisting that I do it, and then he wanted Jessica to do it, too," Shepard recalled. Perhaps Altman was thinking of the onscreen chemistry the two real-life lovers would engender, or the publicity of bringing Shepard and Lange together for another film, especially one about two mercurial lovers.

Shepard was angered somewhat by the fact that Altman took the film to Paris for editing and he never saw it until it was in theaters. This despite a promise from the director that Shepard would be involved in the final cut. In a 1988 feature in *Interview* magazine, Shepard was harsh in his criticism of Altman. "I liked Altman's stuff up to a certain point. And I was fooled into believing that he was going to have integrity in this thing," he said. "Later on, I just felt he kind of shined me on. That surprised me. I just felt like he blasted through the thing and didn't give it everything he told me he was going to give it. But that's all water under the bridge."

Speaking to Mitchell Zuckoff a decade or so later for an Altman oral history, Shepard was more sanguine. "I think Bob did a commendable job," he said.

There was also a bit of a furor over something Shepard said to an interviewer who asked about working with directors such as Altman and Woody Allen. Shepard's response was that neither knew anything about acting. Years later, in Zuckoff's book, Shepard explained that this wasn't a criticism but a truism about many film directors, who unlike those in the theater do not have time to work with actors, talk to actors, or discuss ideas about character. "You don't have that luxury in film," Shepard said.

"Dancing Around the Grave?"

To have had a rich harvest more or less guarantees a comedown later. The issue is the grace with which you fall.

—Adam Gopnik

Most would make the case that by 1986, Shepard's best years as a playwright and actor were behind him. He'd written forty plays; won the Pulitzer; acted in several films, snagging an Oscar nomination for his performance in *The Right Stuff*; and was seemingly ready to settle down with Lange and start a family. The signs of an artist in twilight were already beginning to appear—there were two biographies published around this time, and the Academy and Institute of Arts and Letters notified Shepard that in February he was to be inducted along with Art Buchwald, Morton Gould, and Donald Keene. The first two were well past their prime, and most Americans hadn't even heard of the third. In short, not the kind of company an artist considering himself still relevant wants to keep. Of this transitional time in Shepard's career, the *New York Times* wrote: "In the late 1970s, Mr. Shepard was deeply fashionable, everyone's favorite crossover from the avant-garde. But like all golden boys, he eventually began to tarnish in his public's mind. There was a backlash of feeling that identified him as a relic of a chapter in experimental theater, saturated in symbolism, willfully obscure and given to bashing the American Dream with two heavy hands."

Flash forward, and such sentiments were in the air in May of 1993 when Brussels hosted the first International Sam Shepard Conference. One of the critics in attendance commented upon "Shepard's cultural moment," identifying it as securely in the past. To this observation came the question from one of those in attendance: "Are we dancing around the grave?" Fifteen Americans joined more than thirty European scholars, critics, theater types, and students at the conference. Shepard biographer Don Shewey was there and commented upon the light attendance. "Making the whole enterprise more comically pathetic was the fact that a hotel conference room the size of an average university classroom could house the entire 'Shepard industry.'" Scholars were giving the playwright credit for his longevity but then discussed his "fall from grace."

The fact is that Shepard from this point on, despite the slackening of output and dropoff in the quality of his plays, remains as interesting an artist and personality as ever. The facts are that he still had another very good family play in him and three books of prose, including his best short story. And despite dozens upon dozens of forgettable films, there were still some gems to come. Late in life, he'd actually find himself being sought after by a new generation of filmmakers, racking up countless good reviews. One critic wrote in 2016 of the film *Midnight Special*, in which Shepard is featured only in the first fifteen minutes, that the director should have understood "one of cinema's cast-iron rules: Any film with Sam Shepard in it will seem a lot worse once Sam Shepard is no longer in it."

These years also feature the ups and downs of his relationship with Lange and Shepard's struggles with alcohol.

It would be films that took up most of Shepard's time in these years. But they weren't the kinds of movies he'd originally gravitated to—that is, rural portraits and well-executed character studies. From now on, most of Shepard's film work would be nothing more than a way to pay the bills. (For the remainder of this narrative, only the films that Shepard clearly had an artistic stake in or that can be considered standouts will be dealt with at length.)

The year 1986 would be a time of transition for Shepard, marked at the start with the arrival on January 13 of his first daughter, Hannah Jane. The other big event of the year was moving with Lange and the couple's two children to Charlottesville, Virginia. Santa Fe had simply become too commercialized, Shepard felt. "Well, the town just got inundated with Texas oil people. And the face of it changed into this shopping-mall thing with adobe siding," he said. "It was getting weird. You couldn't even get across the downtown plaza it was so full of tourists. But it's amazing country. The town itself used to be great back in the 50s and 60s."

Charlottesville around this time was becoming, for a select group of show business folk, a refuge from Hollywood and New York. Expensive, yes, but still retaining a small-town feel, "where there is a good balance of intellectual stimulation and lazy-dog relaxation," a 1991 *New York Times* feature put it. There were mountains rolling off to the west and real estate offerings that mixed million-dollar mansions and sprawling horse farms. Among the other glitterati living in the university town was Sissy Spacek, who may have been the one who tipped off Shepard and Lange about the place. Lange has spoken often about not wanting to raise children in Hollywood, and two decades after moving to Virginia, it was a choice she did not regret. "I wanted them to have a childhood that had nothing to do with what I do," she said. "I think it worked out. They came with me on movie sets or sat backstage at the theater. I allowed them into that world, but they were never exposed to the politics of it."

With the birth of his daughter and his move to the Virginia countryside, the ever press-wary Shepard became even more concerned about his privacy. Around this time, he continued to ask anyone to whom he granted a rare interview to be sure not to mention where he lived, or even to refrain from mentioning where they met to talk. Most went along without a complaint, but some poked fun: "This is a man for whom 'How do you do?' constitutes an invasion of privacy," one journalist wrote.

Shepard took on film roles but eschewed serious writing for the most part. There were a few attempts: In his notebooks is the start of a screenplay for a "blues movie," and he and Tom Waits were writing back and forth about collaborating on a film. At this point, the furthest they got was an idea involving a raving lunatic, well dressed and highly intelligent, who is "crushed by his imaginings" and who ultimately breaks down at a rest stop outside Oklahoma City. There he decides to run for elected office and sets up his headquarters in town. The songs should be "stark and jagged, quietly disturbing," Waits writes. They would continue the correspondence, always planning to get together and work on something.

One day in the fall of 1986, Shepard's kitchen phone rang and on the other end was one of Woody Allen's secretaries. She said the director was looking to recast one of the male leads in the film he was currently shooting. Christopher Walken wasn't working out, or, as Allen put it, "We couldn't get copacetic on what to do and decided that instead of his making concessions and my making concessions, we'd work on something else down the line." Hence the call to Shepard. "I was his next idea," he said. Allen thought Shepard could bring a bit more subtlety to the role.

Shepard told the secretary he was interested, and she replied that a special driver making the trip from New York to Virginia would bring a copy of the script to him. Shepard, privacy concerns to the fore, balked at having a stranger drive up to his house and instead had it dropped off at the hardware store the next town over, where he often had his mail sent. Shepard found the script "melodramatic and verbose, but very interesting." He signed on for the role of the lovelorn writer Peter and not long after found himself in New York City being picked up at his hotel in a Ford van and driven to the set with one of the film's other stars, Mia Farrow, sitting in front.

September would be the Allen's most Chekhovian film, set entirely inside a summer home (actually a set constructed on a soundstage in Queens, New York). Finding himself cast in a Woody Allen film proved to Shepard that life was "strange and totally unpredictable." In the end, however, he did not actually end up in a Woody Allen film. The director was unhappy with the results of the ten weeks of shooting involving Shepard and eventually decided to start from scratch.

One reason Shepard didn't make the final cut may have to do with an episode related by writer John Lahr years later in a *New Yorker* profile on

Allen. "On *September*, Sam Shepard was granted permission to improvise a speech, and, according to [actress Dianne] Wiest, ended up talking about leaving Montana to go East to medical school. As Wiest and Allen were walking back to the dressing room, Allen turned to her. 'Montana? Montana?' he said. 'The word "Montana" is gonna be in *my* movie?'" It wasn't.

Ultimately, Allen blamed himself for the first version of *September* needing to be scrapped; the fault was in what he'd written, he said. For round two, some of the original actors couldn't return; others weren't invited back. Ultimately, three of the principals were replaced, including Shepard, who had a commitment that prevented him from coming back for the reshoot. Instead, Sam Waterston played Peter in *September*, which was released in December of 1987.

Those who have seen the film probably have a hard time imagining Shepard in the role of Peter, who, like all the other characters in the film, leaves nary an emotion unspoken or examined to death. In that role Shepard, the actor known as the new Gary Cooper and the embodiment of the "strong, silent type," would seem to have been a serious case of miscasting. The part of Peter, as portrayed originally by Shepard, was very different from the one that made it to the version of *September* that was released. Allen rewrote it when Waterston came aboard, because, as the director put it, "Sam Shepard's quality is that of a kind of inarticulate, attractive loner from the plains, whereas Sam Waterston has a more Eastern, Boston quality."

A few months after Shepard's stint on the set of *September*, he gave Allen a box of old jazz records left behind by his father when he died. The filmmaker is a well-known aficionado of the music and a clarinetist of some ability. Afterward, Allen wrote to Shepard to thank him for the gift, saying he found the collection "very eclectic" and full of surprising selections. He also mentions the fact of Shepard being cut from *September* and looks ahead to a time when the two will get together and "have some laughs over it." Allen also wishes Shepard luck in his first time directing. (He was already planning to direct his own script of *Far North*.)

"Action!"

L

I'd like to write, direct and make my own films. And I'd like to find a way to do that without being eaten up by the system. I'm certainly not willing to crawl around an office floor and beg and do 30,000 rewrites.

—Sam Shepard

The first time Shepard wrote and directed a film, he purposely set out to let the women have their say. In November of 1986, he completed a first draft of the screenplay. While he was recovering from a polo accident, Shepard finished the final script. It was a film he wrote for Lange; as a member of the film's crew told a reporter, it was his "homage" to her family.

Lange, however, remembers the genesis of *Far North* differently and dates it to a few months later. She was pregnant at the start of 1987 and eager for some project that she and Shepard could work on together. Being pregnant limited her options. She was thinking of something for cable television, maybe a play she could star in and he could direct. "He said, 'Yeah, but if I'm going to do that, let me write something for you,'" Lange recalled. *Far North* wouldn't go before the cameras until months after Lange had given birth.

The film's storyline was inspired by a horse riding accident that left Lange's father, Al, hospitalized. Shepard turned the incident into a story where after just such an accident, the man demands the killing of the horse. How true was the story? The accident surely happened, Shepard said, and while in the hospital Lange's father may have considered ordering the demise of his unruly mount, he eventually softened. He soon regretted this: "Then, when he got out of the hospital, he was throwing hay to that horse—who repaid his kindness by kicking a fence, and a railing spun off and hit Jessie's father in the eye and dislodged his retina," Shepard recalled. Al Lange sold the horse after that.

For his first time behind the camera, Shepard wanted to portray a family less dysfunctional than his own. The clan in *Far North* is not without its issues, but Shepard decided to play things not for tragedy but for comedy. "I wanted to start right," Shepard said. "The first one out of the gate should be a little light, you know?"

As *Far North* was in preproduction, one of Shepard's representatives sent a script to Marlon Brando along with a videocassette of Lange's films. He wanted the troubled star to play the father in the film. He got a courteous reply from Brando, saying he enjoyed the script but that it wasn't the kind of part that would be "the right choice" for him at that time. It had been more than seven years since he'd acted in a movie, Brando reminded Shepard.

A sure sign that he was coming off a few years of career highs, *Rolling Stone* magazine published in its 1986 year-end issue a long and wide-ranging interview with Shepard, conducted by Jonathan Cott. It was the kind of piece that would typically augur for an upcoming year of great promise. Yet in 1987, the public would see little of Shepard or his work. This doesn't mean, however, that he wasn't busy. There was a baby boy due, he was living in Virginia on a farm, playing polo and living the life of a true horseman; he was reading *King Lear* and continuing to work on the screenplay for what would become his first film. He picked his mail up at a True Value Hardware store in the next town over and once told a journalist he was late for an interview because "the creek stopped up and we had to get some horses through."

Over the next few years, Shepard would divide his time between family, acting in films, tending to his horses, and getting his own movies made. The part of being a family man would not always come easy. Between his work and his restless nature, being a parent is something Shepard would have to work at, for he found it a "24-hour task with hardly any let up."

June 14, 1987, brought the birth of Samuel Walker Shepard, and suddenly Shepard and Lange were facing "lots of shitty diapers." Shepard reported to a friend that despite this, he and Lange sometimes held their two young children in their arms and couldn't help but laugh at their good fortune and how far they'd come as a couple in the past five years. Life at this time for Shepard was a "rollicking good time."

He began the year wrapping up work on a film that would become one of his most popular, *Baby Boom*, featuring Diane Keaton as a love-starved career woman whose life changes when she "inherits" a baby from a distant relative. When Keaton's character moves to Vermont to give motherhood a try, she meets Dr. Jeff Cooper, the local veterinarian, played by Shepard. He's well cast as the small-town guy that Keaton's yuppie would seemingly never fall for, but of course does.

By the time they met, Keaton had harbored a crush on Shepard for more than a decade. The actress had a wall at her home covered with photos of famous men, from Abraham Lincoln to Gary Cooper. She called them her "prisoners," and front and center in this gallery of more than fifty faces was a photo of Shepard. "I was thirty-one when I went to see a matinee of Terrence Malick's *Days of Heaven* at Cinema 1 on Third Avenue," Keaton remembered. "The movie seemed to glide through a brilliantly lit travelogue until Sam Shepard walked onto the screen and took my breath away. His face bore the imprint of the West in all its barren splendor." She became a fan and followed his career from afar.

They first met on the set of *Crimes of the Heart*, the first of four films they'd appear in together. Shepard's real-life love interest, Jessica Lange, played opposite him as the girl who got away. Keaton and Shepard had few scenes together, but someone had the idea to pair them for *Baby Boom*, filmed shortly after. The film opened in October of 1987 and did well at the box office. As predictable as the film is, critics applauded it mainly due to the strong performance delivered by Keaton. Shepard proved up to the task in this romantic comedy. Overall, the film feels like a sitcom, as one critic noted, and feels a lot longer than its 103 minutes. None of this was Shepard's fault.

Despite sharing movie sets four different times with Shepard—whom Keaton calls "a mesmerizing man"—the actress says, "I never really got to know him. Just as well."

One interesting thing about *Baby Boom* is the reaction it triggered in Shepard's old friend and collaborator Wim Wenders. Aboard a jet over the Pacific, the director watched the film and admits to being "embarrassed" for Shepard. He was "speechless," he wrote, and felt that *Baby Boom* was less a movie and "more like a commercial." Wenders remembered their time spent working on a much better film, *Paris, Texas*, and was clearly hoping for future collaborations. In fact, Wenders had already sent Shepard a partially completed script for what would become his 1991 film *Until the End of the World*, hoping to lure Shepard into working on it. That hope was in vain. The two men would work together, but it wouldn't be for almost twenty years, this time with Shepard as both writer and lead actor.

Whether writing plays, acting, penning screenplays, or directing his own work for the stage, Shepard has had one belief when doing something for the first time: jump right in. So it was with directing his first film. Though he didn't jump without first doing some preparatory work. In one of his journals, he scribbled notes not unlike those a freshman film student might make. "Elements of a Shot," heads the page, and below is information about lenses, lights, framing, continuity, and more. He repeats these in another notebook, along with some of his own ideas about how the film should look and the way the actors should interact.

From these, it's clear to see that Shepard was bringing some of his theatrical experience to bear on his direction of *Far North*. There are notes about letting the actors "freely play within the scene" and using their full bodies to convey emotions. Lastly, the film shoot wasn't to be all work and no play. On Shepard's take-along list to the set in Minnesota were such things as golf clubs, fishing gear, and horse riding equipment.

When *Far North* went before the cameras in October of 1987, with a budget of $5 million—small even for back then—it starred Charles Durning as the father and Lange as his eldest daughter, as well as Tess Harper, Donald Moffat, Patricia Arquette, Ann Wedgeworth, and Nina Draxten as the grandmother. (Shepard originally asked Jessica Tandy to play the latter.) Shepard said he wanted to make a light film, and indeed he did. The overarching problem with the film is, as with Altman's film version of *Fool for Love*, that Shepard's stories are not expansive enough for the cinema. *Far North* has its charms, but there are scenes and bits that go on much longer than necessary. It seems as if Shepard knows he has a small story to tell and a big screen and almost two hours to fill. Watching it today, it reminds one of the kinds of films shown on the Hallmark Channel. He also made the common first-timer's mistake of not shooting enough coverage (additional footage shot around each scene) and had to use some stock footage, "an awful predicament," Shepard said. He also had trouble shooting interiors. As a director, inside four walls he was lost, he said. For his next film, there would be no interior shots to speak of.

The production company was happy enough with the results. Even before *Far North* hit theaters, it pledged enough money for Shepard to have another go at writing and directing his own film. Though, according to Shepard, this would later change.

When *Far North* was released, it was met with tepid reviews, for the most part. The *Boston Globe*'s critic, as if having seen Shepard's cheat sheets in his notebooks, said his filmmaking skills were "rudimentary." Shepard would admit a few years later to getting "fried by the critics." When these wounds were fresh, he said, "I haven't read a lot of the reviews. But people were shocked, I think, because it wasn't a regurgitation of my previous work. It was new and different from what I'd done before and they didn't know how to accept it. As soon as you accumulate a body of work—say, more than six pieces—an expectation begins to be accumulated along with it. You feel like you're chained to this . . . thing . . . and you don't want to be. I refuse to be locked in like that. Hell, the screenings I attended, the audience seemed to enjoy it thoroughly. I sat there and watched their reactions to it. They seemed to be genuine. . . . Maybe they were pulling the wool over my eyes. . . . But I guess you can expect to get hammered along the way and this was the perfect time, because it was my first shot at filmmaking. Hell, there were only two good reviews out of the whole batch."

Shepard was defiant as the critics' arrows flew. He said he had no regrets. He'd made the film he wanted to make, had fun doing it, and did it with the cast, crew, and producers he wanted. Besides, he added, comedy is difficult. His resolve? "So my next film is going to be a tragedy," he said.

It was while driving home to Virginia from Los Angeles after wrapping up the postproduction work on *Far North* that Shepard began to think of his next film, initially conceived as a western shot in black and white. As he crossed the Painted Desert, the starkness of the vistas fired his imagination. His next film would be darker and truer to his personal vision, and he would set it here in this "ruthless country" known as the Badlands.

War Story

I'd rather rope steers than talk politics with you.

—Sam Shepard

The American playwright should snarl and spit, not whimper and whine.

—Sam Shepard

S hepard next took a role in the film *Steel Magnolias* because he needed the cash. "I'm busted," he said at the time. He claimed the producers had written a little part for him in the film, and indeed he doesn't have much to do but drive around in his truck and add some much-needed testosterone to the very feminine goings-on. Critics and ticket buyers were mostly kind to the film when it was released in November of 1989.

Shepard and Lange's relationship was meanwhile defined by extremes, from very hot to very cold. He reflects in January of 1989 on a recent period when he was still madly in love with Lange, but "did some stupid things," which he put down to a "desperate state." This was during a time when Lange was in Iowa and he was in Mexico. He concludes this notebook entry: "Things were not going well between me and the object of my desires."

Early 1990 found the couple again navigating some troubled waters, and it seemingly lasted most of the year. A film director Shepard worked with noted that he "was in a difficult situation at the time with Jessica Lange." Volker Schlöndorff recalled that emotions spilled over during one critical scene. The film was *Voyager*, in which Shepard played the lead opposite Julie Delpy, his love interest in the film. Schlöndorff recalled: "At some point when we were shooting in the streets of Paris, and he'd just said good-bye to Julie Delpy in the little restaurant where they had lunch, and he is leaving her and most likely never to see her again. He walked out of the café and I yelled 'cut,' and we waited for him to come back and do another take. He didn't come back. So I walked outside and I saw him leaning against the wall, face against the wall, and I asked, 'Sam is everything OK?' And after a long pause, he said, 'I just realized I couldn't tolerate another loss in my life.'" Six months later, in a letter to his friend Johnny Dark, Shepard admits going through some "heart-wrenching stuff" around this time and claims he's feeling this way because of "her," likely meaning Lange. By May of 1991, however, he tells Dark in another letter that he and Lange are in love once again and that "everything is hunky-dory."

The shooting of *Voyager*, begun in March of 1990, necessitated a great deal of travel for Shepard. It was the kind of travel he couldn't do behind the wheel of his pickup, his preferred method. Shepard correctly identified *Voyager*, adapted by his friend Rudy Wurlitzer from the novel *Homo Faber* by Max Frisch, as having the potential to be something special, and he wanted the role badly enough that he agreed to fly. The film's far-flung sets meant traveling between Los Angeles, Mexico, Paris, Perugia, Rome, Greece, and New York City. One leg forced him to take the Concorde from New York to Paris. The good news is that the many miles were well worth it. *Voyager* is a gem in Shepard's film oeuvre. It's a movie about an American engineer named Walter Faber, played by Shepard, who at loose ends travels to Paris. On the boat he meets a young woman, Sabeth, played by Delpy. Touring together from France to Italy, they fall in love. After the young woman is gravely injured in Greece, something the audience has already come to suspect is revealed: Sabeth is Walter's daughter from a broken relationship of two decades earlier. She dies, and Faber, who at the start of the story was a lost soul, ends up even further adrift. The film demands the most of Shepard's range as an actor, and he deftly portrays Faber's withdrawn nature, his joy at finding new love, and the heartbreak that nearly destroys him.

The filmmakers paid a hefty price for having Shepard as their star. Eating away at the budget were Shepard's travel expenses. His refusal to fly, other than the Concorde flight, meant that cars, trains, and boats had to be booked to get him from place to place. Days and weeks were spent waiting for him to arrive in Mexico or New York. But director Volker Schlöndorff took this in stride. He knew going in that Shepard's travel would take up as much as half of *Voyager*'s budget but said, "I took him anyhow, because I thought he was the right choice for the part and it gives me a little time to breathe in between the different sections."

The hero of the novel, *Homo Faber*, was originally Swiss, but for the film he was changed to American. Author Max Frisch had doubts about casting Shepard, as he was still clinging to his idea of having a blue-eyed, blond "Bergman" actor, as he'd imagined in his book, according to director Schlöndorff. He remembered trying to convince the author: "I showed him some photographs of Sam Shepard . . . and I said, but he is a writer like yourself, and I left him a few of Sam's plays. The next morning he says he's been looking into his plays and he had a feeling that he might be right for the part. I could never find out what connection he made between Sam Shepard's style in writing as a dramatist and this part. But he said, 'If it's him, it's OK.'"

His costar Delpy found working with Shepard a bit of a guessing game. "To work with as an actor, Sam Shepard is a very sensitive man, I believe," she recollected years later. "And I believe he's a bit more of a writer than an actor, so sometimes the writer would take over the actor and he would get a little moody or insecure. But at the same time he was very giving and very sensitive, like really hypersensitive and sometimes very moody as well, so you never knew what day it was going to be in the morning, when you went on set, whether it was going to be the moody guy or the, you know, very sweet, sensitive person in front of you. So it was unsettling, but after a while I got used to it."

The film won several European awards, but in the United States, when it arrived in late January 1992, it came and went with a whimper, barely earning a half million dollars at the box office. Shepard's performance almost universally drew raves. His old friend Wurlitzer astutely summed up Shepard's performance: "He inhabits the space with a great deal of confidence. He exists on many levels, not just physically but mentally."

Despite the number of film roles he was taking, Shepard's need of money again would be a common theme over the next few years. In the spring of 1991, he was still lamenting to a friend that he was "in deep shit" financially and in need of an acting paycheck. It's hard to believe that two movie stars living together with their three children would be in such straits. Yet one has to remember that Shepard and Lange were living in an expensive enclave on a large farm, and occasionally taking pricey vacations. Add to this the livestock Shepard kept, and it's easy to figure out where all the money went. During these years, he kept up to fourteen feeder steers and seven horses. These numbers fluctuated, as Shepard often bought and sold livestock like any rancher. Though expensive to maintain, the farm was "beyond his wildest dreams." He loved the fact that he could be riding a tractor in the middle of a giant Virginian field or clearing land one day, and on Forty-Sixth Street in Manhattan working with the cast and crew of his latest play the next. Around the house, he was learning to be a good dad to the couple's three children. He sang to the youngsters his favorite old western songs, like "I Ride an Old Paint." Meanwhile, the house was filled with their own version of music, as Shura practiced her cello lessons and the younger kids bounced around the house. Like many parents, Shepard drove the kids to and from school, piling them into the truck for the daily treks. When he had free time, Shepard would take one of his horses out and go foxhunting.

His writing during this time, however, was a cause of concern. A case of writer's block, dating to the fall of 1989, had set in. Shepard reports having "one hell of a time," unable to finish the four plays and seven stories he had under way. It wasn't until the following summer that his next play would begin to take shape, if not on paper at least in his mind. The genesis of this work can be traced to a trip to a Kentucky bar he frequented, where on this occasion instead of the usual horse talk, the place was silent. It "felt like doomsday," Shepard recalled. America was at war with Iraq.

Shepard had just returned from eight weeks on the Pine Ridge Indian Reservation in South Dakota, where he had shot one of his better mid-career films, *Thunderheart*. While there, he saw American fighter jets flying over-head to and from Ellsworth Air Force Base in nearby Rapid City as the nation was gearing up for war. The incongruity of the devastation he saw all around him on the reservation and these multimillion-dollar war machines soaring above, heading off to destroy people of another devastated land, set him off. The fact that so may Americans had bought into the need for war, the "hoax" of it, is what really steamed Shepard.

It had been six years since he'd premiered a new play when *States of Shock* opened at the American Place Theatre in New York in April 1991. He had forgotten how much "simple fun" his first vocation could be. Critics and audiences found the experience of watching this one-act play less so. Set in a diner, *States of Shock* gives us an older man known as the Colonel (a "monster fascist," in his creator's words), dressed in a hodgepodge of military outfits, and Stubbs, a soldier in a wheelchair, whom we are told was with the Colonel's son when he was killed in action. There's also a married couple in a booth waiting for food and a waitress named Glory Bee. The upstage wall is comprised of a cyclorama that flashes different colors and images of war at various points. Behind it are two drummers who occasionally add wild percussion.

Seated at a table, the Colonel wants Stubbs to describe in great detail the moment his son was killed. Stubbs keeps getting stuck on how the bullet went through him first and then into the Colonel's son. There's lots of yelling, and at one point it seems as if Stubbs may actually be the Colonel's son.

As a one-act play, *States of Shock* could have been viewed as a return to Shepard's earliest glory days—a short, sharp attack to the senses, levied with dark humor. It certainly had some of the hallmarks of those wild and woolly Off-Off-Broadway works, including identity swapping and an overload of sights and sounds that might be conjuring the apocalypse. However, the play typifies problems that would mar many of Shepard's late works, where a coherent idea or narrative drive is lacking and the playwright instead tries tossing in some of his signature conceits. The events in *States of Shock* seem to pile up randomly, occasionally touching on a central idea, but then becoming submerged under more noise. The play may seem pervaded by the idea of the high cost of war, but it never crystallizes. Shepard's ideas seem randomly tacked on one after another, and although occasionally the old sparks fly, *States of Shock* comes to little.

Rereading the play in 2016 in light of U.S. foreign policy under the second President Bush and the aftermath of his eight years in office, Shepard seems nothing less than prescient. These days we do indeed live in a state of shock, when war is constant, torture acceptable, and terrorism routine. However, in 1991, Shepard's ideas and anger about the First Gulf War were too much for this seventy-five-minute play to carry. Or at least he didn't elucidate them coherently enough. "The explosive humor soon gives way to narrow preaching," wrote Frank Rich in the *New York Times*. Most agreed that the play seemed half-baked.

As the Colonel, John Malkovich nearly stole the show. He was devilishly funny and even when attempting to charm, had a hint of menace just below the surface, like a smiling land mine. "Extremely intelligent, fearless, and enthusiastic," Shepard said of Malkovich, who had also starred in *True West* a few years earlier. "He just does not give a shit about how this fits into somebody else's idea of what it should be, just goes for ideas that are completely off the wall." Acting in Shepard plays took a toll on the actor. "The big challenge of it in my experience is the incredible amount of energy" those roles take, Malkovich said. "I was tired for a year after [*True West*]. *States of Shock* was the same. So many nights I was saying, 'Jesus, am I going to be able to make this?'"

However, even Malkovich's bold and energetic performance couldn't save this one. *States of Shock* came as a letdown, especially after Shepard's string of successes crowned with *A Lie of the Mind*. Shepard claimed that some critics were at a loss in dealing with the new play, in light of the steps toward naturalism he'd taken with *Lie*. "They couldn't find a place to put it," he said. "They couldn't put it. . . . Some of them called it absurdism or . . . they couldn't fit it into anything. It was so radically different from *A Lie of the Mind*, and I guess their expectations were in that vein." In a later interview, he blamed himself. "I think there was an intrinsic misunderstanding about it," he said, "which was probably my fault. I think the audience, and obviously everybody else, had a hard time realizing that this was indeed about a father and son relationship."

Shepard has long acknowledged that he lacks a gift for the traditional narrative, the ability to write the type of story that follows an arc and has a beginning, middle, and end. In fact, he claims to have little interest in producing such standard fare. Writing screenplays forced him to do this. Still eluding him to this point was the novel. He'd fiddled with the form over the decades and came close to finishing a long work of fiction titled *Stray Hand*. Written between July 1991 and early 1993, including one burst of writing while he was on the set of *Thunderheart*, these 250 unpublished pages give us Shepard's version of a crime novel. It features a waitress from the Happy Chef restaurant who goes missing. Much of the action takes place, in typical Shepard fashion, on the road, in cheap hotels and amid the wide-open spaces of America's Badlands. Why it was left unfinished is unclear. The seeds of a decent story are here, but much rewriting would be required to make it worthy of publication. Perhaps Shepard's time was being taken up by acting and preparing for his second time behind the camera, shooting *Silent Tongue*.

At this time, the American Academy of Arts and Letters awarded Shepard the Gold Medal for Drama, which recognized his entire body of work to date.

Take Two

SHEPARD: *Do you want to make movies?*
DYLAN: *No, not really. You mean direct them?*
SHEPARD: *Yeah.*
DYLAN: *No . . .*
SHEPARD: *It is kind of a pain in the ass.*

—Shepard interview with Dylan

S hepard's first film, *Far North*, disappointed at the box office, and after first agreeing to finance a second film, for a time the "money heads," as Shepard called them, rejected his second project. However, seeing it was an ersatz western ghost story, Hollywood delivered a fortuitous one-two punch in Shepard's favor: *Dances with Wolves* won the Best Picture Oscar in March 1991, and *Ghost* topped the box office for 1990. It added up to "an odd twist of fate," as Shepard termed it. By May of the following year, his second film had been green-lighted. It was set to be shot that October but was pushed back to the following summer.

Written in just ten days, and then put through multiple rewrites, *Silent Tongue* is set in 1893 on the Llano Estacado ("Staked Plains"), a piece of near-barren desert not far from Roswell, New Mexico, or, as Shepard described it: "Probably the most terrifying piece of real estate west of the

Mississippi." The film tells the story of a young man, played by River Phoenix, whose Native American wife has died in childbirth. In the aftermath, he begins to lose his mind, tying her body to a tree limb because he can't bear to bury her and refusing to eat or sleep. His father, Prescott Roe, played by grizzled veteran Richard Harris, had traded a few horses for his son's first wife. The dead woman's father, Eamon McCree, an outrageous Alan Bates, runs a traveling medicine show in the same area of the desert. Roe seeks to make the same kind of deal with McCree for his other daughter, hoping this will alleviate his son's grief.

McCree refuses to let his second daughter go, and so Prescott kidnaps her. She eventually accepts horses and gold herself to do his bidding and marry his son. However, the ghost of her sister, angered that her body has not been burned or buried and that her sister is now involved, wreaks havoc on just about everyone in sight.

Darker than his first film, *Silent Tongue* shows that Shepard's skills as a filmic storyteller had grown. Is his story a bit slight for the 105 minutes of running time? Or, put another way, is there too much desert wandering in the middle of the movie? Sure. But the acting is strong enough that one doesn't really mind. Shepard is clearly invested in the material and it shows. The film brings together many of his long-held thematic concerns about family, identity, the plight of Native Americans, and ideas about the land and destiny. "One of the amazing things about this clash of cultures—the European and the Native American—is you have absolute opposite mentalities," he said. "The European wanted to acquire land, thought that God was in the sky somewhere, the lowly sinner had to aspire to heaven. . . . For the Native American the land wasn't owned by anybody; the holy spirit moves through every animal, every plant, every living thing, including human beings. Those two mentalities could never see eye to eye."

Those familiar with Shepard's early work could be forgiven for the sense of déjà vu, seeing River Phoenix's character sitting around his campfire with a corpse, sometimes joined by its ghost. It has clear echoes of Shepard's 1969 play *The Holy Ghostly*. There, a son sits with his father, who appears to be alive but is, we are told, dead. That relationship doesn't end happily—no surprise there—but in *Silent Tongue*, the father succeeds in rescuing his son. The final scene finds the boy and his father wandering off across the desert toward the horizon.

A reporter visiting the set that July, when filming was in full swing, said Shepard was an intimidating presence, even with such legendary tough customers as Bates and Harris onboard. If his attitude reflected more confidence, it shows in the film. The dreaded interiors of *Far North* that were problematic for Shepard as a first-time director were gone, traded for the wide-open plains of the New Mexican desert. He clearly feels more at home here. Also, this time Shepard shot plenty of footage. *Silent Tongue* looks gorgeous through and through, and each shot is invested with care and demonstrates an impressive attention to detail.

Upon wrapping up production, Shepard had good reason to feel like he'd accomplished something special. However, it turned out that the film would not be released for nearly two years. The delay meant that it was the final film to feature River Phoenix. The promising actor died of an overdose in the early hours of Halloween 1993 at the age of twenty-three.

Silent Tongue finally premiered at the Sundance Film Festival in January of 1993. Shepard was on hand at the Egyptian Theatre for its initial showing and took questions afterward. Four minutes in, he said the experience was "incredibly awkward." He then thanked everyone for coming and disappeared. No distributors picked up the film during the annual festival, known as a place where deals are made on every street corner and in every coffee shop and five-star restaurant. Shepard took the film in November to the Native American Film Festival and to a London festival. It would take the better part of a year for the film to find a distributor. When it was released in February 1994, the successes of *Dances with Wolves* and *Ghost* were distant memories, and *Silent Tongue* was unduly drubbed by most critics and avoided by moviegoers. It would be the last film Shepard directed himself.

About the time Shepard returned home from shooting *Silent Tongue*, his up-and-down relationship with Lange was evident once again. In August of 1991, she pulled out a journal that she bought for him during a solo trip to Paris. On the inside cover, Lange wrote about how sad she was during that trip, being away from him. She wrote that she "wanted to be inside

[him]." She bought the journal hoping it would help her get close to him, despite the thousands of miles of ocean and land separating them.

Compare that with an unpublished poem Shepard wrote in September of the following year that recounted a battle royal with Lange. Differing political views, his drinking and self-absorption, along with what she perceived as his lack of interest in her career and the fact that they had nothing in common, were the kindling that lit this particular fire. "I can't live like this," he quotes Lange as saying. She ends up getting on the phone, ordering plane tickets, and packing the kids up for an impromptu vacation. It was "a major impasse," Shepard writes. It actually turned out to be just another bump on a long and rocky road.

Lange was not the only one referencing Shepard's drinking at this time. A letter to Shepard from a friend, signed only "R.J." and dated October 8, 1992, has a telling PS. The writer tells Shepard to feel free to reach out, "Re: the AA program." The correspondent then goes on to praise the benefits of sobriety.

Shepard's last play, *States of Shock*, may have been ripped by the critics, but it didn't dissuade him from going right back to the well. In fact, before that play's run had concluded, he was back home in Virginia thinking about the next one. The first version of what would become *Simpatico* was written in early September of 1992 as Shepard was driving his pickup west on Route 40, heading to Los Angeles. With the pages pinned to the steering wheel, using his free hand he scribbled out the first draft of what was then titled *One Last Favor*. "I think I wrote twenty-five pages by the time I got there, which was about five hundred miles of driving," he said. At first it seemed like another one-act, but soon after climbing out of his truck, a second character popped into his mind and a second act became necessary. The play would take another year to finish, and it would ultimately become a three-act play involving old friends, racehorses, and betrayal. Vinnie would be based on Shepard's longtime friend and former father-in-law Johnny Dark, who, like the character in the new play, liked to impress strange women by pretending to be a detective.

Shepard and Lange had busy careers, three children, and a home and farm to manage between them. Earlier years found them fighting frequently, but judging by Shepard's notebooks and letters, these tiffs were balanced by passion and a near-desperate love. An example of the latter, from 1986, can be seen when Shepard, after being separated from Lange for two weeks, writes to a friend: "I don't know what to do without her. She's my whole world. I never thought I'd be this way with anyone."

Beginning around 1993 he'd change his tune: The troubles began to run deeper, and last longer. One of Shepard's notebook entries, dated March 7 of that year, notes that his and Lange's relationship is marked by a "state of constant flux and shuffle of emotion," and he describes her "impenetrable aloneness." Also from that September there's what appears to be an apology for his not knowing Lange was suffering and his being too "consumed" to notice. Talking on the phone on April 12, 1994, with Johnny Dark (the conversation was recorded and transcribed by Dark), Shepard reports having another "falling out" with Lange. Dark reminds him of two other recent fights where Shepard was ready to "pack it in and move to Texas." "And then there was the time you drove back to Santa Fe nonstop . . . before you cooled off," Dark reminded his friend. When Shepard was pressed as to the source of his and Lange's recurring battles, he said, "Just these feelings, as though there's some grudge or something. But I don't know what the grudge is about."

The following month, Shepard wrote a poem, unpublished, about how often he'd crossed the Appalachian Mountains. The second stanza breaks from the rumination and goes right to his relationship with Lange, or at least it would seem to be about her. In this telling, Shepard writes of how she's begun "withholding something." As he becomes more desperate, he writes, she becomes more ruthless, until in his desperation he falls again into her little trap. After which, she'd "pull away and drift into [her] long, solitary walks."

There were, of course, good times too. Between 1993 and 1995, Shepard was fully invested in the role of family man. Rising at 6 a.m. to make the kids' lunches, cooking breakfast, and then driving them to school was "a good way to start the day off." His son Walker was now old enough to beat him in chess, and Shepard took the boy to his weekend soccer games. There were trips to New York alone to help get productions of his plays up and running, as well as time spent around the United States on movie shoots.

In the spring of 1995, Shepard was also putting the finishing touches on his next book of poetry and prose, *Cruising Paradise*. With Jessica and the children there were many family trips—like a quick jaunt in May 1995 to watch the Kentucky Derby, and to her parents' home in Minnesota for the big holidays. Around this time, Shepard and Lange began what would become a family tradition—an annual spring break trip to Mexico.

Shepard would later write to his friend and former father-in-law Johnny Dark that he and Lange were going to get married in Minnesota and asking him to be the best man. This blessed event never occurred.

Shepard was in a hit movie as 1993 came to a close. He played Professor Thomas Callahan in *The Pelican Brief*, opposite marquee stars Denzel Washington and Julia Roberts. His character is the mentor and lover of Roberts's law student. It took in nearly $200 million at the box office, despite the reviews being decidedly mixed. Shepard is more than serviceable in the film, but his commitment to the project is perhaps best summed up by his description of his role: a "constitutional lawyer having an affair with what's her name." In other words, *The Pelican Brief* paid the bills.

Losing Game

My Mother loved the sea
To be by the sea
We would drive sometimes for hours
Just to get there

—Sam Shepard

S hepard traveled in early 1993 to a cemetery surrounded by hay-
fields overlooking Lake Michigan in Door County, Wisconsin.
His maternal grandparents were buried there decades earlier in
an unmarked grave. He and his oldest son, Jesse, had brought a slab of
limestone from the shores of the nearby lake in hopes of marking their
forebears' final resting place. They took a guess as to the right location and
planted it between two red cedars and later brought Shepard's mother out
to inspect their work. She looked around, felt the location was wrong, but
couldn't remember the exact burial spot. It had been a long time. They left
the stone that day between the two trees. Not long after, Shepard learned
that his mother was herself terminally ill.

Shepard wrote in his journal on February 25, 1994, about being on
the forty-first floor of a hotel overlooking Central Park and hearing his

mother's voice. These four melancholy-tinged lines indicate that Shepard knew at this point about his mother's illness. It didn't take long. The news arrived on March 10 that Jane Rogers had died. She'd remained living in California after selling the family home in Bradbury upon her retirement from teaching in 1986. In a letter to Chaikin after her death, Shepard said his mother had accepted that her "body was finished with life" and that she didn't suffer much. "Both her living and her dying were precious gifts to me."

Shepard wrote a poem in his mother's honor that remains unpublished, detailing her love of walking along the beach and feeling the sea-kissed wind on her face. She would stare out at the sea, drive for hours sometimes just to get to the shore in time to catch the sunset and to feel the wet sand beneath her "tiny feet." He writes of her sweet nature and how she was devoid of bitterness and was always there for anyone who needed a helping hand. Shepard concludes:

> For this life now
> And always
> She will never die inside me

A year after that visit to the Wisconsin cemetery, Shepard writes, "we buried my mother's ashes slightly to the left of the two red cedars." They checked with the caretaker and found the right spot for her parents' grave and moved the stone again. "It lined up right behind my mother's grave," he writes.

A decade later, Shepard would write in another of his notebooks, totaling the losses over the years. By then his friend and mentor Joe Chaikin was gone, as well. Shepard wonders whether "they're hovering around or just gone."

Simpatico, Shepard's first full-length play since *A Lie of the Mind* nearly a decade earlier, was targeted for Broadway. The cast was certainly strong enough—Ed Harris, Jennifer Jason Leigh, Frederick Forrest, and Beverly D'Angelo—but the $800,000 budget for the production couldn't be met. Or, as Shepard put it, "the deep pockets didn't present themselves." So the play's opening was delayed until November 14, and a new venue was found Off-Broadway at the Public Theater. The cast changed, with Harris joined by Marcia Gay Harden, Fred Ward, James Gammon, and Welker White.

Shepard directed *Simpatico*, and if he was an intimidating presence on the set of *Silent Tongue*, working once again in a New York City theater he was polite, even "courtly," one observer wrote. Ed Harris found him to be "more comfortable, easier" than a dozen years earlier when Shepard had directed him in *Fool for Love*. Yet he was definitely in charge. When Harris asked Shepard if there was a point in the play where his character could come clean, it must have felt too "on the nose." Shepard told him, "Sorry Ed, I can't let you off the hook."

Shepard had toyed with ideas involving the two lead characters of *Simpatico* for years, and had the eight or nine abandoned plays to show for it. He described the play as being "about the rivalry between two close friends who have known each other their whole lives, and involves women and horses, gambling, deceit, envy, jealousy, rage: the stuff I can't help writing about." *Simpatico* riffs on the Gurdjieff-inspired notion that each person contains multiple selves, and just as in *True West*, the two main characters trade places by the final scene. At one point, a character says, "How many lives do you think a man can live?"

Carter and Vinnie are the old friends. Years earlier they'd pulled a scam that involved switching racehorses, substituting a faster one for a cheap claimer and cleaning up at the betting windows. The only hitch was that a racing judge named Simms had caught wind of the fraud. Vinnie and his wife, Rosie, then set the judge up for a tryst, which they had photographed, using the X-rated images to blackmail him. Simms was ruined, and Carter and Vinnie walked. Things got complicated quickly, and Carter, the smoother of the two, ended up with Rosie. Now, years later, Carter and Rosie are living the life of Kentucky royalty and Vinnie is stuck in a California hovel subsisting on the money Carter sends him. *Simpatico* kicks into gear when Vinnie tires of this situation and tries to betray his friend and settle old scores.

Early on, the play promises to feature one of Shepard's most compelling plots—a story of betrayal, with much hanging in the balance. True to his nature, and to avoid the predictable, Shepard doesn't let the cards fall this way. That isn't to say that *Simpatico* gets lost along the way; it just takes a different path. At no point is there a climactic scene where the cops come busting in and haul the bad guys off to jail. Instead, the jail these characters face is of the more existential kind. Shepard lays all the elements down and then lets us observe what happens to the different players, some of whom have had to live with a lie all these years. There are reversals of fortunes, characters who come through intact because they've made peace with the past, and even a happy ending for at least one of those involved. The play is a series of character studies with just enough of a through line to pull it all together.

Giving voice to the idea that each characters is stranded with the fate he or she has earned is Rosie. When Vinnie arrives to confront his ex-wife about the misdeeds of the past, she reminds him there's no going back.

> ROSIE: Oh Jesus, Vinnie. Give it up! Everything has already happened! It's already taken place. This is it. There's no "running off" anymore. It's a done deal. You're in your little hell and I'm in mine.

Simpatico received plenty of good notices. Vincent Canby in the *New York Times* called it one of the best plays of the year, and it sold out its initial run but did not hold enough promise to move to Broadway. When the play traveled to Europe, the reviews were even better. It was made into a film that, despite some A-list talent in Jeff Bridges and Sharon Stone, was hollow-seeming. Again, a filmmaker struggled to make Shepard's small story into a feature-length movie. Where the play is stripped to bare essentials, the film invokes flashbacks to fill in the backstory, adds multiple locations, and introduces other diversions that slowly strangle the subtle points Shepard achieves in his original.

The following year did not get off to a great start for Shepard, with the release of *Safe Passage*, in which he costarred with Susan Sarandon. Shepard plays a husband and father who suffers a form of temporary blindness. Watching his character feel his way around the house, one feels for Shepard, selling himself to Hollywood once again. The movie crept quietly and mercifully off into obscurity.

Shepard had a larger stake in the film version of *Curse of the Starving Class*, based on his 1977 play and featuring James Woods, Randy Quaid, and Kathy Baker. An early version of the film script in Shepard's archives indicates that he had a chance to comment on the adaptation, a chance he forswore for the most part. The script had only a few basic suggestions in Shepard's hand. However, it should be noted that this was a very early draft. The celluloid version of *Curse of the Starving Class* came and went with barely a stir.

The Shepard–Lange household picked up stakes and headed for her home state of Minnesota in the summer of 1995. After thirteen years on the farm in Virginia, Lange wanted to be near her aging mother. The family's new home was a six thousand-square-foot mansion built in 1892 on two and a half acres, located at 903 Fourth Street North in Stillwater. The property included a guesthouse, carriage house, swimming pool, orchard, ponds, woods, and tiered gardens, according to the *St. Paul Pioneer Press*. It provided "sweeping views of the town, the St. Croix River and the historic lift bridge," the newspaper claimed. The house needed a lot of work, as did the land—two acres of scrub had to be torn out. Locally procured limestone was brought in for new terraces and to round out the new and existing landscaping. Lange created a garden for each of her three children, and in the coming years, when the weather was warm, she'd sometimes spend eight hours in a single day planting and caring for the flowers. In time, Shepard and Lange would purchase the adjoining lot, fix up the swimming pool, and build another guesthouse.

The decision to move to Minnesota was brought on by a mix of nostalgia and practicality. "I had this kind of romantic image of the children growing up not dissimilar to the way I grew up, in a small town where they could walk to school," Lange said. "And I wanted to raise them close to their extended family."

The one thing the new home didn't have was room for horses and cattle. Shepard would soon enough purchase a three-hundred-acre ranch just over the state line in River Falls, Wisconsin. He told the *New Yorker* in 1996 that he had fifty head of cattle. When journalists managed to lasso him for an interview, the resulting articles invariable fueled his cowboy image—the Camel-smoking man of few words who, due to his weathered skin, would seem to be as comfortable on a tractor or saddle as seated behind a typewriter. (In 1995 Shepard would fortify this image, donning a cowboy hat in the movie *Good Old Boys* and the TV miniseries *Streets of Laredo*.) He enjoyed the physical work that came with owning a ranch, be it cleaning stalls, cutting hay, working in the barn, or riding one of his many steeds. This labor didn't excuse him from his duties as a dad. He continued to awaken most mornings at six, cook for the kids, pack their lunches, and drive them to school. Then he'd come home and get to his typewriter, or relax by playing the piano.

Lange, who precipitated the move, strangely enough approached the family's new life in the north with some trepidation. "She was suddenly profoundly depressed about returning to the land of her childhood and that everything she'd imagined about being here in Minnesota was a total fantasy and the actual reality of being here was something she couldn't foresee," Shepard wrote to a friend in September 1995. He found it hard to believe that just as he was settling into his new life, his partner, after just a few months, was "getting sick of this place." Complicating the thought of picking up and moving again was the fact that the couple had just sunk $2 million into real estate between the new homestead and his nearby ranch.

This depression of Lange's is something Shepard, other than in this instance, doesn't specifically mention in his letters and notebooks. While he often references the difficulties in their relationship, he is more likely to blame the impossibility of love, the general instability any couple might face, or himself and his habits. However, Lange's behavior comes into sharper focus in light of a 2016 interview with *Closer Weekly* magazine, given while the actress was starring on Broadway in *Long Day's Journey into Night*. The magazine claimed the then–sixty-seven-year-old had for years struggled with depression. "I had really tremendous mood swings, and still do," Lange said. "Though my dark side is dormant right now, it continues to play a big role in whatever capacity I have to be creative." Some of the incidents Shepard describes in his journals and letters do suggest that Lange displayed mood swings and bursts of anger. Usually, he claims responsibility for causing her outbursts.

Regarding their new life in Minnesota, Shepard convinced Lange to at least stay through the winter, reassuring his partner that as long as they were together, "we can't stray far from what's right."

At Last, Paradise

L

Every so often in the evening I am unsettled by small, fleeting
memories that are perhaps authentic.

—Jorge Luis Borges

Since the mid-1960s, Shepard had rarely stepped onto an airplane. The two exceptions he'd made were in 1985 when he flew to California to interview Bob Dylan for *Esquire*, and a Concorde flight to Europe to keep the filming of *Voyager* on schedule. There was pressure to do so again, and a family trip to Mexico—Tulum in the Yucatan, to be specific—hanging in the balance. The weeks leading up to the vacation were filled with uncertainty. Shepard considered his options. "End[ing] up 35,000 miles above the earth, flying to the tropics *or* sitting alone at home, hovering over coffee, wishing you'd gone," as he put it. He decided to go and had "about the best trip I've ever had." Aided by a Xanax Lange had given him, Shepard's anxiety eased and he felt like he'd conquered his fear of flying once and for all.

That is until the return flight, when a passenger at the back of the plane had some sort of medical issue and Shepard found himself face to face with a corpse and a pleading wife. He grabbed the body and lifted the man into the aisle, where two doctors who were on board tried to help. The plane made an emergency stop so the dead man and his wife could be let off. "Everything about this trip was remarkable," Shepard remembered. The encounter with a corpse notwithstanding.

The year 1996 would be a big one for Shepard, with most of the focus on his older work. He would be celebrated at the Atlanta Summer Olympics, in New York City, and in England.

It was the summer of Shepard in London. Even though he hadn't lived in the city for more than two decades, his work had regularly been performed there. The Sam Shepard Festival at the Battersea Arts Centre spread out over most of July and featured *A Lie of the Mind*, *Suicide in B♭*, *Geography of a Horse Dreamer*, and *States of Shock*. Performances of one kind or another (from one-man versions to staged readings) were also presented of *Curse of the Starving Class*, *Action*, *Savage/Love*, and *Killer's Head*. Shepard was too busy Stateside to attend, but he did select the music for the plays. Some of what he chose he did so through a personal connection to the artist (Patti Smith, Charles Mingus, and Nina Simone); the rest was based on his love of jazz, blues, and old country.

The festival was widely covered by the press, with previews and reviews, and Shepard agreed to several interviews, including one with the BBC. One journalist said the mere mention of Shepard's name in culturally aware sections of London provoked shivers of excitement. Others called the festival a return to Shepard's roots, or even a home-coming due to the formative years he spent in England in the early 1970s.

Shepard's third book of prose, *Cruising Paradise*, was published at the end of April 1996. It is in this collection that he takes a giant step forward in his storytelling. An epigraph from Juan Rulfo, the great Mexican novelist and short story writer Shepard had come to admire, indicates that perhaps he'd been studying the form more closely. This would continue the fol-lowing year, when he'd binge on Chekhov's stories.

While his previous collections were filled with interesting anecdotes, sharp observations, and well-drawn scenes that clearly conveyed a sense of place, in *Cruising Paradise* Shepard regularly manages to conclude his tales in a completely satisfying manner.

Shepard admits he's not much of a poet (and he's right), and here he forgoes the poems, replacing them with a handful of entries, comprised only of dialogue, that lie on the page like verse but manage to do a fine job in depicting characters and telling stories. These bits bring to mind what he'd said years earlier about being drawn to playwriting because of an affinity and love for writing dialogue.

The book begins with two vignettes about his late father. In the first, "The Self-Made Man," Shepard traces the generations of men on his father's side of the family, sharing stories most likely passed down to him through the years. It ends with his father standing on the back porch facing the dark backyard and its nocturnal creatures. Realizing how alone he is, the old man feels panicky. "There was no border suddenly between his skin and the night; between his own breath and the surrounding thick air," Shepard writes. His father seeks peace, but it is denied.

The second story, "The Real Gabby Hayes," tells the story of a ride Shepard took with his father out to California Hot Springs, where Sam Rogers had evidently purchased a piece of worthless land. This is the parcel that plays a significant role in *Curse of the Starving Class*, the junk property that the play's patriarch buys from the crooked lawyer, Taylor. "Anyhow, this would be the perfect kind of spot for a little hideaway. Just the two of us," the father says, feeding his own sense of escape and engaging his son's growing sense of adventure.

There are more stories from Shepard's life, about the first band he played in as a teen; his job at a nearby horse farm, where it was rumored the 1955 Kentucky Derby champion, Swaps, was kept; a neighborhood barbecue at his family's house that goes awry in several ways. "See You in My Dreams" is Shepard's retelling of his father's accident, subsequent death, and burial. The stories that comprise roughly the last quarter of the book are the funniest. They are accounts drawn from the set of the 1991 film *Voyager*, in which Shepard played the lead. They deal with the problems created by the need to transport Shepard from Los Angeles down to Mexico via a rented sedan driven by a madman and with trying to get right a very serious scene about a suicide that turns into farce, in part because of the unrealistic "corpse" used as a prop.

Cruising Paradise is a turning point. Three of the *Voyager* pieces were published in the *New Yorker* the month before the collection came out. The principals of the magazine must have liked what Shepard could bring to its pages, for in August of 1998, when David Remnick took the helm, fiction editor Meghan O'Rourke wrote to Shepard, asking him to keep the *New Yorker* in mind whenever he had a story he'd like to have considered for publication. The magazine, under the new regime, was going to be "a more literary place," and if Shepard had something he wished to submit, "We'd be delighted to see it," O'Rourke wrote. She closed by saying that he had many fans at the magazine.

Shepard's next trip to the Great White Way began sometime in 1994, when the actor Gary Sinise, a hot commodity after his costarring role in the hit film *Forrest Gump*, started talking to Shepard about his Steppenwolf Theatre Company reviving *Buried Child*. "I think it's Sam's best play," Sinise said. "It has all the elements—mystery, horror and pain—and it's hysterically funny. He doesn't write things that are all logical and linear. Just like life, he leaves many questions unanswered." Shepard may have had his doubts at first. He'd long considered the play "verbose and overblown" and "unnecessarily complicated." However, the chance to rewrite the play, making significant changes concerning the character of Vince; removing some of the ambiguity over who had fathered the child buried out back; and having such an accomplished troupe as Sinise and Steppenwolf stage it convinced Shepard to revisit the Pulitzer Prize winner. "I think I solved it," Shepard said, once it was ready to go. Even as rehearsals got under way, he drove from Minnesota to Chicago on a few occasions to continue sharpening some of the dialogue.

The work paid off. In October of 1996, *Buried Child* was reborn, and under Sinise's excellent direction, it earned rave notices and large crowds. The *New York Times'* Ben Brantley called the production "spectacularly funny," proving Shepard's long-held belief that humor was key to making the play work.

It's hard to believe that a writer of such accomplishment and acclaim as Shepard, who had been producing plays for thirty-two years by this point, wasn't regularly produced on Broadway. Then again, when one considers how different his work is from most mainstream American theater, believing becomes easier. Shepard made it in a big way when Steppenwolf's production of *Buried Child* transferred from the company's Chicago home base to the Brooks Atkinson Theater. "This is a total surprise to me," Shepard said. "I'm not denying that it's exciting to have a play on Broadway. But this play just happens to fit here. It's not that I'm going to start writing plays for Broadway." Indeed he would not, but a few of his older plays would eventually follow the same path uptown.

Shepard rewrote *Buried Child* drastically enough—roughly half the lines were tinkered with in some fashion—that it qualified as a new play as far as voters for that year's Tony Awards were concerned. Still, the producers had to convince Shepard that the play should be submitted for consideration. Finally, he told them, "O.K., enter the S.O.B." *Buried Child* garnered five Tony nominations, including Best New Play.

Rewriting one of his other great plays, *The Tooth of Crime*, did not work out as well. Shepard felt his 1972 rock 'n' roll play was incomplete. "There's a strength to the play, and it doesn't go where I hoped it would go," he said. Indeed, Shepard said he was dissatisfied with the play's second act, feeling the character of Hoss was too sentimental and full of self-pity. To correct this, Shepard tried to add a Miltonesque twist. "The demonic aspect of the other character [Crow] became more interesting to me than the falling hero," he said. *Tooth of Crime (Second Dance)* also replaced Shepard's original songs from 1972 with new music composed by T Bone Burnett.

The play was presented in New York as part of the Signature Theatre's 1996–1997 season, which was devoted to Shepard. James Houghton had founded the Signature in 1991, with a focus on the playwright. There, Shepard would find a home for his later plays. The theater's season dedicated to Shepard included not only *Tooth of Crime (Second Dance)* but also *Chicago, Action, Killer's Head, The Sad Lament of Pecos Bill on the Eve of Killing His Wife, Curse of the Starving Class,* and *When the World Was Green (A Chef's Fable).*

Second Dance takes what made *The Tooth of Crime* special and runs it into the ground. The life and spontaneity of the language that gave flight to the original was laboriously worked over by Shepard in his revision. He may have achieved the greater rhythm he sought, but at the expense of coherence. Those familiar with the 1972 play can likely follow the action of *Second Dance*, for it shadows the original. Those coming to this story for the first time are left hanging on for clues as to what's going on. A sample:

> BECKY: He's choogin, Hoss. Loopy but choogin.
>
> HOSS: He's dead meat. Look at this Vector shit on the wall! How do you make hide or hair outa this data mush?
>
> MEERA: Patterns, Hoss. Matrix Mesh out there that needs new modes to conjure. I'm playing all this off the wall. Same as the rest.

That pretty much sums up the problems with *Tooth of Crime (Second Dance)*. Shepard took the hip lingo of his original and tried to update it but succeeded only in making it obscure. Critics and audiences were confused and unimpressed. However, around 2004, the Coen brothers expressed interested in turning the play into a film.

A bright spot was Burnett's music, which was more dense and provocative than Shepard's originals from a quarter century earlier. "An unexpected shamanistic world of sound in the dark conjure of the blues" is how Burnett described the music. In 2008 he released *Tooth of Crime*, an album featuring his songs for Shepard's rewrite along with a few others.

The Signature series drew from the entire range of Shepard's catalog, which gave audiences a chance to measure how far he'd developed as a playwright while still hewing closely to a few key themes. However, others felt that his early work, once brilliant and startlingly fresh, felt dated three decades on. All the same, *Chicago*, *Killer's Head*, and *Pecos Bill* each received good reviews in their respective revivals.

When the World Was Green (A Chef's Fable) was part of the Signature series, but the short play by Shepard and Joseph Chaikin had actually premiered during that year's Summer Olympics. It was commissioned and produced by the Cultural Olympiad, part of the Atlanta Committee for the Olympic Games, and played from July 19 to July 23 at the 14th Street Playhouse. It was to be Shepard's final collaboration with his old mentor, whose health was never good during these years, despite his managing to maintain an active schedule of workshops and directing.

At first the pair was trying to write something about the devil. Also, the war in Bosnia was in the headlines and was hanging like a dark cloud over the two men's early discussions. Ultimately, Chaikin's obsession with all things culinary took over. "Every time we'd get together, it was always about the food, and I just went along with it," Shepard said. The idea of a chef as food poisoner interested him, and the story evolved from there.

The chef of the title is serving a long prison sentence for murdering a man, who it turns out was not his intended victim. The chef had meant to kill his cousin to avenge a family feud over the death of a mule dating back many generations. The play begins with the chef in jail being visited by a young woman who claims to be a reporter. She questions him about the murder over the course of eight visits. In between these sections, each character takes turns delivering a monologue detailing aspects of his or her past. It turns out that the man murdered by the chef was the reporter's father. In the end, the two find a way to resolve their differences and share a meal cooked by the chef with help from his visitor.

Reviewers liked the early productions of this play, giving nearly equal credit to Chaikin's direction and the text itself. It also helped that theater legend Alvin Epstein was featured in the role of the cook. The play invokes a bygone world, a more pastoral existence, and celebrates the small accomplishments of this life no matter what fate has decreed. The two interlocutors share a story and the preparation of a meal, two familial rituals that close the gap between them.

Shepard and Lange took the family overseas in January so she could appear in a London production of *Streetcar Named Desire*. He took the kids to Ireland, where he walked the streets near Trinity College and along the River Liffey. Shepard, a Joyce fan from way back, felt Dublin to be steeped in literature and history. There were also the "absolutely devastating lassies."

While there, Shepard received a package from the United States, from his friend James Houghton of the Signature Theatre in New York. He provided the playwright with an update on the theater's "Shepard series," which was still unfolding. He also sent back a copy of Shepard's play then titled *Sangre de Cristo*, asking him reconsider letting it be produced. "I know you feel it's the same old stuff," Houghton wrote. The producer thought the play was not only highly original but also ready for the stage. He told Shepard how he'd showed it to Joseph Chaikin, who "loved it." Shepard did not grant Houghton's request: He felt the play as it stood seemed "old and repetitious." He would continue to work on *Sangre de Cristo* (a name taken from a mountain range that bridges New Mexico and Colorado) for a bit longer. It would become his family play, *The Late Henry Moss*, which would premiere in 2000.

Shepard's drinking must have become a more serious problem at this time, for he admits to hitting "that very severe bottom," enduring "a kind of terrible emotional crash." He claims that alcohol had nearly ruined his life and the lives of those around him. It proved to be a turning point, for on February 2 he quit drinking. As part of this renunciation, he recounted in a February 24, 2000, letter his reasons for drinking, the toll it had taken on his life, and his reasons for stopping. It is remarkable for its insight and candor. Despite entering Alcoholics Anonymous twice in his life, Shepard had trouble accepting the fact that he was an alcoholic. "It was my pride more than anything," he writes. "I had a hard time seeing myself in the same exact bag as my old man." His image of himself and his drinking was that of an "underground hero" using alcohol to cope with a fucked-up world, or of a "fascinating fellow" holding court before a rapt gathering.

Once he quit drinking this time, it took three months, he estimated, for his body to adjust. The physical withdrawal was one thing; hardest for Shepard was the psychological crutch he no longer had recourse to. "It all has to do with this thing of loneliness and the inability to have easy relationships with other people. It's the very reason I started drinking in the first place—THE BAR, the 'Nightlife'; the excitement of meeting strange women; the 'Adventure'—this whole notion that there's something out there I'm missing out on and booze was definitely the ticket that opened the door."

Alcohol gave him courage as well. It helped him with his anxieties and insecurities. Plus, as a writer, wasn't a drinking problem part of his birthright, he wondered? The cost of all this boozing always outweighed the actual fun of it, Shepard claims, at least in sober hindsight. Blackouts behind the wheel, sleeping in ditches, fights, hangovers that lasted until the drinking began anew, pool games with disreputable (and probably armed) men, fights with loved ones, the shakes, nausea, and shitting his pants in public are among the incidents he can remember from his drinking days. "Sounds like fun, huh?" he writes.

Sitting around a Toronto restaurant night after night in early 2000 with Sean Penn and Jack Nicholson, while filming *The Pledge*, was a particularly onerous test of his resolve, Shepard said. He would have loved to join the boys in a shot of bourbon, but he told himself that to do so would lead to him being "long gone down the lost road again." Meanwhile, when driving home from British Columbia, where he'd shot the film *Snow Falling on Cedars*, Shepard stopped in Sheridan, Wyoming, and passed a place he remembered from his "long-ago boozing days" called the Mint Bar. He had no urge to go inside.

His sobriety would last nearly three years. Shepard would often fill the void by revisiting something he'd never fully left behind, the teachings of G. I. Gurdjieff. He spent time rereading the books of Lord Pentland, who was president of the Gurdjieff Foundation in New York until his death in 1984 and a teacher of the Work whom Shepard had known personally.

These days he was also busy with parental duties. He still drove the children to school, took Walker to his different games, enjoyed the annual vacations to the Yucatan with Jessica and the children. The farm also kept Shepard busy, weaning calves (Walker was old enough to help now) and taking off with friends for cattle drives. As for his relationship with Lange, it seemed the pair had settled into a comfort zone, albeit with a lot of turbulent water under the bridge. Throughout, Shepard claims he was seeking "quietness of mind" and pursuing it through Gurdjieff, readings in Buddhism, and what sounds like Zen meditation, all in hopes of drowning out the noise and chaos of his mind.

"Blue" Days

I straighten my papers
I set up a schedule
My days will be busy
I don't have a minute to lose
I write.

—Blaise Cendrars

S hepard continued to write. However, for once it was on a project that did not originate in his own imagination. He came upon a story, "The Blue Bouquet," by Nobel Laureate Octavio Paz, in an anthology titled *Short Shorts*. The story is less than 860 words long, yet Shepard saw great meaning in the "mysterious accidental meeting between the two men and the terrifying proposition that ensues." He was already working on two different plays at the time—including one that would become *The Late Henry Moss*—but the Paz story kept haunting him. Eventually Shepard set aside his own work and on December 6, 1996, wrote to Paz for permission to adapt "The Blue Bouquet" for the stage. Noting the story's brevity, Shepard writes, "There are so many evocative qualities to it that I could not resist expanding it." At the time of this correspondence, Shepard had already been working on an adaptation of the 1949 short story for about a month, a fact he shared in his letter to Paz.

Shepard's affinity for writing small stories himself may have led to his fascination with "The Blue Bouquet." The story is about a man who in the steaming heat of night leaves his boardinghouse in a rural South American town against the advice of his landlord. As he walks, the man feels at one with his surroundings. "I thought that the universe was a vast system of signs, a conversation between giant beings. My actions, the cricket's saw, the star's blink, were nothing but pauses and syllables, scattered phrases from that dialogue," Paz writes. After the man walks on for a while, he feels a knife at his back. When he asks the stranger what he wants, the man replies, "Your eyes, mister." The first man asks why, and the stranger tells him that his girlfriend has a "whim." "She wants a bouquet of blue eyes. And around here they're hard to find."

The first man turns around as commanded, lights a match, and shows his accoster that his eyes are brown and not blue. The man makes him kneel down as he grabs his hair and pull his head back as if he is about to decapitate him. The man's machete comes down but merely grazes his eyelids. The man lets him go. The story finishes with the first man recounting how he got to his feet, stumbled, and ran through the town back to his lodgings. "I saw the owner of the boardinghouse, still sitting in front of the door. I went in without saying a word. The next day I left town."

The blue eyes signify the Americanness of the man, for he is a visitor, an outsider, someone from a highly developed part of the world. This man sees the world differently than the locals do. To take his eyes would symbolically turn this relationship on its head, leaving the "gringo" without his superior station and outlook.

Shepard's idea was to continue the story beyond where Paz leaves off, using the same characters and setting. Six weeks after the letter to Paz, the Mexican master and Nobel Laureate sent his initial blessings. After saying he was an admirer of Shepard's work, Paz added that he never considered his short story as the source material for a play. "I am flattered but also deeply moved by your insight," he wrote, citing Shepard's reading of "The Blue Bouquet" as depicting the "sympathies and oppositions" inside Paz himself.

The play would become *Eyes for Consuela*, a minor work in Shepard's canon, finished on his fifty-fourth birthday. It opened at the Manhattan Theatre Club in April 1998. The Paz story comprises part of Shepard's play, but instead of ending with the release of the man, his assailant follows him back to the boardinghouse. As they approach, they find the landlord, Viejo, on his rocking chair on the porch. Henry, the boarder, says to him, "This man is a bandit." Viejo's reply is, "What man isn't?"

Shepard appends to Paz's short story by having the American and the bandit talk about their situations. We learn that the American is estranged from his wife back home and that the bandit, Amado, also has an American wife, but his true love is a local girl named Consuela. He accidentally killed her years earlier, and her ghost dances across the stage at various points in the play.

The beauty of Paz's story is its precision and the way it says so much with so little. Shepard's play robs the story of its magic by trying to clarify what the great Mexican writer and poet was saying and adding details and backstory. He also heaps on the eye-related metaphors, some of them downright clichés. Still there are points where *Eyes for Consuela* almost justifies itself with Shepard's touches of humor, irony, and mystery, but in the end the entire enterprise comes across as ham-fisted and unnecessary when compared to the source material.

The critics, for the most part, were nothing short of scornful. "This is such a slack little play from the author of *True West*, *Fool for Love* and *Buried Child* that one wonders what's got into him," wrote John Heilpern of the *New York Observer*. Indeed, what had gotten into Shepard? Was he stretched too thin with his role as family man and rancher, combined with his short story writing and film acting? Was he relying too much on past glory, believing the magic of his earlier successes could still be conjured at will? It's a truism of American drama that the powers of our great playwrights often fade as they age. Was this happening to Shepard? If so, why? Was it his drinking? Was the absence of his father—his longtime muse, the wound he could always turn to for fresh blood—leaving him without the grist he needed to create compelling drama? For a writer who so often relied on reworking his autobiography, settling down with his family and livestock, with fewer money worries, may have been the worst thing that happened to Shepard. It's impossible to say for sure. However, it's likely that the answer lies in a combination of these things.

Shepard in his mid-fifties began experiencing health problems. Pain in his lower back and hips made sitting for long stretches of time difficult, and in the near future he would have minor heart surgery. Not surprising, given his longtime cigarette habit—interviews over the decades quite often mention him lighting up a Camel—and the drinking and drugging he readily admits to. Then there were the mental pressures that come with time. Like many people entering this stage of life, Shepard was enduring the death of loved ones, from his mother in 1994 to Jessica's mom in 1998.

The highlights of the next two years would include the naming of a performance space in his honor at San Francisco's Magic Theatre, where Shepard was once playwright in residence and premiered some of his best plays. Meanwhile, another St. Patrick's Day approached in 2000, which would mark Shepard and Lange's seventeenth anniversary. He felt they'd finally settled into a stable relationship. "Hard to believe there's so much water under the bridge but here we are, still together and much more tolerant of each other's differences. Still in love and sort of stunned that we've managed to raise kids, maintain a family, have two separate careers moving all over the world and still together!" However, he also conceded that when Lange was away, he was still depressed and anxious. When the couple was in New York City in early 2000 and Lange had to leave for a role overseas, Shepard says he "fell into a deep depression—got the lonesome, self-pitying blues again." When he leaves her behind for a trip to Oregon, he is "almost verging on despair and then sliding into terrible anxiety about leaving . . . almost to the point of some emotional breakdown."

Despite this evident need for companionship, the coming years would find Shepard and Lange drifting further and further apart, and before the new decade's end, they'd be history as a couple. The seeds of the drift may have been planted the day after Christmas in the year 2000, when the couple was in London. Leaving the kids at a rented flat watching *The Simpsons*, Shepard and Lange walked arm in arm around St. John's Wood. "After all these years, they finally felt at home with each other," Shepard confided to his notebook, coyly referring to himself and Lange in the third

HENDERSON LIBRARIES

when Lange out of the
next live. The couple
mother, but she'd died
ern winters was getting
places he favored were
and they should stay put
igh school. When
v York City and he
ark the beginning

f a new play. In it,
father, specifically
But first he would
er of one, in Michael
d already cast Ethan
ched Shepard about
had a habit of reciting
his truck," Almereyda
eart of the character,
the ghost's lines—he
s guy is crazy,' he said

mous praise from the
id story but transposes
spiring filmmaker who
e in the Denmark Cor-
so married his recently
y turns pinning Hamlet
around the space, all the
sper. Shepard gives the
t forward.
ald be very physical and
Hamlet and the ghost
nguage just took on this

incredible velocity. Sam started yelling his lines and had to cool down between takes," Almereyda said.

Fate and destiny, two things that Shepard has long been interested in, are central in *Hamlet* and likewise in Almereyda's film. Shepard's take on the play was that Hamlet has no choice but to fulfill the revenge his father's ghost asks of him. It goes without saying that the familial aspects of the story attracted Shepard as well. "I've always been fascinated by fathers and sons and by this thing about revenge," he said. "In a way, the film makes clearer than anything I've ever seen about trying to rectify a wrong from the past through violence. The violence gathers force in the play, and nobody can see how they are getting swept up in this brushfire, in this death."

Coincidently, around the time Shepard was working on *Hamlet*, Lange was in Rome shooting the film version of *Titus Andronicus* with Anthony Hopkins.

That March, things were going well. Shepard and the family enjoyed their annual trip to the Yucatan, and *True West*, featuring Philip Seymour Hoffman and John C. Reilly, was a hit on Broadway at the Circle in the Square Theatre, garnering a handful of Tony nominations to boot. The actors famously took turns playing the leading roles. Shepard, not one usually impressed by such things, seemed pleased. "I finally have a smash hit production on Broadway of *True West*—(only twenty some years after it was written)," he wrote to his friend Dark. "The sucker is sold out and got the best, across-the-board reviews I've ever had in my life. I'm in a state of shock." The production broke box office records.

His sideline with the horses was keeping him very busy as well, with upward of fifteen steeds to his name, including weanlings, yearlings, broodmares, and a few in training. Shepard spent part of the summer in Calgary filming *After the Harvest* for Canadian television. Its story was very close to that of *Days of Heaven*, with Shepard playing an overly strict father who pays the price for his inflexibility. He spent his downtime reading the short stories of a favorite author, Graham Greene, as well as Dante's *Inferno*.

"Late" Show

L

There's no law against bringing brothers into plays several times. [Chuckles] I like this predicament, one brother sitting with the corpse and the other one coming from a long distance and meeting around the death of the father. I thought it was an important predicament.

—Sam Shepard

For his next play, Shepard couldn't resist raising old ghosts. Literally. The play that he'd been writing on and off since at least November of 1989 with the working title *Sangre de Cristo* (as well as *The Original Liar* and *A Drowned Man*) was finally finished on January 29, 2000. It was called *The Late Henry Moss*. Broaching head-on the subject of his father's death was easier said than done. "It took me five years to even consider writing about it," Shepard said. "Finally, I came to the point where I thought that if I don't write about it, some aspect of it may be lost."

The play's roots can actually be traced to a 1931 short story by Frank O'Connor called "The Late Henry Conran." Henry, a drinker, huffs off to Chicago after a nasty spat with his wife, which leads to her locking him out of the house. After many years away from his family, he reads in the paper his son's wedding announcement, which lists him as dead. Henry returns home and threatens to sue his wife for defamation. Finally he's allowed to rejoin the family. Shepard's story, naturally, lacks such a happy ending.

The Late Henry Moss premiered the following November at Theatre on the Square in San Francisco as a production of the Magic Theatre, featuring a star-studded cast that included Sean Penn, Nick Nolte, Woody Harrelson, Cheech Marin, and two actors Shepard had often worked with, James Gammon and Sheila Tousey. The fact that his latest play once again involved dueling siblings even amused Shepard, who wrote to a friend about his new play, "brothers again—what a surprise!"

The brothers are Earl and Ray, and when the latter turns up unannounced at his father's apartment in New Mexico, he finds his brother there with his old man's corpse laid out in an upstage alcove. Ray wants to know what happened and doesn't believe that Earl is telling the whole story. The facts surrounding the death of Shepard's father play a pivotal role in the play. Like Sam Rogers, Henry Moss had a few extra bucks and called a taxi to take him and a female friend fishing and then to downtown Bernalillo. However, instead of having the old man stumble out of a bar and into traffic, in *The Late Henry Moss*, the father's final moments are left a mystery until the end of the play.

The three acts are filled with Ray's attempts to get to the bottom of his father's death. He even goes so far as to summon the taxi driver who participated in his father's final escapade to see what he knows. Along the way, he fights with Earl about the elder brother's abdication from the family home years earlier, when he was most needed. The play seamlessly weaves flashbacks from Henry's last day into the present and culminates with the explanation of the cause of his death just before the final curtain.

The play received mixed to negative reviews. Some critics were put off by Shepard's return to his old stamping ground of the troubled family. Others harshly criticized Penn's performance. Many found highlights along the way or praised the power of the play's final scene. The problem with the play is that, like Shepard's movies, he takes a simple story and stretches it too far. Three acts of bickering brothers and mysterious flashbacks were simply more than the story could support. The slackness announces itself at several points, such as when Ray endlessly grills the taxi driver, or when the two brothers argue over who should get the old man's tools. All that being said, the play is often funny and is interesting for its "meta" features, vis-à-vis the way Shepard weaves into the plot his father's real-life accident.

There are other autobiographical elements. The younger brother, Ray, keeps accusing Earl of leaving, of running away, a charge the older brother denies throughout. Shepard, like Earl, left the family home for good at the age of nineteen after the so-called holocaust, or final blowout, with his father. The playwright here seems to put himself on trial for leaving his family and never looking back. *The Late Henry Moss* is reminiscent of *The Holy Ghostly* from 1969, where the character of the father faults the son for running off to New York and making a name for himself. In real life, had Shepard stayed, perhaps the old man's downward trajectory would have turned out differently. Shepard discounts this, contending that his father had been on a long descent by the time he left. The implication being that, like Henry Moss, Sam Rogers long knew that he was "doomed."

Director and Shepard friend Michael Almereyda produced a documentary called *This So-Called Disaster*, which chronicled the rehearsal process and Shepard's directing of *Moss*. Shepard had requested the proceedings be filmed, and at first he had the consent of the cast to do so. However, lawyers got involved, and it "was a nightmare just to get the film started," Almereyda said, adding, "Sam finally said that the camera was going to be on and he didn't want to hear anything more about it."

Shepard wrote to his friend Johnny Dark on November 19, 2000, that he was going through a "rough spell." Chances are the troubles Shepard was alluding to were related to his health. Some time around December 2000, he underwent some sort of heart procedure. He joked to his friend about how his "new reamed out heart artery" made him feel invincible. The next month, he wrote a rather melancholic poem in his notebook that reflected his current state of mind mixed with a hefty dose of nostalgia. Perhaps the heart surgery, minor as it was, along with Lange's being away in London, or the simple fact of his aging, was getting the better of his emotions. The essence of the poem, never published, is that he hadn't changed since his early days in New York City. "He isn't happy with who he is," he writes. In the scribbled lines, Shepard continues, wondering who was that person walking the streets of the Village back then and what was the big idea that drove him. He remembers the jazz artists he hung out with and would see at various nightclubs, including Coltrane, as well as a friend who was also a musician and hooked on heroin. The poem's final line, "Something lost up there," underscores the melancholia he was feeling about times long past.

The mood proved to be less than conducive to his continued sobriety. The previous February, Shepard remarked that he'd been three years sober, but he hastened to add, "There's still always the possibility that the maniac could leap up one day and decide to have a 'little drink.'" Finding himself alone in Santa Fe on a chilly night in mid-January 2001, Shepard fell off the wagon. (This is when he admits his years of sobriety ended, but in the documentary *This So-Called Disaster*, filmed in the fall of 2000, Shepard is seen sipping from what appears to be a glass of wine.) But that January evening, at a Canyon Road bar, he purposely set out to indulge, choosing a red cabernet from Healdsburg, California, to do the job. "Suddenly I know without a doubt that I am going off with the full intention of getting absolutely smashed," he said. He remembers the scene turned sad very quickly, from the fat guy singing Dylan songs in the corner to the "slightly pathetic middle-aged ex-hippie types" lined up at the bar. This drove him out into the night air and back toward the Santa Fe Plaza, where he pulled up a chair at La Fonda Hotel's bar, a place he had once partied with Dark and two strange women, and where his father had been a custodian. Another glass of wine. Shepard leaves and hits another hotel bar before making his way back to the Plaza, where he thinks about his father and begins feeling sorry for himself. "At one point, I'm crying out to the moon and the heavens in a drunken wail," he recalled.

Standing in the Plaza, Shepard was overcome by the familiar feeling of aloneness: "It sometimes feels as though I am absolutely unaware of anyone else existing in this life [and I] wonder to what extent I am cut off from other people—how far have I removed myself into this totally ridiculous state of isolation???"

The story has a happy ending, when three days later, Shepard flies to London to be with Lange and his children, and "it feels like everything is exactly in place and this is where I'm supposed to be and it's all perfect."

"Hell"

I just want to win something!! I don't care what it is. I just want to win. I like winning. Winning is fun. Losing is not fun. I always feel like a loser.

—Sam Shepard

Like the rest of the nation, the events of September 11, 2001, and the inevitable fallout of war shocked and outraged Shepard. His notebooks are filled with concerns that another Vietnam was nigh, that Americans would be force-fed a war, "although no one can figure out exactly why," and that "something at the very core of our being has been savaged." His anger would fuel his next play, *The God of Hell*. However, by this time he was already working on another screenplay, which would mark his reunion with director Wim Wenders and feature parts for both him and Lange.

The winter in Minnesota that year seemed endless. Everything was still covered in snow and ice in mid-March, and Shepard's body hurt, and he and Lange were fighting again. They celebrated their nineteenth anniversary together on St. Patrick's Day, and then "it's like the bottom fell out on us," Shepard reported. This was just days before the annual family trip to the Yucatan, and he and Lange weren't speaking to each other. Reading Beckett's short stories didn't help matters, as they exacerbated Shepard's orneriness. Eventually, he tells of how self-pity set in: "I don't know what to do with myself. I have no friends, I feel alienated from my own family and all of Jessica's relatives, I can't stand Minnesota—the climate, the people, the whole stupid place. . . . This is really the pits."

Around this time, one of his most popular films, *Black Hawk Down*, was released. Shepard puts forward his best steely glare for this military film, where he plays a general trying to commandeer a difficult rescue mission. This, along with a handful of other roles in lesser films, would keep him busy. Asked around this time how he chose his films, Shepard was honest: "Well, sometimes I just need a job," he said with a laugh. "I would like to be able to say I have the luxury of picking my material but sometimes I need the work. But it would be great to pick and choose. I pick and choose as much as I can but sometimes you can't be too picky." Again, Shepard demonstrates an amazing ability to compartmentalize his artistic life. For him, writing is an art; acting more of a craft and a way to get by. He'd be in other popular films in the coming years, including *Swordfish* and *The Notebook*. These and the lesser-known fare were nothing but paychecks, where he plays a man in a uniform or a version of wise, old Dad.

The money from these films was necessary to some degree to keep his horses, cattle, and chickens and to finance trips to riding competitions and rodeos. In May of 2002, he traveled 250 miles to compete in a cutting-horse show, where he claims to have "rode the hair right off my mare." He paid a physical price himself in competing so hard this time: He reported that his hand was bleeding from pressing on the saddle horn so hard.

That same month, Shepard would get a call from his doctor saying his recent stress test had turned up "a glitch of some sort" in the same area of his heart that had been treated eighteen months earlier. What was done about this, if anything, is not recorded, and in 2007 Shepard reports getting a clean bill of health after a checkup.

As had been his wont, every few years, Shepard collected his notebook jottings, short stories, poems, bits of dialogue, and *mishegoss* into a book. *Great Dream of Heaven* was published in October 2002 and was a finalist in England for the W. H. Smith Literary Award. This collection, like the previous ones, had a rural backbone, but Shepard included many scenes of domestic life. Often, a man coming unmoored populates these stories and scenes. "Berlin Wall Piece" has become a favorite at the rare public readings Shepard gives. Told from the perspective of a teenage girl, the story sounds autobiographical, and throughout Shepard revels in self-deprecation. It begins: "My dad knows absolutely nothing about the eighties." Said dad then goes on to reminisce about the decade, embarrassing his kids every stop along the way. In the story "The Stout of Heart," a man sequesters himself in the family attic with his horse auction catalogs and breed directories. He's evidently traded drinking for this new addiction. As with the father in Shepard's first play, *The Rock Garden,* who locks himself away with a collection of cats, we're not sure if it's passion or lunacy behind the behavior. "Coalinga ½ Way" depicts a man leaving his wife for another woman only to find out his new love ultimately can't rendezvous because she's flying off to meet an old flame. Shepard will often use only dialogue to tell a story. Since his earliest days as a writer, dialogue has been his preferred métier. *Great Dream of Heaven* contains a couple of bravura performances demonstrating Shepard's continuing gift for the way people talk, what they mean but don't want to say, and what they don't mean but wish they did.

The collection was well reviewed and featured a beautiful cover photo, taken by Lange, of Shepard and his youngest son sitting at the end of a dock, a big lake unfolding before them.

Shepard, despite any health concerns, was as restless as ever, burning up the highways as he pursued his career and hobbies. Some years he kept track in his notebooks of all the places he'd been. In 2003 that list included St. Paul, Minnesota; Kentucky; back to St. Paul; Las Vegas; New Mexico; Tulum, Mexico; Houston; Albuquerque; back to Las Vegas; Fort Worth, Texas; Montgomery, Alabama; back to Fort Worth; Los Angeles; back to Fort Worth; to Montgomery again; Charleston, South Carolina; back to Kentucky; back to St. Paul. For most of these miles Shepard was behind the wheel of his pickup. During years when Shepard had a new play or an important revival being staged, there were trips to New York as well.

Shepard's world was shaken on June 22, 2003, when his friend and mentor Joseph Chaikin, cursed with ill health most of his life, died in New

York. Chaikin's "whole life was about living with death from day to day," Shepard felt. Shepard also recalled how Chaikin once told him he wasn't interested in collaborating with any artist who "didn't include mortality in their work." The shock Shepard faced at the memorial service, held in New York City, wasn't so much that his friend was gone—though he'd struggle with this for some time—but in the way his old colleagues looked after thirty-five years. Shepard remembered "hunting through their ravaged faces for who they were." Time, he concludes, is "merciless." Many spoke at the service, but the consensus was that Shepard's words honoring the "truly courageous soul," as he considered Chaikin to be, carried the day. "Sam's eulogy was very special," said former Open Theater member and composer Marianne de Pury, who talked with friends who'd attended the ceremony.

Chaikin always provided Shepard with a connection to the avant-garde. No matter how much of a movie star he became or how many Broadway revivals he chalked up, their shared and enduring love for Beckett, and devotion to craft for craft's sake, allowed them to produce work, alone and together, that was bold and uncompromising. Chaikin also brought out the best in Shepard's humanity. While Shepard is often self-critical, and even his oldest friend would refer to him as "a renowned asshole," with Chaikin he was kind and caring. His former mother-in-law, also stricken with severe health problems, likewise regularly brought out this side of Shepard.

Chaikin's sad ending was followed later that summer with a new beginning. Lange's daughter with Mikhail Baryshnikov, Aleksandra (Shura for short), was married at the family home on July 5. Shepard wore a white suit—something he figured only men of a certain age could get away with. Baryshnikov was in attendance, and he and Shepard got on famously. The only trouble came toward the end of the night when Shepard, who admits to being "pretty drunk," saw his daughter Hannah's boyfriend talking with another young woman. He kicked him out, and when Lange and his daughter angrily confronted him about doing so, Shepard jumped into the pool, white suit and all.

That November, Shepard turned sixty, and the family gathered in downtown Stillwater for a celebratory dinner. The guest of honor read a poem he'd written for the occasion, poking fun at his inability to jump barbed-wire fences or hop up into the saddle anymore, about his "leathery chicken-neck" and the "glassy film now between [his] eye and the shimmering human shapes" of his loved ones. He concludes with a loving tribute to his family:

> *Right now here is all we've got*
> *and it's just good and lucky to be in the flow*
> *of kinship, kindness and the human friend*
> *and not be stuck out somewhere deep like Big Bend*
> *in some wasted Super 8 without room service, TV*
> *or a chrome hot plate*
> *it sure is damn good and lucky*

The year 2004 started on a high note for Shepard the rancher: "16 heifers," he wrote in his notebook in mid-January, "some of the best I've ever raised." Around the same time, he was outside his Wisconsin barn weaning one of these heifers when he saw a "female red-tail [come] hard in the horse pasture, snatching a field mouse." It was a scene reminiscent of the most famous section of his 1977 play *Curse of the Starving Class*, where an eagle plucks off the ground a screeching cat and flies away. It was an image that would thrill theater audiences and mystify critics and scholars for years. In 2004, standing in the cold Wisconsin morning, Shepard took the visitation of the feeding hawk as a good sign.

Sadly, he would be mistaken; the next year would prove to be a very painful one. The breakup of his and Lange's relationship began in earnest that spring. On April 10, he took down a bunch of pictures from his writing room, including the ones of himself and Lange when they were "madly lost in love." When the wall was bare but for the hooks that once held the photos, Shepard began weeping, lost in the "sensation of absolute exile." Two days later, he'd again take to his notebooks to ask, "Have I wrecked everything between us?" and to claim that during an argument Lange told him, "You're stupid and I hate you."

The couple put the house in Minnesota up for sale, as they'd discussed doing during that walk in London a few years earlier. The kids were grown, for the most part, and both Shepard and Lange were eager to live someplace warmer than Minnesota. As to where this would be, they were divided. They purchased two places in the spring of 2005, the first being an apartment at 1 Fifth Avenue in New York City for $3.4 million. The corner apartment in the co-op building actually consisted of two original units, a one-bedroom and a two-bedroom. The other home was a farm in Midway, Kentucky, which Shepard claimed was once the home of Jesse James's mother. These would shortly become "his" and "her" residences. Lange would retain a cabin near Duluth.

Lange indicated that the empty nest cleared the way for the change: Daughter Hannah was done with high school and off to Sarah Lawrence College in Westchester County, and Walker would be moved to a private school in Brooklyn. "I'm ready to move back to New York," Lange told a local Minnesota reporter. "This is a nice place to raise children. But there's no reason for me to be here anymore."

The new apartment was situated across from Washington Square Park. Shepard stayed often with Lange, actually enjoying his time in the city once again, after years of hating it. When he would stay in Kentucky, he claimed, "Jessica feels as though I'm abandoning her or something."

Shepard spelled out clearly in a letter to Dark near the end of April the trouble between himself and Lange, during what he called an "enormously painful time." His drinking was driving them apart. "I don't know why I keep returning to these horrible bouts of drinking and bad behavior," Shepard writes. "I've ruined an amazing relationship just out of a callous disregard for anyone else's feelings." Lange had come to the "end of her rope," he claimed. The plan was to stay together for the sake of the children, and Shepard was hopeful the relationship could be salvaged in the long term.

The Minnesota house was put on the market that spring for $3.3 million. That July, Lange auctioned off many belongings, including about forty antiques and paintings. The most expensive piece, a Daum Nancy cameo glass lamp, fetched $9,500. The house itself failed to sell and was taken off the market for a time. It finally sold at the end of September 2008 for $1.825 million.

The year 2004 was not all doom and gloom for Shepard and Lange. The family traveled to Australia for a vacation at one point, Shepard had a new play slated for New York, and he would make his return to the stage as an actor.

Ultimately, Shepard's response to the attacks of September 11, 2001, to judge from his writing anyway, was distaste for the patriotism-cum-jingoism that accompanied the U.S. response. To him, it was the epitome of cynical salesmanship by political leaders, and he was saddened to see so many of his countrymen eat it up. "We're being sold a brand-new idea of patriotism," he said. "It never occurred to me that patriotism had to be advertised. Patriotism is something you deeply felt. You didn't have to wear it on your lapel or show it in your window or on a bumper sticker. That kind of patriotism doesn't appeal to me at all."

This was the theme for a play originally titled *Pax Americana*, but that when it made its premiere in October 2004 at New York's Actors Studio Drama School Theater, was titled *The God of Hell*. Shepard's influence for the play was the late playwright Joe Orton, specifically his 1964 play *Entertaining Mr. Sloane*. He also had the idea of working into the play the phenomenon of static shock, something that afflicted Shepard whenever he walked on rugs.

With *The God of Hell*, Shepard set his sights on a particular kind of politician: The play is, he said, "a takeoff on Republican fascism, in a way." He hustled it from the page to the theater in time for the November 2 elections. The play opened with well-known names like Randy Quaid and, making his first U.S. stage appearance, Tim Roth. However, the play's flimsy plot and lack of original, animating ideas doom it from the start. Frank and Emma are a nice but dull couple living on a Wisconsin dairy farm. They've let Frank's old friend, Haynes, live temporarily in the basement. Haynes is hiding out due to some secret government project he's involved with that has to do with plutonium. (He's the one suffering from chronic static shock.) A crazed patriotic bureaucrat named Welch keeps showing up, asking questions about the house and who lives there, meanwhile trying to sell Frank and Emma all sorts of red-white-and-blue paraphernalia. Welch's real intent, however, involves the capture and torture of Haynes.

There are parts of *The God of Hell* that are funny and interesting, and critics mostly found a few things worth praising. Shepard's anger comes screaming through every scene, but the ninety-minute diatribe against Bush's foreign policy and domestic scare tactics mostly misses the mark.

Around the same time, Shepard was readying for a return to stage acting. He'd famously curtailed his last such performance after a few nights, when he fled shortly after the opening of his and Patti Smith's 1971 play *Cowboy Mouth*. Now, with dozens of films to his credit, he decided he'd try again, playing the father in Caryl Churchill's *A Number*. Like Shepard, Churchill was an acolyte of Brecht, but the main reason for his signing on was to stretch himself as an actor. "Film acting is really the trick of doing moments," he said. "You rarely do a take that lasts more than 20 seconds. You really earn your spurs acting onstage. I needed to do that for myself. . . . Still, it's frightening to confront the audience." *A Number*, though nominally about cloning, also dealt with a longtime Shepard concern, identity. Shepard confided to his notebook that he thought Churchill's play was "incredibly smart." He also found it derivative of Beckett. "But, so what? He inspired us all," he wrote.

Ben Brantley of the *New York Times* said Shepard's being in the cast made the production "an essential ticket for theater lovers." The play opened at New York Theater Workshop in December 2004. Brantley called it "stunning" and called Shepard's performance "terrific."

It took three years to get the screenplay to *Don't Come Knocking* into shape, which was fine because it took director Wim Wenders time to get the roughly $8 million shooting budget pulled together. Shepard got the acceptance call while out in his barn, holding one of his horses as an equine dentist filed away at the animal's back molar.

The film stars Shepard as Howard Spence, an aging actor known for western dramas who one day simply goes AWOL from the set. Realizing he needs to get his life together, he first visits his mother (played by Eva Marie Saint) in of all places the casino city of Elko, Nevada. Clearly, this is the wrong place for a man hoping to reject a life of vice. When Howard's mother lets on that he has a grown son he never knew about, he sets out to find him and the kid's mother, an ex-flame played by Lange. He locates them in Butte, Montana. The reunion does not go smoothly. Adding to Howard's conundrum is a young woman who follows him around with an urn containing her mother's ashes. She may or may not be his daughter. The film was based in reality of a sort. "I don't remember a movie where I haven't wanted to run away at some point," Shepard said.

Wenders was disappointed when Shepard refused to play the lead character, Travis, in their previous collaboration, *Paris, Texas*. With *Don't Come Knocking*, the director didn't push and got a nice surprise. "This time I didn't ask and that was a sneaky thing from me," he said. "And after a few scenes, [Shepard] casually said, 'By the way, I think I could play this.'" Wenders may have had an inkling that Shepard would step up for the role. From early on in the planning of the film, Shepard had a vision of what the film's final scene should be: a "cowboy on the rearing horse." It sounded like an ending he couldn't refuse.

While working on *The God of Hell* with Tim Roth, Shepard had floated the idea of Roth appearing in the film, warning him there was no money. Roth nevertheless signed on to play the film's insurance company investigator, who doggedly tries to find Howard.

The film can be read as addressing one of Shepard's long-held themes, the curse of heredity. Howard's son is also sullen and prone to escaping when the going gets rough. His supposed daughter isn't spared: she seems, like Howard, to be a lost soul. However, Shepard was going for something else. "It's about estrangement more than anything else," he said. "It's about this American sadness that I find, the aloneness that Americans feel. . . . I'm haunted by that American character."

Don't Come Knocking premiered at Cannes on May 19, 2005, and traveled to another half dozen film festivals. Even critics who liked the film called it "strange" or "odd." Shepard's performance drew plenty of positive notices, and the pleasure of the film isn't derived only from the plot; Wenders' breathtaking cinematography and T Bone Burnett's haunting score add much to the film's charm.

The difficulties with Lange continued after Shepard returned to New York City from Cannes. The couple went for breakfast at a favorite Twelfth Street restaurant, and soon afterward, Shepard confided to his notebook, "She likes to try to punish me with her indifference." He goes on to say that Lange learned this passive-aggressive trick from him.

Shepard was in Virginia that year for the Fourth of July. He stopped somewhere along Highway 81 and again jotted a few words about his relationship with Lange, admitting in so many words that he could not live without her. The same month, he wrote with seeming sadness about the days when he and Lange "were entirely focused on each other" and how those times "will never come again." Meanwhile, that September, he wrote a short, unpublished poem while he was fishing in Edmonton, Alberta, that addresses "the impossibility of us" and concludes wondering about "the impossibility of it continuing."

During this trip, Shepard almost drowned in the Bow River. He first got knocked down by the strong current and found himself in water up to his neck, "flailing for my life in the icy water." Once he recovered from this, he was stuck on the other side of the river. Trying to cross back what looked like shallow shoals to where he'd parked his vehicle, the current knocked him down again, and this time he was in over his head. If not for a small gravel island upon which Shepard was able to get a foothold, who knows what might have become of him. He worried about hypothermia as he finally made his way to the car. Back at the hotel, it took an hour-long hot shower to get him back to normal.

The year 2005 had its share of good news. Shepard was back on Broadway with *Fool for Love*, which Ed Harris directed, and after seventeen years of breeding and buying horses, he'd finally bred a thoroughbred "mare to beat the colts," named Two Trail Sioux. She "just punishes horses if they challenge her," Shepard noted. That April she won the Bayakoa Stakes at Oaklawn Park in Arkansas. With this accomplished, Shepard mused that he could now go back to simply raising cattle and saddle horses.

A 2010 profile of Shepard in *Daily Thoroughbred News* detailed his side career as a breeder. He has had horses most of his adult life, but in early 1987 Shepard attended a thoroughbred sale with a check for $3,500 in his pocket, part of his payment for his aborted role in Woody Allen's *September*. With that, he bought his first racehorse. Over the years, Shepard's breeding operation has produced nearly seventy thoroughbreds that have made the races. Some of these have sold at auction as yearlings for hundreds of thousands of dollars. His stable has produced racehorses that together have earned more than $3 million for their owners. (Shepard himself only keeps and races a handful of horses at any one time; many of those have been big earners as well.)

A Late Trilogy

Seems like playwrights hit a certain place where they're either repeating past work or trying to invent new stuff that has nowhere near the impact of the earlier work.

—Sam Shepard

I t was a long-distance phone call around 2006 that inspired Shepard to embark on a handful of shorter plays. His old friend, the actor Stephen Rea, asked Shepard to write something for him to perform at Ireland's Abbey Theatre. Shepard obliged with *Kicking a Dead Horse*, which he directed himself. It is basically a one-hander, and it premiered in September 2007, moving to New York's Public Theater the following summer before traveling to England.

Reuniting with his old friend led Shepard to write another one-act for Rea and another Irish actor, Sean McGinley. *Ages of the Moon* opened at the Abbey in March 2009, directed by Jimmy Fay. The cast and crew traveled to the United States in January 2010, when the play was revived at the Linda Gross Theater in New York.

Shepard's last play to date, *A Particle of Dread*, had its gestation years earlier in his notebooks, as he pondered the works of the ancient Greeks. But it was another call from Rea that set the one-act play in motion. Invited to put his legendary theater company, Field Day, back together, Rea quickly agreed but wondered what to stage. "I thought, 'I'll speak to Sam,' so I called him up and asked if he would do something and he quickly agreed," Rea said. "This was what he was working on." *A Particle of Dread* also premiered at the Abbey Theatre in November 2013 before coming to New York's Signature Theatre the following January.

The keeper of the trio is *Ages of the Moon*. Two old friends, Ames (Rea) and Byron (McGinley) reunite at a cabin in the woods. Ames is experiencing a bit of a crisis. His wife has tossed him out for a simple indiscretion, proof of which was a name and phone number found among his possessions. As he explains to Byron in an early, hilarious exchange:

> AMES: Some girl I would never in a million years have returned to for even a minor blow job.
> BYRON: Minor?
> AMES: Well, you know—
> BYRON: No, I don't know. They're all major, as far as I'm concerned. At this point.

And so it goes. The two friends joke and reminisce as they get drunker and drunker throughout the day. They tussle at one point, but the comedy of the battle and all the talk that went before is soon obliterated by Byron's story of his wife's death. It's a strange tale, about how he carried her dead body piggyback around town. It ends with Byron voicing the problem both men face with the loss of their companions. "[It] stopped being home to me after that. Anywhere—" And later, "There's nowhere to go." We leave the old friends waiting for the full eclipse of the moon, knowing they're lost but in some ways realizing that we in the audience are no better off.

The critics were almost unanimous in their praise for *Ages of the Moon*, as much for Shepard's tale of existential melancholy as for the two actors who bring the story to life. It is perhaps Shepard's best attempt at putting his own spin on Beckett's vision.

Kicking a Dead Horse does not fare as well but has its moments of humor and existential seeking. Rea plays Hobart Struther, an art dealer from New York in his mid-sixties, who sets out into the desert only to have his horse die on him. Standing next to his prostrated mount, a hole dug awaiting the body, Hobart talks to himself, trying to figure out his life during this botched "quest for authenticity."

The story brings to mind a short item Shepard wrote around this time that would be published in his next story collection, *Day out of Days*. Simply titled "Horse," it tells of how he had to bury a favorite horse. It begins: "Dragging my dead gelding by tractor on a chain down to the deep ditch, crying like a baby."

In the play, Hobart is angry at his horse, for letting him down but also for mocking his attempt to achieve some sort of authenticity. This is a term Shepard has used often, and a trait he holds in the highest regard. The play is best read as Shepard poking fun at himself and commenting on the impossibility of being honest and "real" in the world. This, of course, has its roots in Gurdjieff's teachings, where the entire goal is to shed one's masks, or learned personalities, to get to one's true essence.

Through his monologue, often arguing with himself, Hobart gives the impression that he has let himself down and sold out—before making a living as an art dealer he worked on a farm—and is taking the easy path through life. That's what this "grand sojourn" was all about, reconnecting with the authentic, but of course it fails. Authenticity is not something one can simply ride across the desert to attain. Especially when your horse is dead.

Critics were, for the most part, united in dismissing the short play as Shepard spinning his wheels, covering the same old territory with nothing much new to say or an interesting way to say it.

They would be even less impressed with his final play, *A Particle of Dread*. It presents Shepard's take on Sophocles's *Oedipus Rex* and themes the playwright had been kicking around since the mid-1980s. The Greeks are "all about destiny! That's the most powerful thing. Everything is foreseen, and we just play it out," he had told *Rolling Stone* years earlier. Shepard actually outlined in one of his notebooks, back in 1981, a film about Oedipus. The tale of the cursed king fighting against destiny is central to Shepard's understanding of life—it serves as a prism for much of his thinking. His other major themes—the inescapability of heredity and even the seeking of the authentic—also resound in Sophocles's great play.

Despite his long-held fascination with this story, most agree that in putting it onstage, using Sophocles's original as a jumping-off point, Shepard came up short. The play left many members of the audience in New York confused and shaking their heads, and only Shepard aficionados likely appreciated what he was trying to do. Instead of simply giving us his version of a classic tale (as he attempted to do decades earlier with *Man Fly*, his take on *Dr. Faustus*), Shepard slices and dices the story of Oedipus and shows it to us in various contexts. "[Sam] calls it *Oedipus Variations* and that's exactly what it is," said Nancy Meckler, a longtime Shepard friend and director who helmed the play both in Ireland and New York. "The thing about Shepard is that he loves jazz, and this is almost like a jazz improvisation, where you take something that's thrown up by the story, follow it, and then you come back. Sometimes we're in ancient Greece with Oedipus. Sometimes we're in a modern version. It's like Sam's riffing on the myth, but it's still about a man who does not know his origins and gets caught out trying to get to the truth. He doesn't realize that the truth is going to destroy him."

There are times in the play, particularly when a pair of modern-day investigators is on the case, when it seems *A Particle of Dread* is ready to take flight. However, soon enough it leaves that thread and picks up on another, never fully gaining momentum. It's interesting to a point, but only to those who are fans of Shepard's work. The reviewers were, for the most part, not charmed.

This trilogy of late plays allowed Shepard, with varying success, to explore themes that had long interested him from the perspective of the sixty-something-year-old man he now was.

Break

I need four walls around me/to hold my life/to keep me from going astray.

— James Taylor, "Bartender's Blues"

The essence of being human is . . . to be defeated and broken up by life which is the inevitable price of fastening one's love upon other human individuals.

— George Orwell

Acting was taking up a fair amount of Shepard's time these days. He nearly stole the show in *Walker Payne*, a dogfighting movie in which he plays a slick hustler and even gets to do some impressive a cappella singing in an empty ballpark. In *The Assassination of Jesse James by the Coward Robert Ford*, Shepard had a tougher time stealing the show, thanks to its fine cast, but he still shone brightly as the doom-saying Frank James, bringing a gravitas to every scene he was in. He is featured only in the earliest sections of the film, but Shepard makes a strong impression in a cinematic triumph for all concerned.

When *The Assassination of Jesse James* traveled to the Venice Film Festival in early September 2007, Shepard went along, and at one point he hitched along on the yacht of his costars Brad Pitt and Angelina Jolie. Five boats full of paparazzi chased them, and Shepard commented in a notebook entry that Jolie looked worried. "It's not the face she puts on magazine covers," he wrote.

Shepard felt right at home playing a horse trainer in the television film *Ruffian*, based on the true story of a champion horse pushed too far for its own good. Shepard's copy of the script had a handful of notes, many focused on trying to make the dialogue and settings more authentic to life at the racetrack.

At the start of 2007, Shepard and Lange traveled to Rome and then Ireland, where *Kicking a Dead Horse* was having its premiere. While there, they visited their daughter Hannah, who was attending the University of Ireland–Galway. The backdrop was perfect for his rereading of Beckett (yet again) and enjoying Seamus Heaney's translation of *Beowulf*. The sojourn ended with Shepard heading to London, where Lange was featured in *The Glass Menagerie*.

Shepard's looks changed markedly that summer back in Kentucky, when he had all his teeth pulled and replaced with a perfect set. Gone was the front-and-center snaggletooth he was famous for. He'd set the entire month of June aside for the procedure, which was performed by a dentist who looked like Kim Novak, a fact that Shepard did not complain about. Despite this, it was far from pleasant. "My whole face swelled up like I'd gone ten rounds with Mike Tyson," he said. He was healed in time for the late summer wedding of his first child, Jesse.

Around this time, Shepard feared he was becoming too reclusive, even for him, happy to sit alone in his Wisconsin-made Adirondack chair on his stone porch at his Kentucky farm sipping coffee and reading his favorite poets instead of being part of Jessica's busy life in New York City. At the same time he wrote, apropos of his recent dental work, that they could replace every part of him and they'd never get near his "utter isolation, solitude." This may have been the pain pills talking. However, by late August he was worried about his alcohol consumption. "I've been drinking way too much and too often," he wrote to Dark. "Can't ever seem to learn the lesson of it, whatever that is." He also came to the realization that most of his life had been "consumed by flight. Initially from the nightmare of my father's wrath, which I never understood and still don't. . . . The frantic futility of constantly searching for a new place; a new life, a new partner. As though change itself were some kind of elixir."

The world would learn about Shepard's drinking early in 2009. He was having a few drinks the night of Friday, January 2, at Fat Jack's, a bar at 511 North Main Street in Bloomington, Illinois. He departed as closing time approached and climbed into his late-model Chevy Tahoe, where his poodle was waiting for him. Driving on North Main Street in nearby Normal, Shepard was clocked going 46 in a 30 mph zone. Lieutenant Mark Kotte of the Normal Police Department pulled him over around 2 a.m. The officer administered a Breathalyzer test and found Shepard's blood alcohol level to be twice the legal limit of 0.08. Shepard told the officer he was on his way to the local Best Western. Instead, he spent the night in jail.

Shepard had been at Fat Jack's before, stopping over the years as he made his way back to Kentucky from Minnesota. He wrote about his night in jail in a piece that was published in his next story collection. He describes the cell he was put in and the sad fact that he was not only $150 short of making his bond but had no one to call for help. In his cell, he thought of a writer that Patti Smith had introduced him to back in 1971, Jean Genet, and how when Genet was in prison, guards found the manuscript of his great novel *Our Lady of the Flowers* and burned it. Genet rewrote the whole thing from scratch, on toilet paper.

Shepard was released the following afternoon. He went home to Kentucky, but still his "loopy mug shot [was] all over CNN and *People* magazine." He felt like a laughingstock and was glad to be back in his rural paradise, a "sanctuary," especially "in times like these when the media loves parading your vagaries all over the country and your old lady won't talk to you and your children begin to wonder just how insane their father might have become."

If Shepard sounded flip about his arrest and his newfound notoriety, it was quite a different tone with which he wrote in his notebook the following month. It was true, Lange was not speaking to him, and indeed the arrest would eventually be the final straw in their relationship—even if the world didn't learn about the breakup until nearly two years later. This entry, written in Ireland that February, is full of self-loathing and self-recrimination. It's almost painful to read, and it's reminiscent of a Blaise Cendrars quote Shepard had written in his notebook not long before the arrest: "I am an uneasy man, severe with myself, like all solitaries." Under an entry titled "The Height of my Lowest Low," he wrote, "She's had enough of me, that's clear enough. . . . Why shouldn't she? All those years of tolerance beyond the call of duty." Shepard goes on to write of himself as treacherous, untrustworthy, and demonic. He's sober now, he continues, rejecting as "distasteful" any kind of booze. He ends the entry decrying his "continuing repetition of disaster and recovery."

Around the same time, Shepard wrote to his friend Johnny Dark and was very candid about his relationship to alcohol: "I used to think I could maybe give up booze altogether. But I may have been fooling myself. Little did I know that aging and alcohol are sympathetic. I must admit that I like getting drunk. I like the feeling that comes over me. The numbness. . . . Now I'm justifying alcoholism. This is really getting bad." Another letter would find Shepard admitting that he'd been driving drunk "for 50 years and just now got caught." He also swears he will never do so again.

Shepard didn't have a local lawyer but recalled that a man named Patrick Jennings had sent him a screenplay to read, hoping Shepard would play the lead if it were produced. Remembering that the writer's father was a lawyer, Shepard retained the veteran litigator, Hal Jennings, who had an office in Bloomington.

When his day in court arrived during the second week of February, Shepard stayed in Peoria, forty miles west of Normal, to avoid the media. When it came time to explain his behavior to the judge, Shepard made up a story that was at least partly true. He told of how at the bar he'd met some helicopter pilots who had been involved in the real-life *Black Hawk Down* incident and was drinking with them. Shepard had indeed been in the movie, but the fact was that he'd actually met the soldiers the year before.

The verdict was no conviction, meaning Shepard received one hundred hours of community service, a thirty-day loss of his driver's license, and nothing on his record. There was a bit of embarrassment associated with all this, as Shepard's lawyer suggested he get letters of reference to present to the court from a handful of people. He got at least one: from his publisher.

Shepard was still part of Lange's life, if barely. He was with her in New York in early spring 2009 while he did his community service at

New York University. Twice a week he had to show up at an alcohol-counseling center on Forty-Sixth Street, where he had to sign in, give a urine sample, and sit around with a bunch of "raving addicts," as he called them.

Also that spring, Lange broke her collarbone during a fall at her cabin in Minnesota, and Shepard played nursemaid. By May he was back in Kentucky and broke. His accountant had told him he was running out of money, and Shepard despaired that there were no film roles out there for guys his age. (He'd soon be proved wrong, as the next decade would find him playing many roles in very good films and getting great notices.)

The exact date of Shepard's split from Lange is hard to pinpoint. They were still talking on the phone as late as Mother's Day 2009, when Shepard called her with good wishes. Lange even talked then of coming to Kentucky the following year to see his peonies bloom, since in Minnesota they did so much later in spring. That same day, Shepard was evidently thinking back over his past, specifically the days of his marriage and the birth in 1970 of his first son. "We were all living that extraordinary life in Marin County and Jesse was just a wee toddler. It's all heartbreaking to me now. The way things have just come and gone. I truly don't know what to do with myself. Writing has really been my life and when I'm not doing it I feel worse than useless."

That September Shepard sat in a Mexican café near his farm in Kentucky and watched on a television behind the bar the broadcast of that year's Emmy Awards. When Lange came onstage to accept yet another award for her acting, Shepard was moved to think, "How wild and wonderful my life has become and here come my tamales steaming on the plate and my iced-tea and I'm trying to see over the waiter's shoulder at this woman I've had this long on-going torrid love affair with for more than 25 years."

Shepard and Lange traveled to Mexico in September of 2009 and were also together in New York with extended family the following month for Thanksgiving. Most likely they called it quits for good in early 2010. Shepard saw her on March 5 of that year but then didn't see her for at least six months. Whenever it became official, it's fair to say the break with Lange was a long time coming, beginning with increased friction between the two around 2004 and underlined by the mostly separate lives they lived after the spring of 2005, when they sold their place in Minnesota and purchased the apartment in New York and the farm in Kentucky.

The media finally caught up to the separation in mid-December of 2011. *People* magazine carried the story and quoted a source saying the couple had split nearly two years earlier. A spokesperson for Lange said, "They both are pursuing independent lives." In a July 9, 2009, interview with the *Daily Beast*, writer Amanda Fortini had asked about Shepard, but Lange gave a nonanswer. "When I ask about the secret to her enduring relationship with Shepard—the pair, who met in 1982 on the set of *Frances*, have never married but have been together for more than 25 years—she coils up ever so slightly. 'I don't know,' she says, growing quiet and charmingly flustered, 'You've got to have some deep connection . . . it's a lot of history and knowing somebody really well, and . . . it's being interested in somebody after 25 years; they still fascinate you.'"

Beginning in 2010, Shepard had even more reasons for spending time in one of his adopted hometowns, Santa Fe, where he now also had a residence. The Santa Fe Institute awarded him its most prestigious honor, the Miller Distinguished Scholarship. As a so-called Miller Scholar, Shepard had access to an office within the nonprofit research institute and was encouraged to share ideas with the institute's postdoctorate researchers and scientists. Shepard joked about the kinds of highbrow conversations he had with some of these scholars. The person he spoke to most often was actually novelist Cormac McCarthy, who is a trustee of the institute. "I have a real difficult time having dialogues with writers," Shepard admitted, adding with a laugh that with McCarthy their conversations had "mostly to do with dogs or cunt."

While at the institute, Shepard worked on his 2013 play *A Particle of Dread*.

Shepard was back in New York on February 7, 2010, sitting in his car in a parking garage on Pier 40, overlooking the Hudson River, when his phone rang. It was his friend Johnny Dark: His wife, Scarlett, was dead. A burst blood vessel in her brain in September 1979 had left the onetime actress and Shepard's former mother-in-law with lifelong physical challenges. She'd beaten the odds and lived more than three decades. "You know, everybody knew Scarlett was dying," Shepard said. "She'd been dying for years. It was extraordinary she could hang on as long as she did."

It's worth remembering that when Scarlett was first recovering, Shepard played a major role in her care. Dark has old footage of the two of them together; Shepard clearly demonstrates his tender side when he is with his ailing mother-in-law. "Sam gave us money for a cot and whatever we needed," Dark recalled. "Sam was a big help." For a man known to be difficult and ornery, the illnesses of Scarlett and Joseph Chaikin brought out the best in Shepard. These were important people in his life, and when they were down, he was there.

Shepard seemed less concerned with privacy after the kids had moved out and he and Lange had split. He invited of all things a team of filmmakers into his life in 2010 to follow him around. Director and first-time filmmaker Treva Wurmfeld had met Shepard on the set of a film in which he had a small role. She interviewed him and later sent him a handwritten letter proposing a documentary. He called her and invited her to Santa Fe, where he was giving a reading, and allowed to her to film it. Soon after, the cameras were rolling. They kept rolling for eighteen months.

The resulting documentary captures Shepard and his friend Johnny Dark as they pored through their decades of correspondence and readied it for sale to the Wittliff Southern Writers Collection, an archive housed at the University of Texas in San Marcos. In one scene, Shepard is on the phone to a friend saying the sale is necessary due to his own financial situation. (Dark says on camera that he and Shepard each got $250,000 for their letters and photos.) *Shepard & Dark* not only captured the two friends coming to terms with their lives together and apart but also caught Shepard while he was still dealing with his breakup with Lange. At one point, he looks at the camera while going through one of the letters and says: "My life is falling apart, coming apart at the seams. I can see it. It's just that I continue to make the same mistakes over and over again, which is pretty obvious. But still not often enough to prevent me from making them. And I don't quite understand it. I can see the mistakes and shit I continue to make are in these letters."

The blues hit hard at another point in the film, when Shepard reads a letter he wrote about the first time he walked with Jessica through her hometown in Minnesota. He stops after a few sentences, sets the letter down, and turns away from the camera. "I can't do this right now," he says.

Wurmfeld's documentary caught Shepard and Dark dealing with the losses in their lives, having fun, and goofing around like teenage boys. Her takeaway was that there was evidence of arrested development in both men. "What I learnt was that Sam and Johnny had made such an effort to not turn into their fathers that they themselves had never quite grown up," she said. The film ends with Shepard writing a final note to Dark, which was accompanied by a box filled with all the letters they'd been working on for the archive. The letter from Shepard says he'd "come to the end of this obsession and long[ed] to be free of it. I'm no longer interested in poring over the past." It ends giving Dark free rein to do as he pleases: "Take it away, Johnny and good luck!" The letters eventually were published by the University of Texas Press as *Two Prospectors*. Both the documentary and letters collection are musts for anyone remotely interested in Shepard's life and work.

Early 2010 saw the publication of Shepard's fifth collection of prose, *Day out of Days*. Created for the most part by going through the notebooks and journals he'd been keeping since the 1970s, the stories reflect their author's rambling ways. These are stories tied to specific places Shepard has traveled to over the years, mostly around the American Southwest. Some are straight-up reports from his life, while others are true tales that have been somewhat fictionalized for heightened effect. There are fragments; a handful of short, linked items about a detached head; humorous pieces, like the one about a man caught in a restaurant bathroom while the sound system plays Shania Twain tunes all night; farm and racetrack tales; bits of dialogue depicting troubled relationships; and lots more. As disparate as these pieces sound, they cohere due to Shepard's unmistakable voice.

Two stories from the collection appeared in the *New Yorker* in 2009, including one that is easily Shepard's most satisfying work of prose. "Indianapolis" tells the story of a traveler forced to hole up in a hotel until a blizzard passes. There he meets an old flame, and while not much happens between them, Shepard still manages to capture the sense of loss that the passing of time invariably brings and the what-ifs each of us must face in life. Like his other collections, *Day out of Days* received its share of excellent reviews.

Stumbling

*It's an old terror of mine that I will wind up totally alone, some-
what mad and dying in a motel room somewhere in Nevada.*

—Sam Shepard

Mixed reviews greeted Shepard's attempt to write a play about a group of women living together on the outskirts of Los Angeles. *Heartless*, as some critics noted, is for Shepard fans only. It opened in July 2012 at New York's Pershing Square Signature Theater.

Heartless is the story of a sixty-five-year-old professor named Roscoe who has left his wife and is temporarily living with the family of his much-younger lover, Sally. He may be brilliant in the classroom, but the good professor suffers from that malady that Shepard, in referring to his own life, calls "lostness." The matriarch, Mable (Shepard's old friend Lois Smith), sees through Roscoe and plays upon his conscience and his guilt over abandoning his family. (Sound familiar?) She's in a wheelchair, still recovering from a bad fall and is tended to by Liz, a nurse who is mute (at least in Act 1).

Sally has a scar across her chest from a heart transplant years earlier that saved her life. It's a secret she's keeping from Roscoe. They have a falling out, bringing Roscoe's sense of lostness into sharper focus. When in Act 2 Liz has sex with him, we see that she has the same scar as Sally. Liz suddenly begins speaking, and we learn that she was somehow the dead girl whose heart Sally has. In the end, Roscoe is driven off, literally driven away, with Sally's oddball sister Lucy behind the wheel.

The play raises many questions Shepard refuses to answer, as many reviewers and audience members noted. It seems as if Shepard "threw a lot of shit on the wall and hoped some of it stuck," which was how in 1996 he described the writing of his earliest plays. Critic David Cote perhaps best summed up the problem. "*Heartless* is a mysterious play speckled with clues, but one has little desire to put them together or look for a solution. Instead, the stream-of-consciousness monologues and absurdist plot twists feel like cryptic vamping for their own sake."

Shepard the actor entered his eighth decade on a high note, several of them in fact. Aging may have taken a toll on his leading-man looks, but it paid dividends in another area: it heightened his aura of authenticity. Directors and film buffs alike agree that onscreen, Shepard delivers something particular about the American spirit and the mythos of the Old West. "His acting has to be grounded in something real, and he never tries to force it," said Jim Mickle, who directed Shepard in the fine 2014 film *Cold in July*. "He's very honest and real in that kind of stuff. There is a hyperawareness of the physicality of the role." In the film, Shepard plays the ex-con father of a man who was murdered during a housebreak. His character then haunts the family of the man who shot his son, played by Michael C. Hall. It was a role that required little dialogue but a big presence, Mickle said. "I think our movie was kind of built on the idea that whoever that guy was, he had to have that cowboy swagger."

The director also shared his memories of working with Shepard on the film. Where actors often provide directors with a long list of special requests, Shepard's needs were simple: a lamp, a chair, and a desk for his typewriter. Walking past Shepard's dressing room, one could count on hearing him busily clacking away. At one point, Mickle's dog was running up and down the hall near the dressing rooms, causing Shepard to open his door and holler for quiet. There were also occasions for humor, such as Shepard asking before every scene if it "was before the tape"—in other words, was the camera rolling? This became a running gag. Meanwhile, costar Don Johnson kidded Shepard about being cranky, while Shepard kept referring to Johnson's time as a TV star in *Hawaii Five-O*. (Johnson was actually in *Miami Vice*.) "He and Don had a really beautiful relationship," Mickle said.

Many of the roles Shepard took on after 2010 were in better-than-average films and television shows. A project close to his heart was 2011's *Blackthorn*, in which he played the title character. The film's premise is that Butch Cassidy was not killed in that famous shootout in Bolivia, instead escaping to South America. The film catches up to him as an older man going by the name of James Blackthorn. He crosses paths with a young robber, which almost leads to his undoing.

The film reunited Shepard with his old friend Stephen Rea. But there was another reason Shepard probably signed on so quickly after reading the script—mucho time in the saddle. "When he knew he was going to be riding horses that day, you could feel his smile from when he woke up in the morning. He just wanted to ride his horse all the time," remembered director Mateo Gil. One critic called the film a "valedictory performance" for Shepard.

One of Shepard's highest-profile roles was featured on the streaming-video service Netflix. Once again, he garnered strong notices for his performance as the patriarch of a troubled family living in the Florida Keys. *Bloodline* debuted online in March of 2015, with a second season premiering a year later.

Off screen, recent years have not brought the best of news for Shepard. In early 2013, what has to be viewed as the final chapter in his relationship with Lange closed when he transferred to her his shares in their Fifth Avenue co-op for $1.63 million. His problems with drinking also once again became very public.

La Choza is a popular New Mexican restaurant on Alarid Street in Santa Fe. On Memorial Day 2015, at about 7:45 p.m., Shepard was arrested in the parking lot after he failed a sobriety field test. A security guard from the restaurant had called the cops, and when they arrived they saw Shepard's blue Tacoma pickup with its brake lights on "and the vehicle making a jerking motion forward," according to police. News reports indicated that his emergency brake was engaged. Shepard refused the breath test and was charged with aggravated DUI. Once again, Shepard's mug shot went around the world, this one being far worse than the one from 2009. In it, Shepard's eyes are practically closed.

The charges were dismissed in December of 2015 after the district attorney ruled that the case had "no likelihood of success at the trial." Shepard was a regular at the restaurant, and his lawyers claimed that eyewitness accounts indicated that he did not drink enough to put him over the state's blood alcohol limit. Video and audio recordings also factored in the decision. Shepard's lawyers successfully argued that the field sobriety test issued to their client was not appropriate for someone over sixty-five. He was seventy-one at the time of the arrest, and his lawyers claimed he should have been given an alternative test, one that accounted for a decrease in balance typical for older adults.

Shepard's lawyer Dan Cron said, "This whole incident has unjustly tarnished Sam's reputation, and we hope this dismissal serves as the vindication he deserves."

Since his breakup with Lange, Shepard has been seen in public with at least two different women. The paparazzi still snap his photo whenever they see him in New York, and in 2014 they spotted him with these younger women. However, those who thought Shepard and Lange were history would have been surprised that in the wake of his 2015 arrest, he and his former paramour were seen together on three occasions. The first was cozying up on a park bench on July 27, 2015, near her cabin in Duluth, Minnesota. Also, Lange attended the opening night of *Fool for Love*'s revival on Broadway in October 2015. Shepard avoided being photographed with his ex-lover on the red carpet, but they were captured sharing a quiet moment later that evening. Lastly, the couple was spotted riding bikes in New Orleans in January 2016.

The Road Ahead

I could go on and on about death. One of my favorite subjects—so long as you can keep it at arm's length.

—Sam Shepard

*B*uried Child headed back to a New York stage in early 2016. It would next travel to London for a West End engagement. Shepard's old running mate, Ed Harris, was starring with his wife, Amy Madigan, and the author was on hand again tweaking his Pulitzer Prize–winning play. In a New York rehearsal space, he sat listening to the cast work, feeling the rhythm of his language, making changes to match the beat he was hearing in his head, buttressing the humor where he could.

When the rehearsal was finished, Shepard sat with a *New York Times* reporter to talk about the play. She also asked the seventy-two-year-old about his lifelong quest: "Did you try not to become your father?" Shepard, dressed head to toe in dark blue, his face showing lots of hard miles and his gray hair askew, said he had, but that in the end there's no escaping fate, destiny, heredity. "Yes," he said. "It doesn't help. You find these portions in you that are beyond the psychological, beyond what you think you can control. And then suddenly you are your father. You look at really old photographs, photographs that date back to the 1800s, the bone structure of the face is pretty much implanted. Where does it come from?"

Fans of the Netflix drama *Bloodline* got a pleasant surprise when in the finale of Season 2 they saw a face from the series' past. Robert Rayburn, the patriarch of the clan, played by Shepard, who died before Season 1 had reached its halfway point, returned in a flashback. He sure had changed. Sitting at a dining room table and sharing the scene with actor Ben Mendelsohn, Shepard looked sickly. His words came sluggishly, and it seemed his mobility was limited. Instead of gesturing in a normal fashion, he awkwardly moved his shoulders like a man in a straightjacket. It came as a shock to those who remembered how Shepard looked in the show's first season—sun-kissed and vital, able to strum his guitar on the beach and even do a little kayaking.

Shepard's appearance caused at least a few fans to take to the Internet to wonder if he was seriously ill. There were other troubling signs. His professional life had seemingly slowed to a crawl. After a flurry of film roles in recent years, Shepard did not go before the cameras in 2016 (other than the *Bloodline* cameo), and he has nothing scheduled for 2017 or beyond. There are no new plays in the offing. Tellingly, Shepard gave up his beloved Kentucky farm in late 2016. Those who know the family say the seventy-three-year-old moved to Northern California with his eldest son. Nothing has been said publicly about his health. He was not heard from in the latter half of 2016 upon the deaths of fellow playwright Edward Albee or Signature Theatre Company founder and close friend James Houghton.

There was some good news. As 2016 neared its end, there appeared seemingly from nowhere on retail book websites a new work of fiction by Shepard called *The One Inside*. The author's publisher says that Shepard did not want it referred to as a novel but rather a "longer work of fiction." Judging from "Tiny Man," a story culled from the book and published in the December 5, 2016, issue of the *New Yorker*, Shepard's flights of imagination, descriptive powers, and humor are all intact.

The story begins with a young boy holding his father's miniaturized corpse, wrapped in plastic, which a group of men driving a 1949 Mercury has pulled from the car's trunk. After the boy gives the titular tiny man back to the men, the story moves to the boy's house, where his father, now alive and well, is having sex with his "girlfriend," an underage prostitute named Felicity. The young woman keeps returning to the boy's house only to find time and again that the father is not home. This narrative is interwoven with further bits about the shrunken dead father. In the end, Felicity is gone and the father goes searching for her. The ending is ambiguous:

> I thought about Felicity—where she might have gone. Maybe she hadn't gone at all but just got bored with waiting around. Boredom was a real event in those days. What's going to happen? That was the question. What's going to happen.

"Tiny Man" is a fun enough linguistic ride that one never feels the need for concrete answers, or even a narrative through line. Shepard's late story contains some of his old autobiographical bits: life in Southern California, his father picking at the shrapnel marks on his neck, his own youthful imaginings of becoming a famous golfer or veterinarian, and the Indian blood in his family background. It was an interesting enough taste of *The One Inside* to whet the appetite of Shepard fans for its February 7 publication date. "Cheerless but atmospheric and precisely observed," claimed a reviewer for *Kirkus*.

More than a half century after he climbed off that bus in Times Square and began making a name for himself, Sam Shepard's impact on the theater world remains large. Actors and directors love staging his work. And while he's never brought in the crowds like other legendary playwrights, his name is still revered among theatergoers, critics, and members of the cultural cognoscenti. In the world of film, those who appreciate authenticity over scenery-chewing superstars and special effects look to him as one of the best actors in a generation. Late in life, he was still able to carry a certain kind of film, such as *Blackthorn* from 2011, or to come in and make an immediate and lasting impression as a character actor, as he did in 2015's *Midnight Special.*

Shepard has scaled the heights in drama, cinema, fiction, screenwriting, and music. He conquered each on his own terms. In a publicity-crazed world, he doesn't do talk shows, red carpets, social media, or even many interviews. He's always put the work first and allowed it to speak for itself. That's a quality in rare supply these days. In his twilight years, Shepard has been viewed as not only an elder statesman of the theater and cinema but as a venerated man of letters, even a public intellectual.

His legacy is assured, though you wouldn't know it to ask him. Queried about this in 2016, whether as "the greatest living American playwright," as many have called him, he's achieved something substantial, "yes and no," he said. "If you include the short stories and all the other books and you mash them up with some plays and stuff, then, yes, I've come at least close to what I'm shooting for. In one individual piece, I'd say no. There are certainly some plays I like better than others, but none that measure up."

Shepard made a bit of a stir in September 2014 when in an interview with the *Guardian*, he claimed America was on its way out as a culture. Sitting with a reporter at a bar in Santa Fe, Shepard let loose on the ills of modern society. Strip malls, the Internet, mediocre writing, and this country's penchant for outsourcing—he seemed to take aim at everything that smacked of the inauthentic. As the interview was winding down, Shepard was asked why a play like *True West* continues to have such a hold on audiences. He conjured his best aw-shucks expression and again chose to duck and dodge his own legend. "Oh, because they all believe the American fable," he says. "That you can make it here. But you don't make it."

"You've made it pretty well," the reporter says.

"Yeah but I've also . . . I've . . . yeah," he hesitates, laughs, a long rich wheeze. "But you know, oddly, I wasn't even fucking trying."

Acknowledgments

I t was while reading reviews of Bob Dylan's 1986 album *Knocked Out Loaded* that I first encountered the name Sam Shepard. Just about every critic mentioned this well-known playwright who had cowritten with Dylan the best song on the album, an eleven-minute track called "Brownsville Girl." I wanted to know more.

A few years later, when I began going to the theater regularly, eventually becoming a reviewer, I gravitated toward plays by the likes of Samuel Beckett and Harold Pinter. Shepard's work seemed of a piece with that of these masters, in that his plays left me contemplating for days afterward just what I'd seen. Shepard's plays were funny, tinged with darkness, and held at their center an ineffable touch of mystery. Watching his performances in different films and reading his prose works left me further intrigued. Several years ago, I began studying Shepard's life and work assiduously, with the thought in the back of my mind that perhaps there was a need for a new and comprehensive biography.

It was a disappointment that Shepard did not participate in this project. The good news is he's given many interviews over the decades and has recently shared some of his correspondence and other materials with the world. I remain indebted to him for his body of work. After years of working on this book, my interest in him has not diminished—in fact, quite the opposite. He's an American original and a subject any biographer would be lucky to have.

I am indebted to many people who helped me along the way: Michael Townsend Smith, Lee Kissman, Peter Stampfel, Joyce Aaron, Jean-Claude van Itallie, Geri Houlihan, Tony Barsha, Nancy Meckler, Jim Mickle, Peter Feldman, Peter Coyote, Jim Haynie, Jacob Brackman, Rudy Wurlitzer, Claudia Carr Levy, Gail Papp, Stephen Facey, Sara Allen Wilson, Mike White, William D. Wittliff, George Ferencz, Marianne de Pury, Mary Theriot, Lawrence Cole, Linda Stowitts, John Brantingham, Ron Ownbey, James Haire, Joyce Ellen Davis, Ira Ingber, Britt Bacon, Robert Brustein, Mary Lou and Tony, Jack Tarlton, Troy Word, Chip Monck, Brooke Adams, Michael Roloff, Thelma Holt, Diane Byer, Michelle Tabnick, Claudia and Alan Heller, Jason Golding, Chelsea Clark, Claire Brunel, Amanda Faehnel, and Nancy Webster.

The following institutions provided materials important to my research; I am thankful to their staff members, who made researching a pleasure: Sam Shepard Collection, Howard Gotlieb Archival Research Center at Boston University; Harry Ransom Center, University of Texas–Austin; the Wittliff Collections, Texas State University–San Marcos; Billy Rose Theatre Division, New York Public Library; Kent State University Libraries, Special Collections and Archives; Highland Park Public Library; Victoria and Albert Museum, London (Open Space Theatre Archive); and the South Pasadena Public Library. The staff of Bridgewater State Library provided me with hard-to-get materials. Some who especially went out of their way to help or were just exceedingly pleasant to deal with are mentioned above.

Thanks to the previous Shepard biographers Don Shewey and Ellen Oumano. Their work made my journey all the easier.

Acknowledgments

I can't forget to give kudos to the folks who maintain sam-shepard.com. Though unaffiliated with the man himself, it was a wonderful resource for me and is the place to go for information about his work for the stage, onscreen, or on the page.

Thanks also to my agent Don Fehr of Trident Media and editor Jack Shoemaker of Counterpoint Press and their able staffs. Last but not least, thanks to my family, especially my wife, Karen, who kept the home fires burning while I was off in some archive or bent over my laptop for what seemed like years at a time. A special thank-you to my sister Susan, without whom this project (and much else in my life) would have been beyond impossible.

Endnotes

Abbreviations of frequently cited titles:

AC: Sam Shepard, *Angel City, Curse of the Starving Class* and Other Plays (New York: Urizen, 1976).

BU: From the Sam Shepard Collection, Howard Gotlieb Archival Research Center at Boston University.

Cambridge: Matthew Roudané, ed., *The Cambridge Companion to Sam Shepard* (Cambridge: Cambridge University Press, 2002).

CP: Sam Shepard, *Cruising Paradise: Tales by Sam Shepard* (New York: Knopf, 1996).

Day: Sam Shepard, *Day out of Days* (New York: Knopf, 2010).

Disaster: *This So-Called Disaster: Sam Shepard Directs the Late Henry Moss*, documentary, dir. Michael Almereyda, 2003.

Dreamer: Ellen Oumano, *Sam Shepard: The Life and Work of an American Dreamer* (New York: St. Martin's Press, 1986).

Endnotes

DS: Don Shewey, *Sam Shepard* (updated edition) (New York: Da Capo Press, 1997).

Five: Sam Shepard, *Five Plays* (New York, Bobbs-Merrill, 1967).

Fool: Sam Shepard, *Fool for Love and Other Plays* (New York: Dial Press, 2006).

Fool 2: Sam Shepard, *Fool for Love and the Sad Lament of Pecos Bill* (San Francisco: City Lights Publishers, 2001).

HM: Sam Shepard, *Hawk Moon: A Book of Short Stories, Poems, and Monologues* (New York: PAJ Publications, 1981).

Kent: Kent State University Libraries, Special Collections and Archives.

Lie: Sam Shepard, *A Lie of the Mind (A Play in Three Acts).* Also includes "The War in Heaven" (New York: Plume/Penguin, 1987).

Logbook: Sam Shepard, *Rolling Thunder Logbook* (New York: Penguin, 1978).

MC: Sam Shepard, *Motel Chronicles* (San Francisco: City Lights, 2001).

OS: Open Space Theatre Archives, London.

Playing: Stephen J. Bottoms, *Playing Underground: A Critical History of the 1960s Off-Off-Broadway Movement* (Ann Arbor: University of Michigan Press, 2006).

Ransom: Harry Ransom Center, University of Texas–Austin.

Rose: Billy Rose Theatre Division, New York Public Library.

S&D: *Shepard and Dark*, documentary, dir. Treva Wurmfeld, 2012.

Seven: Sam Shepard, *Seven Plays* (New York: Bantam, 1981).

Stalking: *Sam Shepard: Stalking Himself*, documentary, dir. Oren Jacoby, 1998.

Texts: Barry Daniels, ed., *Joseph Chaikin and Sam Shepard: Letters and Texts, 1972–1984* (New York: New American Library, 1989).

Two P: Chad Hammett, ed., *Two Prospectors: The Letters of Sam Shepard and Johnny Dark* (Austin: University of Texas Press, 2013).

Unseen: Sam Shepard, *The Unseen Hand and Other Plays* (New York: Vintage, 1986).

Wittliff: The Wittliff Collections, Texas State University–San Marcos.

www.sam-shepard.com: a website unaffiliated with Shepard that is an excellent resource for information on the artist and his work. The site bears no outward signs of who the author is, but I am indebted to this individual's work.

Preface

"generally acknowledged genius" and information on Off-Off-Broadway: Elmore Lester, "The Pass-the-Hat Circuit," *New York Times Magazine*, December 5, 1965, pp. 90–108. Hereafter Hat.

"a veterinarian with": 2P, p. 310.

"One day": 2P, p. 266.

"I find destiny": S&D.

"sweeping road movie": Ransom, letter to S from Michael Almereyda dated "7/13"; most likely 2009.

"forged a whole": Michael Earley in Bonnie Marranca, ed., *American Dreams: The Imagination of Sam Shepard* (New York: Performing Arts Journal Publications, 1981), p. 126. Hereafter AD.

"gorgeous north star": Ransom, e-mail message dated June 24, 2009, sent to S via Jesse Alick of the Public Theater.

"As an actor": Joe Leydon, "Renaissance Cowboy," *Cowboys & Indians*, April 2006, pp. 94–101. Hereafter C&I.

"essential feelings of": 2P, p. 330.

"Still I feel": 2P, p. 211.

"desert-haunted cowboy": Jonathan Cott, "The Rolling Stone Interview: Sam Shepard," *Rolling Stone*, December 18, 1986–January 1, 1987, p. 166. Hereafter RS.

"I believe in": Seven, p. 232.

Discovery

"We all felt": author interview.

"institutionalized professionalism": Playing, p. vii.

"I always tried": author interview.

Description of seeing S's first double bill assembled from interviews with Michael Smith and Lee Kissman, as well as DS. Historical information about the Off-Off-Broadway scene comes from Playing.

"derivative": Jerry Tallmer, "Tell Me about the Morons, George," *New York Post*, October 12, 1964, p. 16. Hereafter Tallmer.

"When I come": Unseen, pp. 50–51.

"had the sound of the day": Dreamer, p. 34.

"Theatre Genesis has": Michael Smith, "Theater: Cowboys and The Rock Garden," *Village Voice*, October 22, 1964, p. 13.

Beginnings

"a huge house," S's birth details, and Rogers family life from around that time: Wittliff, from a forty-fifth birthday card sent to him from his mother, early November 1988.

Fort Sheridan history: Encyclopedia of Chicago online.

"My mother tracked him down": "America Is on Its Way Out as a Culture," by Laura
   Barton, *Guardian*, September 7, 2014. Hereafter Culture.

"poet laureate of": Stephen Coe, "Sage of Sam Shepard," *New York Times*, November
   23, 1980, online. Hereafter Laureate.

Birth announcement: *Highland Park News*, November 11, 1943, p. 11. The same issue
   provided details of fort life at the time.

"impotent and inconsequential": 2P, p. 330.

Information concerning S's ancestors: genealogical study commissioned by the author from
   the New England Historical Genealogical Society. Note: This study shows that
   S is the fifth Samuel Shepard Rogers in the line; however, if Robert Rogers (born
   circa 1800), father of the first Samuel Shepard Rogers in the line (born 1823), had a
   brother named Samuel Shepard, it would make our playwright the sixth such named
   in the family but still only the fifth in his direct line of descendants.

"That had gone on": Pete Hamill, "The New American Hero: Writer Sam Shepard is a
   movie star for the eighties," *New York*, December 5, 1983, pp. 75–76, 78, 80, 84,
   86, 88, 90. Hereafter Hamill.

"A woman named Susanna" and S's claim to be descended from the original settlers: 2P,
   p. 276.

"redneck grandfather" and information that follows: MC, p. 46.

"He smokes and": Ibid.

"That side's got": Benjamin Ryder Howe, Jeanne McCulloch, and Mona Simpson,
   "Sam Shepard, the Art of Theater No. 12," *Paris Review*, Spring 1997. Hereafter
   Paris.

"My old man": Unseen, *The Holy Ghostly*, pp. 199–221.

"I was born": Stalking.

"irascible": CP, p. 3.

"the mysterious glint": Ibid.

"the daughter of": Ransom, notebook entry circa May 2005.

"deep black eyes": Ibid.

"sorrowful smile": Ibid.

"And my grandmother": RS.

The Dark Muse/Father

"I mean every": HM, p. 17.

"The male influences": John Lahr, "The Pathfinder: Sam Shepard and the Struggles of
   American Manhood," *New Yorker*, February 8, 2010. Hereafter Pathfinder.

Endnotes

"I listened like": Seven, p. 137.

"I find myself flinching": Ransom, notebook entry dated January 2006.

"Perhaps every life": Edmund White, *Genet: A Biography* (New York: Vintage, 1994), p. 7.

"the medicine was": Pathfinder.

"was raised on": 2P, p. 171.

"He'd wind up": CP, pp. 146–147.

"the deed": Ibid.

Samuel Rogers's military service information: records obtained by the author from the U.S. Army and National Archives and Records Administration.

"dropping bombs on Italy": CP, p. 17.

"No wonder he": 2P, p. 123.

Scene from *Buried Child*: Seven, pp. 73–74.

"the sheet metal": Ransom, notebook entry dated April 2006.

"You-Name-It-USA": Lie, p. 36.

"My dad came": Pathfinder.

Information on Samuel Rogers's career at San Marino High School comes from the school's yearbooks from 1952 to 1969.

"Mr. Rogers": author interview.

"good natured and patient": Ibid.

"rather cute": Ibid.

"I found him": author interview.

"a poet himself": Kevin Sessums, "Sam Shepard: Geography of a Horse Dreamer," *Interview*, September 1988, p. 70. Hereafter Geography.

Cruelty to dogs: BU, notebook entry titled "Brush Fire Season," dated August 15, 1998. Hereafter Brush.

"emblem of his": Ibid.

"I just went": Seven, Curse of the Starving Class, pp. 133–200.

"I suppose it": *Fresh Air* interview with S, WBEZ radio, original broadcast date March 31, 1998. Hereafter Fresh.

The Rock/Mother

"It's a curious": Scott Donaldson, *The Impossible Craft: Literary Biography* (University Park: Penn State University Press, 2015), p. 21.

"a strong, solid": Jack Kroll, Constance Guthrie, and Janet Huck, "Who's That Tall, Dark Stranger," *Newsweek*, November 11, 1985, pp. 68–74. Hereafter Stranger.

Endnotes

Mother's ancestry: BU, handwritten genealogy.

"She was just": author interview.

"I just remember": author interview.

"She was my": Andrea R. Vaucher, "The Secret of Indie Success," *Washington Post*, July 23, 2000, online.

"She was a": author interview.

"She also had": Ibid.

"She was a pretty": Ibid.

"He was a good": Ibid.

Go West

Tales of Charlie and Grace Upton: Ransom, notebook entry dated September 7, 1980.

"half raised me": Ibid.

Life at aunt's house details: Ransom, notebook entry dated December 16, 2001.

"dressed up like Arabs": Ibid.

Trips with Aunt Grace: Ransom, notebook entry dated October 1979.

"small-town-America": Ransom, transcript of 1986 *Rolling Stone* interview by Jonathan Cott.

Coca-Cola bottle story: RS.

Juvenilia: BU.

"He was very": DS, p. 17.

Schoolyard rhymes: Ransom, undated notebook entry titled "Highway 64."

Rose Bowl Parade: Ransom, notebook entry dated September 12, 1980.

"haunted": MC, p. 40.

"entered the world": Ibid.

"There was this": Hamill.

"got whipped three": MC, p. 31.

"It wasn't until": AC, p. 144.

"how or when": Ransom, notebook entry dated April 1980.

"starving for a": Ibid.

"Old rancho California": Paris.

"for the purpose": R. Aloysia Moore and Bernice Bozeman Watson, *On the Duarte* (Duarte, CA: City of Duarte, 1976), pp. 145–160.

History of Duarte and Bradbury area: Claudia and Alan Heller, *Duarte Chronicles* (Charleston, SC: The History Press, 2013); *On the Duarte*.

"dry, flat, cracked": HM, p. 71.

"It was the first place": Kenneth Chubb, "Metaphors, Mad Dogs and Old Time Cow-
    boys: Interview with Sam Shepard," in AD, p. 189. Hereafter Chubb.

"a Rock Town": Seven, *The Tooth of Crime*, pp. 201–251.

Life in Duarte: BU, undated notebook entry titled "Brush Fire Season."

"Apache Indians" and peeking in windows: Ransom, notebook entry dated October 1979.

"He couldn't hold": Disaster.

"like a little": Ransom, notebook entry dated March 2006.

House details: author interview and Ransom, notebook entry dated March 2006.

Sheep and flock book information: BU.

"I was mucking": C&I.

"He was one": Robert Goldberg, "Sam Shepard: American Original," *Playboy*, March
    1984, pp. 90, 112, 192–193. Hereafter Playboy.

American Place Theatre newsletter: BU.

"My history with": Paris.

"He was nice": author interview.

Yearbook: Ibid.

"He would have": Ibid.

"Beer and cheap": Ibid.

"loading buckets of": Day, p. 56.

High school activities: Duarte High School 1961 yearbook.

"just because I": Unseen, *The Unseen Hand*, pp. 3–38.

"I actually aspired": 2P, p. 310.

"a perfect cruising": *Playboy*.

Pawnshop drums and first band: RS.

"A rock 'n' roll": Ibid.

"on the skids": Ransom, transcript of 1986 *Rolling Stone* interview by Jonathan Cott.

"I remember being" and other details of Mingus III's early life: Gene Santoro, *Myself
    When I Am Real: The Life and Music of Charles Mingus* (New York: Oxford Univer-
    sity Press, 2000), p. 75.

"That really stunned": Fresh.

"There was something": Michael Almereyda, interviewer, "Sam Shepard," *Interview*
    magazine website, October 10, 2011.

"The fifties sucked": HM, p. 58.

On the Road

"I didn't have": Chubb.

Endnotes

"I had the": *Magician: The Life and Art of Orson Welles*, documentary, dir. Chuck Workman, 2015.

"probably shatter my": BU, letter to grandmother circa August 1961. Other information about S's post-graduation plans comes from this letter.

Mt. SAC information and Beulah L. Yeager biographical information: Barbara Ann Hall and Odette Marie Pietzsch, *Mt. San Antonio College: The First Fifty Years* (privately published, undated), pp. 48–49; as well as various press reports.

"She was a": author interview.

"This proved quite": undated, unnamed newspaper article retrieved from Mt. San Antonio College archives.

"beatnik": DS, p. 23.

"After *Godot*, plots": quoted by Mel Gussow in *Conversations with and about Beckett* (New York: Grove Press, 1996), p. 67.

"It just struck": Hamill.

"Once I started": Sylvia Drake, "Sam Shepard: A Play for Every Lifestyle," *Los Angeles Times* calendar section, October 21, 1977, pp. 1, 58, 62. Hereafter Lifestyle.

The Mildew, S's first play: retrieved from the Mt. San Antonio journal, *MoSAiC*.

"There was always": DS, p. 18.

"Don't starch the": Ransom, undated notebook entry.

"holocaust": Fresh.

"I had a": Paris.

Father's behavior on S's last night at home and description of leaving: Ransom, notebook entry circa May 20, 2008.

"I've done my": S&D.

"I walked out": 2P, p. 69.

"I found out": Paris.

"I think they": Pathfinder.

"Lots of one-night": author interview.

History of Bishop's Company: James Wheaton, *Masks before the Altar* (privately published, 1999).

"We performed nearly": author interview.

The Boy with the Cart: selected lines from Christopher Fry, *Selected Plays* (New York: Oxford University Press, 1985), p. 9.

Description/review of Shepard acting with Bishop's Company: afternoon edition of the October 18, 1963, *Daily Intelligencer of Doylestown*, Pennsylvania, online.

"The most subtle": Ibid.

"It was actually": Paris.

Endnotes

"It showed me": Stalking.

"led to rhythm": program note to S's play *Red Cross*.

"One day we": Paris.

"One of the": Jamie Brisick, blog post, *Wrestling Elephants*, December 11, 2013.

"people who knew": Suze Rotollo, *A Freewheeling Time* (New York: Broadway Books, 2009), p. 4.

Arriving

"dullest and dreariest": Jim F. Heath, *Decade of Disillusionment: The Kennedy–Johnson Years* (Bloomington: Indiana University Press, 1976), p. 5.

"rogues and outcasts" and historical information about Greenwich Village: John Strausbaugh, *The Village: 400 Years of Beats and Bohemians, Radicals and Rogues, a History of Greenwich Village* (New York: Ecco Press, 2014), p. 3. Hereafter Village.

"The Village in": Ibid, p. i.

"crest of the": Mel Gussow, *Edward Albee: A Singular Journey: A Biography* (New York: Simon and Schuster, 1999), p. 129. Hereafter Albee.

"In effect, the" and history of Off- and Off-Off-Broadway from Playing, p. 20 and thereabouts.

"defining Off-Broadway": Playing, p. 21.

"That was quite": author interview.

"greedy landlords, union": Playing, p. 83.

"Thus, for the": Ibid, p. 23.

Dating of the start of Off-Off-Broadway: Ibid.

"A return to": Ibid.

"We were all": author interview.

"The experience of": Michael Townsend Smith, ed., *The Best of Off-Off-Broadway* (New York: E.P. Dutton, 1969), p. 17. Hereafter Best.

"American theater has": David A. Crespy, *Off-Off-Broadway Explosion: How Provocative Playwrights of the 1960s Ignited a New American Theater* (New York: Back Stage Books, 2003).

"made America theater": Paris.

"I had a": Disaster.

"I didn't know": *La Mama: A Theatrical Tapestry*, documentary, dir. Robert McCarty, 2006.

"We were all": Michael Smith, *Johnny* (New York: Fast Books, 2011), p. 27.

"None of us": author interview.

Endnotes

"Now I'm really" and description of arriving in NYC: S, "My First Year in New York City," *New York Times Magazine*, September 17, 2000.

"My immediate mission": Ibid.

"scoop mounds of fried": Ibid.

"It turned out to be": Paris.

"Fear of the Fiddle": *Cruising*, pp. 55–59.

"every random hallucination": Wittliff, notebook entry dated January 4, 1994.

"Famous for something": 2P, p. 231.

"Actually, I was": Brian Bartels, "Sam Shepard's Master Class in Playwriting," *Missouri Review*, Summer 2007, pp. 72–88.

"I always thought": Hamill.

"It looked like": author interview.

"the weirdest apartment": Michael ver Meulen, "Sam Shepard: Yes, Yes, Yes," *Esquire*, February 1980, pp. 79–81, 85–86.

4-H Club: Unseen, pp. 93–114.

"Just about froze": 2P, p. 205.

"quite shaggy": author interview.

"I rode anything": Stranger.

"But these women": Ibid.

"I also may": Marc Meyers, Jazzwax.com, October 13, 2008.

Village Gate history: Ronald D. Cohen and Stephen Petrus, *Folk City: New York and the American Folk Music Revival* (New York: Oxford University Press, 2015), p. 159.

Untitled story about Nina Simone: MC, pp. 79–80.

"If there was": author interview.

"Jazz could move": Hamill.

"I used to": Lifestyle.

"Our group never" and other information about the staff of the Village Gate: Lee Kissman, "50 Years On: Theater Genesis and Sam Shepard," *Contemporary Theatre Review*, 2015. Hereafter Genesis.

"I don't know" and history of St. Mark's: David W. Dunlap, *From Abyssinian to Zion: A Guide to Manhattan's House of Worship* (New York: Columbia University Press, 2004), p. 224.

"If I could": "Rev. J.C. Michael Allen dies; activist priest who once had no religion," *St. Louis Post-Dispatch*, September 8, 2013, online.

"My father was": author interview.

"The doors to": Gerald Astor, "Chaplain to the Cool World," *Look*, October 31, 1967, p. 79.

Endnotes

"That day, I": Michael Allen, "This Time, This Place" (New York: Bobbs-Merrill, 1971), p. 80.

"back into the": Ibid, p. 81.

"Here, now, in": "Ralph Cook, a Pioneer of Off Off Broadway, Dies at 85," *New York Times*, October 18, 2013, online.

Genesis

"womblike sweatbox": Playing, p. 111.

"You could use": Ibid.

"Downtown experimental theater": Genesis.

"It was sort": author interview.

"a bunch of": Playing, p. 119.

"It was pretty": author interview.

"Sam Shepard's plays": Five, p. 10.

"I used to": Chubb.

"You threw a": Brian Case, "Slay 'em Again, Sam" *Time Out*, July 3–10, 1996, p. 24. Hereafter Slay.

"It wasn't a": Ibid.

"There were so": Paris.

"pain in the ass": Lifestyle.

"I was extremely": Ibid.

"Attentive and helpful": Genesis.

"We didn't spend hours": author interview.

The Rock Garden, quotations from and descriptions of: Unseen, pp. 39–51.

"apocalyptic orgasm": Michael Bloom, "Visions of the End: The Early Plays," in AD, p. 73.

"living on Mars": Stalking.

"Character is something": Pathfinder.

"If you go": Don Shewey, "Rock-and-Roll Jesus with a Cowboy Mouth (Revisited), *American Theatre*, April 2004, online. Hereafter Jesus.

"leaving my mom": Dreamer, p. 32.

"Albee's *Zoo Story*": Jeremy Gerard, *Wynn Place Show: A Biased History of the Rollicking Life and Extreme Times of Wynn Handman and the American Place Theatre* (New York: Smith and Kraus, 2013), p. 63. Hereafter Wynn.

"less alive": Genesis.

"He was unique": author interview.

"various dialects from": Tallmer.

"was really an": Playing, p. 109.

"One day you": Ibid.

"Generally Acknowledged Genius"

"The next thing": author interview.

"I don't think": Ibid.

"Needless to say": Unseen, p. xi.

"I just have": Dreamer, p. 8.

"I used to watch": Day, p. 149.

"disposable": Clive Barnes, "Theater: A Sam Shepard Double Bill; Dramatic Cartoons Are Displayed in Village at Intermission, Author Plays Rock Drums," *New York Times*, April 2, 1970, p. 43.

"With the early": Joe Penhall, "The Outsiders," *Guardian*, June 14, 2006, online. Hereafter Outsiders.

"crystal methedrine, crème": Ransom, notebook entry dated September 1, 1980.

"You just knew": author interview.

"didn't even consider": sam-shepard.com.

"The play is": Ibid.

"The author draws": Richard F. Shepard, "Drama: 3 New Arrivals; Theater 1965 Offers Test for Writers," *New York Times*, February 11, 1965, online.

"Sam got hysterical": author interview.

"The conventional logic": Joyce Aaron, "Clues in a Memory," in AD, p. 172. Hereafter Clues.

"Sam was a": author interview.

"He told me": Ibid.

"Dog was about": Chubb.

"We were always" and details of her life with Shepard: author interview.

"paranoid": Ibid.

"It was impossible": 2P, 133.

"I just think": Ibid.

"In the early days": author interview.

"traumatized crazy people" and biographical information on Chaikin: Eileen Blumenthal, *Joseph Chaikin* (New York: Cambridge University Press, 1984), p. 6. Hereafter Chaikin.

"radical change": Joseph Chaikin, *The Presence of the Actor* (New York: Theatre Communications Group, 1993), p. 49. Hereafter Presence.

Endnotes

"I liked the": Ibid, pp. 53–54.

"We did a": author interview.

"I started attending": *The Presence of Joe Chaikin*, documentary, dir. Troy Word, 2012. Hereafter PJC.

"Sam always said": author interview.

"When Sam suggested": author interview.

"I think that": author interview.

"the theater of": Presence, p. 3.

Chicago, quotations from and description of: Unseen, pp. 53–69.

"I love the bathtub": Jesus.

"The reading of": Stephen J. Bottoms, "Shepard and Off-Off-Broadway: The Unseen Hand of Theatre Genesis," in Cambridge, p. 41.

"They were just": Stalking.

"blazing, youthful, like": Jennifer Allen, "The Man on the High Horse: On the Trail of Sam Shepard," *Esquire*, November 1988, pp. 141–151.

"I never knew": Clues.

Dedication to Aaron: author interview.

"The play still": Ben Brantley, "Sam Shepard of Today, and of Many Days Ago," *New York Times*, November 8, 1996, online.

"forlorn and funny": Hat.

"You can be": Chubb.

"Sam got me": author interview.

"I tried to" from text of story: MC, pp. 73–77.

"amoebic dysentery": Lifestyle.

"terrifying": author interview.

"For me, these": Unseen, p. xi.

Sense of dread in *Icarus's Mother*: Chubb.

"his fear of": author interview.

"is more interested": Five, pp. 71–72.

"I remember Sam": author interview.

"generally acknowledged genius" and information on Off-Off-Broadway: Hat.

"a lifelong devotee": "Agent Toby Cole dies at 92," *Variety*, January 3, 2008, online.

Fourteen Hundred Thousand, quotations from and description of: Unseen, pp. 115–136.

"taking steps into": "American Experimental Theatre, Then and Now" in AD, p. 212.

Endnotes

Musical Interlude

Except where otherwise noted, details and quotations in this chapter are from an interview the author conducted with Peter Stampfel.

"I write at": DS, p. 50.

"I really hated" and Stampfel and band history: Chris Boros, radio interview, "Holy Modal Rounders: Oddly Influential Folk," National Public Radio, February 24, 2009, online transcript. Hereafter Folk.

"Our first album": Ibid.

"People were so": *The Holy Modal Rounders: Bound to Lose*, documentary, dir. Paul Lovelace and Sam Wainwright Douglas, 2006.

"I heard it": Ibid.

"We were on": Ibid.

New Territory

"To be responsible": John Lahr, *Astonish Me: Adventures in Contemporary Theater* (New York: Viking, 1973), pp. 102–103. Hereafter Astonish.

"truly contemporary images": Ibid.

"chamber plays": Dreamer, p. 50.

"We were sitting": Ibid.

"I thought the": Wynn, p. 63.

"I said, 'Listen": Ibid.

"In that state": Stephen J. Bottoms, *The Theatre of Sam Shepard: States of Crisis* (Cambridge: Cambridge University Press, 1998), p. xi. Hereafter Crisis.

"fourth-degree burns," more quotations from, and description of *La Turista*: Seven, pp. 253–298.

"Jacques was very": author interview.

"Why should everything": Associated Press, "Playwright Foe of Reviewers, *Independent* (Long Beach, CA), April 27, 1967, online.

"I was a": Wynn, pp. 64–65.

"dazzling production": Elizabeth Hardwick, "Word of Mouth," *New York Review of Books*, April 6, 1967, online.

"superlative interest": Ibid.

"Our new American": Ibid.

"tone and style": Ibid.

"possesses the most": Ibid.

Endnotes

"The most hostile": Paris.

"We lost lots": Wynn, p. 67.

"most of them": Ibid.

"It's still kind": Ibid.

"I was brokenhearted": author interview.

"Tall, lean, angular": Unseen, p. 291.

"impressionistic scenario": Tony Barsha and Murray Mednick, *The Hawk*.

"He was unique": author interview.

"He was a quiet guy": Ibid.

Split or dual nature theme: Cambridge, p. 47.

"I mean, it's": S&D.

Johnson family information: DS, p. 69.

"like a guy": 2P, p. 268.

"He was a tricky guy": author interview.

Shepard sought the rawer and more direct sounds of rock: Crisis, p. 66.

"Never in poetry": Leslie Stainton, *Lorca: A Dream of Life* (New York: Farrar Straus and Giroux, 1999), p. 36.

"First of all," Crisis, p. 66.

Forensic and the Navigators, quotations from and description of: Unseen, pp. 175–198.

"You couldn't see": Dreamer, p. 80.

"The noise was": Cambridge, p. 233.

"jolly good": Clive Barnes, "Theater: A Sam Shepard Double Bill; Dramatic Cartoons Are Displayed in Village at Intermission, Author Plays Rock Drums," *New York Times*, April 2, 1970, online.

"I'm getting fucking": Unseen, *Mad Dog Blues*, pp. 289–341.

"It's like real": Best, p. 21.

Early Film Work (1968–1970)

Joyce Aaron's belief that Shepard would become an actor: author interview.

"Playing music, you": Chris Wallace, *Interview* website, "Culture: Sam Shepard" podcast, April 27, 2015, online. Hereafter Podcast.

"had bottomed out": Mark Harris, *Pictures at a Revolution: Five Movies and the Birth of the New Hollywood* (New York: Penguin Press, 2008), p. 9.

"My ideas about": Roger Ebert, "Interview with Michelangelo Antonioni," rogerebert.com, June 19, 1969.

Connection between *Icarus's Mother* and *Zabriskie Point*: Dreamer, p. 69.

Endnotes

"It is difficult": Sam Rohdie, "Antonioni," littlerabbit.com.

"I started to": Bert Cardullo, *Michelangelo Antonioni: Interviews* (Jackson: University Press of Mississippi, 2008), p. 71.

"go out in": BU, Soren Agenoux, "Sam Shepard," *inter/View*, no. 1, 1969, pp. 6–7, 28. Hereafter inter/View.

"a girl goes": Ibid.

"emaciated and worn": Ibid.

"I like Michelangelo": Dreamer, p. 71.

"I think people": inter/View.

"Hollywood's most expensive": Ibid.

"wants it to be": Ibid.

Reassessment: John Burks, "14 Points to *Zabriskie Point*," *Rolling Stone*, March 7, 1970, pp. 36–39.

"heavy," "groovy," and information about working with Richards: inter/View.

"a distorted Western" and additional details about and quotations from *Maxagasm*: BU, unproduced script.

"a really great": inter/View.

"dated": Ibid.

"I remember a": author interview.

"It has some": Dreamer, p. 63.

"So what began" and additional information about the film's genesis: Brigitta Burger Utzer and Stefan Grisseman, eds., with Robert Frank, *Frank Films: The Film and Video Work of Robert Frank* (Göttingen, Germany: Steidl, 2009), p. 60.

"It was about": Naseem Khan, "Free Form Playwright," *Time Out London*, July 13–17, 1972, pp. 30–31.

"a reflection of": Ibid.

"a really nice": Ibid.

"You can't be": Ibid.

Dazed and Confused (1968 and 1969)

"He thought it": Culture.

"went out to": Disaster.

"the tail end": 2P, p. x.

"was for the": author interview.

"everything began looking": 2P, x.

Endnotes

S's homophobic utterances can be found, among other places: Ransom, notebook entry
  December 11, 1981; Ransom story "Synthetic Tears"; and 2P, p. 331.

Operation Sidewinder, quotations from and description of: Unseen, pp. 223–287.

"serious racial tensions": "Law Faculty Tries to Meet Demands of Black Students," *Yale
  Daily News*, January 10, 1969, online.

"either no reference": "'Sidewinder' Cancellation Sought by Drama Blacks," *Yale Daily
  News*, December 20, 1968, p. 1, online.

"pre-censorship": Ibid.

"whether plays of": Ibid.

"If they want": Ibid.

"convinced it could": Ibid.

"festival of upheavals,": Ibid.

"create a theater": Robert Brustein, "Politics and Theater," *Yale Daily News*, February
  21, 1969, p. 2, online.

Frankenstein: Josh Greenfield, "The Man Who Gave Us Hair," *Life*, June 27, 1969,
  p. 50.

"a very beautiful person": Ibid.

"In a broken" and other marriage details: Mel Gussow, "Sam Shepard: Writer on the
  Way Up," *New York Times*, November 12, 1969, p. 42, online. Hereafter Up.

"My dad's favorite" and other details of S's marriage: author interview.

"I don't know": Dreamer, p. 81.

"It was like": Ibid.

"a collection of": BU, program note from a later production at Touchstone Theater.

The Unseen Hand, quotations from and description of: Unseen, pp. 3–38.

"The people are": Wittliff. Tom Morris, "Reality on a Small Scale," *London Evening
  Standard*, July 4, 1996.

"Sam came to": author interview.

"rescue him" and information about the "kidnapping attempt": Tony Barsha interview
  and Joey Skaggs, "Lucky Loser: My Aborted Attempt to Kidnap Sam Shepard,"
  Huffington Post, April 22, 2013.

"We didn't give": Ibid.

"As we went": Ibid.

"He thought I": author interview.

"the most prolific": Up.

"There is not": Quote appears in Five, but was retrieved from sam-shepard.com.

"The main theme": Carolee Schneeman, "American Experimental Theatre: Then and
  Now," *Performing Arts Journal*, Fall 1977, pp. 21–22.

New Directions

The Holy Ghostly, quotations from and description of: Unseen, pp. 199–221.

"As far as": Playboy.

"enemy territory": Pathfinder.

"My idea was": Up.

"our country's identity": George Stambolian, "A Trip through Popular Culture," in AD, pp. 79–89.

"deservedly so": Michael Smith, "Underground Landscapes," *Guardian*, online.

"It was very": Clive Barnes, "Stage: Lizard vs. Snake": *New York Times*, March 13, 1970, online.

"possibly significant": Ibid.

"A glorious piece": Pathfinder.

"The theater needs": Astonish, pp. 107–119.

"The world premiere": BU, *New York Times* ad.

Operation Sidewinder program: Repertory Theater of Lincoln Center.

"Terrible, terrible, terrible": Pathfinder.

"I'm not worried": Ibid.

"We lost about": Jasper Rees, "American Playwright in London," *Independent*, June 25, 1996, online. Hereafter Playwright.

"That blew it": Hamill.

Patti

"He was actually" and details about the first meeting of S and Smith: author interview.

"Apparently the blind": Ibid.

Smith biographical details: Patti Smith, *Just Kids* (New York: Ecco/Deckle Edge, 2010). Hereafter Just; and Dave Thompson, *Dancing Barefoot: The Patti Smith Story* (Chicago: Chicago Review Press, 2011). Also various media reports.

Chelsea Hotel information: Sherill Tippins, *Inside the Dream Palace: The Life and Times of New York's Legendary Chelsea Hotel* (New York: Houghton Mifflin Harcourt, 2013).

"being at an Arabian": Just, p. 171.

"I fixed on": Ibid.

"the heart and": Ibid.

"Rock 'n' roll": Ibid.

"fellow with the": Ibid, p. 173.

Endnotes

"What are you": Ibid.

"Patti possesses a": James Wolcott, *Critical Mass: Four Decades of Essays, Reviews, Hand Grenades, and Hurrahs* (New York: Doubleday, 2013), p. 114.

"penetration draws blood": Ibid.

"We'd have a": Patricia Morrisroe, *Mapplethorpe* (New York: Random House, 1995), p. 92. Hereafter Mapplethorpe.

"Me and his": Ibid.

"Essentially Patti was": Sam Shepard Q&A, *Details*, July 2008. Retrieved from sam-shepard.com. Hereafter Details.

"stabbed the lightning": Just, p. 183.

"I remember a": Mapplethorpe, p. 94.

"Let's write a," quotations and description of writing *Cowboy Mouth*: Just, pp. 184–185.

"it just kind": Ben Brantley, "Sam Shepard: Storyteller," *New York Times*, November 13, 1994, online. Hereafter Storyteller.

"Patti was devastated": Mapplethorpe, p. 95.

Patti "screaming": Ibid.

"Like any snake": BU, Smith's diary, dated 1971, dedicated "To Sam."

Three decades' separation etc.: Ransom, notebook entry dated October 2006.

"as sweet as": 2P, p. 270.

"She had a": Details.

"best friend . . . precious": Podcast.

"He looked at": Just, p. 186.

Mad Dogs, Splits, and More (1971 continued)

Shaved Splits quotations from and descriptions of: BU, *Screw*, July 21, 1971.

"Ideas spring to": retrieved from sam-shepard.com.

"He had a": Dreamer, pp. 86–87.

Mad Dog Blues quotations from and descriptions of: Unseen, pp. 289–341.

"The abstract quality": Jack Gelber, "Playwright as Shaman," in AD, p. 47.

"hung himself on," *Cowboy Mouth*, plus other quotations from and descriptions of: Fool, pp. 145–165.

"Before Patti, you": author interview.

"said to me": 2P, p. 301.

"The thing was": Don Shewey, "Patriot Acts: Back in New York with a New Play and Starring in Another, Sam Shepard Reflects on the Dangerous Farce of Contemporary Politics," *Village Voice*, November 17, 2004, online. Hereafter Patriot.

"He came up": author interview.

"felt embarrassed by": Ransom, notebook entry dated March 4, 1980.

Back Bog Beast Bait quotations from and descriptions of: Unseen, pp. 343–377.

Tennessee Williams letter: BU, letter to S dated September 10, 1971.

Gurdjieff

"messenger of the spirit": Jacob Needleman, "The Gurdjieff Work," Gurdjieff Foundation of California website.

"help human beings": Ibid.

In-laws introduce S to the Work: 2P, p. 245.

Roots of the Work: Seymour B. Ginsburg, *Gurdjieff Unveiled* (Lighthouse Editions,
2005), p. 4.

"another approach, another": Jennifer Allen, "The Man on the High Horse: On the
Trial of Sam Shepard, *Esquire*, November 1988, p. 141. Hereafter Horse.

"arbitrary mindlessness": Ibid.

"the most informative": Ibid.

"shifted the direction": Ibid.

"bad boy trying": 2P, xi.

"dumb ballet shoes": 2P, p. 5.

"little, wooden soldiers": Ibid.

"the English twerps": Ibid.

"Still there's something": Ibid.

"like a little": Ibid, p. 13.

"At last I'd": Ibid.

"Now it almost": Ibid.

"never feeling really": Texts, p. 7.

"has been in": Ibid.

"totally mapped out": 2P, p. 87.

"Don't you have": Wittliff, *Silent Tongue* preview/report from Sundance, "a big voice for
a big place," Spring 1993 (no publication, headline, or byline visible). Hereafter
Sundance.

"It's an amazing": Disaster.

"I know the": 2P, p. 69.

"personality is everything": Michiko Kakutani, "Myths, Dreams, Realities—Sam
Shepard's America," *New York Times*, January 29, 1984, online. Hereafter
America.

"comprendo": 2P, p. 150.

"on an almost": Ibid, p. 192.

"it lasted about": Ibid, p. 271.

"have gone up": Ibid, p. 305.

London

"I had this fantasy": Chubb.

"I was just": Slay.

"nutty, juvenile scrawl": Charles Marowitz, "Sam Shepard: Sophisticate Abroad," *Village Voice*, September 7, 1972, p. 59. Hereafter Sophisticate.

"trying to find": "Sam Shepard on Why He Came to London," *Independent*, June 26, 1996 (taken from a BBC 3 transcript of a *Nightwaves* interview with director Tom Morris. Hereafter Nightwaves.

"a laconic, dry": Playwright.

"My sense was": Ibid.

"detached": Michael Coveney, "Shepard's Delight," *Observer Review*, June 30, 1996, p. 10.

"the most unostentatiously": Ibid.

"long, lanky and": Ibid.

"A lot of": Nightwaves.

"I left": Beth Whitaker, "Sam Shepard: A Fascination with Fate," *Signature Stories* (a publication of Signature Theatre), Autumn 2014, pp. 13–17.

"three years in": 2P, p. 330.

"how much work": Laureate.

"They're all about": RS.

Nancy Meckler biographical information: author interview.

"I found him": Ibid.

"I got the": Ibid.

"It was meat": Ibid.

"Sam came to": Ibid.

"One didn't approach": Lost.

"I had a conversation": Stranger

"[He] once said that": Ibid.

Dog racing information: Jerome Taylor, "After 75 Years, Dog Track Has Finally Run Its Course," *London Independent*, May 18, 2008, online.

"Greyhound racing is": Stephen Fay, "Renaissance Man Rides out of the West," *Sunday Times Magazine* (London), August 26, 1984, pp. 16, 19. Hereafter Renaissance.

"romantic impulse": Chubb.

"So those few": "Less Than Half a Minute," *Time Out* (London), July 12–18, 1974, pp. 16–17.

"It struck me": *Tooth of Crime (Second Dance): A Play with Music in Two Acts* (revised edition) (New York: Vintage, 2006), p. ix. Hereafter Dance.

"is never defined": Chubb.

"At the end": Laureate.

Description of *The Tooth of Crime* and music's ability to communicate emotion: Chubb.

"the finest American" and other thoughts about *The Tooth of Crime*: Sophisticate.

"I didn't know": author interview.

"Shepard was enchanting": Ibid.

The Tooth of Crime quotations and description: Seven, pp. 201–251.

"I would up": Dance, ix.

"In 1972, it": Ibid.

Opening delay: OS.

"uncomprehended": Sophisticate.

"It not only": Ibid.

Hoss as too sentimental: Jesus.

"as classically rendered": Florence Falk, "Men without Women: The Shepard Landscape," in AD, p. 94.

"Sam's always had": author interview.

"run its course": James M. Harding and Cindy Rosenthal, eds., *Restaging the Sixties: Radical Theaters and Their Legacies* (Ann Arbor: University of Michigan Press, 2006), pp. 77–78.

"It's only dog": 2P, p. 15.

Blue Bitch quotations from and description of: BU, copy of unpublished radio play.

"brilliant": Allen Crossett, "With Michael Kahn's Arrival in Princeton This Year," *Bernardsville (New Jersey) News*, November 21, 1974, p. 47.

"He has no": DS, p. 85.

"open the space" and other information about his technique: Richard Schechner, *Performance Theory* (New York: Routledge Classics, 2003).

"patterns of movement": Ibid, p. 76.

"far from what": Ibid.

"should respect the": Richard Schechner, "Drama, Script, Theatre, and Performance," *Drama Review*, vol. 17, no. 3, September 1973, pp. 5–36.

"It was so": Peter Crawley, "Dramatic Awakenings: The Theatre That Changed My Life," *Irish Times*, February 29, 2016, online.

Endnotes

Geography of a Horse Dreamer quotations from and description of: Fool, pp. 277–307.

"using language from": Chubb.

"opened up lots": Texts, p. 12.

"the actor being": Jesus.

"When I first": Wittliff. Bob Hoskins, "On . . . The Sam Shepard Festival at the BAC," *London Evening Standard*, June 28, 1996.

"He gave you": Sundance.

"Sam said, 'Practicing": Ibid.

"For my character": Ibid.

"very willing to": Renaissance.

Proficiency of London's actors: Lost.

"It was a": Outsider.

Little Ocean information: BU, Peter Ansorge, review of *Little Ocean*; copy did not have other details. Hereafter Ocean.

"One day [Shepard]": Playwright.

"He's an American": Ibid.

"a revivifying influence": Ocean.

"I'd been writing": Horse.

The Last American Gas Station: BU, unfinished manuscript.

Mill Valley Days

"Darks and Sheps": 2P, p. 19.

"Back then, Mill": author interview.

"I'm filled with": Logbook, p. 3.

"Cycles, weed, convoluted": 2P, p. 231.

Details about life in Mill Valley: Ibid, pp. 113–114.

"I remember the": Ibid, p. 189.

"Those were indeed": Ibid, p. 282.

"a set for *Buried Child*" and description of the Evergreen Avenue house: Dreamer, p. 130.

"It was darling": Ibid, p. 131.

"works for me": Ibid.

"alive": Texts, p. 14.

"some kind of": Ibid.

"starting a 'new'": 2P, p. 330.

"It's very special": Texts, p. 12.

Action, quotations from and description of: Fool, pp. 167–190.

"Sam . . . helpfully talked": author interview.

"The improvs eventually": Ibid.

Killer's Head, quotations from and descriptions of: Unseen, pp. 379–383.

"It is so": author interview.

"bizarre" and "It was the": Judith Davis, *Richard Gere: An Unauthorized Biography* (New York: Signet/New American Library), p. 37.

Magic Theatre history: magictheatre.org.

"an even more": Magic.

"I started to": Ibid.

Curse of the Starving Class outline: BU, Rolling Thunder notebook.

"Theater is a": Stalking.

Dylan

"Dylan called": Logbook, p. 3.

"It's a long": Ibid, p. 2.

"protection from intellectual": Ibid, p. 62.

"I believe in": Seven, p. 232.

"He was better": Robert Shelton, *No Direction Home: The Life and Music of Bob Dylan* (New York: Ballantine Books, 1986), p. 513.

"He's OK for": S&D.

"make it appear": Clinton Heylin, *Bob Dylan: Behind the Shades Revisited* (New York: HarperEntertainment, 2003), p. 415. Hereafter Clinton.

"That's why he": author interview.

"the duality between": John Rockwell, "Dylan: My Film Is Truer Than Reality," *New York Times*, January 8, 1978, online. Hereafter Truer.

"We don't have": Logbook, p. 11.

"My lawyer used": Clinton, p. 428.

"everybody was strung": Michelle Mercer, *Will You Take Me as I Am: Joni Mitchell's Blue Period* (New York: Simon and Schuster Digital, 2009), ebook.

"Dylan has invented": Logbook, p. 100.

"I'm pissed off" and information about Shepard's writing for *Renaldo and Clara*: Larry Sloman, *On the Road with Bob Dylan* (New York: Three Rivers Press, 2002), pp. 117–118. Hereafter Road.

"Ultimately, I think": author interview.

Dylan as genius: Road, p. 161.

"conflict of ideas": Truer.

Endnotes

"spend the rest": Chris O'Dell, Miss O'Dell: *My Hard Days and Long Nights with The Beatles, The Stones, Bob Dylan, Eric Clapton, and the Women They Loved* (New York: Touchstone, 2009), p. 327.

"You know Sam's": Ibid, p. 328.

"My film is": Reality.

"The idea of": Logbook, p. 181.

"Judgment Day": Ibid.

"plastered": Ibid.

"cadaver city": Ibid.

"What a minute!": Logbook, p. 183.

"I don't have": Ibid.

"desperately clicking their": Ibid, p. 184.

"Bob was genuinely": author interview.

"That tour wiped": Wittliff. Recording made by S of Dylan in the summer of 1986 for *Esquire* piece. Hereafter Dylan Tape.

"Well, in the": Bob Dylan during an October 1997 press conference, as quoted on alldylan.com.

"It has to": Clinton, p. 574.

"We felt this": author interview.

"a shitload of": author interview.

"There're too many": author interview.

"I asked him": author interview.

"I love that": Ibid.

"He said, 'It's'": author interview.

"I find it": Ibid.

"I think the": Howard Sounes, *Down the Highway: The Life of Bob Dylan* (New York: Grove Press, 2011), p. 375.

Eight-page treatment of "Brownsville Girl": Wittliff.

"total disregard for": Fintan O'Toole, "A Nod from One Sam to Another," *Irish Times*, February 24, 2007, p. Arts-1.

Quotes from Shepard–Dylan session for *Esquire*: Dylan Tape.

"I once showed him": BU, from S Rolling Thunder notebook, circa fall 1975.

"I need more head": BU, notebook entry from early 1977.

Heavenward (1976)

"He saw it": Disaster.

"I guess the 'Steve'": BU, letter to S from father dated February 24, 1976.

"young kid": Ibid.

"desolate": Ibid.

"This caused a great": Ibid.

"When they leave": Ibid.

"was worth a shit": Ibid.

"three great kids": Ibid.

"damn, selfish Jane": Ibid.

"Sam has a presence": author interview.

"You should see": Ibid.

"I got off on": author interview.

"Terry was very shy": *Days of Heaven*, DVD extras, Criterion Collection, 2010.

Man Fly: BU, manuscript of unproduced play.

"I don't understand": NYPL. Memo on *Man Fly* to Joe Papp, dated February 13, 1976.

"disappointed": Ibid.

"Too little, too": Ibid.

"The movies! I can make": 2P, p. 227.

"I remember also," Ibid, p. 228.

"monumental turning point": Ibid.

Angel City, quotations from and description of: AC, pp. 5–54.

Earlier drafts of *Angel City*: BU.

"Only two-thirds": Review of *Angel City*, *Variety*, April 19, 1977, online.

"Don't try to solve": Reality.

Suicide in B♭, quotations from and description of: Fool, pp. 191–230.

"emotional impact": BU, notebook entry titled "San Francisco '76."

"sensation of deep mystery": Ibid.

"kept cutting people off": Ira Nadel, *David Mamet: A Life in the Theater* (New York, Palgrave Macmillan, 2008), p. 98.

"The aggressive manner": Ibid.

"I didn't feel": "Woodruff on Shepard," *SoHo Weekly News*, October 26, 1978, pp. 74, 79. Hereafter Woodruff.

"holes": Ibid.

"You just have to": Ibid.

The Sad Lament of Pecos Bill on the Eve of Killing His Wife, quotations from and description of: Fool 2, p. 79.

"On this movie shoot," author interview.

"so much spare time": 2P, p. 29.

"orgies of reading": Ibid.

Brooke Adams discussing writing with S: author interview.

"Sam really has a mean streak": author interview.

S leaving the set in the middle of the night: Ibid.

"forever, irrevocably changed": 2P, p. 228.

Family Matters

"I've had this idea": Sylvia Drake, "Inside the Words," *Time Out London*, April 22–28, 1977), pg. 11. Hereafter Words.

"I'm very interested": Texts, p. 18.

"fluid written structure": William Kleb, "Sam Shepard's *Inacoma* at the Magic Theatre," *Theater*, Fall 1977, pp. 59–64.

Inacoma, quotations and descriptions: BU, unpublished typescript.

"I said, 'Hi'": Words.

"All I could visualize": *Inacoma* program note.

"cotton to": Rose. Letter from Toby Cole to Joe Papp, dated August 19, 1971.

Assessments of Shepard's earlier work by Papp's staff: Rose.

"I'm not sure": Texts, p. 34.

"It suddenly occurred to me": Stalking.

"What I wanted to do": Alexis Soloski, "Sam Shepard Takes Stock of 'Buried Child' and the Writer's Life," *New York Times*, January 28, 2016, online. Hereafter Buried.

Royalties from 1977: BU. Letter from S's former agent, Toby Cole, dated March 3, 1978.

"severe": Ibid.

"small fortune": Rose. Handwritten note from S to Joe Papp, dated April 5, 1976.

Curse of the Starving Class, quotations from and descriptions of: Seven, pp. 133–200.

"People often want to": author interview.

"I like to think": Ibid.

"She's very much oriented": Lifestyle.

"With *Curse* people": Woodruff.

"Mr. Shepard has worked out": Richard Eder, "Theater: 'The Starving Class,'" *New York Times*, March 3, 1978.

"disastrous": author interview.

"The lamb had to": Ibid.

"Writing for me has become": Texts, p. 41.

"geographic gap": Texts, p. 34.

"a very exciting time": Ibid.

"I like living out here": Ibid, p. 39.

"has seen fit": Janet Maslin, "'Renaldo and Clara,' Film by Bob Dylan: Rolling
    Thunder," *New York Times*, January 26, 1978, online.

"Contemporary critics write": BU. Dylan was quoted in a letter from S's agent's office,
    written by Minna K. Abernethy, dated March 4, 1978.

Seduced, descriptions of: Fool, pp. 231–276.

"It's not attempting to be": Judy Klemesrud, "Broadway: Rip Torn to be a rich, dying
    recluse in new Shepard play," *New York Times*, July 28, 1978, online.

"I've been following": Lifestyle.

"I think Joe responded": author interview.

"I never felt it was easy": Texts, p. 46.

"He would say things": Chaikin.

"What funny, always unexpected": Texts, p. 40.

Tongues, quotations from and description of: Texts, pp. 76–77.

"Sam looked up to Joe": author interview.

You Can't Go Home Again

"It came from": Buried.

"It was a very odd": author interview.

1977 draft of *Buried Child*: BU.

Buried Child, quotations from and descriptions of: Seven, pp. 61–132.

"They have to laugh": Stephanie Coen, "Things at Stake Here," *American Theatre*, Sep-
    tember 1, 1996, p. 28. Hereafter Stake.

"it manages to be": Richard Eder, "Stage: Sam Shepard Offers 'Buried Child,'" *New
    York Times*, November 7, 1978, online.

"I didn't know": Stranger.

"After the movie": author interview.

"then I saw": BU, letter to S from his father, dated February 24, 1976.

"You are a damn": Ibid.

"We'd watch these scenes": Stranger.

"He has a tall": Harold Schonberg, "Days of Heaven," *New York Times*, September 14,
    1978, online.

"romanced away from": BU, letter to S from Lois Berman, dated November 7, 1978.

"There was this feeling": John O'Mahony, "The Write Stuff," *Guardian*, October 11,
    2003, online. Hereafter Write.

"Not only was he tall": Wim Wenders, "The Inspiration," *New York Times*, online. Hereafter Inspiration.

"Sam and I had to drop": Ibid.

"You can't make a living": Jeff Dawson, *London Times*, June 4, 2006, online.

"I don't go": Robert Coe, "The Saga of Sam Shepard," *New York Times*, November 23, 1980. Hereafter Saga.

"Gary Cooper": DS, p. 161.

"a genius": Ibid, p. 123.

"To me he was": Ellen Burstyn, *Lessons in Becoming Myself* (New York: Riverhead Books, 2007), p. 363.

"the sexuality would": Ibid, p. 364.

True Brothers

"like news of": Lifestyle.

"a kind of conversation with himself": Jennifer Dunning, "A Nagrin Dance to a Shepard Libretto," *New York Times*, May 31, 1979, online.

"I always liked": Ibid.

"My work is not": Robert Coe, "Image Shots Are Blown: The Rock Plays," AD, p. 59.

"realized I'd never learned" and information about Scarlett's illness: MC, p. 129.

"She turned into a child": S&D.

"It was a really arduous": Ibid.

"Scarlett and Sam were great": Ibid.

"one of the greatest": Ibid.

"Voice is the nut of it": Christopher Wren, "Camp Shepard: Exploring the Geography of Character," *West Coast Plays* 7, Fall 1980, pp. 75–106.

"It's a great mistake": Ibid.

"I didn't want to": author interview.

"She said, 'Get down here'": Ibid.

"knew it was going to work": Jesus.

"sprawling, demented snake": MC, p. 121.

"to peel it back": John Dark, "The 'True West' Interviews," *West Coast Plays* 9, Summer 1981, pp. 51–71. Hereafter True.

"I wanted to get on": Ibid.

True West, quotations from and descriptions of: Seven, pp. 1–59.

"I never intended the play": Don Shewey, "Certain Personal Elements: 5 Notes on Biography and Theater," *Lincoln Center Theater Review*, Spring 1995, online.

Endnotes

"I wanted to write a play": Don Shewey, "The True Story of *True West*," *Village Voice*, November 30, 1982, online.

"I got my first taste": author interview.

"I said, 'Are you fucking crazy?'": Ibid.

"It was riveting theater": Kenneth Turan and Joseph Papp, *Free for All: Joe Papp, the Public, and the Greatest Theater Story Ever Told* (New York: Doubleday, 2009), p. 493. Hereafter Free.

"It was a real thrill": True.

"This [play] reminded me": Free, p. 492.

"Sam called her": Ibid.

"If I ever do": Fred Ferretti, "Joseph Papp: A 'Divisive Force' or a 'Healing' One?" *New York Times*, December 20, 1980, online. Hereafter Force.

"He'll never see another": Jane Perlez, "Joseph Papp's Big New Project Is Finding Himself," *New York Times*, December 13, 1981, online.

"Papp said I 'just wouldn't do'": author interview.

"widespread agreement": Force.

"I cast the play": Free, p. 495.

"We ended up with": Ibid.

"The actors weren't doing": Ibid, pp. 495–496.

"He was angry": Ibid, p. 500.

"I got Sam on the phone": Ibid, p. 501.

"I wasn't really delicate": Ibid, p. 498.

"I had difficulty": Ibid, p. 498.

"isn't my vision": Force.

"acting high-handedly": Ibid.

"Some day, when": Frank Rich, "Sam Shepard's True West: Myth vs. Reality," *New York Times*, December 24, 1980, online.

"We had a rudderless production": Free, p. 501.

"I would like it to be known": Ransom, note dated December 15, 1980, titled "S.F. Chronicle statement."

"continued to have": author interview.

"I'm not proud": Playboy.

"magnetic": Stranger.

"a filthy fan letter": Ibid.

Script for *Resurrection*: BU, shooting script dated January 10, 1979, with handwritten comments by S.

"I went to a lot of": Ransom, transcript of 1986 *Rolling Stone* interview by Jonathan Cott.

"It's a self-fulfilling prophecy": Tom Buckley, "At the Movies; A very busy Trevor Howard pauses to visit," *New York Times*, November 21, 1980, online.

"still smacks of soap opera": Ransom, notebook entry circa March 4, 1980.

"I immediately felt I knew": C&I.

"didn't know exactly,": Ransom, notebook entry dated December 22, 1980.

"in a state of panic": Ibid.

"hallucinating earthquakes all": Ransom, notebook entry dated February 5, 1980.

"premonitions of panic": Ibid.

"persistent shaking": Ibid.

"Maybe I'm just plain spooked": Ibid.

Second most produced: Saga.

"all I wanna do": Ransom, notebook entry dated October 13 (most likely 1980).

"Sam didn't want the hoopla": DS, p. 137.

Superstitions review: Frank Rich, "2 Sam Shepard Pieces Open at La MaMa," *New York Times*, September 20, 1983, online.

"glimpses of the unsettled furniture": Benedict Nightingale, "Even Minimal Shepard Is Food for Thought," *New York Times*, September 25, 1983, online.

"I'm ready for a little": Texts, p. 114.

"sustain[ing] a female character": America.

"The play came out of": Paris.

"rural": Laureate.

"In my view, Sam is": author interview.

"Stuff"

"no time for the reader": Ransom, undated letter to S.

"is one of those books": David Thomson, *The New Biographical Dictionary of Film* (New York: Knopf, 2004), p. 824.

"I was looking everywhere": *The Right Stuff*, DVD extra "Realizing the Right Stuff," Warner Home Video, 2005. Hereafter Stuff.

"There's your guy": Alex French and Howie Kahn, "Punch a Hole in the Sky," *Wired*, online. Hereafter Wired.

"cowboy quality about him": Ibid.

"I refused": Ibid.

"He'd excised much of" and information about development of the film: Stuff.

"Tom Wolf started writing": Wired.

"This isn't the tale": Stuff.

"One of the main": "You Can Lead a Horse to Water," from *Moth Radio Hour*, recorded May 29, 2008.

"Be present in every second" and other reminders while acting in *The Right Stuff*: Ransom notebook devoted in part to the film, undated entries.

"Eddie and me were big buddies": Wired.

"It was a real sense": Ibid.

Jessica: The Beginning

Story of Shepard and Lange's first meeting: BU, notebook entry titled "Ruthless," dated November 5, 1982.

"They were getting along": *Frances*, DVD commentary, Lions Gate, 2010. Hereafter Frances.

Lange biography: "Jessica Lange: On Her Own Terms," A&E network, except where otherwise noted below. Includes quotes from Jeff Bridges, teachers, friends, and film historians found in the text. Retrieved via YouTube and Biography.com. Hereafter Lange.

"the beautiful one": author interview.

"That sounds good": *New York Times* Look West interview with Lange and Kathy Bates. Retrieved online. Recorded June 10, 2015. Hereafter West.

"I hated being lumped": Jennifer Rodger, "In Focus: Jessica Lange," *London Independent*, June 10, 1998, online.

"I've always been fascinated": West.

"She runs the show": Lange.

"a cross between a fawn": Lange interview, *Sunday Observer and Belfast Telegraph*, January 2007, retrieved from sam-shepard.com.

"It's just two guys": S&D.

"I could just tell": Lange.

"terrible and impossible": Storyteller.

"BEING IN LOVE" etc.: Ransom, notebook entry circa end of 1982, start of 1983.

"If she truly loves": Ransom, notebook entry dating from the end of 1982.

"magic": Ibid.

"sadness I can't even name": Texts, p. 119.

"celebrate a victory": Ibid.

Fools for Love

"a nervous breakdown a day": TCM.com, "Frances" page.

"I think there's a lot of the rebel": Lange.

"because it is like a Greek tragedy": *The Making of Frances*, online; assembled, edited, and provided by Dario Recla, updated August 1999. Hereafter Making.

"enigmatic sexuality": Frances.

"be someone Jessica would personally": Ibid.

"It was uncanny": Lange.

Fool for Love, quotations from and descriptions of: Fool, pp. 17–57.

"carriers of my emotions": Texts, 119.

"I was desperately looking": Paris.

"force myself": Texts, p. 119.

"I had mixed feelings about it": Paris.

Beckett knows who Shepard is: Mel Gussow, *Conversations with and about Beckett* (New York: Grove Press, 1996), p. 10.

"My dad took it upon": Samuel G. Freedman, "Sam Shepard's Mythic Vision of the Family," *New York Times*, December 1, 1985, online.

"completely strung out": 2P, p. 129.

"Where's my fucking bag?" 2P, p. 65.

"I'm thinking, 'Oh, my God'": S&D.

"ME—I'M IN THE EYE": Ransom, documents dated March 17, 1983.

"SOMETHING IS TAKING ME": Ibid.

"pissed off": S&D.

"I think the main pain": Ibid.

"When we started it": DS, p. 170.

"I'm still in a strange": Texts, p. 120.

"heavily": 2P, p. 61.

"something dark": 2P, p. 62.

"suddenly and irrevocably changed": 2P, p. 111.

"the most powerful influence": Ibid, p. 80.

"Paris"

"what territory we had in common": Inspiration.

"take some of the essence": S, *Paris, Texas* (West Germany: Greno Verlagsgesellschaft, 1984), S interview.

"It was a sentence": Ibid.

List of things *Paris, Texas* is about: Ransom, notebook entry dated November 21. Year was likely 1983.

"rush it or go beyond": Inspiration.

"He adamantly insisted": Stephen Farber, "East Meets West, Take 2," *New York Times*, March 12, 2006, online.

"sort of in the mouth": 2P, p. 85.

"holing up like": Ibid.

"WALK, TALK RHYTHM" and other script notes: Ransom, draft of *Country* script dated September 1983.

"the shit has hit": 2P, p. 88.

"Sam got all pissed": author interview.

"finally starting to feel": Texts, p. 132.

"Jessica's great, and Sam": Hamill.

"fucking nightmare": Ransom, letter to S from Wenders, dated October 20, 1983.

"It is not ONE PIECE": Ibid.

"I sent it to Sam": *Paris, Texas*, DVD extra interview with Wim Wenders, Criterion Collection, 2010.

"He wrote it in one night": Ibid.

"the executives and businessmen": Texts, p. 120.

"go into many different states": Ibid.

Machine Dreams manuscript: Wittliff.

Denial manuscript: Wittliff.

Imaginary Sufferings and "Imaginary Prisoners": Ransom, notebook dated October 1979.

"I go through such inner dramas": 2P, p. 85.

"confrontations" and details of friction: Ibid.

"It's just not my game": Ibid, p. 88.

"Between Two Deaths"

"All the women in the company" and description of S and Lange in Cambridge: DS, p. 147.

"Sam's got the persona": Stranger.

"If he wants it": Playboy.

"It's one of those meetings": Disaster.

"My name is Sam": Ibid, p. 322.

"miserable, contemptible death": Ransom, essay titled "Between Two Deaths," notebook dated April 10, 1984.

"as if he had purposely": Ibid.

"He had a tough life": Write.

"He was sort of looking": Blanche McCrary Boyd, "The Natural," *American Film: Magazine of the Film and TV Arts*, October 10, 1984, pp. 22–26, 91–92.

"wishing for death": *Three Plays: The Late Henry Moss, Eyes for Consuela, When the World Was Green* (New York: Vintage, 2002), p. 111. Hereafter Moss.

"It was not the place": Jesus.

"You may think this": Ibid, p. 146.

"There were all these": Stranger.

"The Black Heralds": Clayton Eshleman, ed. and trans., *The Complete Poetry of César Vallejo* (Berkeley: University of California Press, 2007), p. 25.

"My heart again": Wittliff. Letter from Chaikin to S, dated March 16, 1984.

"quality of the moments": Ibid.

"Sam was there": Chaikin.

"We were doing like word": PJC.

"keep working on": Kent, letter to Chaikin from S, dated September 1, 1984.

"grows stronger": Ibid.

"It was a very important": Texts, p. 154.

The War in Heaven, quotations from and descriptions of: Texts, pp. 158–175.

"extremely moving": Ibid, p. 185.

Toronto review: Ibid, pp. 186–187.

"a blatant propaganda message": Lisa Friedman, "Reagan, the Film Buff," *Los Angeles Daily News*, online.

"I love you more": Ransom, *Paris, Texas* folder, undated entry.

Between Two Families

"some brand new territory of togetherness": 2P, p. 105.

"taking care of Sam": Sally Weale, "Dark Victory," *Guardian*, November 4, 2000, online.

"I think I'm at": Kent. S letter to Chaikin, dated December 23, 1985.

"unbearable loneliness": Ransom, notebook entry circa November 1984.

"dumb animal": Ibid.

"I read this and I thought": *Fool for Love*, DVD extra "Robert Altman: Art and Soul," MGM, 2004. Hereafter Art.

"Looks like it wants to be": Texts, p. 157.

"some kind of final, definitive piece": 2P, p. 105.

"real essence" of it all": Ibid.

"the incredible schism": RS.

A Lie of the Mind, quotations from and descriptions of: Hereafter Lie.

"recurring terror": Ransom, notebook entry dated May 25, 2005.

"a major writer": Frank Rich, "Theater: *A Lie of the Mind* by Sam Shepard," *New York Times*, December 6, 1985, online.

"a considerable amount": Ransom, letter to S. from Lewis Allen dated May 22, 1986.

"right": Ibid.

"screw the cost": Ibid.

"a sense of bafflement": Cambridge, p. 1.

"Onstage it was": Mitchell Zuckoff, *Robert Altman: The Oral Biography* (New York: Knopf, 2009), p. 391. Hereafter Altman.

"Kind of a thing": Art.

"I felt very uncomfortable": Geography.

"giant stride forward": Stranger.

"We shot the scene": Ibid.

"Sam Shepard isn't really": DS, p. 191.

"Bob kept insisting": Altman, pp. 390–391.

"I liked Altman's stuff": Dreamer.

"I think Bob": Altman, p. 391.

"You don't have that": Ibid, p. 392.

"Dancing Around the Grave?"

"In the late 1970s": Ben Brantley, "A Sam Shepard Revival Gets Him to Broadway," *New York Times*, May 1, 1996, online.

"Shepard's cultural moment": Don Shewey, "Shepard Shock: The First International Sam Shepard Conference," *Village Voice*, July 1993, online. Hereafter Shock.

"Are we dancing": Ibid.

"Making the whole enterprise": Ibid.

"fall from grace": Cambridge, p. 257.

"one of cinema's": Nicholas Barber, BBC, retrieved from sam-shepard.com.

"Well, the town just got": Geography.

"where there is a good balance": Drummond Ayres Jr., "College Town of 'Mr. Jefferson' Offers Genteel Haven for Rich and Famous," *New York Times*, August 21, 1991, online.

"I wanted them to have": Ariel Leve, "Sense and Sensitivity," *London Sunday Times Magazine*, April 2, 2006, online.

"This is a man": David Richards, "Sam Shepard Gets a Little Testy When Interviews Get Personal," *Orlando Sentinel* (via *Washington Post*), December 23, 1988, online. Hereafter Testy.

Unrealized Tom Waits collaboration: Ransom; there are a few letters, many without specific dates, circa 1986.

"We couldn't get copacetic": Eric Lax, "For Woody Allen, 60 Days Hath 'September,'" *New York Times*, December 6, 1987, online. Hereafter September.

"I was his next idea": Wittliff. Notebook entry dated April 9, 1989.

"melodramatic and verbose": Ibid.

"strange and totally unpredictable": 2P, p. 111.

"On *September*, Sam Shepard was": John Lahr, "The Imperfectionist," *New Yorker*, December 9, 1996, online.

"Sam Shepard's quality": September.

"very eclectic": Ransom. Allen letter to S dated May 6, 1987.

"have some laughs": Ibid.

"Action!"

"homage": Horse.

"He said, 'Yeah, but'": DS, p. 209.

"Then, when he got out": Neil Scheinin, "Jessica Lange's Balancing Act a Family vs. a Career—Stars Face the Conflict, Too," *Philadelphia Inquirer*, May 25, 1989, online.

"I wanted to start right": Stranger.

"the right choice": BU, letter to S from Marlon Brando, dated June 1987.

"the creek stopped": Horse.

"24-hour task": 2P, p. 113.

"lots of shitty diapers": Ibid, p. 112.

"rollicking good time": Ibid.

"prisoners": Diane Keaton, *Let's Just Say It Wasn't Pretty* (New York: Random House, 2014, p. 8

"I was thirty-one": Ibid, p. 5.

"a mesmerizing man": Ibid., p. 14.

"I never really got to know": Ibid.

"embarrassed": Ransom. Letter to S from Wenders; undated but circa March 1988.

"speechless": Ibid.

"more like a commercial": Ibid.

"Elements of a Shot": Ransom, notebook entry, undated; most likely 1988. Other notes on filmmaking appear in a notebook entry dated August 14, 1987.

"freely play with the scene": Ibid.

Endnotes

"an awful predicament": Wolf Schneider, "Back Home . . . on the Range," *Los Angeles Times,* July 16, 1992, online. Hereafter Home.

"a period Western": 2P, p. 113.

"rudimentary": film review, *Boston Globe,* September 15, 1988, online.

"fried by the critics": 2P, p. 123.

"I haven't read": David Richards, "Shhh! It's Sam Shepard: Secretive and Publicity Shy with No Regrets about His 'Far North,'" *Washington Post,* December 12, 1988.

"So my next film": Testy.

"ruthless country": Home.

War Story

"I'm busted": Horse.

"did some stupid things": Ransom, notebook entry dated January 2, 1989.

"desperate state": Ibid.

"Things were not going well": Ibid.

"was in a difficult situation": *Voyager,* DVD extras, Alliance Entertainment, 2010. Hereafter Voyager.

"At some point": Ibid.

"heart-wrenching stuff" and "her": 2P, p. 121.

"everything is hunky dory": Ibid., p. 125.

"I took him anyhow": "Interview with director Volker Schlondorff," *Bomb,* Summer 1990, retrieved from sam-shepard.com.

"Bergman": Voyager.

"I showed him some": Ibid.

"To work with as an actor": Ibid.

"He inhabits the space": author interview.

"in deep shit": 2P, p. 123.

"beyond his wildest dreams": Ibid., pp. 123, 125.

"one hell of a time": Ibid., p. 118.

"felt like doomsday": Carol Rosen, "Silent Tongues: Sam Shepard's Exploration of Emotional Territory," *Village Voice,* August 4, 1992. Hereafter Rosen.

"hoax": Ibid.

"simple fun": 2P, p. 123.

States of Shock, quotations from and descriptions of: *States of Shock, Far North, and Silent Tongue* (New York: Vintage, 1993).

"monster fascist": Shock.

"The explosive humor": Frank Rich, "Review/Theater; Sam Shepard Returns, On War and Machismo," *New York Times*, May 17, 1991, online.

"Extremely intelligent": Sundance.

"The big challenge": Ibid.

"They couldn't find a place": Rosen.

"I think there was": Storyteller.

Stray Hand: Wittliff. Unpublished novel.

Take Two

"money heads": Home.

"an odd twist of fate": Ibid.

"Probably the most terrifying": Ibid.

"One of the amazing things": Sundance.

"incredibly awkward": Sundance.

"wanted to be inside you": Ransom, notebook inscription by Lange, August 1991.

"I can't live like this": Wittliff. Notebook entry titled "Horrors of the Road," dated September 1992.

"a major impasse": Ibid.

"R.J." letter: Wittliff. Letter dated October 8, 1992.

"I think I wrote twenty-five pages": Paris.

"I don't know what to do": 2P, p. 111.

"state of constant flux": Ransom, notebook entry dated March 7, 1993.

"impenetrable aloneness": Ibid.

"consumed": Ransom, notebook entry dated September 1993.

"falling out": 2P, p. 134.

"Just these feelings": Ibid.

"withholding something": Wittliff, unpublished poem dated May 3, 1994.

"pull away and drift": Ibid.

"a good way to start": 2P, p. 136.

"constitutional lawyer": Sundance.

Losing Game

"body was finished with life": Kent. S letter to Chaikin, dated March 20, 1994.

"tiny feet" and the rest of eulogy: Wittliff, undated document.

"we buried my mother's ashes,": CP, pp. 238–239.

"It lined up right behind": Ibid.

"they're hovering around or just gone": Ransom, notebook entry dated December 12, 2004.

"the deep pockets": Sundance.

"courtly": Storyteller.

"more comfortable, easier": Ibid.

"on the nose": Ibid.

"Sorry Ed, I can't": Ibid.

Simpatico, quotations from and descriptions of: *Simpatico* (New York: Vintage, 1996).

"sweeping views of the town": *St. Paul Pioneer Press*, June 25, 2004, retrieved via sam-shepard.com.

"I had this kind of": *Architectural Digest*, March 2006, retrieved from sam-shepard.com.

"She was suddenly profoundly": 2P, p. 140.

"getting sick of this place": Ibid.

"I had really tremendous": Bruce Fretts, "Jessica Lange: Back on Top at 67," *Closer Weekly*, May 9, 2016, pp. 18–19.

"we can't stray": 2P, p. 140.

At Last, Paradise

"End[ing] up 35,000 miles above": 2P, p. 143.

"Everything about this trip": Ibid, p. 144.

"There was no border": CP, p. 5.

"Anyhow, this would be": Ibid, p. 9.

"a more literary place": BU, letter to S from Meghan O'Rourke of the *New Yorker*, dated August 5, 1998.

"we'd be delighted to see": Ibid.

"I think it's Sam's": Mel Gussow, "Finally Famous in Films, Back to Theater," *New York Times*, October 5, 1995, online.

"verbose and overblown": Stake.

"unnecessarily complicated": Ibid.

"I think I solved it": Ibid.

"spectacularly funny": Ben Brantley, "A Home Where No One Finds Comfort," *New York Times*, October 9, 1995.

"This is a total surprise": Peter Marks, "Sam Shepard Is Happy to Be on Broadway, but It's Just a Visit," *New York Times*, May 28, 1996, online.

"O.K., enter the S.O.B.": Ibid.

"There's a strength": Stake.

"The demonic aspect": Jesus.

Tooth of Crime (Second Dance), quotations of and descriptions of: *Tooth of Crime (Second Dance): A Play with Music in Two Acts* (New York: Random House, 2006).

When the World Was Green (A Chef's Fable), descriptions of: Moss.

"An unexpected shamanistic": Lloyd Sachs, *T Bone Burnett: A Life in Pursuit* (Austin: University of Texas Press), ebook.

"Every time we'd get together": sam-shepard.com.

"absolutely devastating lassies": 2P, p. 149.

"I know you feel": BU, letter to S from James Houghton, dated January 3, 1997.

"loved it": Ibid.

"old and repetitious": Kent, letter to S from Chaikin, August 1998.

"that very severe bottom": 2P, p. 218.

"a kind of terrible emotional crash": Ibid, p. 215.

"It was my pride more": Ibid, p. 217.

"underground hero": Ibid.

"fascinating fellow": Ibid, p. 218.

"It all has to do": Ibid, p. 217.

"Sounds like fun" and list of incidents related to drinking: Ibid.

"long, gone down": Ibid, p. 218.

"long-ago boozing days": Ibid, p. 168.

"quietness of mind": 2P, p. 194

"Blue" Days

"The Blue Bouquet": Octavio Paz, translated by Eliot Weinberger, online.

"mysterious accidental meeting": BU, draft of letter from S to Paz dated December 6, 1996.

"There are so many evocative": Ibid.

"I am flattered": BU, letter to S from Paz dated January 7, 1998.

"sympathies and oppositions": Ibid.

Eyes for Consuela, quotations from and descriptions of: Moss.

"This is such a slack": John Heilpern, "Chekhov without Headphones; Buena Suerte, Mr. Shepard," *New York Observer*, March 2, 1998, online.

"Hard to believe": 2P, p. 215.

"fell into a deep": Ibid, p. 205.

"almost verging on despair": Ibid, p. 211.

"After all these years": Ransom, notebook entry dated December 26, 2000.

"He admitted he had a habit": Patrick Pacheco, "The Man behind the Myth," *Show People*, Fall 2004, pp. 42–46. Hereafter Show.

"Sam seized on something": Ibid.

"The language just took on": Ibid.

"I've always been fascinated": Chris Hewitt, "Play It Again, Sam," *St. Paul Pioneer Press*, May 17, 2000.

"I finally have a smash hit production": 2P, p. 220.

"Late" Show

The Late Henry Moss, quotations from and descriptions of: Moss.

"It took me five years": Kevin Berger, "Sam Shepard," *Salon*, January 2, 2001, online.

Frank O'Connor, *The Late Henry Conran* (New York: Knopf, 2009), pp. 567–574.

"brothers again—what a surprise!": 2P, p. 188.

"was a nightmare just to": Show.

"rough spell": 2P, p. 232.

"new reamed out heart": Ibid., p. 233.

"He isn't happy with who he is": Ransom, notebook entry dated January 2001.

"Something lost up there": Ibid.

"There's still always the possibility": 2P, p. 218.

"Suddenly I know without": Ibid., p. 233.

"slightly pathetic": Ibid.

"At one point": Ibid.

"It sometimes feels as though": Ibid., p. 235.

"it feels like everything": Ibid.

"Hell"

"although no one": Ransom, undated notebook entry (clearly not long after September 11, 2001).

"something at the very core": Ibid.

"it's like the bottom": 2P, p. 245.

"I don't know what": Ibid.

"Well, sometimes I just need": sam-shepard.com.

"rode the hair": 2P, p. 247.

"a glitch of some sort": 2P, p. 249.

Endnotes

"My dad knows absolutely": *Great Dream of Heaven* (New York: Knopf, 2002) p. 19.

"whole life was about": 2P, p. 250.

"didn't include mortality": Ransom, notebook entry dated June 2005.

"hunting through their ravaged": Ransom, notebook entry dated September 20, 2003.

"merciless": Ibid.

"truly courageous soul": 2P, p. 250.

"Sam's eulogy was very special": author interview.

"a renowned asshole": Ibid, p. 76.

"pretty drunk": 2P, p. 254.

Lines and sections of "Sixty": Ibid, pp. 261–262.

"16 heifers": Ransom, notebook entry dated January 12–13, 2004.

"some of the best I've ever raised": Ibid.

"female red-tail [come] hard": Ibid.

"madly lost in love": Ransom, notebook entry dated April 10, 2004.

"sensation of absolute exile": Ibid.

"Have I wrecked everything": Ransom, notebook entry dated April 12, 2004.

"You're stupid and I hate you": Ibid.

New York apartment details: William Neuman, "A Penthouse Closer to the Stars," *New York Times*, May 29, 2005.

"I'm ready to move": *St. Paul Pioneer Press*, June 25, 2004, retrieved from sam-shepard.com.

"Jessica feels as though": 2P, p. 274.

"enormously painful time": Ibid, p. 265.

"I don't know why": Ibid.

"end of her rope": Ibid.

"We're being sold": Patriot.

The God of Hell, description of: *The God of Hell* (New York: Vintage, 2005).

"a takeoff on Republican fascism": Jesse McKinley, "Pointed new Shepard play to arrive just before election," *New York Times*, October 4, 2004, online.

"Film acting is really": Patriot.

"incredibly smart": Ransom, notebook entry dated February 21, 2002.

"But, so what?": Ibid.

"an essential ticket": Ben Brantley, "Her Three Sons," *New York Times*, September 12, 2004, online.

"stunning": Ben Brantley, "My 3 sons: cloning's unexpected results," *New York Times*, December 8, 2004, online.

"I don't remember a movie": Jeff Dawson, "The Write Stuff," *London Sunday Times*, June 4, 2006, online.

"This time, I didn't ask": sam-shepard.com.

"cowboy on the rearing horse": Ransom, letter to S from Wenders, dated August 28, 2004.

"It's about estrangement more": Joe Leydon with Red Steagall, "Sam Shepard—Actor, Playwright, Cowboy," *Cowboys and Indians*, April 2006.

"She likes to try": Ransom, notebook entry dated May 23, 2005.

Can't live without Lange: Ransom, notebook entry dated July 4, 2005.

"were entirely focused on each other": Ransom, notebook entry dated July 2005.

"will never come again": Ibid.

"the impossibility of us": Ransom, notebook entry dated September 2005.

"the impossibility of it continuing": Ibid.

"flailing for my life": Ransom, notebook entry dated September 2005.

"mare to beat the colts": Ransom, notebook entry dated July 2005.

"just punishes horses if they challenge": Ibid.

A Late Trilogy

"I thought 'I'll speak to Sam'": "Meet the Cast of 'A Particle of Dread (Oedipus Variations),'" promotional video. Retrieved online.

Ages of the Moon, quotations from and description of: *Fifteen One-Act Plays* (New York: Vintage, 2012) pp. 3–46.

Kicking a Dead Horse, quotations from and description of: *Kicking a Dead Horse* (New York: Vintage, 2008).

"Dragging my dead": Days, p. 214.

"all about destiny": RS.

"[Sam] calls it *Oedipus Variations* and that's": sam-shepard.com.

Horse breeding information: Bill Oppenheim, "No Ordinary Cowboys," *Thoroughbred Daily News*, July 28, 2010, online.

Break

"It's not the face": Ransom, notebook entry dated September 2, 2007.

"My whole face swelled up": 2P, p. 284.

"utter isolation, solitude": Ransom, notebook entry dated early June 2007.

"I've been drinking way too much": 2P, p. 289.

"consumed by flight": Ibid, p. 307.

"loopy mug shot": Ibid, p. 309.

"sanctuary": Ibid.

"In times like these": Ibid.

"She's had enough of me": Ransom, "The Height of My Lowest Low," notebook entry dated February 2009.

"distasteful": Ibid.

"a continuing repetition of disaster": Ibid.

"I used to think": 2P, p. 318.

"for 50 years and just": Ibid, p. 316.

Swears he will never do so again: Ibid, p. 318.

"raving addicts": 2P, pp. 341–342.

"We were all living that extraordinary life": Ibid, p. 324.

"How wild and wonderful my": Ibid, p. 331.

"They both are pursuing independent lives": Julie Jordan, "Jessica Lange and Sam Shepard Have Separated," *People*, December 19, 2011, online.

"When I ask about the secret to her": Amanda Fortini, "Jessica Lange's Secret Passion," *Daily Beast*, July 9, 2009.

"I have a real difficult": Podcast.

"You know, everybody knew Scarlett": S&D.

"Sam gave us money for a cot": Ibid.

"My life is falling apart": Ibid.

"I can't do this right now": Ibid.

"What I learnt was that Sam and Johnny": sam-shepard.com.

"come to the of this obsession": 2P, p. 369.

"Take it away": Ibid.

Stumbling

"threw a lot": Slay.

"*Heartless* is a mysterious play": sam-shepard.com.

"His acting has": author interview.

"He's very honest and real": Ibid.

"I think our movie": Ibid.

"was before the tape": Ibid.

"He and Don had": Ibid.

"When he knew he was going to be": Marshall Fine, "Mateo Gil takes on the western with 'Blackthorn,'" *Hollywood and Fine*, October 5, 2011, online.

"valedictory performance": Ibid.

Endnotes

Details of the sale of co-op: Kim Velsey, "End of the Affair: Sam Shepard Transfers
  Co-op Shares to Ex Jessica Lange, *New York Observer*, February 7, 2013.
"no likelihood of success": Edmund Carrillo, "Playwright Sam Shepard's DWI charge
  dismissed," *Albuquerque Journal*, December 18, 2015, online.
"This whole incident has": Ibid.

The Road Ahead

"Did you try?": Alexis Soloski, "Sam Shepard Takes Stock of 'Buried Child' and the
  Writer's Life," *New York Times*, January 28, 2016. Hereafter Stock.
"Yes. It doesn't help": Ibid.
"Tiny Man": S, *New Yorker*, December 5, 2016, online.
"Cheerless but atmospheric": "The One Inside," *Kirkus Reviews*, January 23, 2017,
  online.
"greatest American playwright": Stock.
"yes and no": Culture.
"Oh, because they": Culture.

Index

Index

Index